SO-AHE-048

CARL A. RUDISILL LIBRARY
LENOIR RHYNE COLLEGE

301.
5920985
P43

97396

DATE DUE			
May22 78			

WITHDRAWN

PERUVIAN NATIONALISM
A Corporatist Revolution

Peruvian Nationalism

A Corporatist Revolution

Edited by

David Chaplin

CARL A. RUDISILL LIBRARY
LENOIR RHYNE COLLEGE

Transaction Books
New Brunswick, New Jersey

301.5920985

P43

97396

June 1976

Copyright © 1976 by Transaction, Inc.
New Brunswick, New Jersey

All rights reserved under International and Pan-American Copyright Conventions. No part of this book may be reproduced or transmitted in any form or by any means, electronic or mechanical, including photocopy, recording or any information storage and retrieval system, without prior permission in writing from the publisher. All inquiries should be addressed to Transaction Books, Rutgers University, New Brunswick, New Jersey.

Library of Congress Catalog Number: 73-85099
ISBN: 0-87855-077-1 (cloth); 0-87855-573-0 (paper)

Printed in the United States of America

ACKNOWLEDGMENTS

Grateful acknowledgment is made to the following authors and publishers for permission to reprint selections from copyright material.

Julio Cotler, "The Mechanics of Internal Domination and Social Change in Peru," Copyright © *Studies in Comparative International Development,* vol. 3, no. 2 (1967-68). Reprinted by permission of the author and publisher.

Daniel Goldrich et al., "The Political Integration of Lower-Class Urban Settlements in Chile and Peru," Copyright © *Studies in Comparative International Development,* vol. 3, no. 2 (1967-68). Reprinted by permission of the author and publisher.

Sandra Powell, "Political Participation in the Barriadas: A Case Study," *Comparative Political Studies,* vol. 2, no. 2 (1969): 195-215. Copyright © Sage Publications. Reprinted by permission of the author and publisher.

David Bayer, "Urban Peru: Political Action as Sellout" *trans*action magazine (now *Society*) (November 1969). Copyright © Transaction, Inc. Reprinted by permission of the publisher.

William F. Whyte, "Rural Peru: Peasants as Activists," *trans*action magazine (now *Society*) (November 1969). Copyright © Transaction, Inc. Reprinted by permission of the publisher.

Georgio Alberti, "Peasant Movement in the Yanamarca Valley," *Sociologia Ruralis*, vol. 12, no. 3-4 (1972). Translated and reprinted by permission of the author and publisher.

Shane Hunt, "Distribution, Growth and Government Economic Behavior in Peru," abridged from *Government and Economic Development*, ed. Gustav Ranis (New Haven: Yale University Press, 1971). Copyright © 1971 by Yale University. Reprinted by permission of the author and publisher.

David Chaplin, "La Convencion Valley and the 1962-65 Guerrilla Uprising," excerpted from "Peru's Postponed Revolution," *World Politics*, vol. 20, no. 3. Copyright © 1968 by Princeton University Press. "Blue Collar Workers in Peru," *International Journal of Comparative Sociology*, vol. 10, no. 1-2 (March–June 1969). Copyright © 1969 *by International Journal of Comparative Sociology;* reprinted by permission of K. Ishwaran, editor.

DEDICATION

To my closest critic: my wife, Joyce Whittier Chaplin.

Contents

Economic Growth and Development

The Military and the Church

National
Sociopolitical
Structure

David Chaplin

1.

The Revolutionary Challenge and Peruvian Militarism

During the industrialization of Latin America, various countries have enjoyed center stage. The first was Argentina, now suffering a prolonged economic and political stagnation. Mexico, Brazil and Cuba were the next leaders. The first two countries have sustained absolute economic growth and structural transformation at the expense of a heavy infusion of foreign investment. In Mexico's case, this has meant the substantial abandonment of the social ideals of the 1911 revolution—so far as the bottom third of the population is concerned—and involves the end of rapid economic growth, largely due to the neglect of the population growth rate and related social reforms. Cuba's abortive effort to industrialize collapsed, owing to mismanagement, the U.S. blockade and her small population base—plus the need for capital, which had to come from her enormous comparative advantage in sugar production and export.

At the close of the 1960s, Peru and Chile offered the most interesting models for social and economic development. The military junta that has controlled Peru since 1968, and the Allende regime in Chile were more seriously committed to eliminating some of the structural obstacles to industrialization than any other regimes these countries have ever had. The two governments' approaches and their populations differed considerably, but their goals were sufficiently similar to merit systematic comparisons. Thus, although this volume is primarily about Peru, several papers also discuss other countries, especially Chile, in relation to Peru.

Approximately one-third of this chapter is a revision of "Peru's Postponed Revolution," which originally appeared in *World Politics*. I wish to acknowledge the valuable comments of my wife, Joyce Whittier Chaplin, and Scott Palmer on this chapter, but as usual absolve them of any responsibility for the final version.

The governments of both Peru and Chile were seeking social justice, defined generally as social equality within their countries and between them and the economically developed nations, especially the United States. The Allende regime, however, was attempting to achieve this goal through a legally elected parliament and mass mobilization, with social justice taking precedence over economic development and productivity. Peru's military junta is managing a "corporatist-nationalist revolution" from above, with no elections or other conventional forms of mass "democratic" participation. Its primary goal appears to be national independence, and the question of social justice is dealt with primarily as a means to this end.

Counterrevolutionary Factors

Before we deal at greater length with the junta's program, Peru's continuing failure to experience a violent mass revolution requires some explanation, in view of the persistent expectation since the early thirties that such a revolution was about to occur.

Since Carleton Beals (1934), observers of Peru have been predicting "fire on the Andes." [1] When Bolivia began its social transformation in 1952, a Peruvian conflagration seemed all the more inevitable. Then, in 1962, what appeared to be Peru's version of the Sierra Maestra phase of "the revolution" began in the densely populated mountainous southern areas. This movement culminated in a series of abortive revolutionary actions during the summer of 1965. These efforts were resoundingly crushed by the Peruvian army as it finally rose to the challenge of guerrilla warfare from the lethargy of its traditional subservience to Peru's "oligarchy" and its ceremonial, riot-control and border-skirmish functions.

The relative ease with which this uprising was repressed (compared to similar revolts in Venezuela and Colombia), and the still-unrealized violent revolution in Peru, require special explanation. How could a serious student of Peru such as Bourricaud write in 1966 that

> this apocalyptic vision ... of illiterate masses ... determined to sacrifice everything to their rage for destruction ... which in the 30's and 40's engaged [the] oligarchy in fierce resistance to the APRA [the leftist reform party] is far less widespread today. The most current attitude is that with a

little luck and a lot of skill the basis of traditional positions can be preserved.[2]

The basic factors which account for Peru's relatively peaceful past are:

1. The historical role of APRA (the Alianza Popular Revolucionaria Americana) in insulating Peru's industrial proletariat from Communist influence. More recently (1963–68), this role was partially taken over by Acción Popular, Belaúnde's party, leaving the APRA to a coalition with its former archenemy, the ex-dictator, General Ordrìa.
2. Peru's unusually diversified economic structure, which provided a relatively strong and stable currency and employment situation.
3. Peru's geography, which makes guerrilla warfare extremely difficult. (The 1962–65 peasant revolt, dealt with in Chapter 11, expands on this problem.)

Besides these unique and extreme factors, Peru shared with many Latin American countries certain other revolution-dampening characteristics:

1. An urban middle class more prone to aping passé elite values and behavior than to seeing itself, together with the lower class, in opposition to "the oligarchy." Latin America's middle class is extremely divided by ambivalent attitudes toward the traditional elite, capitalism and modern bureaucratic norms, preferring a reliance on powerful patrons and clique favoritism, rather than merit, in the pursuit of career success.[3]
2. An "unfavorable" openness of class structure, with respect to race. The much-touted tolerance of Latins on the matter of race does in fact function in Peru to facilitate the passage of some Indians into the category of *cholos* (racially Indian, culturally aggressive participants in local political affairs).[4] The same primarily behavioral acculturation requirement permits some second-generation *cholos* to become middle-class *mestizos* (who are of mixed blood and culture). Potential leaders of either of these classes are thus subverted, by a "too-easy" accession to the next highest level, from what could otherwise have become a racially based opposition to the status quo. In the same manner, the oligarchy has been quite open to invasion by postcolonial

immigrant entrepreneurs, in rural areas as well as Lima.
3. Extensive U.S. military aid since 1945, followed, since 1960, by U.S. assistance in the strengthening and retraining of Latin American armies for the conditions peculiar to antiguerrilla warfare.[5]
4. The large split within the revolutionary camp, from the Peking-Havana-Moscow division at the top, down to local aggravation on the basis of the endemic personalism that infects all Latin American political activity. In a survey of extremist politics in Peru from 1956 to 1961, Payne distinguishes seven separate factions: (1) the Trotskyite party (the old Fourth International faction), (2) the Trotskyite party (the new Pablo faction), (3) the Leninist Committee, (4) the Rebel APRA party, (5) the Communist party, (6) the Progressive Socialist party, and (7) the Socialist party. Similar divisions persist under the present military regime with the Moscow-oriented Communist party, in favor of the junta and the various radical Left parties in opposition. In addition to dissension, Peru's extremist leadership demonstrated extraordinary incompetence—especially in its post-1956 dealings with organized labor. Payne points particularly to the Communist-dominated Cuzco Workers' Federation (operating in the area of the 1962 uprising), as an example of bungled opportunities.[6]

In addition to both sets of characteristics listed above, we should note the erosion and splintering of opposition to organized urban lower-class demands. Even before 1968, Peru was no longer run by a united, conservative and all-powerful coalition of the army, the church and the landed aristocracy. Such a weakening of a once-dominant elite is often viewed as a revolution-precipitating factor. However, in this case it should be viewed more broadly, as permitting change—either violent or gradual.

We shall now discuss these factors in more detail, under the following headings: (1) the APRA's insulating role, (2) diversified economy, (3) geography, and (4) the weakening of "the oligarchy."

The APRA's Insulating Role

APRA stands out in Latin American political history as the first significant South American radical reform party on the Left after the Mexican Revolution.[7] During the twenties it took public positions that were not advocated by comparably organized and widely based populist parties in other Latin American countries (except Mexico) until 1945. APRA claimed to be anticlerical, socialist and pro-Indian and, as such, absorbed the left wing of Peruvian intellectuals as well as most of the nascent labor movement. Its strength lay not only in its "populist" ideology, but also in its highly centralized and disciplined party structure. To this day it is the only real political party in Peru.

Until 1945 the APRA party was outlawed; even after that it could not run its own candidates. For three years, however (1945–48), it did have an opportunity to try and control the country by supporting President Bustamante, a non-Aprista compromise choice, but all interested groups were disappointed in the results. The Apristas were burdened by the difficult postwar readjustments, but this fact alone does not account for their failures. No significant reform projects were undertaken on behalf of labor or the Indians (except for the very important unionization of the sugar plantation workers), nor was the power of the church or the army in any way curtailed. Rather, the interests of the urban middle classes seemed to be the major concern of the Apristas, as they concentrated on currency exchange controls. It must be admitted, however, that, facing the implacable hatred of the army, they could not have accomplished much more at that time.

In 1948 the APRA underwent a severe repression, under the otherwise relatively mild dictatorship of General Odría. Again in 1956, APRA took the opportunity to govern in a *convivencia* ("living together") arrangement with a president who was clearly a member of Peru's urban commercial oligarchy. It was during this latter period (1956–62) that the APRA began to lose its appeal to the younger generation of radicals, since it had greatly compromised its original goals in return for legitimacy and some degree of respectability.* By

---

* The following assessment would seem most appropriate to the APRA during these 1956-1962 *convivencia* days, but it was written in 1934: "Unfortunately, the APRA movement has already compromised its program. It has been trying to conciliate the

1960 it had swung so far to the Right that a Castro-oriented splinter group, the Rebel APRA party (the Movimiento Izquierdista Revolucionario), split off, while the majority of Young Turks of this period became Belaúndistas (members of the president's party between 1963–68) or Christian Democrats. Within the universities, APRA began to lose out to openly Communist student parties. By 1966 it had even lost the University of Trujillo, although the city of Trujillo had long been the APRA's hometown.

Thanks to its moderation, APRA won the overt support of the U.S. government (or at least of the Kennedy-appointed U.S. ambassador) during the 1962 election. This belated, but well-intended, "recognition" of a party long stereotyped as "Communist" by many U.S. citizens in Peru came too late to bolster its declining appeal. It was misperceived by Ambassador Loeb as still embodying the ideals attributed to it by Harry Kantor's 1956 book on the APRA.

By 1960, APRA was no longer deflecting the radical reform element in Peruvian politics from a revolutionary course. It became extremely anti-Communist, in an apparent attempt to achieve a rapprochement with the military, as its only hope of ever achieving full power. (It has, however, won the warm support of the AFL-CIO in the U.S.) At the same time, its current drift to the Right should not obscure its historical role, which was especially significant during the height of Communist popularity in the early post-World War II period.

Diversified Economy

Peru has one of the most diversified portfolios of export products of any underdeveloped country. It includes significant quantities of copper, silver, lead, sugar, wool and cotton, as well as fish meal (of which Peru is the world's leading producer). In addition, Peru is

---

church; instead of propagandizing against the militarists, it has advocated justice and efficiency for the army; and it has soft-pedalled its whole anti-imperialistic position, especially with reference to British capital. This opportunism is largely due to Haya de la Torre, now entirely too enmeshed in the intrigues of Lima politics. It is doubtful if this attempt to win the sympathy of the poorer clergy and the army has brought enough effective support to compensate for the loss of mass faith in the Aprista movement itself." [8]

almost self-sufficient in oil. It is extremely unlikely that the prices of all these commodities would fall simultaneously. Thus, although a sizable portion of Peru's rural labor force has been "proletarianized," all of its workers would rarely be in the same market situation at once. Therefore, while Peru's manufacturing sector is still quite underdeveloped, the country does not have a "banana republic," monocultural economic structure. The better-paid urban workers, at least, can afford a wider range of imported consumer goods and experience fewer disrupting economic cycles than is true in most other Latin American countries. The organized blue-collar workers in Lima have enjoyed a relative as well as an absolute rise in income since 1950.[9]

Geography

As the 1962–1965 guerrilla uprisings made clear, the Peruvian *sierra* is not the Sierra Maestra—nor the Colombian *selva* (jungle), in which there is sufficient cover, food and water to protect and sustain small bands of guerrillas.[10] The Peruvian middle and southern sierra, where most of the Indians live, ranges from 6,000 to 12,000 feet at the higher altitudes where the guerrillas were fighting, and requires a period of acclimatization to carry on even normal activity—to say nothing of a running battle. In addition, on the western slopes facing the coastal region (and the country's urban power centers), these mountains are without water and hence bare of vegetation. Therefore, parachute squads and helicopter-borne troops, aided by aerial surveillance, can easily pursue and capture bands of fleeing guerrillas, whose only respite is found in Peru's large but politically unimportant jungle.

In fact, even jungle cover is not sufficient to guarantee the guerrillas' success in societies dominated by urban power. Even after more than a decade of extreme violence, the government of Colombia remained amazingly stable in the face of rural anarchy (especially in forested areas), because it has held the cities. In the 1965 Peruvian guerrilla uprising, even those units operating at the edge of the jungle were quickly captured. In an attack on an isolated hacienda, one group of guerrillas and jungle Indians *(Campas),* led by Guillermo Lobatón were all apprehended and killed by troops using a combination of aerial surveillance (assisted by U.S. Protestant missionaries familiar with the area) and local informers. The original assistance of the Campas had been enlisted on behalf of the guerrillas, through the efforts of a "renegade" U.S. Protestant missionary, but subsequently many of this tribe turned informer for the army. The peculiar problem with this jungle area is that the presence of strangers is very quickly noticed and communicated. Only total support by all local inhabitants can afford real protection. The feeling of isolation in the jungle is quite illusory.

The guerrillas would have had more luck if they had remained in the jungle and concentrated on sabotaging the government's efforts at agrarian reform through colonization, since one of the objectives of this program is increased food production. At present, Peru's highly productive irrigated coastal agriculture is not supplying enough of the country's food. Already scarce foreign exchange must be diverted from the purchase of manufactured goods to basic food imports. (However, it must also be noted that most major Latin American metropolises are not so dependent on a local hinterland as their size would suggest. They have long purchased many basic commodities from abroad, and hence could survive a brief loss of control over much of their rural areas.)

One further geographical factor is unfavorable to rebel activity: Peru's population is divided internally by high mountain ranges and a long, extremely barren, coastal desert. As a result, the military can bottle up major portions of the country with relative ease.

The Weakening of "The Oligarchy"

The landed aristocracy

Probably the least instructive stereotype which one might use to classify Peruvian politics prior to 1968 would be: a simplistic power coalition consisting of a landed aristocracy, supported above by the church and below by the military. Actually, the plutocratic elite whose primary wealth has always been in land had been substantially displaced by an urban commercial oligarchy, which in turn is extremely fragmented, due to differing foreign orientations, personal rivalries and political contacts. The significant turning point in the shift from a rural, land-based oligarchy to an urban commercial one came during the Leguía dictatorship (1919–1930). Such a displacement was deliberately pursued by Leguía, to the extent of exiling some of the old guard and developing a new elite to take their places.

The landed plutocracy itself has been going through drastic changes ever since national independence was achieved in 1821. During the early years of the nineteenth century, the withdrawal of the somewhat protective hands of the church and the crown meant the further encroachment of private haciendas on the lands of Indian communities. This occurred partly because of the private owners' desire to own land per se, but equally often it was due to a need to acquire the virtually free labor of Indians, who "came with" the land. The biggest landholdings during the first half of the nineteenth century were in the mountainous regions, where local labor was available. In addition, the decay of the pre-Columbian irrigation system along the coast meant that only the land immediately adjacent to the few small streams there could be utilized.

During the second half of the nineteenth century, the development of the guano fertilizer industry, together with the growth of export markets for Peruvian cotton and sugar, encouraged the development and consolidation of enormous commercial plantations along the coastal desert. From this time on, the interests of the *sierra gamonal* (the large landowner in the mountains) and the coastal agricultural entrepreneur began to diverge. The latter was different, not only in his activity, but also in his origins: the most successful entrepreneurs were of immigrant rather than Creole origin.

The property of the sierra *gamonal* produced largely subsistence crops for a local or, at the most, a national market,* while the coastal agricultural entrepreneur was devoted to export cash crops. The former's main asset was control over a large, cheap and presumably docile labor supply that yielded as much political power as financial profit. The latter, on the other hand, experienced an unstable labor supply until well into the twentieth century (a situation complicated by the emancipation of Negroes in 1854, and only temporarily relieved by the subsequent importation of Chinese coolies), and

* Excluding wool.

hence he relied more on mechanization and efficient business practices to make a fortune. In recent years, the cleavage between these groups has been revealed in the pre-1968 governments' clear unwillingness to defend the interests of the inefficient sierra *gamonal* as vigorously as it had protected those of the modern coastal plantation owner. In particular, APRA, whose unions control most of the sugar mill and plantation labor force, had fought successfully for the special exemption of coastal plantations from the agrarian reform law.

We should not assume, however, that even during the nineteenth century the sierra *gamonal* constituted a stable, traditional, all-powerful, landed aristocracy. In the first place, Indian unrest and resistance against land encroachment never ceased. Life in the sierra was closer to the U.S. frontier relations with its Indians than is generally supposed. The main point about this Indian resistance is that it was largely sporadic, unorganized and "conservative"—that is, it had no revolutionary goal of remodeling society, but only wanted to protect or try to take back the Indians' traditional landholdings.[11] Even the formation of peasant unions in the early 1960s near the old Inca capital of Cuzco had a conservative orientation—which the 1962–65 guerrilla leadership failed to recognize. Solid historical evidence concerning the isolated, pre-twentieth-century uprisings is difficult to obtain. There are reports, however, of "hundreds" of incidents during the nineteenth and early twentieth centuries, and these attacks helped accelerate the development of patterns of absentee land ownership.[12] These patterns of flight also arose from changed definitions of an acceptable elite life-style. The difference between the domestic amenities available in Lima and *la casa grande* (the main house) of a plantation was minor in the early nineteenth century, but with the arrival of paved streets, plumbing, gas and electricity in Lima near the turn of the century, life in the country suddenly became intolerably primitive. Absenteeism, of course, had been an established pattern since colonial days. However, before the present century it meant seasonal visits by the landowner, whereas more recently the owner stayed away from his land altogether, sending the hired manager to collect rents.

Another factor that increased rural instability during the nineteenth century was the abolition of *mayorazgo* (entail). During the colonial period, this rule kept large estates in one piece under the control of a single descendant, whereas the republican inheritance laws required the division of property among all children, male and female, legitimate and illegitimate. It was therefore extremely difficult for one "line" to maintain a sociopolitical position in a local area, generation after generation. Moreover, the Latin family structure (similar in this respect to the Western family structure) is of the bilateral kindred type—that is, the opposite of a unilateral extended corporate clan, such as exists in China. In the latter type of system, real property could easily be held together and passed down one line (paternal or maternal) of a family, whereas in the Western system, relations among extended kin are not as strong, because even first cousins don't share a single family head. In addition, without primogeniture, property disperses with each generation and can be held together or reassembled only if a given set of parents has the "right" number of children of the right sex and makes favorable matches for them. Otherwise the inevitable tendency is a progressive fractionalization of their property.

As a result of this inheritance and kinship structure, there has been a high level of social mobility within the provincial middle and upper classes in Peru. For those facing a declining status as landholders, flight to the city has usually seemed the best course of action. At the same time, absentee ownership of even large tracts of land does not usually yield an income sufficient to get someone with provincial upper-class status a comparable position in Lima. Urban migration usually means a relative decline, to middle-class status. Even this can be tenuous, as Indian unrest and mismanagement, or embezzlement by hired managers, gradually decrease the liquid income that can be derived from distant landholdings.

The church

Like the "landed aristocracy," the Peruvian Catholic church is still credited with exerting more influence than it actually enjoys or than it has probably exercised at any time since Independence. The best available estimates of the church's landholdings suggest that it probably owns three or four percent of nongovernmental land, only slightly more than the Beneficencias Publicas (Public Welfare Societies).[13] Moreover, the poor use to which most of this land has been put presumably limits the liquid income the church could obtain from it.

It is probably because of these weaknesses that the Peruvian Catholic church has clung to its formal position as the established, state-protected church in Peru. In 1874, after a postindependence period of church estrangement from republican governments (but not active governmental anticlericalism, as exists in Mexico), the colonial *patronato* system was reestablished, giving the Peruvian president and congress the power to name bishops. Even prior to this, in 1854, when General Castilla freed the impoverished Indians from their special burden of tithing for the church, the government had taken over the payment of clerical salaries. These payments persist today, but are so insignificant that they can be interpreted only as a gesture of polite contempt. They probably produce even fewer public contributions than the church would receive if it were independent.

In the area of legislation, virtually all the matters over which the church had enjoyed a monopoly during the colonial era—namely, marriages, burials, schools and charities—have escaped its exclusive control. The lowest point of church influence was probably reached in 1957, when President Prado won a Vatican-sanctioned annulment of a 30-year-old marriage, which included children, in order to marry the woman who had long been his official lady-of-honor at state functions. This rather traditional arrangement had been quite acceptable, *until* the president's de facto "divorce." His actions so outraged Lima's first families that some cabinet officers' wives refused to attend official dinners with the new First Lady, now that she was the president's legal wife. Some even took to the streets barefoot to demonstrate in front of the presidential palace, an action ordinarily unthinkable for women of this socioeconomic level.

In general, it can be said that the Peruvian Catholic church was largely on the defensive, until 1968. Such foreign assistance as it received was usually shunted off to isolated Indian provinces, while national priests, whose number is diminishing, were concentrated in Lima. Most of the foreign Catholic clergy in Peru, unlike those of Chile, were until recently excluded from positions of responsibility in the national hierarchy. In Chile, a liberal archbishop brought large numbers of European clergy into high positions within the hierarchy as the prerequisite for a rejuvenation of the Chilean church. The current Peruvian archbishop, Cardinal Landazuri, although one of the youngest in Latin America, felt incapable of any decisive action until the *golpe* of 1968.

If, on the other hand, one were to include the Christian Democratic party, the "Christian" labor movement, and students at the Catholic University as part of "the church" (an assumption which the people involved would generally not accept), then Catholicism would seem to have risen to the challenge of the times. These groups, according to Frederick Pike, a historian at Notre Dame, have taken such extremely "demagogic" and "irresponsible" stands against capitalism that he feels—as a North American Catholic—that he must take them to task for not being more concerned with inculcating

> natural virtue among all classes, from aristocracy to proletariat. . . . All too often . . . the long-term, slow approach of helping the poor classes to develop their own spiritual and material resources is shunned in favor of dramatic measures which allegedly make possible overnight solution of social problems without imposing any burdens, obligations and responsibilities of self-improvement on the poor classes. . . . The economic problem of Peru is in part a moral problem involving not just the hard-heartedness of the wealthy but the laziness, irresponsibility and lack of natural virtue of the lower classes.

Pike does admit, however, that "the Catholic Church in Peru undertook the modernization process at a late date. The first important joint pastoral letter of the hierarchy attacking social evils . . . was issued only in 1958." [14] (In this respect, at least, the Catholic church in most of the rest of Latin America was equally slow moving.)

The ideological divergencies existing within Catholicism are probably at least as serious as those outside it. On the far Left in the early 1960s stood MOSICP (the Movimiento de Sindicatos Cristianos del Peru), while the more recent left wing is described by Astiz in Chapter 17, and on the far Right a Peruvian branch of Opus Dei is developing. All these are essentially imported organizations, although each has found significant local support. The operations of Opus Dei other than certain charities are, "confidential," so any estimate of its importance is impossible at this stage. It is, however, possible that Opus

Dei, through its influence on the post-1968 junta, is fostering a tech-
nocratic-developmentalist policy in Peru, rather than being an-
timodern, as some of its religious pronouncements would suggest.
MOSICP, on the other hand, claimed a far larger success than it had in
fact achieved. The liberal Archbishop of Cuzco did give this union his
official support at its beginning in 1963, but by 1965 no traces of the
organization remained in the area under his jurisdiction.

In view of the recent and extraordinary turnabout on the part of
President Echeverría of Mexico with respect to birth control, which
received public support from 80 of Mexico's bishops, it will be very
interesting to see if and when Peru's church will act on this issue. Will
it merely second the government, if the junta openly supports family
planning clinics, or would the church actually take the initiative in this
area? The Mexican bishops define the situation of their poor as an
"emergency," requiring a modification of the anti-birth control position of the Papal Encyclical, *Humanae Vitae*. Since Peru's poor are
certainly no better off, the remaining difference between Peru and
Mexico is apparently the ideology of the Peruvian religious hierarchy.

The military

The domestic modernizing institution currently favored by most
U.S. policy writers is the military. In the late 1950s, some people
hoped that the middle sectors of Peruvian society would replicate the
Western entrepreneurial, or at least the bourgeois, role in modernization. J. J. Johnson,[15] typifying the fads and fashions of this
prime-mover approach, turned to the military, thus helping to provide
a new rationale for U.S. support of counterinsurgency and internal
control activities, once the external Communist military threat was no
longer credible. The Brazilian military, of course, has not disappointed
U.S. private business expectations, but the early populist-nationalist
actions of the current Peruvian junta came as a rude shock. Peru's
above-mentioned advantage of resource diversification has been offset
by heavy U.S. control—both direct and indirect—over most of its export
sectors: oil, mining, sugar and shipping, as well as sources of credit.
Therefore, given Peru's extensive dependence on trade with the United
States, the apparent radicalism of their nationalist actions dismayed

the U.S. officials prepared to view military regimes as their last, best bulwark against Communism.

Due to the extensive treatment by this volume's contributors of the military, both historically and since the 1968 golpe, a summary would be redundant. Instead, some of the unresolved issues will be delineated, and hopefully they will encourage further research in this area.

The Issue of the Junta's Merit Orientation

Astiz and García take issue with another aspect of the "middle class" interpretation of the Peruvian junta's origins and behavior—namely, its alleged "achievement" orientation. For those aware of the weaknesses of McClelland's achievement model for interpreting economic development, criticizing such a reductionist psychologistic explanation for national economic growth could seem like beating a dead horse. But such interpretations are so persistent among students of this regime that they must be dealt with again. Astiz and García cite Einaudi and Whyte as emphasizing the greater commitment of the Peruvian military to merit, via formal education and objective tests, than is found elsewhere in Peruvian society. Astiz and García's attack on this emphasis takes the following form:

1. Achievement is meaningful only in the context of the legitimate means and ends of a given institution. Among the formalized standards for promotion in the Peruvian military, good conduct—defined as discipline—is five times as important as intellectual achievement on academic examinations. Given the presumably universal tendency for the intellectually gifted to be restive under the usual constraints of military conduct and collegiate sociability, a rationalistic genius would probably not be recognized as such in Peru. This characteristic of the military has long been taken for granted—as in the cases of Gen. Billy Mitchell, Admiral Rickover, etc. How or why, then, should the Peruvian military have been able to escape this meaning of "achievement"?

2. Like all professional military groups, the Peruvian armed forces are constitutionally subordinate to civilian control. In normal times, or at least during eras of constitutional democracy, the

president has the right to influence promotions and retirements.
Hence, his preferences and external "political" influence inevitably affect the behavior of achievement or promotion-oriented
officers. In fact, the highest achievers among those officers
promoted since 1914 have been those on the winning side of the
many golpes which have taken place since then.
3. The number of military officers related to other officers in the first
degree of kinship is far too high to have occurred by chance.[16]

Overall, then, the Peruvian military, notwithstanding its high commitment to formal education, has not demonstrated any special merit
in the area most strategic to industrialization—namely, economics. The
regime has yet to recognize its need to force a drastic reorganization of
Peruvian manufacturing, so that it can increase its domestic market—to
say nothing of withstanding even Andean Common Market competition or the much more threatening Asian imports. The military's
ineffectual effort to control (or understand the basis for) rising food
prices following agrarian reform also attests to its economic incompetence.

Social Mobilization and Revolution

The most controversial aspect of the junta's insistent claim to being
"revolutionary" is its program of social mobilization. In the first year
after the golpe the widespread disgust with the Belaúnde regime, and
parliamentary democracy in general, together with a well-orches-
trated series of spectacular populist measures, provided sufficient
legitimacy for the junta. This was so, despite its persistent inability to
provide either a charismatic leader or a coherent program of social
development. The sizable number of vulnerable internal oligarchs
and foreign interests which then existed provided a sufficient number
of unpopular targets so that attacks on lower and middle-class obstacles to development could be postponed.

As time went on, the junta's left-wing supporters began to realize
that it was impossible to make a real revolution without mass
mobilization to offset the inevitable counterrevolutionary reaction.
The first expression of this new perspective on their part was the
Committees for the Defense of the Revolution fostered by the staff of

Expresso, a newspaper expropriated from one of Belaúnde's cabinet ministers. Once the potentially disruptive nature of this organization became evident, the government phased it out of existence and replaced it with SINAMOS (The National System of Support for Social Mobilization),[17] headed by a general and staffed by many of the junta's left-wing critics—including some jailed guerrilla leaders such as Hector Bejar.*

SINAMOS clearly fits the historic Latin corporatist model of social organization/regimentation. Class conflict is ruled out, in favor of vertical segmentation integrated at the top. Such a structure fits the regime's claim to pursuing a middle path between communism and capitalism. Potentially inconsistent with this goal is the Industrial Community Program for worker control over domestic industry. Workers (defined as *both* labor and management) could eventually buy controlling stock ownership in their own firms. This suggests, of course, a formally classless corporatist structure, but if it took the Scandinavian-Jugoslav route it could also involve radical decentralization and lower-class worker control over economic enterprises.

There is good reason, however, to believe that the military government has no intention of permitting anything like direct democracy, even at the plant level. To begin with, one of the major goals of its "cooperative" model has been to eliminate the need for unions, especially Aprista unions. This was clearly demonstrated in the structure of the sugar plantation producer's co-ops, in which former union leaders were disqualified and field workers received only 25 percent representation on the councils. After a year of poor harvests and mismanagement, the workers staged a number of violent protests. Many workers and some so-called foreign agitators were jailed. After this effective show of force, the government relented, released the imprisoned workers and even allowed them to run for office as councilmen. This pragmatic mixture of an immediate use of force and subsequent compromise has been repeated in many other areas, notably university reform, and appears to be a reasonably viable tactic for momentarily defusing general unrest, leaving the government free to pursue its essentially technocratic model of development.

---

* The details of SINAMOS' organization and ideology are well described in Chapter 16 of this volume.

Whyte's major objection [18] to the worker ownership program is that, so far, it offers no effective means for the workers to *control*, or even significantly influence, their immediate working conditions—to say nothing of making a contribution to improved organizational and technical efficiency. At present the workers' interest and influence is focused solely on the distribution of profits. This defect in worker participation Whyte sees as a specific case of the regime's disinterest in external feedback [19] on the functioning of its reforms. Faced with failures, the regime's response too often has been coercion, political compromise and greater efforts at indoctrination. This is not to deny the many organizational successes of the regime, but rather to note that it cannot respond effectively to instances of failure, except in the short-run sense of quelling unrest without extreme repression.

Besides the limitations now imposed on serious worker influence—even over the distribution of benefits, there are a number of other weaknesses and inconsistencies in the participatory structure:

1. The problem of national planning and societal welfare. There is no reason to suppose, even if the worker communities fully controlled their enterprises, that they would pursue policies which conformed to any rational national growth plan or that would not disadvantage other groups in the society. Organizing a polity solely on the basis of employment, especially where the already heavily favored industrial workers are a small minority, explicitly disenfranchises the majority and lures the favored minority into narrowly defining their own interests. The most obvious flaw in this process would be their inevitable failure to solve the problem of growing unemployment, since a more capital-intensive type of investment would best enhance the income of those already employed. The current structure of military control avoids this outcome, at the cost of making a mockery of plant democracy, so this criticism would be relevant only if worker control were taken seriously. Full worker control would also probably accentuate the already privileged status of industrial, workers relative to other lower-class workers, as is explained in Chapter 7; thus it would further decrease labor turnover, already dysfunctionally low in an economy in need of drastic changes. This latter tendency would be increased by the way in which a worker's rights in his job or the ownership of his firm were defined.

2. As is explained more fully in Chapter 7, most Peruvian plants are not economically viable enterprises if treated as independent units. Drastic technical and organizational reforms should *precede* social reform, but this priority is pursued only by a few of the many ministries which share the responsibility for this program. In addition to a diversity of ministerial approaches, there is also a variety of forms of participation—social property, compensation communities, etc.—which could affect firms in the same industry differently, often burdening some with more "advanced" schemes, thus forcing them to compete on unfavorable terms with other, less constrained, companies.[20] The special advantages retained by foreign capital in mining is the outstanding example of this situation.

3. The role of SINAMOS vis-à-vis the mobilization of the workers is as yet unclear. The industrial communities and their counterparts in other sectors as explored by Palmer and Middlebrook, were created before SINAMOS, hence conflict between them has been maximized. SINAMOS is variously referred to as a "red guard" and a "gestapo"—indicative of its highly uncertain political function. Clearly SINAMOS had the support of President General Velasco, but it also has aroused growing opposition among its targets: unions, especially the Aprista (although it enjoys the support of the Communist party, for the latter's own tactical reasons), "old guard" bureaucrats and the private owners of industry. Its field of operations is in fact unlimited. In late 1972 it "unionized" the Peruvian employees of Foster Parents in the impoverished port city of Chimbote, in an apparent effort to drive out this embarrassing and paternalistic symbol of Yankee charity.[21]

Before taking up the most hostile criticism of the regime's programs for mass mobilization, the official ideals of its supporters should be presented. The Industrial Communities were defended in July 1972 by General Alberto Jimenez de Lucio, Minister of Industry, as follows:

Industrial Communities contribute to the fundamental solution of the problem of humanism—the creation of a just society which in turn is free, a society in which all are seen as ends and not as means. It thus constitutes an example of necessary gradualism in order to avoid contradictions between theory and practice—it is a grave error to consider the industrial community as an attack on the firm. It tries to turn the enterprise into a human community in which the worker is not reduced to a mere tool—the dogmatists of the ultra-left believe that it is a subterfuge to enervate the working class by impeding the expression of its revolutionary force. The dogmatists of the ultra-right feel that it is a hidden effort to destroy private enterprise. These ingrained misunderstandings are difficult to overcome.[22]

The origin of the belatedly tacked-on section concerning worker participation in the Industrial Community Law is interesting. Although precursors of this idea can be found in the writings of Christian Democrats as early as 1963, the first (May 1970) version of the General Industrial Law contained no mention of this radical provision.[23] Whatever the full explanation for its sudden appearance in the final July 27, 1970 law, this "delay" had the double function of: being another of the regime's surprise reforms, analogous to the early dawn paratroop seizure of sugar plantation and bank records; and eliminating the usual period of public airing for intended changes, which would have permitted unofficial feedback from affected interests. Since then, however, the SNI (National Industrial Society) has reacted vigorously and has come up with counterproposals. By late 1972, the involvement of SINAMOS in the Industrial Communities and the decreasing tolerance of the regime for criticism resulted in the "reorganization" of the SNI to include both labor and management in order to be "adequately representative" of the industrial sector in what could be called the full-scale classless corporate model.

As the controversy over SINAMOS increased, Quijano, Cotler and others publicly discussed the corporatist and capitalist issues in a new journal called *Sociedad y Politica* (Society and Politics).[24] The essence of their overall criticism of the junta's program could be summarized and paraphrased as follows.

Thanks to the advanced state of decay of the traditional oligarchy and the impotence of the working class, no violent mass-bourgeois revolution was required to destroy the remnants of primitive capitalism in Peru. However, the administered reforms which dislodged the traditional domestic oligarchy have neither eliminated foreign capitalist influence nor moved beyond a modernized bourgeois capitalist system. In fact, a more insidious collaboration between the less unified and less powerful U.S. interests and local capitalists has developed with the full support of the government. The Industrial Community reforms, in particular, attempt to blur the reality of labor management conflict and the antisocial aspects of private property. In effect, the state will be subsidizing this reformed version of modern capitalism. In so doing, it will hide the growing inequality of income and unemployment, since only a fraction of the labor force will enjoy the benefits of these "reforms." The state is thus evolving a private property welfare paternalism, or corporatist model of modernization, sufficient for the present to maintain its populist legitimacy. This token "participationism" on the part of the privileged proletariat can only lead to the *demobilization* of the masses—the antithesis of the presumed goal of SINAMOS—by means of diverting workers from their real class interests.

Worker ownership of industry, even if realized, would only be a semisocialized variant of capitalism, while the reality of the government's corporatist style suggests fascism—although Cotler, in particular, correctly disclaims the explicit use of this label.[25]

The progovernment editor of *Oiga* responded in an editorial entitled, "Is This a Fascist Process?"[26] In it, he defended SINAMOS as an exercise in political education, and the revolution as a humanistic path between the "insensitivity of communism" and the "egoism of capitalism," leading to a "free society, administered with justice and equal security and opportunity for all." None of the issues raised above, however, was adequately answered by *Oiga*'s editorial. This left the ideological issues of socialism a matter of the observer's personal politics, and the limited analogy with fascism (especially the Spanish variety, in its heyday) a fruitful comparative framework. Cotler's contention [27] that this "revolution" is merely a military technocratic substitute for Western bourgeois modernization, which Peru's native middle class was unable to attain, is difficult to refute. The actual beneficiaries of the regime's populist reforms are so few that no significant alteration of Peru's class structure is likely to result.

In summary, SINAMOS is an extremely disingenuous, yet apparently viable, effort to co-opt most potential or actual leaders of mass opposition. We cannot understand whether or not SINAMOS will function to slow the reformist thrust of the regime's "revolution" merely by looking at its structure. Although the "revolution" has certainly not fulfilled all the expectations that reformers and radicals held for it during its early years, its persistently pragmatic style makes any conclusive judgments premature.

Cotler ends his rebuttal, as does Quijano in *Nationalism and Capitalism*, by predicting that this pattern of corporatist demobilization of the masses cannot endure, given the exigencies of capitalist accumulation and inflation, without an increasing resort to violent repression and hence eventually revolution. Mexico's political pattern, however, suggests that this demobilization model may be quite viable, whatever its social costs.

Predictably, critics on the Left refrain from mentioning a related failure of humanistic reform, the junta's resistance to family planning via birth control. Peru's population growth rate, therefore, continues at more than 3 percent annually, thus ensuring a continuous increase in unemployment, an unproductive expenditure on education and the misery of lower-class urban women who, as in all such countries, must therefore resort to illegal abortions.[28]

Urban Politics

The study of local politics in Latin America has received far less than its share of scholarly attention, especially in urban areas. Most political research conducted during the 1960s was either hemispheric, national or sectoral—i.e., concerning peasants, miners or residents of the *barriadas*. In contrast, the essays included in this section focus largely on metropolitan Lima, except for Bayer's chapter on Ica. In addition, the three essays specifically about Lima complement each other, in utilizing different but interrelated types of data and analysis, while Doughty's chapter describes national urban structure and the concentration of people and services in Lima.

Chapter 4 carries forward our Chilean comparison, paralleling Strasma's in chapter 13, on the basis of a field survey conducted from May to July, 1965. (Readers should bear in mind the following contemporary events: the Peruvian guerrilla uprising was developing during this period, to be decisively crushed only after the end of the field research; U.S. troops had invaded the Dominican Republic; and the Camelot project in Chile was exposed. There is no direct evidence of urban lower-class awareness of these facts, but perhaps this is only because no questions were asked about specific current events.)

Powell's project followed Goldrich, Pratt and Schuller's in 1967 and complements it by concentrating on aggregate voting patterns, especially the crucial municipal elections of 1963 and 1966. Both of these chapters should be read in the context of the various explanations offered by many of the contributors as to why the Belaúnde regime failed. Both also illustrate the limitations of a person's residential role on his identity and behavior as a citizen—since neighborhood organizations held together only as long as they faced basic service and land title problems.

Both of these chapters should also be read in the context of the continuous decline in the unity of both the Popular Action-Christian Democratic Alliance and the Apra-UNO (Odría) Coalition, from 1964 to 1968. At the same time, the U.S. was losing interest in Latin America, in general, and in reform as a requisite for development. In the U.S., efforts were also being made to organize the poor on their own behalf—with even less effective results.

A point not made by either author, however (although it is implied by Powell), was the conservatizing effect of the government's action in permitting and aiding urban squatters. Collier's chapter proves that the Peruvian experience contradicts the widely held notion that squatters are likely to be more favorably treated by liberal democratic regimes than by military dictatorships. Collier's study also complements those of Goldrich, et al., and Powell, by focusing on the (neglected) role of official support for squatter settlement formation, and by following the two previous studies in time—1965, 1967, 1970—and in covering essentially the same barriada or "suburban slum" populations.

These three studies of Lima's barriadas by political scientists do not deal with some of the longer-range, partially political consequences of official permissiveness toward squatters, which conventionally are of greater concern to urban planners and economists. Like agrarian reform, urban squatting co-opts certain segments of the lower class, by involving them in petit bourgeois concerns with land titles and local public utility services—at the expense of foregoing systemically rational economic planning. Economies of scale are often surrendered in rural areas, especially where production requires larger and better integrated units of land, to say nothing of the delivery of health and educational services. In urban areas the latter cost is far more evident and harder to postpone. The low-density, dispersed structure of Lima's newer barriada settlements makes the provision of minimal electricity, water, sewage, public transportation and health and education much more expensive than it is in the high-rise apartment complexes in Caracas. (The latter, in turn, could serve as a functional substitute for the factory, in creating alienated class consciousness based on residence, rather than occupation.) Thus a regime which opts for this short-term populist strategy is really only preparing to load heavier expenses on some subsequent government. Lima is already suffering diseconomies of scale, due to its absolute size relative to the size of its water mains, and the inadequacy of its transportation system and water supply. These problems are compounded by the rate of the city's growth, and the longer-term economic irrationality of permitting dispersed, detached, one-story single family dwellings to be the predominant type of new housing.

An additional aspect of Lima's "crisis" is its possible role in legitimating a concern for family planning, as has recently been the case in Mexico. The need for a subway to solve the transportation crisis, the rising levels of air pollution, the large additional investment required to maintain Lima's water supply and similar physical crises—together with the publication of the 1972 census—may alert the junta to Peru's population problem. As in the case of Mexico City, urban "overpopulation" will thus become a visible reality which is far more persuasive than all the efforts of economists and demographers using statistical abstractions as a declining real average income if the growth of GNP is not a multiple of the population growth rate. Mexico's extraordinary post-1970 turnabout with respect to family planning is apparently partly the result of the physical crises of growth in Mexico City. Lima may play a similar role, with the economic irrationality of permissiveness toward squatting providing an accelerating factor.

The above speculation should not be interpreted as suggesting that even a successful crash program of birth control could have much immediate effect on the problems described above or on unemployment, since it would be 15–20 years before a decline in the birth rate would have an adult-age payoff. Thus, birth control would be a desirable, but an ineffective solution to Lima's immediate problems.*

Chapter 7 on Blue-Collar Workers in Peru follows Collier's explanation of barriada deradicalization and focuses on the reasons for the conservatism and weakness of urban factory workers. Bayer (Chapter 8) contributes a valuable study of both provincial urban politics and the ineffectiveness of the Belaúnde administration.

Finally, in viewing the urban political arena during the Belaúnde administration, the present writer has long been struck by what could be defined as a major lost opportunity. One of Belaúnde's major campaign promises in 1963 was to give cities the right to elect their own mayors, a right rescinded by the dictator Leguía in the early 1920s. (In the intervening years, even during democratic constitutional periods, the president appointed all mayors.) By restoring municipal elections, Belaúnde threw away his best opportunity to create a genuine grassroots base for his personalistic Popular Action Party. He also set in motion a process of administration decentralization, and escalation of demands for central government resources, which became major internal obstacles to all his other development plans.

Dew's study of the Puno-Juliaca feud [30] is the best available report in English on the extent to which this decentralization diverted funds to unpromising areas (such as Puno), and complicated the efforts of regional development programs.

Radical reforms have always required an era of increased centralization, even when "home rule" was the long-run goal. This is especially necessary in a country like Peru, where illiterates are not enfranchized and rural areas are still overrepresented. Turning the local majority over to the tender mercies of the local mestizo Creole elite was an abdication of responsibility for mass welfare.

Austin and Lewis [31] provide an interesting, if more technical, discussion on the provision of urban services in central Lima during the Belaúnde period. Major credit for Lima's successful development (at least in physical terms, and in middle-class services) belonged, not to

---

* A projective model based on Mexico (1970–2015) dramatized the probable delayed benefits accruing to peasants, and perhaps city workers, of birth control, as the decreased demand for food increases the possibility for urban savings.[29]

Belaúnde, but to Luis Bedoya, the man who many observers feel would probably win a presidential election if one were held in the near future.

A final observation is in order with respect to the junta's urban policy. It is evidently not destined to be an arena of social reform, especially with respect to real estate ownership. Bayer and others have speculated that the extent of real estate holdings by military officers precludes any "urban reform" paralleling the recent agrarian reform.[32] In any event, the Junta's urban policy consists largely of the physical reconstruction of Lima's streets and public utilities, with SINAMOS taking over the squatter organizations described in the section on urban politics (see Chapter 16).

The Role of U.S. Influence or Domination

The absence of a chapter devoted primarily to U.S. or foreign influence over Peru does not mean that such influence was either minor or benign. The most salient and best-documented case of U.S. pressure on Peru was certainly its premature and unofficial invoking of the Hickenlooper amendment due to the threat of nationalizing the Esso-owned International Petroleum Company. The primary result of this policy was to accelerate the collapse of the otherwise pro-United States, democratically elected Belaúnde regime. The relative neglect of U.S. influence in this volume arises from the following considerations.

1. Daniel Sharp's 1970 volume on *U.S. Foreign Policy and Peru* is a fairly up-to-date and thorough examination of the major issues except, unfortunately, the International Petroleum Company nationalization and the continuing effort of the United States to persuade Peru to commence family planning. Carlos Astiz also has a useful chapter on "External Factors Influencing Peruvian Politics," in his *Pressure Groups and Power Elites in Peruvian Politics,* published in 1969.

2. To the best of the editor's knowledge, no well-researched study has been made, or is probably possible, of either the inside view" on U.S. business influence over the State Department or on local politics in Peru—or the internal workings of United States-Peruvian military aid relations. Most of the works which

deal with these issues are polemical interpretations of official data, and press reports by writers rarely trained in economics and without access to the relevant facts.

3. The major point about current United States-Peruvian relations (conceded by both the political Left and Right) is the relative weakness of the United States and the longstanding divisions among its business interests in Peru. The military junta has clearly enjoyed an era of "benign neglect" which could be better described as the same sort of salutary neglect the 13 colonies enjoyed from English domination prior to the U.S. War of Independence.

Some Academic Issues

The 1970 earthquake

The May 30, 1970 earthquake in the Callejon de Huaylas was not only a historical disaster, killing an estimated 60,000 people and leaving 800,000 homeless, but, like the flooding of Bangladesh and the earthquake destruction of Managua, it had a major political impact, as yet unresearched, on the national and international status of the junta's revolution. The earthquake came as relations with the United States were at their lowest point, and when the various populist reforms had so shaken the confidence of both the national and international private sector that new investments had declined sharply and per capita economic growth stagnated. The junta's rapport with the students and the Left was declining, as it began to move beyond the easier anti-U.S. objects of reformist activity.

Richard Patch and Paul Doughty [32] provide graphic descriptions of the immediate events surrounding the quake, as well as touching on some important themes—such as the differences between U.S., Russian and Chilean aid; the junta's approach to reconstruction, as opposed to that of the survivors; and the effect of disaster on the class structure of several severely affected towns. Overall, it seems that the poorer peasants living in single-story homes on steep hillsides fared much better (and had far less to lose) than members of the urban elite living in multistory buildings in towns located at the bottoms of valleys. In general, it seems that a major opportunity for an imaginative social as well as physical construction is likely to be bypassed.

Constitutional reform

Although the junta has offered no timetable for a return to a civilian parliamentary democracy, its eventual reestablishment seems certain enough to raise the issue of what constitutional reforms would decrease the instability and ineffectiveness of Peru's political regimes. This weakness goes far beyond Latin "character defects," the population problem or even economic crises. One of the primary factors involved here is Peru's uniquely unfavorable combination of the British and U.S. institutional relationships between the executive and the legislative branches of government, which was especially clear during the Belaúnde administration. Peru's presidents are not so powerful as those of most other Latin American countries. The Peruvian congress can "fire" the president's ministers and refuse to finance his programs. Yet these ministers are not members of congress. Furthermore, congress can be, and often has been, of a different party than the president.[34]

Illiterates are disenfranchised in Peru, yet they are counted for purposes of representation, thus causing an overrepresentation of the small rural middle and upper classes. The junta has moved toward preparing illiterates for suffrage by giving them the right to vote for the directors of the rural cooperatives. Whether they will be allowed (or rather *required,* like the eligible voters before 1968) to vote in the future is still uncertain. Meanwhile, unlike the far more repressive Brazilian military dictatorship, the Peruvian junta has *not* mounted a mass rural, adult literacy campaign.

Civilianization and the junta's middle-class orientation

José Nun, in a much-quoted essay,[35] views most of the current Latin American military regimes as creatures of the middle-class, because, at least initially, they have been so well received by that class; and the officers are of predominantly middle-class origin. As Nun and other analysts of recent Latin military regimes have demonstrated, the professionalization of the military need not lead to their retreat from politics (in spite of the Mexican experience). Rather, it may lead to a greater involvement. Furthermore, the new middle classes do not, at least initially, disapprove of military rule, since the only alternative appears to be populist-elite coalitions which have been less favorable to middle-class educational and economic aspirations.

However, Nun's categorical rejection of C. Wright Mills's model of the military as a semiautonomous institution seems overdrawn in the Peruvian case. To begin with, the "middle-class origins" of most officers obscures the salient fact that a high proportion of them are also the sons, and grandsons, of military officers. Thus, they are primarily military, and only secondarily middle-class. There is more outward than inward career mobility, since entry into the military must occur at an early age, while early retirements could militarize the civilian world by stocking the middle managerial ranks of business and industry with ex-officers. In addition, despite their many nationalist-populist moves, the caste privileges of the military remain inviolate. In fact, the major exceptions to their otherwise relatively loose control over the press have dealt with exposés of military salary increases, early and increased pension benefits and other institutional privileges.

The primary issue of interest at this point, however, is the net flow of influence during the deep and prolonged interpenetration of the civilian and military worlds in Peru. While the current style of Peruvian military professionalism has not led to a withdrawal from politics, a deep and enduring responsibility for daily civilian governmental administration does constitute a threat to the integrity of the military, by introducing civilian partisanship and "corruption" into an otherwise fairly consensus-based institution; and by placing the honor of the military at stake, if economic development should lag with resultant labor unrest. The experience of the Argentine military is, of course, highly relevant on this point.

Therefore, a growing conflict within the military over one or both of these threats will presumably lead to the eventual withdrawal of, or splits within, the military, leaving open the possibility of sharp turns to the Left or Right if one "partisan" faction were to predominate.

University reform

One of the major failures of the junta has been its retreat from a proposed program of university reform. After an abortive attempt to exclude partisan politics from the universities and sharply curtail *co-gobierno* (a system of co-government, in which elected student leaders constitute one-third of a university's "trustees"), President General Velasco returned to this system in a populist performance at the University of San Marcos, traditionally the most politicized of Peru's universities.

A possible consequence of this retreat may be the budgetary and recruitment neglect of the civilian universities and their graduates, in favor of giving more funds and job opportunities to graduates of the military academies. There are already many civilians attending military primary and secondary schools, so the duplication of higher education within military academies seems highly probable. The graduates of the discredited, repoliticized civilian universities may find it increasingly difficult to obtain "appropriate" employment during the junta's administration. Already the early rapport that had existed between the university students and the junta has declined. The future employment of these students may well be the decisive element in the Junta's continued legitimacy.

Throughout this introductory chapter, we have tried to explain why Peru has yet to experience a radical social revolution. No predictions about the course of the current military government will be attempted. It would appear, however, that they have exhausted the populist options which have sustained their legitimacy, given the orientation of the dominant members of the Junta. To sustain their rule, they will either have to turn more sectors of the economy back to foreign capital or move ahead into even more active management of the economy. The latter could be accomplished either by an even greater involvement of military officers in enterprise management, or the military could create a corps of civilian socialist enterprise managers. None of these solutions to economic development, however, comes to grips with social mobilization, or control, the issue SINAMOS was designed to handle. It would not appear at this point that the next five years, if the junta stays in power that long, will be as easily "successful" as its first five.

NOTES

1. Carleton Beals, *Fire on the Andes* (Philadelphia: Lippincott, 1934).

2. François Bourricaud, "Structure and Function of the Peruvian Oligarchy," *Studies in Comparative International Development* 2, no. 2.

3. Luis Ratinoff, "Las clases medias en America Latina," *Revista paraguaya de sociologia* 2 (September-December 1965): 5-31; Anthony Leeds, "Brazilian Careers and Social Structure: An Evolutionary Model and Case History," *American Anthropologist* 66 (December 1964): 1321-47; and Rodolfo Stavenhagen, "Seven Erroneous Theses About Latin America," *New University Thought* 4 (Winter 1966-1967): 32.

4. Gabriel Escobar, "El mestizaje en la region andina: El caso del Peru," *Revista de Indias* (Madrid), nos. 95-96 (January-June 1964): 197-220; Anibal Quijano, "La emergencia del grupo 'cholo' y sus consecuencias en la sociedad peruana," in Asociación Colombiana de Sociologia, *Sociologia y sociedad en Latino-america* (Bogota, 1965): 403-47; and José Varallanos, *El cholo y el Peru* (Buenos Aires, 1962).

5. Carey found that, in Latin America, Peru was second only to Brazil in the amount of U.S. military assistance (not including covert military and CIA assistance) received from 1945 to 1960 ($94,000,000). See James C. Carey, *Peru and the United States* (Notre Dame, Ind.: University of Notre Dame Press, 1964), p. 144. See also Gertrude E. Heare, *Trends in Latin American Military Expenditures 1940-1970*, Department of State Publication No. 2618 (Washington, D.C.: USGPO, December 1971).

6. James L. Payne, *Labor and Politics in Peru* (New Haven: Yale University Press, 1965), p. 109.

7. Harry Kantor, *The Ideology and Program of the Peruvian Aprista Movement* (Berkeley: University of California Press, 1956); and Robert J. Alexander, *Communism in Latin America* (New Brunswick: Rutgers University Press, 1957).

8. Beals, *Fire on the Andes*, p. 428.

9. United Nations, Economic Commission for Latin America, *Analyses and Projections of Economic Development: 6. The Industrial Development of Peru:* 2 (Mexico City, 1959).

10. German Guzman, Orlando Fals Borda and Eduardo Umana Luna, *La violencia en Colombia;* 2nd ed., vols. 1, 2 (Bogota, 1963).

11. Gabriel Escobar, an authority on the social history of the Peruvian sierra, observes that "if the Indians, as Indians, had ever acquired political power it would have taken the form of a 'nativistic' reconstruction of the Inca empire, as revealed by the Puno rebellions of the 1920s" (personal communication, January 27, 1967).

12. Gabriel Escobar, *La estructura politica rural del departamento de Puno*, Ph.D. diss. (Cuzco: Universidad Nacional de San Antonio Abad del Cuzco, 1961).

13. Thomas Ford, *Man and Land in Peru* (Gainesville: University of Florida Press, 1962), p. 80. The Beneficencias Publicas (Public Welfare Societies) were established in the late 1820s, to serve as an alternative to the religious orders for receiving land bequests and directing charities.

14. "The Modernized Church in Peru: Two Aspects," *Review of Politics* 26 (July 1964): 308, 309, 307, 311.

15. J. J. Johnson, *The Military and Society in Latin America* (Stanford, Calif.: Stanford University Press, 1964).

16. Carlos A. Astiz and José Z. Garcia, "The Peruvian Military: Achievement Orientation, Training and Political Tendencies," *Western Political Quarterly* (December 1972).

17. SINAMOS, *Ley Organica Decreto Ley*, no. 19352 (Lima, 1972).

18. William F. Whyte, "Peruvian Paradox: Military Rule and Popular Participation," unpublished manuscript, p. 25.

19. Ibid. p. 33.

20. This discussion has also benefited from Michael Anderson's "New Forms of Worker Participation in the Peruvian Economy: A Report to the Ford Foundation" (Ithaca, New York: September 3, 1972), p. 20.

21. For this and other observations on conditions in Peru during late 1972, the author gratefully acknowledges the observations of Professor Stillman Bradfield.

22. A July 13, 1972 speech reprinted in the July 14 issue of *Oiga*, quoted in Anderson, "New Forms of Worker Participation." (Editor's translation.)

23. Anderson, "New Forms of Worker Participation," p. 3.

24. Anibal Quijano, "Imperialismo y Capitalismo de estado" and Julio Cotler, "La Politica y el Comentario," in *Sociedad y Politica* (Lima), no. 1 (June 1972); and "Bases del Corporativismo en el Peru," *Sociedad y Politica*, no. 2 (October 1972). Anibal Quijano, *Nationalism and Capitalism in Peru: A Study in Neo-Imperialism* (New York: Monthly Review Press, 1971).

25. Cotler, "Bases del Corporativismo," p. 10.

26. *Oiga*, July 21, 1972, p. 11.

27. Cotler, "Bases del Corporativismo."

28. See David Chaplin, *Population Policies and Growth in Latin America* (Lexington, Mass.: Heath-Lexington Books, 1971), for an interdisciplinary examination of the relationship between population growth and social welfare. See especially Chapter 11 on Peru.

29. See John Isbister, "Birth Control, Income Redistribution, and the Rate of Savings: The Case of Mexico," *Demography* 10, no. 1 (February 1973): 85–98.

30. Edward Dew, *Politics in the Altiplano: The Dynamics of Change in Rural Peru* (Austin: University of Texas Press, 1969).

31. Allan G. Austin and Sherman Lewis, *Urban Government for Metropolitan Lima* (New York: Praeger, 1970).

32. David Bayer, personal correspondence with the author, February 1973.

33. Richard Patch, "The Peruvian Earthquake of 1970," part 1, Carhuaz, vol. 18, no. 6; part 2, Marcara to Vicos, vol. 18, no. 7; part 3, Huaraz, vol. 18, no. 8; part 4, Yungay, vol. 18, no. 9; *American Universities Field Staff Reports*, May-July, 1971. Paul Doughty, "From Disaster to Development," *Americas* 23, no. 5 (May 1971), and Doughty, "Community Response to Natural Disaster in the Peruvian Andes" (Paper presented to the November 1971 annual meeting of the *American Anthropological Association*).

34. For an excellent summary of the history and structure of the Peruvian presidency and congress, see Terry McCoy, "Congress, The President and Political Instability in Peru," Chapter 8 in Weston Agor, *Latin American Legislatures* (New York: Praeger, 1971).

35. José Nun, "A Latin American Phenomenon: The Middle Class Military Coup," in J. Petras and M. Zeitlin, *Latin America—Reform or Revolution?* (New York: Fawcett Books, 1968); "The Middle Class Coup Revisited," in Claudio Veliz, *The Politics of Conformity in Latin America* (New York: Oxford University Press, 1967).

Julio Cotler

2. The Mechanics of Internal Domination and Social Change in Peru

Peruvian society is characterized by a structural dualism, based on sociocultural contrasts between the coast and the sierra, the two most important regions of the country.[1]

Those sectors of economic activity with the highest productivity, such as fishing, agriculture for export, manufacturing and financial services, are concentrated on the coast. This concentration is reflected in the income and occupational mobility of the population. In 1961, 47 percent of the country's total population lived on the coast and contributed 67 percent of the national income, while the proportions in the sierra amounted to 46 percent and 34 percent respectively. As a result of this differential participation, the average income per capita on the coast was 23 percent above the national average, while in the sierra it was 29 percent below it.[2] In the same year, 69 percent of the coastal population resided in urban areas, in contrast to only 29 percent in the sierra. Seventy-nine percent of the coastal population over 15 was literate, versus 47 percent of that in the sierra within the same age group.[3] This contributed to the fact that, in 1966, 69 percent of the electorate came from coastal departments, while only 26 percent was from the sierra.

A major part of all newspapers, journals and books (both domestic and imported) are published and sold in the coastal region. Most radio and television stations are installed on the coast. In 1966, only a scant .4 percent of the television sets existing in the country were to be found in two cities of the sierra.[4] All these factors lead to an intense intra- and inter-regional communication in the coastal section of Peru.

The Spanish conquerors carried out an early eradication of native culture on the coast. At the turn of the century, the coast became integrated into the international capitalist market, thus growing further apart from Indian cultural patterns. The result was a variation on Western colonial culture, known as "Creole culture." [5]

These characteristics have given rise to a conception of the coast as a region of "Western modernizing development," while the sierra continues to be branded as a "traditional, underdeveloped region."

With the exception of mining centers, the predominant activity in the sierra is agriculture and cattle-breeding, characterized by a low rate of productivity. This means that a great part of the population participates only rarely in the internal market and lives in widely disseminated areas.

The limited access to the sierra region and its preindustrial forms of production account for that area's precarious internal communication and limited acculturation. There are vast pockets of isolation which allow for the survival of the *quechua* and *aymará* languages and the traditional social forms of organization with which those languages are associated. This situation is largely due to the fact that in the sierra public investment is six times smaller than on the coast.[6]

In the coastal region there is relative diversification and occupational mobility, in conjunction with the development of industrial patterns of production and property. In the sierra preindustrial patterns predominate, with the exception of mining centers, which are enterprises organized and directed from abroad.

Contrary to what happens on the coast, the landholding system in the sierra exhibits two preindustrial patterns of organization: Indian communities and latifundia. The former constitute corporate organizations based on kinship which, through common utilization of land and water, maintain political-religious functions and ties of internal solidarity. Latifundia are characterized by the feudal character of their social relations. These establishments, which emphasize ascriptive criteria, further the continuance of obsolete social and cultural patterns.

The disparity noted between coast and sierra is true to the extent that it does not discriminate internally originated differences within each one of these regions, and in that it endeavors to emphasize the relationship between a geographical region and sociocultural patterns of existence.

This stereotyped image gives rise to a perception of the country as presenting strikingly opposed social situations. Moreover, Peru is often viewed as a nonintegrated nation, with the sierra considered as marginal and the coastal region representing the country. This concept of a lack of national integration has led some authors to view the country as a social archipelago, or as an inarticulate, pluralistic, heterogeneous society.[7]

These concepts are useful to illustrate internal differences through various indicators, such as those mentioned above. Nevertheless, it is important to point out that this perspective overlooks the relations between the regions and their social strata, insofar as they are affected— although in different degrees—by a single historical process.

Although it would be inaccurate to state that the population of the sierra is not incorporated into the life of the nation, this statement must also be qualified by pointing out the context of social relations of dependence. The existing terms of interaction between the two regions and their respective social sectors are unfavorable to the sierra, insofar as its population does not have access to the opportunities and resources of the global society. This does not mean that as a whole the sierra is marginal with respect to the country, but rather that it is *made* marginal by a sector of the latter. In Andrew Gunder Frank's words:

> this "marginal" or "floating" population is in the process of becoming, or in some instances, is fully integrated into the society in a way which prejudices its welfare and opportunities to develop, and which defines the urban or rural economic sector, social position, and economic region or locality as "underdeveloped."
>
> These considerations suggest that Latin America is not a "dual" society, but rather an integrated one, and that many of its members are not so much marginal as they are integrated in a way that prejudices their most vital interests. . . .[8]

Some writers have suggested that, just as relations between developed and underdeveloped countries are set in metropolitan-colonial terms, the same relationship exists between the developed and underdeveloped regions of a particular country.[9] In addition to this regional stratification, within each one of the regions stratification relationships of the same nature are produced and successively repeated in a branching pattern. Thus, "developed" social sectors may include both metropolitan and colonial social sectors, which may in turn have their own area of influence as a single unit, thus performing a metropolitan role with respect to other social sectors.

> The structure of relations between the developing metropolis and the underdeveloped periphery of the international market appears, in the course of the historical development of Latin America, to have been duplicated within the continent, within each of its countries, and indeed within many of the latter's internal regions. Within each of these there developed a metropolitan center and a corresponding underdeveloped periphery. At the same time these national metropolises, as is the case with the world metropolises, maintain structured economic relationships with their respective provincial peripheries, which is an extension of the relationship between the world metropolises and themselves. A similar relationship can be observed in turn at the regional level, whose commercial centers are in an economically disadvantageous position, being in the periphery with respect to national and international metropolises—yet performing a metropolitan role in terms of their respective peripheral rural hinterlands. The metropolis-periphery relationship at the national, regional, and in certain cases sectoral levels, no less than at the international level, exhibits a transfer of capital from the periphery to the metropolis, as well as the determination of the fortunes of the periphery by the metropolis.[10]

Rodolfo Stavenhagen, in his description of dualist societies in Latin America, points out that the "underdeveloped" regions of these countries remain in this state because of the human exploitation in underdeveloped areas: "The underdeveloped regions of Latin American countries perform the role of internal colonies. Instead of stating the problem of Latin America in terms of dualism, it would be better to speak of internal colonialism." [11] In the same sense, the person appointed by the Mayor of New York to rehabilitate Harlem declared that "Harlem has many of the features of underdeveloped countries. . . . The basic similarity between Harlem and an underdeveloped nation is that the local population does not control the area's economy, and therefore most of the internally generated income is rapidly drained out. That money is not returned or applied to any local community improvement." [12]

Various writers have described the deprivation of the Indian sectors in Latin America—in the Mezoamerican region as well as in the central Andean region—on the basis of the dependence and domination imposed upon the Indians by the immediate "superior" element, the ladino or mestizo. François Bourricaud refers to the status of the Indians in terms of their dependence upon the mestizo. Stavenhagen and González Casanova define the status of the Indians as that of a colonized class or a *Lumpenproletariat* with respect to the ladinos.[13]

Wolf points out that the marginality of the Central American communities stems from the Indians' unwillingness to establish relations with the ladinos, inasmuch as it might entail patterns of domination.[14] Bourricaud, on the other hand, defines the Indian community as essentially alien with respect to the mestizo.[15] The Regional Plan for the Development of Southern Peru states that "the Indians . . . in many cases appear to have conducted a war of exhaustion, consisting of a passive resistance, or of retiring into areas where there is a minimum of contact with the higher classes." [16]

These authors have endeavored to explain the relations between metropolitan and peripheral social strata—without explaining how this situation is linked with the metropolitan region and its different social sectors. In other words, if as stated among others by Bourricaud and the Plan del Sur, the Puno mestizo is the dominant element in that circumscription, the question could be raised as to what extent his status is sustained by and at the same time dependent upon the metropolitan area and social strata established in the coastal region. If such relations exist, which are the mechanisms that furnish the mestizos with such regional standing? And what consequences does that situation entail for the social system as a whole, and for the coastal peripheral elements in particular?

The purpose of this analysis is to provide some tentative answers to these questions, within the Peruvian context, on the basis of bibliographical sources and—in some cases—primary sources.

Indians and Mestizos

Bourricaud characterizes Indians and mestizos as sociocultural groups having their own particular attributes and constituting a sort of caste. These attributes include traits such as language, place and status of residence, consumption and occupation. Thus, the Indian speaks only *quechua* or *aymará,* is always bound to rural areas, has a distinctive style of consumption (generally characterized by its reduced ties with the market) and is always a shepherd or farmer. In other words, he fills social positions of minor social prestige. Conversely, the mestizo always speaks Spanish and masters some other aboriginal tongue, resides in or is attached to urban areas, his consumption is linked to the market and he is never a shepherd or peon.

> Nobody would classify a lawyer or a physician in the Indian group, nor an army or police officer. "Occupations which do not require previous instruction are regarded as the exclusive property of the Indians. Inversely, we could say that the fact of being white or a *'misti'* is incompatible with certain activities. The peon of the hacienda is always an Indian. Also the *'misti,'* even of the lowest status, will have a position which confers upon him a minimum of authority; he will be at least a warden, or a gatherer. Should he descend in the social scale to the status of peon, he would suddenly find himself in the same status as the Indian. We would even go as far as to assert that an Indian is never the holder of a position that entails high prestige. . . ." [17]

Likewise, in the Plan del Sur it is stated that, "in Puno there is a pronounced dichotomy between the mass (85 percent) of the population who live in rural areas, speak an indigenous language, perform manual tasks and are regarded as a separate class (almost a caste), and the dominant urban society of three intermediate classes which participate to different degrees in the Peruvian economy and culture." [18]

But, as these writers point out, within the Indian group there are internal differences, if one considers the institutional framework within which the Indian status is located. Though the Indian is always a shepherd or farmer, these activities can be performed within the hacienda or in the Indian community, which involve different patterns of social control in the mestizo-Indian relationship.

Among the mestizos there are different social gradings based on class criteria, such as education, occupational prestige, income, place of residence, etc., but they always have one common trait: the domination of the Indian peasant. The distinctions between Indians and mestizos are therefore discontinuous in nature, since the latter, despite their internal differences, are characterized by their control over the Indian.

In 1961, the region commonly referred to as "Mancha India," which included the departments of Ancash, Apurímac, Ayacucho, Cuzco,

Huancavelica and Puno, comprised 29 percent of the country's total population. Within this group 87 percent of those over five years of age communicated with each other in an Indian language. Sixty-nine percent of the economically active population was dedicated to agriculture and cattle-breeding, whereas the average for such occupations in the rest of the country was only 42 percent.

These occupational conditions entail a reduced diversification and are reflected in the average income of the population of the area, which is 39 percent lower than the national average.

Table 1
DISTRIBUTION OF LANDHOLDINGS IN
"MANCHA INDIA" AND IN THE REMAINDER OF THE COUNTRY

Hectares	Mancha India		Rest of Country	
	Productive Units %	Hectares %	Productive Units %	Hectares %
0 – 4	87.5	7.8	79.3	5.8
5 – 9	6.6	2.7	11.4	3.3
10 – 19	2.5	2.0	4.6	2.9
20 – 99	1.9	4.6	3.5	6.2
100 – 499	0.5	8.5	0.7	7.2
500 – +	0.4	60.7	0.2	65.4
Within incorporated communities	0.03	13.1	0.03	8.8
Total	99.43	99.4	99.73	99.6

Source: Primer Censo Nacional Agropecuario, Lima, 1961.

The agricultural and cattle-breeding activities were carried on within a system of property characterized by latifundism and a high fragmentation of productive units—a situation which does not differ much from that existing in the rest of the country.

The haciendas

The haciendas of this region are mainly dedicated to sheep-grazing, and in a complementary form to agriculture. While wool is destined primarily for the international market, mutton is shipped to the largest cities within the country. It would appear that agricultural production is aimed chiefly at local consumption or limited commercial circles. In certain cases, however, it has an essential function, especially in the case of haciendas in subtropical valleys, where the cultivation of *coca* and of sugar cane (the latter for the production of vodka) is intended for consumption by the Indians, while coffee and tea are destined for the international market.

The abundance of manpower in the area—due to a landless or minifundist population—makes it cheap, and thereby intensively used with a correspondingly low capitalization. Such an abundance of cheap manpower explains why reinvestment is chiefly aimed at increasing production and not labor productivity.

As a result of this structure of property and of production, the population is scattered—especially in hacienda zones—with only a few important population centers in the area. In 1961 there were only six cities with over 20,000 inhabitants, housing only 61 percent of the total population—while 87 percent resided in centers with less than 2,000 inhabitants, contrasting with an average in the rest of the country of 31 percent and 60 percent respectively.[19]

The conditions of the structure of property and of production, together with the high dispersion of the population and the lack of occupational diversification, favor the existing relations between mestizos and Indians, and do not allow for alternatives to the hacienda system.[20]

The manpower of landless Indians is employed in the haciendas of the region through a peculiar form of debt servitude generally referred to as *"colonato."* By *"colonato"* it is assumed that the mestizo owner offers the Indian worker the use of a plot of land for cultivation or grazing, contingent upon the latter's paying him back through the fulfillment of certain "obligations." The obligations that the Indian is committed to are varied: unremunerated work on the land of the hacienda during a certain number of days per week, grazing of the cattle of the hacienda, domestic service at the farmhouse or in the urban residence of the boss; selling to the owner the produce of his own small plot at a price established by the owner, as well as any surpluses that the Indian may have been able to achieve. This last duty is fundamental in the case of haciendas in the subtropical valleys, since it enables the landowner not only to recruit workers almost free, but also to monopolize the marketing of high-priced goods such as coffee and tea.

This relationship established between landlord and worker determines that the latter will remain in a permanent state of insecurity, unable to anticipate with any degree of certainty the character of his duties, and with no time to accomplish any task of his own: "At plowing and potato-digging time they work for the hacienda during a whole month, and therefore have no time left to tend their plots." [21] The workers' possibilities to migrate temporarily from the hacienda are severely limited, as this would imply a nonfulfillment of their duties—with the consequent loss of their "rights" over the plot of land they use.

The situation of uncertainty which characterizes the tenant-farmer has led some authors to believe that his state of mind probably verges on the pathological. His constant fear that the boss might expel him from the plot or take possession of his livestock, his fear that, through illness, he will be unable to fulfill his duties or tend his plot, surrounds the Indian in a complex of worries and repressions.[22]

> The Vicos manor serf suffered from a number of forms of fear—so many, and often so serious, that we entertain some doubts as to whether the local subculture really worked out effective escapes from danger that permitted the serfs to enjoy a state of relaxation at any time. In the most general terms of personal interaction, the serf regarded all human relationships as hostile, since they were basically power-oriented.[23]

In this situation the boss is perceived as the all-powerful source, whose good graces the Indian must woo in order to maintain his unstable position. Because the Indian has no other possibilities of livelihood within his reach he must accept the asymmetrical ties of reciprocity proposed by the landlord. Toward this end, he seeks to establish paternalistic ties with the boss and also with the figures of authority in general, so as to commit them to a situation which might place him in a preferential status with respect to the other tenants. If he gets the boss to be godfather to one of his children, he may have fewer duties to perform, and there may be a chance that he will obtain a certain degree of indulgence in case of unfulfillment of his duties or, at best, he might even be taken as the boss's man. [24] The landlord, for his own part, uses this paternalistic relationship to strengthen the tenant's ties of personal loyalty—highlighting the latter's exceptional status and thereby constituting himself as the single source of identification of his tenant-farmers—thus avoiding the formation of class identifications.[25]

There is a common ideology between landlords and *japas*. The former regard themselves as protectors of the Indians, whom they call their "little ones"; they offer them economic security in times of famine, and social security when they are summoned to appear before the local authorities on charges of misdeeds or misdemeanors. The Indians call the landlord *"patrón,"* and sometimes look upon him as a father and protector. They do not feel scorned . . . when regarded as servants; on the contrary, on certain occasions they identify with their landlords.[26]

With these conditions of control and social identification, cultural forms proscribe patterns of aggression toward the boss and prescribe instead that these be directed toward the other tenant-farmers competing for the boss's favors. As a result, the Indian views his wellbeing in terms of the deprivation of other workers.[27] This provokes a situation of distrust and envy, characteristic of the "familial amorality" described by E. Banfield,[28] which contributes to social fragmentation. The Indians' lack of social articulation—encouraged by the authority figure on the basis of services and personal rewards which tend to divide the tenant population—determines the establishment of dyadic[29] and asymmetric relationships between landlord and tenant,[30] suggesting the existence of multiple disconnected radii which converge on one single vertex.

This situation of structural and normative dependence of the Indian upon the *"mistis,"* gives rise to considerable social and cultural distance between these two sectors of the population. If for the mestizo "the Indian is the animal which most resembles man," the Indian, on his part, internalizes his subordinate condition. Thus, of 499 Indians interviewed in six communities and one hacienda of the department of Cuzco, 52 percent agreed that "Indians are born to serve and obey the *"misti."*[31]

The Indian communities

Along with the hacienda, the Indian community is one of the two types of rural social organizations characteristic of the area. Indian communities, in contrast to what happens in the hacienda, exhibit a high population density and an incipient occupational differentiation.

Indian communities are characterized by the ties that exist between their members, ties which encourage them to regard themselves as particular collectivities. The identifications developed in these centers have a local-familial character, as indicated by the fact that an individual belonging to a certain community may be recognized by certain distinctive aspects of his clothing.

Despite the existence of such internal solidarity, the situation of these communities continues to be precarious. Indian communities are generally located in the most barren lands, on hillsides with a large degree of erosion. As a consequence of the distribution of communal plots, there is a high degree of fragmentation and dispersion of the land, which is the chief, if not the only, source of capitalization. This forces the commoners to seek land in neighboring areas, and there are cases of status combinations, as when commoners rent land from the haciendas, which they in turn sublet to other tenant-farmers who are thus committed to render service both to the hacienda and to the commoner-renter.[32] Yet another arrangement is that of a community collectively integrated into the hacienda system, which has been called a "dependent" or "captive" community.[33]

Another alternative for commoners facing the problem of land shortage is to emigrate. This does not affect their rights or affiliation in the community, in contrast to the situation of tenant-farmers.[34]

Thus the communities in "Mancha India" constitute a reservoir of manpower for the haciendas whenever the latter want to extend their areas of work or replace any number of tenant-farmers.

The intense fragmentation and dispersion of the commoners' farmland favors the existence of a permanent state of anxiety among them, expressed by manifold internal conflicts. These same circumstances account for the existing discord between communities, to which must be added their ethnocentric identifications, all of which favors the development of endless lawsuits.[35] Moreover, with no new occupational opportunities, these circumstances are aggravated by population growth.

Under these conditions a new form of Indian dependence is generated: this time with respect to the mestizo. In order to resolve lawsuits, the Indian woos the favors of a mestizo to obtain (through the latter's good offices) a favorable judicial ruling—since the Indian does not speak Spanish, is illiterate, and there is a generalized belief that juridical proceedings are not subject to universalist criteria. Thus, of 499 Indians interviewed in Cuzco, 56 percent considered that judges base their rulings on personal influence and on the amount of money paid by plaintiffs.[36]

> The Indian seeks the (mestizo) middle-class member as a protector and, above all, as an influential factor to tilt justice on his side in his all-too-frequent lawsuits with other Indians or with people of higher strata.[37]

The mestizo's role as middleman and "protector" of the Indian extends not only to judiciary cases, but also to all the relationships that the Indian must establish with official institutions. Under such conditions, commoners are in effect clients of the mestizos, whom they must reward in some way. They are tacitly committed to sell them their products, thus becoming dependent upon the *"atajadores"* ("intercepters"). They are recruited to perform tasks of a private nature gratis, and "public" labor in district capitals under the pretense of retribution for favors that it is in the hands of the mestizos to grant. Such recruitment is carried out through the indigenous authorities of the haciendas or communities. Thus, in contrast to what some "indigenists" assume, community autonomy is spurious, in that Indian authorities channel the landlord's or the district authorities' orders and the requests for favors—in addition to the fact that the commoners are also clients of the town mestizos.

> In the communities or in the haciendas, the Indians have their own traditional authorities designated annually by the commoners, whose duty it is to maintain relationships within the system in force. They receive orders from the *"mistis"* and see that they are carried out, and seek to obtain the mestizo's favors.[38]

As a result of the structural and normative conditions of dependence in which tenant-farmers and commoners find themselves with regard to the mestizos, the predominant personality trait is one of fatalism. They also exhibit political lethargy and an inability to modify this situation, since the designs of the mestizos appear to them as uncontrollable, a perception which is manifested through the servile behavior that is usual among subordinate groups.

The Mestizos and the National System

Even though property is a sufficient condition to establish a relation of domination over the Indians, this condition is not necessary since, as we have already seen, those commoners who are in no direct relation with the hacienda system are nonetheless equally involved in ties of dependence. The necessary and sufficient requirements of the system of domination described are a function of the mestizo's access to the system of authority through his knowledge of Spanish, and through literacy which allows him to elect or be elected and to designate or be designated to fill positions within the system of "national" authority or within the public administration—thus securing state resources to legitimize his lineage and his domination of the Indian mass.

As stated above, the mestizo is not only the owner or administrator of the hacienda; he is also lawyer, middleman, judge, governor, policeman, trader. As expressed by Bourricaud: "the 'misti,' even of the lowest strata, occupies a position which bestows upon him at least a minimum of authority. . . ."

Monolinguism and illiteracy

In 1961 there were in Peru 1.8 million inhabitants over five years of age who spoke *quechua* or *aymará*, 87 percent of whom were concentrated in Mancha India, constituting 19 percent of the total population of the country within this age group.[39] These departments, especially Huancavelica, Apurímac and Ayacucho, lead all departments in their degree of illiteracy, since there is a correlation of .84 between literacy and the ability to speak Spanish.[40]

Despite the relative weight of Indian languages among the population of the country, those who speak them are discriminated against in all spheres of the institutional life of Peru. The educational system ignores the *quechua* and *aymará* languages and imposes Spanish universally. Teachers sent to Mancha India usually do not speak Indian tongues, and if they do, being mestizo, they only use them in personal relations in which they invoke their privileged status. The help rendered by government and university institutions for the study of Indian languages is insignificant, and the scarce research in this field is subsidized by foreign foundations.

Table 2
DISTRIBUTION OF POPULATION IN TERMS OF TOTAL AND RURAL ILLITERACY AND BY DEGREE OF FUNCTIONAL LITERACY

Departments	Percentage of illiterate adults, 15 years or older, in the total population	Percentage of illiterate adults, 15 years or older, in rural areas	Percentage of functional literacy
Ancash	51	82	19
Apurimac	76	86	10
Ayacucho	72	81	10
Cuzco	72	80	16
Huancavelica	66	88	9
Puno	64	66	10
Average-6 departments	65	81	12
National average	39	78	31

Source: Censo Nacional de Población, volume 2, 1961.

Indians themselves appear to recognize that their lack of knowledge of the Spanish language and illiteracy are associated with their status. Of 495 Indians interviewed in Cuzco, 76 percent felt that if Indians had the same level of education as mestizos they would be on equal terms to perform any occupation; and 91 percent agreed that "through education a man can achieve what he wants." [41] Mario Vázquez likewise testifies:

Vicosinos recognise the importance of the Spanish language as an instrument of communication and knowledge, for at present Spanish is the chief barrier between the Indian and the mestizo, and is perhaps one of the causes of Vicos' isolation and cultural backwardness. The following confirm our statement: "I am afraid of going to other towns because I do not speak Spanish. . . . I am ashamed of being unable to answer when spoken to in Spanish. . . . Many people scoff at us when we cannot answer their questions . . . they keep saying, why do you come here if you cannot speak Spanish? If I could only speak Spanish I would not be afraid because I would feel equal to the others. . . . Mestizos have better opportunities to make money because they work more with their eyes, while we are tied up in the fields.... If I knew Spanish perhaps I would be more courageous and the educated would not humiliate me." [42]

Public administration lacks the necessary mechanisms to communicate with this population. The Ministry of Labor and Communities has only one official *quechua* or *aymará* translator at the Indigenist Institute of Peru. Regarding the administration of justice, the situation is truly pathetic, as the Indian defendants have no possibility of understanding their cases since they are carried out in a language unknown to them. It goes without saying that the Indians lack the means to learn about their rights, and as a consequence are at the mercy of the mestizos, their obligated middlemen.

The electoral system

Due to Peru's electoral regulations, which stipulate that only literate individuals have the right to elect or be elected, the Indian population has no access to the polls or to true representation. Nonetheless, in accordance with those regulations, they are considered in the computation of the number of representatives that each area sends to Congress—for which the total population of each department is taken into account. Thus, Mancha India, which holds 29 percent of the total population of the country, has 14 percent of the electoral population—since only one out of every five of its inhabitants over twenty years of age is entitled to vote. This fraction of the population, however, elects 50 (27 percent) of the 185 representatives who constitute Congress. Likewise, these departments require an average of five times less electors to elect a representative than those required for the department of Lima, which has the highest proportion of electoral population in the country—86 percent of its population over 20 years of age are electors.

This electoral mechanism, besides contributing to the discrimination against the population of Mancha India, discriminates against the peasant population of the country as a whole, be it in sierra or coastal departments: 78 percent of the rural population over fifteen years of age is illiterate. Thus, there is a positive rank correlation of .83 between the economically active population dedicated to agri-

cultural activities and the illiterate population—and a negative correlation of .87 between the population dedicated to agricultural labor
and the electoral population, at the national level.*

Ignorance of the Spanish language, the strong incidence of rural
illiteracy, the dispersion which characterizes the population of
Mancha India, the situation of structural and normative dependence
that the Indian suffers in relation to the mestizo, are all factors which
suggest that both the electors and the elected are mestizos. In this way
the mestizo authority is institutionalized and the Indian population
placed outside of the institutional resources.

"Gamonalismo"

Through their own knowledge of the Spanish language, education,
and through withholding these resources from the Indian population,
mestizos are able to control economic, political, juridical, repressive
and cultural resources: they are the representatives and senators,
hacienda owners or administrators, departmental prefects, sub-
prefects and governors; they are likewise the judges and teachers,
dominating all authority spheres, a fact which defines the *gamonal*
system.

Mestizo domination over the Indian separates the two along
castelike lines. Both the mestizo and the Indian sectors have their
own well-defined values, activities and relations. From this it may be
concluded that mestizo activities in Congress, the bureaucracy,
tribunals, etç., are aimed at strengthening the position of their own
group.

Thus, mestizos have access to decisions at local and regional
levels—and through these at the national level—without having to
take into consideration a dominated mass incapable of autonomous
initiatives or decisions.

This privatization of power exists at different levels. The mestizo
group is free to act in accordance with its own initiatives, even re-

---

* In 1965 the electoral population was about two million. At the same time there were
six million people of voting age.

interpreting dispositions which could reduce the range of its attributions.

> In the Chawaytiri hacienda (Cuzco), as a result of a movement which brought about tenant-farmer syndicalization, district authorities appointed a literate tenant-farmer as lieutenant-governor. . . . Upon his visiting the hacienda owner in order to inform him of his appointment, he was told by the owner: "Who do you think you are, to have yourself appointed lieutenant-governor. . . . I do not know you. . . . You should know that in this hacienda there can be no lieutenant-governor or any other authority for that matter, so go and paper the walls of your house with your appointment. In the hacienda the only authorities are those appointed by me.[43]

Moreover, the owner or his administrator, even without holding any political office, through the control they exercise over the tenant-farmers and their affinity and closeness with those in authority, do in fact perform such functions.

> Until three years ago, the landlord was the maximum political, social and juridical authority. When quarrels broke out, theft, or even crime was perpetrated, the administrator or his representative were the first to intervene. If the case warranted it, it was then transmitted to the competent authority. Traditional local authorities were appointed by and took oath before the administrator; there was no need to travel to the Pisac governorship in order to receive a ruling of the case.[44]

This privatization of power has geographic connotations. V. Landázuri states that at La Convención the district capital is but a village within the hacienda, which constitutes the real seat of authority.[45]

Due to lack of social diversification in Mancha India, and also to a lack of peasant mass articulation, whole regions are under *gamonal* domination, thus the popular saying: "Abancay is the only hacienda with a Prefecture." * A district, province, or even a department may be dominated by a single family or group of families.[46]

There are ample possibilities for the mestizo group to expand its economic resources, either through illegal, coercive means, or through legal means. Of particular importance is the renting of land owned by

* Abancay was a city of 9,000 inhabitants in 1961.

the government, religious congregations, public charities, universities, schools, etc. In fact, extensive holdings belonging to these institutions are rented in "public auctions" at rates which have not changed through several decades. Thus, in mid-1966 the Ministry of Public Education "discovered" that it owned nearly a million hectares (about two and a half million acres of land) which were rented at ridiculously low rates. In order to participate in such auctions it is necessary, among other things, to be literate, to be the holder of a voting card, and to possess a commercial guarantee—requisites which only mestizos of certain status are able to achieve.

The bureaucratic clientele

One of the manifestations of the rigidity of the social system existing in Mancha India is the well-preserved consistency of the criteria by which the population is classified. Wealth (land and/or cattle), education, place of residence, type and prestige of occupation and scope of influence remain the important criteria. Indians either do not possess land or are very small landowners, they are always agricultural laborers, monolingual or illiterate, they reside in rural areas and their scope of personal influence is limited to their fellows or relatives. In contrast, as the mestizo moves upward along the social scale, the wealthier he is, the higher his level of education, the less time he dedicates to activities related to agriculture; he resides in increasingly important urban areas, filling positions of increasingly wide political influence.

> The political participation of the social classes is circumscribed by the geographical categories where their personal influence exists. The lowest class (Indians) is circumscribed by the community and the neighborhood; the low class (called *"chola"* class) plays a dynamic role in village politics, while the middle class acts in provincial politics, with a good degree of participation in departmental politics.[47]

The big landowners reside in cities, departmental capitals such as Arequipa, Cuzco, Puno, Huaraz or in Lima, holding important positions in the public administration, magistrate or Congress, dedicating themselves to a lesser degree to trading. Different authors point out the existence in provincial cities of Mancha India, of a "white" group, with lineage, wealth, education and positions of prestige, closely tied to Lima.[48]

The Pisac district,[49] for example, in the department of Cuzco, has 10,000 inhabitants, of whom 84 percent are Indians. The population of the district recognizes the existence of four district social strata: landowners, mestizos, the *Cholada,* and the Indians. In this district there are ten haciendas, one of them the property of a religious congregation, and 15 communities spread over the hillsides, which, administratively, constitute extensions of the district capital. The landowners rent or own the haciendas. They do not reside in the district capital but in the departmental capital, occupying positions as judges, high functionaries of the public administration, or as university professors—their holdings being rented and managed by mestizos. The latter constitute the high class of the town, jointly with the small and medium-sized landowners, traders and public officials. They maintain close contact with the high class at provincial or departmental levels—for they must remain "in their good graces" if they wish to continue their climb up the social ladder.[50] Through the electoral mechanism and the particularistic pattern in which juridical and political authorities are designated, the Pisac mestizos become political figures, owing to the support of other, "high class" mestizos.

> Taraco is a district ... and as such, authority within its jurisdiction is exercised by a governor who is appointed by the departmental prefect, having been proposed by the sub-prefect of the province. The latter suggests three "neighbors," one of which is chosen to fill the post in question. Ostensibly, the chief requisite in order to qualify for the post of governor is to be a "prominent neighbor" in the district, i.e., a prominent mestizo residing in the district capital, who enjoys certain prestige amongst the group constituted by mestizos; but in fact the man who gets elected is he who has the best relationship with sub-prefect or prefect.[51]

High-placed officials secure appointments for teachers, post office employees, judges, prefects and sub-prefects, irrigation administrators, etc. These are the key positions at local and regional levels, and thus these officials take care of individuals who wish to promote their own status through politics. It is understood that the appointees will perform their jobs in such a way as to avoid severing these ties, for this would leave them in a helpless situation.

This system of recruitment and promotion in the public administration is not limited to the level of local or regional decisions, since the big landowners place ("recommend" is the currently employed euphemism) their allies in positions connected with decision-making at the national level. It could be surmised that in the public adminis-tration of Peru there exists the phenomenon of "clientelism," similar to the *"panhelinas"* of Brazil,[52] since the livelihood of a bureaucrat depends on the personal protection he is able to secure from an influential person—who must be rewarded in an equally personal way. Influential figures take it upon themselves to distribute favors among their kin or close friends with the understanding that the latter, once placed in key positions, will not only reinforce the formers' positions, but that they will also help their protectors in contacting new entities, thus expanding their economic and political opportunities.

If the recruitment of the bureaucracy and of individuals in positions of authority is carried out among the clients of powerful figures, it may be concluded that the bureaucracy is characterized not only by its origins, but also by its class orientation—and that identification with their patrons and the distance that separates them from the dominated sectors, favors their association with the situation and with the culture of domination. In other words, the value orientations of public employees are characterized by their discrimination against the In-dians and all other underprivileged sectors.

Although favoritism within the public administration occurs all over the country and at all social levels, it undoubtedly loses its aspect of "clientelism" as the social environment presents a greater diversifica-tion and the social mobility of the population increases. In fact, under these conditions it is possible to alternate between different sources of influence, and the population is able to develop institutional resources which limit the power of patronal figures.

Neutralization of "Participants"

The "participant" sectors, or sectors integrated within the "na-tional" society—namely, manufacturing, mining and agricultural workers; governmental and private-sector employees; professionals, who live in urban sectors with access to education and to the polls, who are incorporated into the internal market and participate in unions or political organizations—in sum, those who have means of representation, have achieved considerable gains with regard to the unorganized peasant mass, the Indian mass, and the unemployed population of the cities.

The sociocultural distance between the participant and the marginal sectors explains why the gains that the former are trying to secure are exclusively for themselves. They ignore any type of massive redistribution which could immediately affect their consumption. Their aspirations follow the life-style exhibited by the higher classes.

Segmentary incorporation

The privileges of the system of domination are expanded by incorporating various segments of the population into that system, extending the number of social sectors which directly or indirectly benefit from the peasant marginality. Thus it can be argued [53] that, although the basic problem "underdeveloped" societies confront is that of creating ways and means for new population sectors to gain access to social and political resources—it might be added that, to the extent that such incorporation is partial or in progressive steps, it favors the maintenance of the system of domination as it expands, neutralizing the activities of those "promoted" by alienating them from the marginal sectors.

In seeking to improve the income of their members, unions gain many advantages to the impairment of nonorganized sectors. The pressure they originate in enterprises often brings about a greater mechanization and a stabilization in the number of employees.

> The reduction or at least the strict limitation of individuals employed is very probably the counterpart of the advantage gained by the higher-paid and better organized agricultural workers. Their privileged status is very high in comparison with that of their non-unionized fellows—even more so if it be considered that those who might have found employment in the exploitation of sugar and have been unable to do so due to mechanization, have had to remain on their miserable plots.[54]

Although unionized workers have achieved a certain degree of autonomy from patronal constraints, as evidenced by benefits gained

—such as social security, improved working conditions and higher salaries than the nonunionized, [55] paradoxically, they have fallen into new patterns of dependence as their demands for improvement and benefits are directed exclusively toward the unionized workers, without taking into consideration the national context. For example, the agricultural unions on the northern coast and the central sierra mining unions, after tough and protracted struggles, have achieved relatively high wages and improved their standards of living through legal dispositions that bind enterprises to provide lodging, medical assistance, education, etc., which transform such enterprises into "company towns." Consequently, leaving the enterprise would entail loss of the right to use those public services which are in fact private, inasmuch as they are a "property" of the enterprise.[56] In fact, there are still places where it is necessary to produce a special permit to gain access to them.

To the extent that such organized sectors do not promote an "opening" of the system, but only particularized benefits, they determine the inflexibility of their own possibilities in terms of market consumption, production and employment, thus creating a low rate of occupational mobility, all the more evident because there is a growing demand for employment. Thus, recruitment in enterprises is based on favoritism and family connections, which encourages a familial-regional climate, as well as an arrangement in which employer-employee relations are in fact a new version of the old style.[57]

Narrow and segmentarily-oriented worker groups push for state investment in urban development projects, chiefly in the coastal region, thus creating not only a greater sociocultural alienation between the coast and sierra, but also a more acute stagnation of agricultural production, as the greater urban demand is opposed by a rigidity in the supply of food. Thus the growing demands of the participant sectors to improve their standards of living—without implying redistributive measures at the national level, especially in the rural sector—lead to an inflationary pressure which works against their own aspirations.

The rural sectors' marginality and the narrow and specific orientation of the participant sectors leave the road clear for individuals with access to large property, to the control of production and marketing of exports, and of credit—items in which foreign capital plays an important role. They are the ones who establish economic restrictions within the political sphere, thus redirecting the economic policy of the state to suit their own ends.[58]

One reason why the Peruvian economy is based on the export of raw materials is the lack of an effective mass movement advocating national economic development, along with a redistribution of income and wealth, and a "nationalization" of the government, placing the latter in a position to control industrial development.

The political parties

The tendency toward segmentation and state privatization is favored by the political parties. These organizations characteristically recruit their members and orient their activities in terms of the participant sectors, with an exclusive insistence upon measures conducive to increasing the latters' income. At present, for example, no party has made universal suffrage an issue in its political platform. We once asked an Apra leader why his party had not sought to organize the Indian masses, and he replied that "there was no interest in it, in view of the fact that Indians do not count politically, as they do not vote...." We obtained a similar reply from another leader, this time of Acción Popular: "there is very little interest in this matter as it would arouse too much opposition.... Internally, many in the party would oppose such a measure.... The vindication of such a measure would be unpopular, we would be very much criticized and moreover we would have major opposition from the Army."

During almost 35 years, Apra sought to combine the different strata of the population: agricultural and urban workers—whom it helped unionize—clerks, students and professionals, in order to break down the control that the "oligarchy" exercised over the government. This situation met with a stubborn opposition from the *"fuerzas vivas"* and the armed forces, as the achievement of the objectives that Apra pursued would lead to the emergence of the former social sectors to state power, with the subsequent subordination of the armed forces to civil authority.

In view of the strong opposition of the *"fuerzas vivas"* and armed forces, Apra retained a segmentarian orientation in order to obtain their support. Its alliance with these sectors was made with the understanding of an adherence to the rules of segmentarian incorporation and a rejection of any attempt at a "massification" of society. The new parties constituted during the last decade have adjusted to the same rules, resulting in what is referred to in journalistic jargon as "superaccommodation."

With the incorporation of political parties into the political system, which grants representation to the participant sectors—thus offering a new legitimacy to the state, the mechanism of segmentation has become institutionalized, as shown, for example, by "parliamentarian initiatives" and "surname laws." Parliamentarian initiatives consist of the power given each representative to personally mobilize a given budget assignation for any purposes he chooses. "Surname laws" refer to laws which exclusively affect—benefit, or hurt—a particular individual, or sector of the population. The national budget is compounded through such legal mechanisms. It seems to benefit a determined "political clientele," without taking into consideration the national requirements. It can truly be said that there are two budgets: one compounded by representatives in order to neutralize and win over a specific social sector, and another based on international loans devoted to furthering new possibilities in order that new sectors be segmentarily "incorporated" into "national" life.

Dynamics of Social Change

Despite the dependence of the peasant mass, especially the Indians, the segmentary orientation of the participant sectors, and the privatization of power by the "oligarchy"—the chief axis of the social system, new social forces are emerging within a context of social and political mobilization,[59] exhibiting an organized confrontation and an awareness of the limitations of the prevailing social order.

Urban ruralization and rural urbanization

During the last 25 years the country has undergone great urban growth and physical mobility of the population. While in 1940 the urban population (residing in localities of over 2,000 inhabitants) comprised 25 percent of the population, the proportion had by 1961 swollen to 42 percent, with an annual average growth rate three times above that of the rural population.[60]

Migration originates chiefly from rural sierra zones and moves toward urban coastal zones, especially in the central area, Lima being the main focus of this movement.[61] In 1961, about 15 percent of the total population of the country resided in departments other than those of their birth, with the strongest movement being to the Lima-Callao complex. During the last 25 years Lima has tripled its population, of which over half is made up of first-generation immigrants. Likewise, the country has witnessed the sprouting of two cities, Chimbote and Huancayo, chiefly composed of immigrants and which are competing in importance with those (excepting Lima) that were founded by the Spaniards.

Urban growth due to internal migration has produced "city ruralization," a phenomenon consisting of an accommodation to the new habitat—without eradication of the old rural social and political behavioral patterns. The industrial labor characterizing the urban and "modern" world absorbs only a small number of these immigrants —insofar as industrial recruitment tends to select literate individuals from urbanized areas.[62]

> Very few textile workers come from densely populated rural areas, from mines or plantations. Most come directly from urban areas . . . or from other mechanized labor. The growing number of rural migrants in Lima and in Arequipa is chiefly employed, as might be expected, in nonindustrial "entry" occupations, such as construction work, domestic service and the Armed Forces.[63]

Immigrants perform chiefly service activities or crafts of a family variety, and are often underemployed. Due to the political pressure originated by their presence, the state has been forced to develop housing construction, destined especially for the high-income sectors, and to grant facilities for industrial development, in order to create stable and gainful employment for the immigrants. Thus, a part of this "migrant" population is introduced into unions and political life, with the consequent arousal of class-consciousness and ideological interest. But even this new occupational pattern and the political participation it encourages does not sever the ties that this sector maintains with rural areas, either because they have dependents in those areas, or

because such ties are reinforced through the arrival of other immigrants that they attract.

The rural areas, however, especially the communities, continue to
be sources of social identification for the immigrants. The city slums
witness patterns of traditional reciprocity, cooperative labor, and fes-
tivities, reflected in a reinforcement of the original regional and
communal solidarity ties. This identification is also seen in the high
rate of participation in regional and local provincial "associations"
which exist in Lima.[64] Likewise, the occupational instability of these
sectors, the holdings that they preserve in their communities of origin
and the family and communal links of solidarity they maintain, act to
provide a very fluid residential mobility. Many city slums group people
from one part of the country together in a pattern of extended families.
They often are all engaged in one single occupational specialization.
On the other hand, due to the marginal status of these slums and to the
social and political mobilization of their dwellers, the latter tend to
become increasingly interested in local problems, as manifested by the
"associations of dwellers."

This new type of urban proletariat has the opportunity to become
politically socialized at quite different levels. There is both class-consciousness and a party context, and both urban and rural contexts.
Multiple loyalties and identifications are developed, and thus their
social and political mobilization is devoid of any segmentarian
character. The organization which groups the construction workers, for
example, stands out as one of the most aggressive in two very different
areas: personal benefits and the advocating of political change at the
national level.

As a result of this urban ruralization, there is a growing "sierraniza-
tion" of the coast. Because of the large population originating from that
region and residing on the coast, a great number of radio and television
stations dedicate a large part of their programs to news and music from
Mancha India, to advertising in *quechua,* and to creating a stereotype of
urbanized "Indians." The production of recordings of sierra music has
achieved a considerable volume, sierra folk programs have increasingly gained interest and are now combined, for the first time,
with Creole groups.

This new urban proletariat also leads in great measure to the inverse
process: rural urbanization. The close links which immigrants main-

tain with their places of origin encourage the diffusion of new social, cultural and political customs into the rural areas, as well as diverse social innovations, propagating new technologies and styles of consumption, diffusing new mass communications media, and re-creating identifications with the rural society by means of a new cultural style. It is important to notice that this group, with its traditional values, is determined to achieve a position of civic equality within the national context.

Further, a new and autonomous group is being formed which incorporates modern values, without destroying all of the traditional patterns, encouraging a climate of civic equality which is creative in its form, and not just a copy of that part of the culture from which it has been borrowed.

These immigrants spread new organizational and ideological patterns which emphasize the relationship between population and country, family and peasant status in general. This movement has been fostered by the state, the church, and other international organizations, which have sent representatives to direct this social mobilization. Cooperación Popular, United States and Canadian missionaries and the Peace Corps, by making an appearance in rural areas, have also influenced the process of peasant urbanization, leading to the development of social diversification and of new patterns of social stratification.

On the other hand, due to the occupational demands of the urban population and of rural urbanization, the state has been forced to develop a policy of public works, opening new regions to communications facilities and connecting a greater number of the rural sectors. Finally, the growth of the urban population itself has had repercussions in rural areas. The expansion of urban centers has increased the demand for agricultural goods, and because these could not be met under the prevailing structure of property and production,[65] technical innovations have been introduced and further occupational diversification has occurred, especially in those areas close to population centers and free of the encroachment of the traditional haciendas.

The marginal urban population and the state

The social and political mobilization which characterizes the marginal urban population has also affected the character of its relations with the authorities and with the state. Due to the massive scope of its claims, and also because of the existence of numerous spheres which compete to satisfy the requirements of the population of marginal slums (with the purpose of expanding their clientele), this group has avoided situations of dependence, since their members alternate between different power figures. Though the associations of dwellers seek to use influential middlemen in order to achieve their claims, the terms of reciprocity achieved through such links do not result in personal identifications or loyalties.

Moreover, this population reinterprets and adapts to its own interest the ties originated through the rendering of services, in order to avoid relations which could result in a condition of dependence or in the restriction of its activities. Thus, government functionaries, political parties and "prominent" figures have felt defrauded by the reaction of this population once it had been granted certain services.

Due to the type and magnitude of the demands of this population, only state entities are in a position to offer a convincing answer, which leaves no place for the middleman.

"Cholification"

As a result of the confluence of urban ruralization and of rural urbanization, there has been a change in the patterns of social stratification of Mancha India, with an emphasis upon the elimination of caste lines. These new patterns of social stratification have come about through the phenomenon of *cholification*. [66]

This form of social mobilization, which affects both urban and rural populations, has resulted in an increasing number of Indians who, through contact with urban areas, learn Spanish, become literate and are thus able to perform new occupations—this time independently of mestizo patronage. Thus, in 1959, the Plan for the South estimated that *cholos* constituted 70 percent of the urban population and 13 percent of the population in the department of Puno.[67]

The *cholo* is characterized by an incompatible status: due to his social origins and the low prestige of his occupation, he resembles the Indian; yet in terms of his income and the occupational independence he enjoys with regard to the mestizo, he does not fit into either of these ethnic-social groups. His reference group is ambiguous, for he maintains many Indian cultural traits while adopting some of the mestizo's, adding to them a new, elusive element. While the *cholo* often settles in his own local area and engages in agricultural labor, he also undertakes new occupations which involve residential mobility, and which provide him with the means of obtaining a larger income and discovering new opportunities. He appears to be indifferent to the sacred character of agriculture and to the relations of communal solidarity—all of which occasions a loosening of ties with the extended family, typical of the Indian kinship structure.

As the mestizo social system prevents the Indian from achieving prestige, wealth and power through the traditional roads of access to authority and property, the Indian moves upward socially to the *cholo* status—without severing his original roots—through the performance of new occupations unhindered by mestizo patronage, such as laborer in public works, truckdriver, door-to-door salesman, trader of meat and wool, etc. These occupations afford the *cholo* the means and status which make him important in the eyes of his family, friends and countrymen who remain in the Indian status, and also in the eyes of the town mestizos. The *cholo* adopts an aggressive and mobile behavior which differentiates him from both the "polite" mestizo, and the "servile" and "apathetic" Indian.

This new social type is most frequently encountered in places unhindered by the domination of the hacienda—the Mantaro valley, for example. There, the *cholo* carries on intensive commercial activity and contributes to the formation of new population centers. A good example of the latter, outside Mancha India, is the city of Huancayo.

It is significant in this sense to note that in Sicuani, where the process of *"Cholification"* is more evident, there are but few haciendas; there is a certain alienation from the control of Cuzco and a very important commercial movement. Such a process resembles greatly what happened at the end of the middle ages, when opportunities for commerce and for crafts-manship arose and the serf became a free citizen.[68]

But due to the political-economic limitations in Mancha India, social opportunities for the *cholo* are somewhat limited, although this is not the case in the Mantaro valley. The mestizo blockade against the *cholos* of Mancha India forces them to direct their aggression toward trade union and political activities, in an effort to develop a national orientation. The proximity of the *cholo* group to that of the Indians—fundamentally due to their social origin and family connections—and their estrangement from the mestizos, has led to a form of political activity geared toward the mobilization of the rural, communal and tenant-farmer masses. The growing political importance that the *cholo* sector has achieved by "grabbing political initiative as a representative of the peasant indigenous mass with the purpose of dominating the upper classes," [69] has conferred upon this sector a certain prestige in the eyes of some sectors of the lower mestizo class, which would favor the development of "a pressure tending toward the amalgamation of the middle class downwards and of the *cholo* class upwards." [70]

This situation suggests that the *cholo* group in fact organized and heads the peasant movement existing in Mancha India,[71] which determined a series of hacienda invasions by the communities, and of tenant-farmer strikes, which had to face mestizo repression.[72]

The political importance of the Puno *cholos* is shown by the success achieved by the Frente de Trabajadores y Campesinos (Workers' and Peasants' Front)—a regional organization which is made up chiefly of *cholos*—in the municipal elections of December 1966, in which it won in all the provinces, with the exception of the chief mestizo bastion, the city of Puno.

As this new agrarian union movement originating in the Indian region takes on a political character, and as it pushes for distribution of property and of regional power—in contrast with the guild benefits characteristic of the coastal unions—it conditions the articulation of the Indian peasant, who thus appears ready to sever the patterns of domination previously described.[73]

On the other hand, the entrance of the *cholo* sector into economic and political activities, creating new occupations and symbols of prestige, has brought with it signs of competition with the village and town mestizos, since the latter are not always able to adequately compete with the *cholo* either in terms of consumption or politics. This is at least one reason why the small and medium-sized landowners in the area, who face an uncertain and threatening situation, have emigrated to urban zones—preferentially coastal—where they seek to fill subordinate positions in the state bureaucracy or in small business concerns, with the help of family connections and friends. This is done after selling, parceling out, or abandoning their holdings in order to avoid lowering their social status. Another alternative left them is to enter the ranks of the official political parties, thus facing peasant articulation with the formers' help.

This weakening of mestizo prestige in Mancha India implies that the support they received from the higher mestizo classes, who in turn were sustained by the Lima "oligarchy," is being eliminated. In fact, spokesmen of the National Agrarian Society have publicly declared the need for parceling out large haciendas in the southern sierra.

To the extent that the weakening of the mestizos in rural areas becomes visible and their power image fades in the eyes of the peasants, the status of the *cholo* will gain stature among the Indians and come to constitute a new model of social behavior.

It should also be noted that some urban left-wing groups have found in this emergence, apparently initiated and led by the *cholo* sector of Mancha India, a reinforcement of their ideology and they too have offered to support various activities.

The Cuban Revolution and the Sino-Soviet conflict have contributed—among other factors with which we shall not deal here—to the rebuff by some left-wing intellectual sectors of the "reformist" styles of political parties, especially of the Communist party, and of their adherence to the "Peking" line of thought.

The affiliation of these new groups has been reinforced by the land invasions, strikes and peasant uprisings which have recurred in the region during the past few years. It is felt that the revolutionary violence of this peasantry is the only road to social change. On the other hand, small and medium-sized landowners, workers, employees and professionals seem to be "bourgeoisified" or neutralized. Thus Hugo

Blanco declared while in prison: "The peasants of La Convención are petit bourgeois; any future uprising of Indians will take place in the highlands, not in La Convención." [74]

Though the frustrated guerrilla activities in the southern sierra have not achieved their final purpose, they have indeed contributed to the political mobilization of tenant-farmers and commoners and to the continuous deterioration of the structural and normative dependence which they suffer at the hands of the mestizos. It would appear that one of the guerrilla groups has been less dedicated to guerrilla activities than to dispelling the image of omnipotence that the boss embodies before his serfs, by scoffing at the former and scattering to the four winds the signs of his authority—at the same time vindicating the local authorities.

Although the guerrillas have been subdued, this activity as well as the peasant organizations have prompted various political, intellectual, economic and even military circles into "discovering" the existence of this "alien" country, with the limitations and dangers that its existence signifies to the social structure. They have pressed for state intervention in the region, not only with repressive measures, but also through the elimination of the dependence of the Indian at the hands of the mestizo. Agrarian reform and communications media in the region would allow the incorporation of this population into the national market and into the mainstream of the "neutralized" sectors.

But such measures are being continuously postponed, even in their most timid manifestations, since, as we have tried to point out, certain previous measures of internal reorganization of the state apparatus would be required, thus necessitating a revamping of the social system as a whole.

The new urban proletariat and its *cholo* counterpart in Mancha India are—both separately and together—breaking in upon the structural and normative dependence of the Indian mass by mobilizing it socially and politically. Such mobilization entails a change from the local-family Indian pattern to another with class connotations. The confrontation with the mestizo system takes place especially in the political sphere as such, since this type of resource is at the very root of the mestizo class status. Therefore, the "access crisis" of the peasantry presupposes the questioning of the legitimacy of the caste system and thereby of the economic, social, political and cultural cleavages which it entails.

If rural marginality allows for the neutralization of the participating sectors and the privatization of state power, the growing incursions of the peasantry into the political sphere demands, with pressing urgency, a new line of social integration based upon the full participation of the different sectors of the population in the distribution of social resources; a form of pluralistic participation. In other words, this crisis pursues the "nationalization" of Peruvian society.

The crisis of participation that is evident in the country seeks to reject a consensus based on domination criteria and to establish in its place one based on the participation of citizens of the different sectors of society.

NOTES

1. *Informe sobre la situación económica y social del Peru* (Lima: Instituto Nacional de Planificación, 1963-64).
2. *Cuentas Nacionales del Perú,* 1950-1965 (Lima: Banco Central de Reserva, 1966).
3. Censo Nacional de Poblacion, 1961.
4. Walter Thompson, *Perfil del Mercado Peruano* (Lima, May 1966).
5. Ozzie Simmons, "The Criollo Outlook in the Mestizo Culture of Coastal Peru," *American Anthropologist* 57 (1955): 107-117; and Richard Morse, "The Heritage of Latin America," in *Founding of New Societies,* ed. Louis Hartz (New York: Harcourt, Brace & World, 1964), pp. 123-177.
6. *New York Times,* March 27, 1966.
7. José Matos Mar, *Idea y Diagnóstico del Perú: La pluralidad de situaciones sociales y culturales.* Instituto de Estudios Peruanos, Serie Mesas Redondas y Conferencias no. 5 (Lima, September 1966); and Augusto Salazar Bondy, *La Cultura de la Dependencia.* Instituto de Estudios Peruanos, Serie Mesas Redondas y Conferencias no. 8 (Lima, October 1966).
8. Andrew G. Frank, "La participación popular en lo relativo a algunos objetivos económicos rurales" (unpublished manuscript), p. 9.
9. François Perroux, "Consideraciones en torno a la noción del polo de crecimiento," *Cuadernos de la Sociedad Venezolana de Planificación* 2, no. 3-4 (1963): 1-10; and John Friedmann, "Core Region Strategy as an Instrument of Development Policy," September 1966 (mimeo).
10. Andrew G. Frank, "La participación," pp. 7-8.
11. Rodolfo Stavenhagen, "7 thèses erronées sur l'Amérique Latine," *Partisans,* no. 26-27, p. 4.
12. *The New York Times,* December 11, 1966.
13. François Bourricaud, *Changements à Puno: Étude de Sociologie Andine* (Institut des Hautes Etudes de l'Amérique Latine); Pablo González Casanova, "Sociedad Plural, Colonialismo Interno y Desarrollo," *América Latina,* year 6, no. 3 (1963): 15-32; and Rodolfo Stavenhagen, "Classes, Colonialism and Acculturation in Mezoamerica," *Studies in Comparative International Development* 1, no. 6 (1965).
14. E. Wolf, "Corporate Peasant Communities in Mezoamerica and Java," *Southwestern Journal of Anthropology* 13 (Spring 1957).
15. François Bourricaud, *Changements à Puno.*
16. *Plan Regional para el Desarrollo del Sur del Perú,* vol. 5 PS/B/9, p. 20, 1959. (Further references below will use the title *Plan del Sur.*)
17. François Bourricaud, *Changements à Puno,* p. 17.
18. *Plan del Sur,* PS/B/9, p. 13.
19. Censo Nacional de Población, vol. 1, 1961.
20. Some descriptions of the hacienda system can be found in: François Bourricaud, *Changements à Puno;* Carlos Ferdinand Cuadros y Villena, "El Arriendo y la Reforma Agraria en la Provincia de la Convención," *Forum sobre desarrollo enconómico* (Sociedad de Ingenieros del Perú, 1966), pp. 61-99; Gustavo Palacios P., "Relaciones de trabajo entre el patrón y los colonos en los fundos de la provincia de Paucartambo,"

Revista Universitaria del Cuzco, year 66, no. 112 (1957): 174-222; Mario Vázquez, "La Antropología Cultural y Nuestro Problema del Indio," *Perú Indigena* 2 (June 1952): 5-6; and *Hacienda, Peonaje y Servidumbre en los Andes Peruanos* (Lima: Editorial Estudios Andinos, 1961).

21. T. C. Cevallos Valencia, "Informe sobre Chawaytiri," Instituto de Estudios Peruanos, *Estudio de Cambios Rurales del Perú* (Lima, 1965).

22. Allan Holmberg, "Relationships Between Psychological Deprivations and Culture Change in the Andes." Paper presented at Cornell Latin American Year, Conference of the Development of Highland Communities in Latin America, March 21-25, 1966; and Jacob Fried, "Social Organization and Personal Security in a Peruvian Hacienda Indian Community: Vicos," *American Anthropologist* 64, no. 4 (August 1962): 771-780.

23. Ralph Klein, "The Self-image of Adult Males in an Andean Culture: A Clinical Exploration of a Dynamic Personality Construct," in A. Holmberg, "Relationships," p. 2.

24. G. Foster, "The Dyadic Contract in Tzintzuntzan: Patron-Client Relationship," *American Anthropologist* 65, no. 11 (1962): 1280-1294.

25. W. Mangin, "Estratificación Social en el Callejón de Huaylas," in *Estudios sobre la Cultura Actual del Perú* (Lima: Universidad de San Marcos, 1964), pp. 298-305.

26. César Fonseca and Juan Murrugara, "Huaychao," in *Sociedad, Cultura y Economia en 10 áreas andino-peruanas* (Lima: Ministerio de Trabajo y Comunidades, Instituto Indigenista Peruano, October 1966), pp. 36-37.

27. G. Foster, "Peasant Society and the Image of Limited Good," *American Anthropologist* 67, no. 2 (1965): 293-315.

28. E. Banfield, *The Moral Basis of the Backward Societies* (New York: Free Press, 1958).

29. Foster, *The Dyadic Contract.*

30. Stanislaw Ossowski, *Class Structure in the Social Consciousness* (New York: Free Press, 1963), p. 149.

31. Instituto de Estudios Peruanos. *Estudio de Cambios Rurales en el Perú* (Lima, 1965).

32. Cevallos, *Informe sobre chawaytiri;* and Virgilio Landázuri, "Informe sobre el problema de los arrendires del valle de La Convención" (unpublished manuscript, 1960).

33. Rodolfo Vizcardo Arce, *Pacaicasa, una comunidad de hacienda.* Universidad Nacional de San Cristóbal de Huamanga, Ayacucho (Ph.D. diss., 1965).

34. Apparently this possibility is conditioned by the relative importance of the hacienda system in a given area. The hypotheses may be suggested that the larger the holdings under hacienda domination, the smaller the amount of immigration. It should also be noted that there is seemingly no relation between the amount of emigration and the number of communities or commoners in a given department. Thus, for example, 21 percent of those born in Ancash, Apurimac, Ayacucho and Huancavelica have emigrated from these departments—while only 11 percent of those born in Cuzco and Puno have chosen this alternative. Similarly, in the first four departments mentioned, 50 percent of the land is concentrated in holdings of over 500 hectares (about 1500 acres)—communities not included, while in Cuzco and Puno this percentage rises to 80 percent.

35. Uldrich P. Ritter, *Comunidades indigenas y cooperativismo en el Perú,* Estudios sobre la economía iberoamericana (Bilbao: Ed. Deusto, 1965).

36. Instituto de Estudios Peruanos.

37. *Plan del Sur*, PS/B/11, p. 28.

38. Cevallos, *Informe sobre Chawaytiri*. See also Mario Vázquez, "Autoridades en una hacienda Andino-Peruana," *Perú Indigena* 10, nos. 24–25 (1963): 24–36.

39. Censo Nacional de Población, 1961, vol. 3.

40. Censo Nacional, 1961, vol. 3, p. 8.

41. Instituto de Estudios Peruanos.

42. M. Vázquez, Cambios en la estratificación social en una hacienda andina, *Perú Indigena* 6, nos. 14–15 (July 1957): 85.

43. Cevallos, *Informe sobre Chawaytiri*, p. 17.

44. Ibid., p. 19.

45. V. Landázuri, "Informe sobre el problema de los arrendires."

46. M. Vázquez, *Hacienda, Peonaje y Servidumbre*, p. 18.

47. *Plan del Sur*, PS/B/11, p. 28.

48. W. Mangin, "Classification of Highland Communities in Latin America," Cornell Latin American Year, Conference on the Development of Highland Communities in Latin America, March 21–25, 1966.

49. F. Garmendia, "Informe sobre Pisac," Instituto de Estudios Peruanos, 1965.

50. One might well ask if these haciendas with low productivity are not maintained more as a political power base than as an economic entity. They may be used to obtain political positions which in turn are a source of wealth and social prestige.

51. H. Martínez, "La subárea quechua de Taraco," Instituto Indigenista Peruano, Programa Puno-Tambopata, March 1958, p. 98.

52. Anthony Leeds, "Brazilian Careers and Social Structure: A Case History and Model," in D. Heath and R.N. Adams, eds., *Contemporary Cultures and Societies of Latin America* (New York: Random House, 1965), pp. 379–404.

53. Gino Germani, *Politica y Sociedad en una época de transición: De la sociedad tradicional a la sociedad de masas* (Buenos Aires: Editorial Paidós), esp. Chapter 3.

54. François Bourricaud, "Syndicalisme et Politique: le cas péruvien," *Sociologie du Travail*, no. 4 (1961): 48–49.

55. David Chaplin, "A Discussion of Major Issues Arising in the Recruitment of Industrial Labor in Peru"; and James Payne, *Labor and Politics in Peru* (New Haven: Yale University Press, 1965).

56. Luis Soberón, "Cerro de Pasco, Ciudad-Empresa," *Revista del Instituto de Planeamiento de Lima*, Universidad Nacional de Ingeniería, no. 1 (1966): 27–35.

57. David Chaplin, "A Discussion of Major Issues."

58. François Bourricaud, "Structure and Function of the Peruvian Oligarchy," *Studies in Comparative International Development* 2, no. 2 (1966)

59. Karl W. Deutsch, "Social Mobilization and Political Development," *American Political Science Review* (September 1961).

60. "Diagnóstico y Programación de los Recursos Humanos Población del Peru," *Servicio del Empleo y Recursos Humanos*, March 1965.

61. Ibid. "Diagnóstico de la Situación de Los Recursos Humanos" (Instituto Nacional de Planificación, January 1966).

62. Alex Inkeles, "Industrial Man: The Relation of Status to Experience, Perception and Value," *The Bobbs-Merrill Reprint Series in the Social Sciences*, S-131.

63. David Chaplin, "A Discussion of Major Issues." See also Stillman Bradfield,

"Some Occupational Aspects of Migration," *Economic Development and Cultural Change* 14, no. 1 (October 1965): 10; and G. Briones y J. Mejía V., *El Obrero Industrial, Aspectos Sociales del desarrollo económico del Perú,* Instituto de Investigaciones Sociológicas, Universidad de San Marcos (Lima, 1964), pp. 29-30.

64. W. Mangin, "Clubes de Provincianos en Lima," in *Estudios sobre la Cultura Actual del Perú* (Lima: Universidad de San Marcos, 1964), pp. 289-305.

65. CIDA: *Perú, Tenencia de la Tierra y Desarrollo Socio-Económico del Sector Agrícola.* Unión Panamericana, Washington, D.C., 1966.

66. José María Arguedas, "Puquio, una cultura en proceso de cambio," *Revista del Museo Nacional* 25: 184-232; "Evolución de las Comunidades Indígenas. El valle del Montaro y la ciudad de Huancayo: un caso de fusión de culturas no comprometidas por la acción de las instituciones de orden colonial," ibid. 26: 140-194; F. Bourricaud, "Aparition du Cholo" and "Cholification" in *Changements à Puno,* pp. 25-27, 215-228; *Plan del Sur;* Aníbal Quijano, "La emergencia del grupo cholo y sus implicaciones en la sociedad peruana," Ph.D. diss., Universidad de San Marcos, Lima, 1965; and Mangin, "Classification of Highland Communities in Latin America."

67. *Plan del Sur,* PS/B/9, p. 16.

68. Ibid., p. 18.

69. Ibid.

70. Ibid.

71. A. Quijano, "El Movimiento Campesino Peruano y sus Líderes," *América Latina,* year 8, no. 4 (Oct.-Dec., 1965).

72. Hugo Neira, *Cuzco, Tierra y Muerte* (Lima: Editorial Populibros Peruanos, 1964); and Wesley W. Craig, Jr., "The Peasant Movement of La Convención, Perú: Dynamics of Rural Labor Organization" (mimeo).

73. A. Quijano, "Contemporary Peasant Movements," in *Elites in Latin America,* ed. S. Lipset and A. Solari (New York: Oxford University Press, 1967), pp. 301-342.

74. Quoted in Craig, "The Peasant Movement of La Convención," p. 33.

Urban
Politics

Paul L. Doughty

3. Social Policy and Urban Growth in Lima

For a variety of reasons, a number of the elements that are considered essential for living the good life in a modern state are most abundant and accessible in urban areas. Many of these things take the form of services, rendered by the government to its citizens. Therefore it is of fundamental interest to know how a nation chooses to distribute the collective wealth in this form in order to understand why cities grow and why some are more attractive than others.

Peru offers a valuable setting in which to explore this aspect of urbanization. It has a time depth that is unique in South America with respect to urban history, and it has had a substantial population during much of this time, that is, of native, rather than foreign origin. In the following pages I shall briefly review some of this urban history, pertinent national conditions, social attitudes toward urbanism and rurality, the distribution of public services and the character of urban policy or the lack of it.

Peru—The Country

All classic descriptions of Peru speak of it as being divided, like Gaul, into three parts. Although in strictly geographical terms this is a gross simplification—there are eight major ecological areas and many microenvironments—the three-part division provides us with the basis for a preliminary analysis. There is an important correlation between these traditional geographical units and the social, political and economic realities of the modern country.

The coast of Peru is a bleak but interesting desert washed by Pacific waters which form one of the world's greatest fishing grounds. The coastal strip contains about 12 percent of the national territory

(161,000 square kilometers) and is broken into sections by the 57 small rivers which descend from the highlands, providing the basis of life in the oasislike valleys they form. By 1972, 44 percent of the country's population lived in these valleys, which contain the nation's largest cities and account for most of its agricultural production, as well as almost nine-tenths of the industrial production. In addition to this, the fishing industry is located here (Peru was first in world fishing tonnage), and the oil industry is concentrated on the extreme northern coast (Piura). In all, despite its environmental peculiarities, the coastal area dominates the rest of the country.

The Andean highlands, which at certain places begin literally at the edge of the Pacific, rise abruptly to altitudes of over four miles within a short distance. The western flank of the mountains is as dry as the coast from which it rises, but gaining the heights, it is pockmarked by habitable niches and arable land. Open pasture lands cover the rolling plains of the *puna* or *altiplano* beyond the treeline, above which tower the snowy peaks of the Andes. The vast majority of the highland population—44 percent of the total population—is concentrated in the intermontane valleys at altitudes between seven and twelve thousand feet above sea level. 1972 was the first time when the highlands did not hold well over half of the nation's people, representing a drop of 8 percent since 1961.

As a whole, the highlands comprise about 30 percent of the national territory, of which only 4.5 percent is arable. This productive land constitutes 52 percent of the nation's total, but it supplies only 33 percent of its agricultural products. Moreover, only slightly over a tenth of the manufactured goods is made here.

The third region, the vast lands of the eastern Andean slope and Amazon basin, constitutes 57 percent of the country's area but contains only 12 percent of the population. Despite the fact that it is located behind the ragged barrier of the Andes and poorly connected by roads to the rest of the country, it nevertheless contributes 15 percent of the agricultural production (mostly coffee, tea, coca, etc.) from useful lands, which amount to 15 percent of the national total in that category. The people of this area produce less than 1 percent of the nation's total manufactured goods.

Predictably, the communications system and transportation patterns of the country reflect these characteristics. The coastal valleys are connected by the paved Pan-American highway, which runs the length of the country. "Penetration" roads snake their way into the mountains on narrow dirt beds whose perimeters are marked by impressive chasms and blind corners. There is no inter-Andean road system paralleling that of the coast, although attempts to complete such a system are always being discussed. Thus, if one were in the city of Huaraz (Ancash) and wished to go to Huancayo (Junín), it would be necessary to travel first to the coast, then turn south to Lima and finally return to the highlands (via the only paved road in the Andes)—the trip forming a great "U" pattern.

The railroads which were built with Chinese and peasant labor in the last century and considered a triumph of engineering in their day, have changed very little and so are restricted in their utility. The main track runs from Lima to Junín and Cerro de Pasco, having been built to handle the mining industry of that area. The second major system runs from the two coastal ports of Mollendo and Matarani on the south coast, through Arequipa to Puno and Cuzco in the highlands. As in other parts of the world, these railroads are presently being eclipsed by truck transportation. Nevertheless, it was the steam locomotive that made wheeled transport a viable item in the Andes.

The overall picture that one has of Peru is heavily influenced by the country's varied geographic character and by the seeming remoteness of the parts from one another. Taken as a whole, the land is not densely populated, with only 10.5 persons per square kilometer, ranking eighteenth in density among Latin American countries. There are 483 persons per square kilometer of cultivated and usable land however, a fact which yields a greater understanding about population pressure in relation to urban growth. The urban population has increased from 35 percent to 60 percent of the national total in the 32-year period ending in 1972.

Part of this change is due to the cumulative factor of sheer population increase. The present population of 13,572,689 has been augmenting at an increased rate of 3.3 percent per year for the past decade—a rate which has been on the rise just as the death rate has dropped to 12.3 per thousand (from a 1940 figure of 32.6), despite a seven-point drop in birth rate to 43.4 per thousand, over the same period. This is a familiar portrait of a country receiving the impact of modern but limited public health care—a combination of vaccinations, penicillin and DDT. These changes have sharpened the edges of both needs and wants, since there are more children to be socialized and schooled and more old people to be retired. Profound as such developments are and can be, they alone do not account for the rate of urbanization. To find out what does, we shall examine the nature of the process as it occurs in Peru and explore some of the assumptions upon which the urban movement is based.

Peruvian Urban Traditions

The city is not new in Peru. There have been several periods in the last four millennia of Andean history when cities have developed and played important roles in regional life. By the time of Christ, numerous small cities were found in Peru, in the coastal valleys as well as in the highlands. Pre-Columbian urbanism in Peru reached a significant new level in the next eight hundred years, with the emergence of, first, regional states, and later the Huari-Tiahuanaco empire which was based upon a military expansion of highland peoples from the Ayacucho area and perhaps the Titicaca region. The urban idea, however, had apparently spread widely by this time, having a particularly significant impact on the north coastal area where, some years after the decline of Huari, and just prior to the rise of the Incas, perhaps the largest city in the preconquest period in the Western hemisphere—Chan Chan—developed.

Despite such longstanding urban traditions, the dominant theme in Peruvian prehistory features—not the rising crescendo of urban life, but rather a cyclical (if that is the word) rise and fall of cities and a clear preference for small, rather than large and urbanlike centers. It is a pattern which encourages the development of ceremonial and administrative complexes (such as Pachacamac, Maranga, Moche and Cuzco) centralized in densely settled valleys where residential concentrations remain distinct and peripheral to the shared centers.

The pre-Columbian population of the central Andean area was far greater than many have traditionally thought.[1] Indeed, according to the most recent estimates, the modern population of Peru is only beginning to approach the size that it had achieved prior to the arrival of smallpox, colds, bubonic plague and the Spaniards.

During much of Andean history, however, regional cultures and states were the rule, with each mountain and coastal valley or complex of valleys retaining certain autonomy despite the fact that all were widely influenced by general developments. While cities were a permanent feature of the Andean scene, particularly from Chavin times, it would be difficult to argue that they were integral to the broad course of development.

The pattern of many small, rather than few large, cities is undoubtedly related to the political and social fragmentation which characterize Andean life—cities are important as such, only during periods of empire. John Rowe points out the parallel here with the abandonment of cities after the fall of Rome [2] and concludes that cities were but one alternative in the management of populations. In fact, the preferred arrangement seems to have been scattered settlements of family groups in combination with small urban centers. The abundant ceremonial centers found at all time periods further show that such organizational style was part of this preference and not a stage, as such, in large-scale urban development.

The effect of the Spanish conquest was profound in this regard. The establishment in 1535 of Lima on the central coast, as part of the Spanish conquest, represented a sharp break with the past in that, for the first time ever, a coastal settlement would dominate the highlands. The elite rulers, representing the colonial power, were a racially distinct "caste" into whose ranks mobility was virtually impossible. They resided in the central portions of the city, organized around the "Plaza de Armas," symbolic center of the viceroyalty. If anything, power was concentrated—officially, at least—to an even further degree in the viceroy than it had been in the Inca, and Lima was more important than Cuzco as a consequence.

The social and political hierarchy of the colonial state became sharply focused on Lima, which developed not so much as an administrative and economic center to serve its national hinterland, as to be served *by* the hinterland. Little reciprocity emerges in the relationship between the city and its environment: the flow of the current is to Lima, where the officious and self-serving accumulation mounts and the bureaucracy becomes a many-layered institution. The history of the colonial period could be seen as a constant battle of the king and his loyal representatives to penetrate the centralized and institutionalized interests in Lima, to find out what was going on in the provinces and to discover some means of controlling the special interest groups. The crown continually compiled data based upon field research (census-like surveys like that made by Iñigo Ortiz de Zúniga in 1567), although it is doubtful if such information was ever analyzed or actually used. As seen from the hinterland itself, the situation was even more difficult to penetrate or influence.

In theory, the governmental process flowed through the hierarchy of the structure, but in practice, this did not occur. Local political and economic interests held firm and operated in collusion with regional officials to further their own ends. The average provincial citizen, regardless of his caste (but especially if he was of Indian or mixed caste) was powerless. The frustrations of dealing with the unresponsive hierarchy began early, eventually developing into one of the most characteristic patterns of behavior from colonial times to the present—that is, to bypass the intermediate officialdom entirely and take one's message straight to the top, or at least, to Lima. The first classic expression of this can be found in Felipe Guamán Poma de Ayala's 1200-page "letter" of information and protest which he delivered to the viceroy in 1615.[3] His letter met the fate of so many others to follow: it was "lost," and not found again until it turned up in 1908 in the Royal Danish Archive.

Lima flourished as the seat of the most important city in South America during the colonial period. Its population was never particularly large, although it was substantial. By the end of the colonial period the concentrations of personages and power, facility and favor, were clearly in Lima. According to Cosme Bueno, chronicler of eighteenth-century Peru, Lima was as follows in 1779:[4]

The shortness of this work does not permit giving an ample description of this city. It will be enough to indicate the most notable. It is fenced by walls with 34 bulwarks, begun and finished by the Duke of Palata about 1685. It is nearly two thirds of a league in length and almost the same in width; including a suburb to the north named San Lorenzo, to which one passes over a bridge of stone, built by the Marques of Montesclaros. It boasts a fountain of handsome bronze, beautifully made, that was cast and placed in the center of the spacious plaza of the Count of Salvatierra; and a beautiful promenade, renovated sumptuously by his Excellence, Señor Don Manuel de Amat in 1762; at the same time a Colesseum for cock fights was founded. It is the residence of the Viceroy and the corresponding tribunes for the administration of justice, which are: the high court of justice and the royal chancellery comprised of eight justices and prosecutor for civil cases; criminal court with its prosecutor; fiscal court; inheritance court; the Holy Office of the Inquisition; the Crusade; the consulate; the municipal council office of the city, comprised of "ordinary mayors" and councilmen; the Ecclesiastic Council headed by the archbishop (and his retinue); the Ecclesiastic court and (its officials); the Protomedicato, with prosecutor and examinor. It has a celebrated University, three high schools (colegios) of which one is major and the other a seminary; six parishes; 27 religious convents; 14 nunneries and 4 for lay sisters; 12 hospitals; a Foundlings Home and a mint.

It is the city of most commerce and enterprise in South America. It is about a league and a half from the sea. Its residential sections have about 54,000 persons of which there are approximately 16 to 18 thousand Spaniards among whom there are families of established nobility, descendents of illustrious Houses of Spain; a few more than 2,000 Indians; and the rest Mestizos, Mulatos and Negros, the last two castes being the most abundant. Within the walls of this city is a town of Indians, named Santiago del Cercado, governed by a Corregidor who has jurisdiction not only over the Indians of the city but also of those of the surrounding towns. The rest of the inhabitants are subject to the ordinary laws of Lima, so that all the district can be considered as a Province, called the jurisdiction of Lima or district of the Corregimiento del Cercado (walled city).

Our meticulous chronicler goes on to elaborate more details, not only for Lima, but for all the other provinces of the viceroyalty as well. A review of these passages leaves no doubt about the supremacy of Lima in virtually everything. Of Cuzco, Bueno notes that it is the second city in importance in the realm; has 26,000 inhabitants and an established mint (not functioning); a municipal council with full mayor and officers, bishop and retinue, various lower courts; some "recognized" families of ancient nobility, but twice as many Indians as Spaniards—despite the fact that many died in a terrible plague in 1720. There are somewhat fewer convents and nunneries; a university and three high schools; a high school for children of the Indian nobles; two general hospitals and one each for "Indians and white women" and finally, some problems with the water system.[5]

Beyond this, there was little else. The population reached its nadir in 1790 with approximately 1,500,000 persons living within the Peruvian territory. Except for the ubiquity of church institutions, other parts of the public establishment were thinly represented beyond Lima, Cuzco, La Paz and Chuquisaca (Sucre). As Cosme

Bueno also indicated, the Spaniards of noble attributes were similarly distributed. The provinces were all equally remote and arduously reached on horseback or litter on trips of several days or weeks. Aside from the few oases of culture and society like Cuzco, Arequipa, Trujillo and Saña, the countryside and its towns were rustic at best. The inhabitants of such places were similarly identified, being mostly of the Indian and mestizo castes, with lesser Spaniards appearing occasionally in their ranks.

It should be pointed out that those of non-Spaniard castes operated under considerable handicaps in colonial Peru. They were not permitted (in theory or in practice) to ride horses, bear arms or wear "Spanish" clothing; instead, they had to serve in such ways as performing the onerous "mita de minas"—working in textile mills and performing the other laborious tasks of the colony, in addition to supplying it with food and tribute. Thus the city, particularly Lima, is identified with the upper classes and ruling elites; it is considered the administrative center, giver of justice, the center of enlightenment and the holder of wealth and well-being, both physical and spiritual. It is a place to be served, rather than one from which service is rendered. Its citizens are the ones who have primary access to whatever services and facilities might exist there, and the assumption further develops that these are the people who can best appreciate their value and utilize them properly.

The translation of such an orientation into ways of life and sets of values which permeate the country is as follows. The late Sebastian Salazar Bondy is a Peruvian essayist who captures this spirit in all its detail and subtlety with his brutal but constructive critique, *Lima, La Horrible*.[6] For him, Lima is egoistic, absorbent, possessed by its royalist past and seduced by its values, metropolitan but also locked in its own provincialism which it projects out over the entire nation, as the model. Its style is *criollismo,* a word that summarizes the ethos and is used to characterize everything that comes from Lima: its food and music, politics and interpersonal behavior.[7] Salazar's words say it all:[8] "Criollism comes to be, then, Limean nationalism, that is, a substitute for real nationalism, since for it Peru is Lima and Lima, the Jirón de la Unión." *

* Jirón de la Unión is the principal commercial street and urban showplace of Lima, which runs between the Plaza de Armas and the Plaza San Martín in the heart of the city.

Political Structure and the City

Modern Peru is subdivided into three diminishing classes of administrative units: departments, provinces and districts (roughly corresponding to our states, counties and townships). Each of these is similarly structured in terms of organizational content and official positions, with the exception that at the departmental level, the prefect (who is always appointed from Lima) does not interact with a municipal council and is not specifically charged with managing urban areas. At the provincial and subordinate district levels which most concern us, however, the chief officials are arranged as follows:

Duty	District	Province
Executive officer to administrate municipal government, especially urban center affairs. Formerly elected, now appointed.	Mayor *(alcalde)*	Mayor
Manage specific aspects of municipal government: treasury, garbage collection, markets, parks, lights, spectacles, etc. Formerly elected, now appointed.	Councilmen *(Concejales)*	Councilmen
Serve as municipal representative in hamlets and outlying areas. Always appointed.	Municipal Agent	
Act as the "political authority": oversee the care of law and order in the province as a whole, initiate action where needed, especially in rural areas. Governor appointed by sub-prefect, who in turn is appointed by the prefect, with Lima's approval.	Governor	Sub-prefect
Represent the governor and "political authority" in hamlet and rural areas. Appointed by governor.	Lieutenant Governor	

There is considerable potential overlap in this administrative structure, but essentially, as it actually works out, the mayors have the chief—but not the exclusive—responsibility for urban areas. In the past, municipal officials have been elected. Until 1919, they were elected in each town or city by an informal, yet official group called the "board of notables" *(junta de notables)*. From 1919 until 1963 they were appointed by the prefect, who received a list of three recommended candidates sent to him by the governors or the sub-prefect of each district. In 1963 and 1966 municipal elections were reinstated, only to be stopped again in 1968 with a return to the former appointment procedure.

Rural hamlets participated in their respective district-level elections but did not, at least officially, elect their own municipal agents or lieutenant governors. Ironically, since 1919, members of recognized *Comunidades Campesinas* (peasant communities)—formerly *Comunidades Indigenas* (Indian communities) have had the right to elect their own officers under the supervision of the ministry charged with overseeing their activities. Such *Comunidades* however, may or may not be rural in character and often are coterminous with the districts in which they are located. For our purposes here, we shall have to omit consideration of these units although ideally they should be discussed, since at the present time they are taking on great importance for life in all provincial areas of the country and their newly developing status and functions will certainly have additional bearing upon urban affairs in the future.

With this political-administrative structure, it becomes evident that the basic unit of management is the district. It is important to realize that there is no city organization or apparatus beyond or supplementary to the district or the province. All districts in Peru are organized in exactly the same manner, no matter where they are; there is only a difference in scale of operations. Thus, districts with very large populations will have large councils, many councilmen and bigger budgets.

In every case, the capital of the district is defined by law as an urban area, no matter what the size of its population. By the same token, in order to be classified as "urban," any population center outside the district capital must have a population equal to or exceeding that of the district capital, and have certain urban attributes—such as plazas and streets. Thus, every district capital potentially has the same political and administrative powers and services to offer the public.

The city of greater Lima is comprised of 32 districts, each with its own municipal structure and all contained within the Province of Lima, which is comprised of a total of 39 districts.*

The office of the provincial government is located on the Plaza de Armas of the district of Lima; it coordinates the larger affairs of the subordinate districts. Thus, the "city" of Lima is essentially the province, adding new districts to its roster in a manner reminiscent of a segmentary lineage. Consequently, it is difficult to know where the city limits are; the last one I recall seeing was engulfed in the center of the district of San Martín de Porras, a prominent new section of the city.

The services that districts offer their residents are several and elastic, as they can be expanded at any time. Basically, citizens of the district capital itself can expect to obtain the following services from their municipal government:

1. the prestige of being classified as "urban"
2. care and management of public thoroughfares and buildings
3. care and management of the marketplace, including price controls; inspection of weights and measures; licensing of vendors
4. collection of fees and taxes
5. organization and care of public libraries, museums, parks, etc.
6. organization and management of public spectacles such as parades, political rallies, patronal fiestas, etc.
7. management of the municipal treasury
8. garbage collection, street cleaning *(baja policia)* and sewerage
9. management and control of drinking water and, often, electricity
10. representation of the urban area and the district in ceremonial affairs

In addition, although it is not required so far as I can determine, any district capital will have a Plaza de Armas or central square, around which are concentrated municipal offices and important public

---

* This is my judgment, in terms of which districts actually form part of the complex which is Lima. Potentially, the whole province could eventually become the "city" of Lima.

buildings. District capitals can also generally count on having, as a result of their political status, the following services which are controlled by national authorities: postal service to the capital, complete primary school (first six years of schooling) and a police post. Population centers which are not district capitals have little chance of obtaining such services for themselves—although a few do, for unpredictable political reasons.

Let us see how this operates in terms of urbanization and political dynamics. In order for a settlement to be considered urban, it must generally be the capital of a political district. If it can become the capital of a district, it can then expect to be imbued *automatically* with the capacity to obtain the kinds of services outlined above, plus others which it will then have an advantage in obtaining as a result of its status. The argument in this regard relies on sensitivity to matters of national pride as much as anything, and not, necessarily, that the people should in fact have access to these services. Thus, indignation is expressed by residents of district capitals and by politicians over the lack of such services, buildings and functions when the place is, after all, a district capital and an urban center.

One way in which we can see the impact of such philosophy and practice is in the formation of new districts and provinces. The following table summarizes this matter rather clearly. The number of districts in Peru increased by 59 percent from 1940 to 1966, but not at all since that time. As we can see in Table 1, this increase has not been uniform and there are many factors which explain the variations: migration patterns, political action and the social mobility of the respective populations being foremost. Thus, Ancash, which is the department which sends the most migrants to the city of Lima (aside from the rural areas of the department of Lima itself) exhibited a 58 percent growth in districts—and perhaps more importantly—a 60 percent increase in the number of provinces. Prior to the suspension of elections in 1968, and the change in electoral constituencies in 1966, the number of deputies in the Congress representing the departments was based upon the number of provinces: one deputy per province. Ancash, with 16 provinces, had far better (more numerous) representation than any other department. The migrants from the departments in Lima play an important role in such changes, since they act as a lobby for their home districts and provinces. With the present government, however, political activity of the traditional sort has cooled; in turn, the number of new districts and provinces created has vastly diminished. Interestingly enough however, the number of districts in the province of Lima increased by 11 percent in the same period.

Table 1
POLITICAL-ADMINISTRATIVE UNITS IN PERU AND THEIR
INCREASE FROM 1940-1961-1966

Department	Provinces No. 1966	% Increase since 1940	No. 1966	Districts % Increase since 1940	Population Centers * % Inc. to 1961
Amazonas	5	25	77	32	39
Ancash	16	60	154	58	34
Apurimac	6	20	69	91	15
Arequipa	8	0	105	25	23
Ayacucho	7	0	101	48	34
Cajamarca	11	37	109	49	25
Callao	1	0	5	60	115
Cuzco	13	0	100	40	16
Huancavelica	5	25	90	130	71
Huánuco	7	16	69	64	90
Ica	5	66	39	95	43
Junín †	7	40	119	62	−30
La Libertad	7	0	72	30	48
Lambayeque	3	50	32	28	83
Lima	7	0	162	60	85
Loreto	6	100	52	135	13
Madre de Dios	3	0	9	12	74
Moquegua	2	0	17	88	4
Pasco †	3	100	26	−	−
Piura	7	16	61	56	34
Puno	9	0	94	13	26
San Martín	6	0	69	97	66
Tacna	2	0	23	91	4
Tumbes	3	200	11	112	7
Total ‡	148	22	1665	59 ‡	35

Source: *Anuario Estadíatica del Perú, 1966, Resultados de 1958 a 1966* (Ministerio de Hacienda y Comercio, Dirección Nacional de Estadística y Censos) Volumen XXVII, de la Nueva Serie, Lima, 1969, pp. 75–76.

* Populated Center includes any place with established residents and a name.

† Junín was divided in 1944, to create the department of Pasco, which was formerly one of its provinces. This accounts for the decrease in the number of populated centers in Junín.

‡ The increase in the number of districts from 1961 to 1966 amounted to 11 percent of the 1961 total. This was a period in which there were municipal elections and intense political activity. Since that time the increases in the number of provinces and districts has been less than 1 percent. Five of the 11 new districts, however, are in greater Lima.

Such changes are less spectacular when considered in light of overall population growth. Between 1940 and 1961, the increase amounted to 59 percent for the nation (2.8 percent per year). Thus the average increment in the number of districts merely matched this figure for the period. Between 1961 and 1972, however, the 36.9 percent population growth (3.3 percent per year) was not matched by the increase in districts. Nevertheless, urban growth continues, whether or not it is as closely tied to district capital creation as it was in the past. As often as not district capitals were frustrated in achieving the services they may have desired. The clear trend, as indicated by the figures in Table 2, is for migrants to enter the larger cities where an urban condition has already been established or where considerable promise for one is held forth.

Table 2 indicates what this growth has been in the cities since 1940. The majority of these (55 percent) are in the coastal region. Of special interest, however, is the overall increase in cities which have populations of 20,000 or more. Before 1940, only 15 percent of the people lived in those 11 urban areas. By 1961 this had increased to 27 percent living in 26 urban centers, and, by 1972, 41 percent of the population were living in 36 cities of that size. Clearly the urban expansion has continued unabated as the percent of yearly increment has remained the same for cities of this size since 1940, 9.3 percent per year. This is, of course, far in excess of the overall average national population increase since 1961, of 3.3 percent per year, although that figure has also risen markedly from the previous period. Consequently, we can conclude that the urban policies of the seven administrations holding office in Peru during the past 34 years have not changed the pattern of urban growth in large cities.

The rush of migrants into the urban coast from the highland provinces is an unwavering stream which develops even greater thrust through the years, especially toward the coast and Lima, whose pull is undeniable. As of 1961, about 70 percent of the greater Lima population was born elsewhere and 16 percent of the national population resided there, representing an increase from 1940 of 7.9 percent per year. It now has 24 percent of the total population and for the last decade Lima has been increasing at the rate of over 9 percent per year. Lima's overpowering attraction seems to be based largely on the availability of "services"—which I define here as any common good which is offered to the citizenry. In a country like Peru, this

Table 2
PERUVIAN CITIES WITH 20,000 INHABITANTS OR MORE, 1940-1972

City	No. Districts 1972	Population 1961	% Increase 1940–1961 Tot.	% Increase 1940–1961 Year	Population 1972	% increase 1961–1972 Tot.	% increase 1961–1972 Year	Rank Increase Order
Lima [C]*	32	1,436,231	175	8.3	2,973,845	107	9.7	5
Callao [C]*	6	204,990	124	5.9	312,332	52	4.7	23
[Greater Lima	38	1,641,221	167	7.9	3,286,177	100	9.0	(7)]
Arequipa [H]*	9	158,685	122	5.8	304,653	91	8.2	9
Trujillo [C]*	4	103,020	170	8.0	241,882	134	12.1	2
Chiclayo [C]*	2	95,667	203	9.6	189,685	98	8.9	7
Chimbote [C]	1	59,990	1313	62.5	159,045	165	15.0	1
Piura [C]*	2	72,096	158	7.5	126,702	75	6.8	15
Cuzco [H]*	3	79,857	96	4.5	120,881	52	4.7	23
Huancayo [H]*	3	64,153	140	6.6	115,693	80	7.2	14
Iquitos [J]	1	57,777	81	3.8	111,327	92	8.3	8
Ica [C]*	1	49,097	134	6.3	73,883	50	4.5	25
Sullana [C]*	1	34,501	63	3.0	60,112	74	6.7	16
Pucallpa [J]	1	26,391	1014	48.2	57,525	117	10.6	4
Tacna [C]	1	27,449	149	7.0	55,752	103	9.3	6
Cerro de Pasco [H]	1	21,363	19	.9	47,178	120	10.9	3
Pisco [C]	1	22,112	55	2.6	41,429	87	7.9	11
Puno [H]	1	24,459	77	3.6	41,166	68	6.1	17
Huánuco [H]	1	24,646	105	5.0	41,123	66	6.0	18
Juliaca [H]	1	20,351	237	11.2	38,475	89	8.0	10
Cajamarca [H]	1	22,705	58	2.7	37,608	65	5.9	19
Huacho [C]	1	22,806	75	3.5	36,697	60	5.4	20
Ayacucho [H]	3	23,768	42	2.0	34,593	38	3.4	27
Tumbes [C]	1	20,885	238	11.3	32,972	57	5.1	21
Talara [C]	1	27,957	115	5.4	29,884	6	.5	28
Huaraz [H]	1	20,345	84	4.0	29,719	46	4.1	26
Chincha Alta [C]	1	20,817	67	3.1	28,785	38	3.4	27
Pativilca [C]†	1	[15,327]	198	9.4	28,369	85	7.7	12
Tarma [H]†	1	[15,452]	110	5.2	28,100	81	7.3	13
Other Cities		24,724†			224,866 s	54	4.9	22
Total		2,766,842	196	9.3	5,624,281	103	9.3	

Sources: *Anuario Estadístico del Perú, 1966*. pp. 75–89; all data for 1972 are derived from: Perú, Oficina Nacional de Estadística y Censos, *1972 Resultados Provisionales: Población del Perú, Censo del 4 de Junio* (Lima).

[C] Coast
[H] Highland
[J] Jungle
* Cities over 20,000 population in 1940.
† Not added in 1961 total; Pativilca includes Paramonga.
‡ The only city was La Oroya.
S Chulucanas [C], La Oroya [H], Barranca [C], Chepen [C], Tarapoto [J], Chocope [C], Ilo [C], Huaral [C], Tingo Maria [J]; listed in order of size.

includes: municipal services, such as water, light and a marketplace; national government services—postal, communications, schools and universities, hospitals, social security, indigent care; and privately owned, public attractions, such as theaters, movies, sports events, etc. Since the government is the nation's largest employer, another major service of the government is providing employment to those who seek it. Justice and religion are likewise Lima-based, official services.

The Distribution of Services

The extreme dominance of Lima and of Peru's cities in general is quite evident. Almost one quarter of the nation's four thousand kilometers of paved highways are in the department of Lima (not including the city streets, however, which would account for much of the total paving). The national highway system focuses upon the capital in hublike fashion; and greater Lima is the only Peruvian city that has a complete and active public transport system leading to all parts of the province and the country.

The cities also monopolize the nation in economic terms, as can be seen in Tables 3 to 7. We note that 75 percent of all industrial wages are paid in greater Lima, 5.6 percent in Chimbote, 4 percent in Arequipa, 3 percent in the mines of Junín and the rest in infinitesimal amounts elsewhere. For anyone seeking employment, the message is clear, and the distribution of technical personnel indicated in Table 3 indicates one result of this fact. The more highly trained the individual, the more likely that person is to reside and work in Lima. The strength of that hypothesis is illustrated by the fact that, of the 731 agricultural engineers "available" to Peruvian farmers in 1961, 40 percent were to be found in the capital.[9] The heavy concentration of managerial, white-collar and professional persons in Lima demonstrates the middle-class character of the city. Of course, the members of the upper class reside in Lima as well, when they are not abroad, a situation which the present government has been examining closely—particularly in terms of financial affairs.

Of interest, too, is the concentration of military headquarters, bases and ministries within the environs of Lima. There is a large base at Chorillos, a suburb of Lima, which serves both the army and the air force; there is also a naval base in Callao and in Ancón and a powerful

Table 3
DISTRIBUTION OF TRAINED PERSONNEL BY OCCUPATIONAL GROUPS IN PERU, 1961

	Professionals, engineers, etc.		Managerial Functionaries		White Collar		Sales Personal		Artesans Total	
	No.	%	No.	%	No.	%	No.	%	No.	%
Lima	39,385		22,742		75,997		76,234		158,838	
Callao	2,814		2,059		8,955		6,851		19,372	
Greater Lima	42,199	42	24,801	54	84,952	63	83,085	36	178,210	38
Rest of nation		58		46		37		64		62
Total	102,712	(100)	45,182	(100)	133,345	(100)	226,300	(100)	476,193	(100)

Source: *Anuario Estadístico del Perú, 1966*, vol. 14. pp. 162–171.

armored division headquarters in Rimac. Nevertheless, while there are important military centers in places like Piura, Trujillo and Arequipa, and many regional headquarters within the departmental capitals, their cumulative size pales in comparison to the bulk of the military establishment in Lima. Because of the size of the military presence within the city, Lima also contains a number of military-related facilities. These include: schools for the children of military personnel (and of course for officer training), special hospitals for members of the armed forces and their relatives, military consumers' cooperatives, military manufacturing industries and special military recreational facilities—such as casinos. Few if any of these services intended for military personnel are so significantly represented elsewhere in Peru.

Table 4
BLUE- AND WHITE-COLLAR WORKERS REGISTERED
WITH SOCIAL SECURITY, PERU, 1966

	Blue Collar *	White Collar **
Total	481,236	568,513
Lima (city)	238,185	316,228
Callao	22,446	25,331
Greater Lima Total	(54%) 260,631	(60%) 341,559
Cuzco	6,661	14,357
Arequipa	18,167	29,499
Chimbote-Casma	12,477	14,760
Ancash other	1,284	
Ica (city)	14,176	15,505
Trujillo	10,793	23,100
Cerro de Pasco	12,987	5,549
Junín	20,387	21,507
Piura	15,881	20,684
Rest of country	46%	40%

Source: *Anuario Estadístico del Perú, 1966.* pp. 911, 915.
* Figures given for cities only.
** Figures for departments only.

The official statistics showing the concentration of blue-collar workers within the cities and in greater Lima are similarly impressive (see Table 4). In fact, like their white collar and military counterparts, virtually no blue-collar workers live in rural areas. The importance of the role played by Peru's national social security system in the country's urban growth should not be underestimated. Peruvian social security law provides for vacations, health care, maternity assistance, specific pay scales, retirement conditions and so forth. Until very recently, a person living in a rural area or a small town had no access to blue-collar social security—there were few regional offices and practically no coverage outside the biggest urban centers. Thus, in order to participate in this program, people had to move into a large city. Once in the city, the manual worker would quickly realize that white-collar workers were covered by a far more favorable social security law and had better, separate hospital facilities. President Odría (1948–56) built a blue-collar workers' resort on the outskirts of Lima, but it quickly gained more general usage.

Table 5
BLUE-COLLAR WORKERS' OLD AGE PENSIONS PAID, 1966

Place	No.	%
Arequipa	84	4.5
Ica	168	9.2
Junín	31	1.6
La Libertad	158	8.7
Chiclayo	253	14.0
Lima city	982	54.0
Callao	74	4.0
Huacho	181	10.0
Cañete	48	2.0
Pasco	20	1.0
Piura	22	1.0
Tacna	3	−.1
	1,795	100.0

Source: *Anuario Estadístico del Perú, 1966*, p. 919.

Table 6
BLUE-COLLAR WORKERS IN PERU ACCORDING
TO WEEKLY WAGES, 1961

Weekly wage	Urban		Rural	
	No.	%	No.	%
S/10.00–150.00 †	192,257	36	303,100	67
S/150.00–3,000 +	335,051	64	153,200	33
Total	527,308	(100)	456,377	(100)

† In 1961, the *SOL* was valued at S/.26.80 per $1.00 (1972 it was S/43.40 per $1.00); wage range was $.37–$5.50 and $5.60 and up, in 1961.

Source: *Anuario Estadístico del Perú, 1966*, p. 308–309.

The difference between urban and rural wages is striking (see Table 6), for they are the mirror images of one another. The poverty of the rural situation vis-à-vis that of urban areas is clear and undeniable. Wages paid in Lima are the highest in Peru, with an average weekly wage of about 1,300 soles per month in 1966.[10] Unfortunately, cost of living indices are not widely collected in Peru and only the statistics for the cities of Lima and Arequipa are reported, an interesting commentary in itself on the subject of centralization. Furthermore, some of the "corresponding" figures cited for the two cities use different units of measure! The nature of the Peruvian marketing system becomes apparent here, as the costs for Arequipa outdistance those of greater Lima. The prices, cost indices notwithstanding, are higher in the wholesale market of Lima (La Parada, also known as La Mayorista), and so they attract producers from all over the country.

Table 7
PRICE INDEX, 1966
(1960 = 100)

	Lima		Arequipa	
	Cost (kilo)	Index	Cost (kilo)	Index
Beef (top grade) †	26.2	151.7	10.51 *	184.3
lard	14.18	119.9	7.80 *	145.3
oil (bottle)	7.20	141.5	10.16	147.2
fresh milk ‡	3.89	123.1	2.89	139.4
evaporated milk (can) ‡	4.69	116.7	4.72	118.0
tomatoes §	4.00	146.5	4.43	246.1
white potatoes §	4.31	189.9	4.06	205.1
General cost rise		166.8		169.5

Source: *Anuario Estadístico del Perú, 1966,* pp. 1383–1405.

* Cost given in pounds, rather than kilos, for reasons known only to the compilers.

†Adjacent to Arequipa is Puno, the nation's leading producer of beef cattle.

‡ Produced on a commercial scale, within 15 miles of the city of Arequipa. Canned milk is exported to Lima, 750 kilometers away.

§ The leading producers are in adjacent departments for both Lima and Arequipa.

The result of this centralized market system is that in Chimbote, the major fishing port of Peru, fish are frequently unavailable, and in Huaraz, the center of the biggest potato-growing area, often there are but handfuls of third-rate potatoes in the marketplace. In Huaraz, for example, the municipal government used police to force producers shipping their goods to Lima to retain a fixed percentage of their highest grade potatoes for local sale—and potatoes are the staple food of the Andes. Thus, it is not surprising to learn that milk products, which are produced in industrial quantity on the very outskirts of the city of Arequipa, cost more there than in Lima! In the absence of data from rural areas, the moral of this story is: if you must migrate to a city, take Lima. Even if you do not actually move to Lima, you will have a much better chance of buying there, since over 80 percent of the nation's wholesalers, and 36 percent of its retailers, operate in Lima. This concentration of the commercial establishment in Lima takes on a new meaning for provincial business with the gradual development of better roads. Wherever possible, local purchasers prefer to bypass the intermediaries in their own district and provincial capitals, and deal directly with the chief suppliers in Lima.

Table 8
ESTIMATED ELECTRIC POWER CONSUMED
IN KILOWATT HOURS, 1966

| | Electricity Consumed | | |
	Kilowatt Hrs.	Percent	Percent of Population
Total	1,956,054,463	100.00	100.0
Lima-Callao	1,449,099,526	72.9	22.6
Rest of Nation	506,954,937	27.1	77.4

Source: *Anuario Estadístico del Perú, 1966*, p. 1110.

Given this background, Peru's patterns of consumption are not surprising, but we must, of course, be careful in interpreting them. For example, Peru's consumption of electric power corresponds almost exactly to the nation's distribution of industrial wages (see Table 8). The dramatic differences in the presence or absence of household amenities according to urban and rural classification is clear (see Table 9). Only 4 percent of rural families, as opposed to 50 percent of families in urban centers, have electricity in their homes. However, there are also significant variations among the cities, with Lima, Callao and Arequipa offering much more to their inhabitants than is generally the case. Unfortunately, data for the other cities are not available, but they almost certainly would show a sharp drop from those presented here, with certain exceptions—such as oil-rich Talara.

Table 9
PERCENTAGE OF HOUSEHOLDS OWNING AND USING
AMENITIES BY DEPARTMENTS AND THEIR
MAJOR CITIES, 1961

Department and City	Electric Lights	Modern Kitchen	Radio	Sewing Machine
Urban Peru (total)	50.7	57.8	43.3	42.23
Rural Peru (total)	4.2	7.2	5.4	15.70
Arequipa (dept.)	43.8	50.0	34.9	34.1
Arequipa (city)	77.9	89.8	58.0	50.0
Cuzco (dept.)	12.9	14.2	10.0	13.2
Cuzco (city)	69.2	77.2	47.6	41.3
Junín (dept.)	23.5	25.3	18.6	29.3
Huancayo (city)	67.6	79.9	50.2	47.6
La Libertad (dept.)	20.7	25.6	19.5	34.3
Trujillo (city)	46.5	66.8	46.0	50.2
Lambayeque (dept.)	30.2	25.3	26.1	34.6
Chiclayo (city)	53.2	52.8	46.0	46.4
Lima (dept.)	63.3	77.8	56.4	45.8
Lima (city)	81.0	88.9	70.7	52.8
Callao (prov.)	78.2	87.6	68.8	49.0
Loreto (dept.)	14.5	7.9	13.0	30.0
Iquitos (city)	46.6	18.8	36.6	53.9

Source: *Anuario Estadístico del Perú, 1966,* Sect. 12, p. xiv.

These data indicate several things. First, they show that the people living in large urban areas are more likely to have use of those items noted than are persons living elsewhere. Second, either because they can better afford them and/or due to their greater access to the sources of these things, urban dwellers acquire luxuries such as electricity, stoves and radios—which quickly become recognized as needs.

It is a mistake to think that people living in the small district capitals do not want to make life easier for themselves where possible. But, as the Peruvians would say, the multiple public services provided at this level, "shine by their absence." (Table 10 demonstrates this situation all too clearly.) The problem for these people is how to obtain even the beginnings of such luxuries. I have heard native Limean urbanites accounting for this lack of "facilities" in the provinces in terms that question not only the people's desires and needs for them, but also their mental capacity to make use of them. Thus, when the district of Huaylas fought to install electricity in 1960, they had to convince the director of the power corporation (the nephew of President Prado) that the people were capable of using it. Once the initial installation was made, however, the people of Huaylas extended the power network to

Table 10
NUMBER AND PERCENT OF DISTRICTS LACKING SERVICES, 1964

Service to District	Nation		Coast		West Highlands		Puna		East Highlands		Jungle	
	no.	%	no.	%	no.	%	no.	%	no.	%	no.	%
Total Districts	1565	—	255	—	378	—	184	—	613	—	135	—
Electricity	944	60	68	27	254	67	122	66	408	67	92	68
Communications	193	12	10	4	36	10	18	10	67	11	62	46
Parish and Church	1047	67	127	50	269	71	106	58	456	74	89	66
Access Road	593	38	17	7	165	44	29	16	285	46	97	72
Complete Primary School	59	4	13	5	7	2	7	4	23	4	9	7
Public Health Officer	1111	71	*	45	*	77	*	90	*	84	*	16
Agricultural Extension	1362	87	*	88	*	86	*	79	*	89	*	89
Credit Union	1424	91	*	73	*	93	*	93	*	96	*	91
Bank	1455	93	*	81	*	97	*	96	*	96	*	90

Source: *Adenda: Datos Distritales Para Fines de Desarrollo* (Cooperación Popular-Alianza para el Progreso) Lima Imprenta del SESP, 1964.

*Number not given in source.

include over 50 percent of all homes in the district, including rural areas—thus equalling the national urban average.[11] Despite such examples, the middle class retains its old attitude of "pobrecitos, porque quieran vivir así?" (the poor devils, why do they want to live like that?). Such rationalizations for the traditional pattern of distribution of public wealth and services form the basis for many of the antagonisms within Peruvian society.

We need not look far into the area of education to find similar problems. It has been demonstrated many times that migrants to the cities, especially Lima, rank high in terms of the level of education available and achieved in their home villages and towns; also, the primary migrants (wage-earners) almost inevitably speak Spanish. Moreover, the migrant who is not moving primarily to get work, is going in order to educate himself and thereby improve his employment status.[12]

It should be noted that the availability of educational facilities, at all levels, is closely tied to urbanism and political administration. Thus, at the district level, about half of the capitals have complete primary schools for both sexes (boys' and girls' schools used to be separate;

Table 11
ATTENDANCE IN HIGH SCHOOLS IN GREATER LIMA
AND PERU, 1961

	High School	%	Vocational High School	%
Greater Lima	106.903	44	17,226	60
Rest of Nation	110,218	56	11,282	60
Total	227,121	(100)	28,508	(100)

Source: *Anuario Estadístico del Perú, 1966*, p. 876.

Table 12
NUMBER OF UNIVERSITIES IN PERU AND APPLICANTS
FOR UNIVERSITY ADMISSION 1965

	Universities		Applicants		Applicants Admitted		% Accepted
Place	no.	%	no.	%	no.	%	
Greater Lima	11	44	22,741	67	9873	62	43
All Other Areas	17	56	11,512	33	5833	38	50
Total	(28)	(100)	(34,253)	(100)	15706	(100)	45

Source: *Anuario Estadístico del Perú, 1966*, pp. 886–901.

since 1971, they have been integrated). A few district capitals have high schools, but these are rare outside the coastal areas. Most of the high schools are found in the provincial and departmental capitals, with the result that students who wish to attend them must leave home in order to do so. This, of course, can be a considerable financial hardship and thus is beyond the reach of many families.

As shown in Tables 11–13, the distribution of advanced educational facilities again favors greater Lima in all aspects. What is only hinted at in these figures, however, is the aspect of relative educational quality. The general public believes that the education offered in Lima is better than that given elsewhere. Therefore, Lima's schools are crowded. And at the university level, students tend to apply for admission in Lima, despite the fact that they have a greater chance of being accepted elsewhere.

All of this serves to reinforce the assumption that the people who live in the towns and provinces are less educated, less interested in education and generally less sophisticated than urbanites. The character of the migrant flow into the cities from these areas demonstrates that, if these things have any truth to them, it is due to a lack of possibilities, rather than choice. For example, it is often difficult to purchase a newspaper in the Andes, particularly if one lives away from the main highways or away from the provincial capitals. Few papers are dispatched beyond the departmental capitals in the highlands, for it is generally assumed that they will not (or cannot) be read there. *La Prensa,* the most widely distributed newspaper in the highland areas, publishes a separate limited edition for each major region of the country, dropping certain international and national news in order to do so. This results in an interesting form of news management, in which each provincial region sees different items on the same day and none gets the full story of what goes on in Lima or the world. Similarly, the people in Lima never get to read much provincial news.

Despite such peculiarities, however, a valiant attempt at true nationwide communication is being made (see Table 13). Perhaps the most interesting and important development in this field is the radio. There are many small town stations, but most of these can scarcely be heard a few blocks away from their transmitters. Instead, several very powerful stations in Lima serve the country at large. The national government runs its own station, and recently has acquired considerable control over all the other stations. It is nevertheless difficult to estimate the impact of radio,[13] especially in rural areas, but we assume it is significant in whetting the people's appetites for things they do not have. In this sense, the radio is an urban tool, instrumental in stimulating the potential migrant.

Table 13
COMMUNICATIONS AND EDUCATIONAL MEDIA, 1966

	% of population	Museums		News-papers		Maga-zines		Radio Stations	
		no.	%	no.	%	no.	%	no.	%
Lima-Callao	24	42	52	36	51	426	86	34	21
rest of nation	76	40	48	34	49	66	14	128	79
total		82	(100)	70	(100)	492	(100)	162	(100)

Source: *Anuario Estadístico del Perú, 1966*, pp. 886–901.

Personal well-being can be best taken care of in urban centers. Indeed, it seems reasonable to assume that a city's medical and spiritual care improve as its rank and size increase. Tables 14–16 indicate how the distribution and availability of these services clearly augment in this manner. The clustering of medical personnel and facilities within Lima and Callao leaves no doubt that these are the places to go when one requires serious medical care, bypassing the provincial clinics and hospitals where understaffing is a chronic trait, and the lack of equipment bewilders medical doctors accustomed to urban facilities. Since there are frequently operating rooms without lights or perhaps scissors, laboratories without modern hypodermic needles, and wards with no nurses, peasants surmise—often correctly—that one only goes to the provincial hospital when he is about to die. A review of hospital statistics supports this observation, only 3 percent of patients succumb in Lima hospitals, which handled 44.5 percent of all the nation's patients in 1965, whereas 4.4 percent of those in other hospitals died. In Lima, medical care can be truly excellent; in rural areas, it may be altogether absent.

Finally, if one needs remedial or custodial care, he will find 75 percent of the facilities, such as they are, in Lima. The entire country of Peru contains only enough places for 4,569 patients in institutions of this sort. The result is that the family is the institution which undertakes this task, where possible. And, since the extended family is still opera-

Table 14
MEDICAL SERVICE DISTRIBUTION IN PERU, 1965

Department	% of pop.	No. of hospitals	No. of beds	% of beds	No. of Doctors	% of Doctors
Amazonas	1.1	3	154	0.5	14	0.5
Ancash	5.8	12	760	3.0	53	2.0
Apurimac	2.9	1 2	146	0.5	11	0.3
Arequipa	3.9	9	1641	7.0	223	8.0
Ayacucho	4.1	5	283	1.2	23	0.8
Cajamarca	7.4	5	354	1.5	27	1.0
Callao	2.1	6	1263	5.4	170	6.4
Cuzco	6.1	4	721	3.1	36	1.4
Huancavelica	3.0	1	130	0.5	8	0.2
Huánuco	3.3	3	302	1.2	33	1.3
Ica	2.5	9	1184	5.0	90	3.2
Junín	5.2	6	966	4.1	78	2.8
La Libertad	5.8	11	1521	6.9	146	5.2
Lambayeque	4.8	4	603	2.6	65	2.3
Lima	20.5	37	10481	45.0	1584	57.0
Loreto	3.4	7	417	2.0	18	0.6
Madre de Dios	.1	1	24	0.5	2	0.0
Moquegua	.5	4	237	1.0	12	0.4
Pasco	1.4	4	359	1.5	26	0.9
Piura	6.5	8	829	3.5	75	2.7
Puno	6.9	5	242	1.0	25	0.9
San Martín	1.6	4	172	0.5	6	0.2
Tacna	.6	2	432	2.0	38	1.5
Tumbes	.5	1	123	0.5	12	0.4
Total	100.0	153	23,344	100.0	2,775	100.0

Source: *Anuario Estadístico del Perú, 1966*, pp. 752–53. The population distribution in 1972 is approximately the same, with Lima having increased to 25.7 percent. Similarly, all other coastal regions increased slightly while highland areas declined in their percent (not in number, however) of the population. Jungle areas increased slightly in 1972 figures. (Source: *Catálogo de instituciones de servicio a la comunidad: Trujillo-Chimbote-Lima-Arequipa*, Oficina Nacional de Desarrollo de Pueblos Jovenes, Lima.)

tive in Peru—even in Lima—this is true in the majority of such cases. On the other hand, the cities have a severe problem with beggars, mental incompetents and orphans wandering the streets—since, to date, there is no other place for them to go.

As a last resort, the *provinciano* can always migrate to Lima in order to find a priest with whom to confess. Roman Catholicism, as the official, protected state religion, is—like all other governmental arms—focused on greater Lima in terms of its numbers and facilities. Provincial parishes are often unstaffed, and it is the rule—rather than the exception—in the highlands, to go to one's grave without any priestly intervention along the way.

CARL A. RUDISILL LIBRARY
LENOIR RHYNE COLLEGE

Table 15
STATE-CONTROLLED PUBLIC MEDICAL WELFARE
INSTITUTIONS, 1966 (OLD AGE, ORPHANAGES,
BLIND AND DEAF, ETC.)

Department	Number	Beds	% Beds
Ancash	1	30	0.2
1 general			
Arequipa	4	510	11.2
1 orphanage			
2 old age homes			
1 blind home			
Cajamarca	1	161	3.6
1 old age home			
Callao	1	90	2.0
1 old age home			
Cuzco	1	110	2.4
1 children's home			
Huánuco	2	20	0.1
2 old age homes			
La Libertad	1	80	2.0
1 old age home			
Lima	10	3,458	76.0
1 orphanage			
1 old age home			
1 blind home			
7 general			
Loreto	1	50	1.2
1 invalid care			
Puno	1	60	1.3
1 orphanage			
Total	23	4,569	100.0

Source: *Anuario Estadístico del Perú, 1966*, p. 964.

Table 16
DISTRIBUTION OF PERUVIAN ECCLESIASTIC PERSONNEL,
1966

	Priests		Nuns	
	Number	%	Number	%
Archdioceses of				
Lima	731	31	2203	44
All Others	1643	69	2389	56
National Total	2374	100	4592	100

Source: *Anuario Estadístico del Perú, 1966*, pp. 908–909.

Urban Policy: Real and Imagined

We have explored the uniform concentration in Lima of services, as well as almost everything else that is given value in Peru. Now we must discover the "policy" which governed such unidirectional growth—which, whatever its original intention, has created a primate city, and one whose growth seems irreversible at the present time.

The city of Lima nourishes itself with new migrants, attracted because of its unparalleled complex of services, attractions and opportunities. As the migrants pour into the greater Lima area, they put pressure on the system that will not serve them elsewhere, to serve them here. Thus, this great migration is a passionate cry for attention and recognition, demonstrating that these people, too, have needs and a right to satisfy them.

The kind of people who come to Lima are generally those who want more participation in the system and who are willing to take the risks required. They know that, in Lima, they will gain greater leverage over the bureaucratic elite that governs the country. Indeed, migration to Lima is the only way to achieve such goals, as countless delegations of peasants have discovered.

What, then, are the policies that made Lima what it is today? Clearly, they have ignored the provincial towns and cities, whose few amenities—where they exist—have been achieved at the cost of great effort and sacrifice by the people in the different localities,[14] and often, in spite of official policy or intent.[15]

The most important urban issue in Peru during the last twenty years has been the problem of what to "do" with the *barriadas* (squatter settlements) and their inhabitants. To the native, middle-class Limean, the *barriada* is often seen as a vicious blight, or—as one writer put it—something equivalent to the ring around the bathtub. Middle-class fears are rife in this respect, for many see the *barriadas* as full of "Indians" who are ready to march on San Isidro or Miraflores, the posh residential sections of Lima. The government's actions—first "recognizing" organized *barriadas,* and then allowing them to gain political status as new districts—were significant urban policy. Lima's growth is continuing in this regard. The squatter settlements are being permitted to achieve formal status within the system, thus entitling the people to urban services, in addition to home ownership, which is no small inducement by itself. Thus water, electricity, police protection, garbage collection, markets and the like, make their way into the "young towns," as they are now officially called. Squatting has been a success for the migrants and, in many respects, a successful policy for the government which "allowed" them to happen. (There have been serious troubles, however, when the government tried to remove squatters by force.)

Just as the government has made attempts to supply housing for the migrants, it has also been successfully argued that the squatter settlements provide a more satisfactory and a quicker solution to the problem.[16] The government has made major investments in middle-class housing, with international loans such as the classic case of "Residential San Felipe," built on the site of the old Lima race track. This enormous complex of deluxe apartments houses a population of 35,000 in one of the most desirable sectors of the city. Such monuments do nothing to slow the flow of migrants into Lima. But they represent a series of decisions, all designed to make Lima a modern capital, complete with arterial expressways, big government buildings and so forth.

There has been much talk about the "Indian problem." For many years, the classic *criollo* remark was "yes, let's raise the Indian up—up to 4,000 meters!" Out of sight, out of mind. A second solution in this vein is "to develop our uncounted riches in the jungle." Colonization projects are quite popular in Peru, so long as it is someone else who actually goes and does the work. In the last century, the Peruvian government tried to induce European farmers to settle in the jungle areas, and some actually did so. Latter-day attempts at this goal inevitably involve highlanders who, it is hoped, will migrate there instead of to Lima. Indeed, a few *barriada* residents were enticed to move into the jungle in exchange for land and a great deal of financial assistance. Those *barriada* residents who took up the challenge unfortunately met the fate of their predecessors: the promises of government support failed to materialize. Thus, the negative image of Peru's colonization projects is difficult to overcome, despite the energetic campaign waged by President Belaúnde from 1963 to 1968.

The much-publicized "carretera marginal de la selva" (jungle perimeter highway) has apparently had some impact, particularly in the northern departments of Cajamarca and San Martín, which traditionally have had very weak ties with Lima and have usually sent most of their migrant workers to the coastal plantations.[17] The call of the *selva*, however, does not generally fall on receptive ears. The enormous investments made in the road with international help have yet to offer more than a promise, and in the current political climate of Peru, that is not enough.

Why should a family who wants a better life for themselves and their children migrate to the jungle? The conditions there are not impressive (see Table 10); indeed they are no better than those in the highlands. Moreover, the patterns of agriculture in the jungle are totally foreign and the crops are different: coffee, tea, cacao, tropical fruit, lumber and coca. The first three are subject to the rigors of world markets and controlling companies like Anderson Clayton. Lumber and fruit production require well-made commercial roads to allow reasonable transportation, and thus far no government has shown any interest in developing first-rate trans-Andean highways connecting the Peruvian coast with the jungle. The future of coca production does not appear bright. With 40 percent of the nation's agronomists and veterinarians in Lima, who will provide the expertise to make the jungle pay its keep? The fate of the "sacrificado" colonist in Peru is accurately portrayed in the devastating Peruvian movie, "La Muralla Verde" ("The Green Wall"). The message is that if one wants schools, movies, good wages and good health care he must go to Lima.

One suspects that the "policy" to avoid investing in the highlands where most of the people have always lived (until 1972), and to put most of the public wealth into urban Lima was not made in a conspiratorial manner, or even as part of a great plan to reorganize the national demographic patterns. It happened as the result of several series of small decisions, some of them based on whims, some made as political favors, and most of them—perhaps—because the problems of Lima were the ones the governing elites saw every day. The people who decided where to place the investments have normally had little to do with the rural areas, even though they were often landholders there. Most of the voters lived in coastal cities, and most congressional representatives lived there permanently. Lurking behind such day-to-day decisions was the omnipresent attitude that the coast was primary in relation to the highlands; that the more Spanish, cosmopolitan, urban people were more entitled to modern improvements, and, that the Indians and Cholos could not appreciate such things or use them well. For policymakers, then, decisions to invest in Lima were entirely logical, and indeed, not seriously questioned.

Augusto B. Leguía (1919–1930), who was probably the first Peruvian president to develop a major public works program, initiated projects all over the country on a most ambitious scale. Under his rule, conscript labor brought vehicular roads to the highlands and contractors built myriad public buildings, bridges, canals and monuments. Yet more than half of the 7.7 million *soles* used for this purpose were spent in Lima. All the details of this project are commemorated in a thick illustrated "Album" that was released on July 4, 1930.[18] This effort was not duplicated until the administration of Fernando Belaúnde (1963–69). Leguía's bias toward Lima pales in comparison to that of Belaúnde, despite his rhetoric about "the conquest of Peru by the Peruvians" and raising the hopes of the *provincianos*. Investments in housing and urban development at the peak of his administration favored Lima, 75.3 percent to 24.7 percent for all other cities.[19] The fast-growing, important industrial city of Chimbote (see Table 2)—already misshapen by advanced urban sprawl of the worst sort—was still having its plans for urban growth developed in 1965, after more than a decade of expansion.[20]

As major national investments were made in urban housing —especially for Lima—the private sector continued to focus its investments on the capital as well. During the Belaúnde period, no fewer than ten automobile companies established assembly plants in greater Lima, and, of course, they were not the only industry to seek its headquarters there.

As the first truly broadly based, popularly elected government in Peruvian history, the Belaúnde administration was extremely sensitive to the mass of its key supporters who were, predictably, the professionals, technicians and white-collar groups of the cities, especially Lima. Consequently, despite his good intentions about developing the jungle and the highlands, the vortex of Lima finally won out. And of course, the migrant flow to that city continued unabated.

Conclusions

The present "Revolutionary Government of the Armed Forces" has been attempting to create a number of fundamental changes in the fabric of Peruvian society. For example, it has introduced a far-reaching land reform, encompassing all the great traditional estates, both in the Andes and on the coast. In theory, it will eventually seek to modify the minifundia systems, as well. In the industrial sectors, the government has made sweeping changes concerning the structure and ownership of businesses. In education, extensive reforms have also been decreed involving not only the scholastic hierarchy and the bureaucracy, but also the substance and character of what is taught in many areas. An important step has also been the move to create a system of bilingual education—principally for native speakers of *Quechua* and *Aymara*. These are just a few of the acts of the present government.

The question remains, however, whether even with its apparent great power, this regime can, or wishes to, affect the trend of urban growth so evident in the preceding pages. The preliminary results of the recent census indicate that the pattern of migration to Lima discussed here is continuing unabated, with the metropolitan area having reached the three million mark in population. The regional cities of Arequipa, Chimbote, Trujillo and Chiclayo, along with Huancayo in the highlands, have also grown enormously. Available census data has not permitted a detailed analysis here of this recent growth, but the present government apparently has not affected the basic pattern that has existed since 1940. Some of the governmental programs and policies have sought to develop the rural areas and alter the social and economic status of the rural population, but others such as the National Office of Development for the New Towns ("squattments"), have worked just as hard to make the new and growing "squattments" in all major cities better places to live. A recent publication [21] listing all the service institutions, both governmental and private, for the cities of Lima, Trujillo, Chimbote and Arequipa demonstrates the continued dominance of Lima in the service field as well. In this listing of the services and agencies available in these cities, Lima had 80 percent of what can be called "national," as opposed to locally based, services—whereas the others offered only 46 percent or less of these services to their inhabitants. In other words, at the level of the squatter settlement, a person's chances for improvement were almost twice as good in Lima as in the other leading cities.

On the other hand, official documents continue to call for rural development and modernization, greater participation in national life and the restructuring of the society.[22] There is no question that urban growth is intimately connected with the basic character of national social cleavages and the differential sharing of wealth, power, well-being and enlightenment that these determine. The sharp contrasts between the highlands and the coast, on the one hand, and among the cities on the other—in light of the broad ethnic and social class distinctions involved—sets the stage for the inevitable urban migration, especially to Lima. This, of course, means a renewed cycle of urbanization—despite occasional talk in planning circles that hints of spending less in Lima and allowing some streets there to crumble so that money can be better spent elsewhere.

The question as to whether this pattern of urbanization will be a positive factor in the long run has not yet been resolved. While the evidence cited earlier indicates that ancient Peru distributed its population among many small cities with their respective hinterlands, a return to this pattern would obviously require the firmest kind of discipline and probably an overriding revolutionary commitment on the part of a strong majority to make it work. And this does not seem to be even a remote possibility, given the present situation in Peru.

In the future, then, Lima is likely to grow and the large-scale migration into that city will undoubtedly continue. Thus, while one may lament the unrelenting growth of the primate city as a grotesque phenomenon complicated by the fact that Lima's climate leaves much to be desired, the mold has now been cast and will be difficult to alter or break. Indeed, it is likely that population redistribution of this sort is essential for the making of the revolution of which so many people speak. Such urban growth places enormous demands upon the traditional system, forcing many changes. Perhaps through this process, however arduous and unsightly it may appear to some, action may thus be devoted to solving the social issues raised by the message that Felipe Guamán Poma de Ayala tried to deliver more than three centuries ago to the king of Spain. Ironically, the urban migration seen in this light represents, at long last, the social and political reemergence to prominence of highland peoples and native culture, however modified since conquest. Finally, through the process of urbanization, Peru is achieving a national unity which in the past has always been elusive.

NOTES

1. Henry F. Dobyns, "Estimating Aboriginal American Population, An Appraisal of Techniques with a New Hemispheric Estimate," *Current Anthropology* 7, no. 4 (1966): 395–416.

2. John H. Rowe, "Urban Settlements in Ancient Peru," in *Peruvian Archaeology: Selected Readings,* ed. J. H. Rowe and D. Menzel (Palo Alto: Peek Publications, 1967), p. 308.

3. John V. Murra, "Guaman Poma de Ayala: A Seventeenth Century Indian's Account of Andean Civilization," *Natural History* 70, no. 7–8 (1961): 34–51; 52–63.

4. Daniel Valcarcel (Publisher), *Geografía del Perú Virreinal* by Cosme Bueno (Siglo 18) (Lima: Imprenta D. M., 1951), pp. 19–20.

5. Ibid., pp. 93–94.

6. Sebastian Salazar Bondy, *Lima, La Horrible* (Lima: Popilibros Peruanos, 1964).

7. Ozzie Simmons, "The Criollo Outlook in the Mestizo Culture of Coastal Peru," *American Anthropologist* 57 (1955): 107–17; and Richard W. Patch, "La Parada, Lima's Market: Part III Serrano to Criollo, A Study in Assimilation," *West Coast of South America Series* 14, no. 3 (1967), American Universities Field Staff.

8. Salazar Bondy, *Lima, La Horrible,* p. 22.

9. *Anuario Estadístico del Perú, 1966, Resultados de 1958 a 1966* (Ministerio de Hacienda y Comercio, Dirreción Nacional de Estadística y Censos), Volumen XXVII (1969), II de la Nueva Serie, Lima, pp. 66–72.

10. Ibid., p. 1406.

11. Paul L. Doughty, *Huaylas: An Andean District in Search of Progress* (Ithaca, N.Y.: Cornell University Press, 1968), pp. 168–75.

12. J. Oscar Alers and R. P. Appelbaum, "La Migración en el Perú: Un Inventario de Proposiciones," *Estudios de Población y Desarrollo* (Lima: Centro de Estudios de Población y Desarrollo, 1968), vol. I, no. 4, pp. 1–43.

13. Paul L. Doughty, "Peruvian Migrant Identity in the Urban Milieu," in *The Anthropological Study of Urban Environments,* ed. T. Weaver and D. White, Society for Applied Anthropology Monograph 1972, pp. 39–50.

14. Henry F. Dobyns, *Comunidades Campesinas del Perú* (Lima: Editorial Estudios Andinos, 1970).

15. Paul L. Doughty, "Engineers and Energy in the Andes," in *Technological Innovation and Social Change,* ed. R. Bernard and P. Pelto (New York: The Macmillan Company, 1972).

16. Carlos Delgado, "Three Proposals Regarding Accelerated Urbanization Problems in Metropolitan Areas: The Lima Case," *American Behavioral Scientist* 12, no. 5 (1969): 34–44.

17. R. F. Hafer, *The People Up the Hill: Individual Progress Without Village Participation in Pariamarca, Cajamarca, Peru* (Ph.D. diss. 1971, Bloomington, Indiana University).

18. Perú. *Album, Obsequiado al Sr. D. Augusto B. Leguia, Presidente de la República*

por el personal directiva de Ministerio de Fomento mostrando las diversas Obras llevadas a cabo de 1919 a 1930: 4 de Julio de 1930 (Lima: Imprenta Torres Aguirre, 1930).

19. Perú. *El Perú Construye: Mensaje del Presidente de la República Fernando Belaunde Terry al Congreso Nacional, 28 de Julio 1965* (Lima: Editorial Minerva, 1965), pp. 362–78.

20. Ibid., p. 352.

21. *Catálogo de instituciones de servicio a la comunidad: Trujillo-Chimbote-Lima-Arequipa* (Lima: Oficina Nacional de Desarrollo de Pueblos Jovenes. 1971).

22. Sergio Chang Auije, *Diagnóstico socio económico preliminar del area rural Peruana.* Dirección general de organizaciones rurales, Sistema Nacional de Apoyo a la Movilización Social (SINAMOS-ONAMS, 1972).

Daniel Goldrich, Raymond B. Pratt
and C. R. Schuller

4. The Political Integration of Lower-Class Urban Settlements in Chile and Peru

A city's crowded, lower-class residential areas are invariably dismissed by the area's middle- and upper-class citizens as slums—with all the negative connotations implied by that term. In fact, however, some lower-class urban settlements do not conform to this stereotype. A true slum is a drain on a city's resources, since it is continually deteriorating, and since its residents very seldom participate in either local- or national-level political activities. This research report concerns four settlements on the outskirts of Santiago, Chile, and Lima, Peru, and the process of national political integration they are undergoing. These areas are not slums, since they are constantly being improved and consolidated, and since their residents—who are clearly oriented toward the process of national development—constitute, not a drain on the city's economy, but a significant human resource. At the time of this study, all four of the settlements had been recently established; all became permanent, and either had obtained or were in the process of obtaining legal title to the land on which they stood. Three of the settlements began with squatters' invasions;[1] the fourth is a government housing project, composed partly of invaders and partly of applicants who qualified through the "normal" channels of the National Housing Corporation.

The two components of national political integration with which we are concerned here are: politicalization—the process of becoming aware of, involved in, and disposed to make use of the political process; and the extent of support for, acquiescence and opposition to the political system and its subsystems. Presumably the more politicalized and supportive these sectors of the metropolitan lower class are, the more likely they are to develop basic national citizenship orientations regarding rights and responsibilities.

We will deal with four problems regarding change in political integration: the role of the local association in the settlements; the impact of severe sanctions on the level of politicalization; the assessment of politicalization as a continuous or discontinuous process; and patterns of political legitimacy orientations.

The data employed here are derived largely from interviews, substantially open-ended in character, conducted with samples of male adult residents of the four communities during the period of May through July 1965.

In Chile and Peru, the work force is divided mainly into workers and employees, with the distinction based on manual versus other labor. Our respondents are all workers in this sense, plus lower-level employees of the janitor, porter and petty service variety. Also included are such occupations as street vendor, small (home) storekeeper, etc. Within each of the four settlements, the initial sampling unit was the household, with one male adult (18 years or over) interviewed in each selected household. In the two Santiago areas, a very recent census was available from which households were randomly selected; then the interviewers selected respondents randomly from the household. In the two Lima *barriadas,* block and dwelling maps were used to assign areas to interviewers, who selected households and respondents by availability, although care was taken to disperse the selection throughout the area. The interview schedule was pretested in Santiago. The same form, with only language changes (suggested by people with experience in the barriadas) to promote comparability, was used in Lima. The interviewers in both cities were social workers and social science students who had had training and experience in interviewing lower-class people.

This report is provisional, in the sense that we are making use of some of the data especially coded for it. Since so little survey research had been done on the political orientations of squatters, or the Latin American urban lower class in general, it seemed desirable to use mainly open-ended interviewing techniques, to avoid constricting the range of responses.

Urbanization and Squatter Settlements

Squatter settlements are a ubiquitous part of the metropolitan landscape in the poorer countries—on the hillsides, river banks, tidal swamps and even garbage dumps within and around the urban zone. These are the residential loci of hundreds of thousands of Latin Americans; they exist widely in Lima and Santiago. An estimated one-fourth of the metropolitan Lima population of approximately two million resides in such areas, as does perhaps one-tenth of Santiago's roughly equivalent population. The lower figure in Santiago is a reflection of a major program of squatter settlement eradication and large-scale, low-cost government dwellings to accommodate those housed in shanties and deteriorating *conventillos* (traditional one-story, multiple-family dwellings with minimal facilities). Through this program, another tenth of the metropolitan lower-class population has been more or less permanently settled. (The cost of the program had, however, severely strained the national treasury at a time when a new reformist government has come into power committed to peaceful but far-reaching reconstruction of the society. Thus, it is questionable whether in Santiago the phenomenon of squatting can be maintained at a level which is lower than elsewhere in Latin America.)

Squatter invasions are the consequence of urbanization and population growth which occur without public or private provision being made to provide dwellings for the massive metropolitan lower classes. Reinforcing the effect of immigration and population factors are such "normal" urbanization phenomena as clearance of the traditional lower-class dwellings in order to build new streets, high-rise commercial establishments and luxury apartments, and the continuous process of dilapidation of the remaining traditional lower-class quarters. As crowding and rent-squeezing of the poor increase, the only outlet for hundreds of thousands is the seizure of unused lands or rental of tiny, makeshift quarters in clandestine settlements run as commercial enterprises.

The prevailing image of these settlements (and also of government housing projects) among middle- and upper-class people and local and foreign social scientists is that of the slum. It is an image of apathy, misery, filth, crime, delinquency, prostitution and family disintegration. It is also commonplace to view these areas as breeding-grounds for political instability and extremism. Their inhabitants are considered the lowest social stratum, mainly recruited from the torrent of emigrants from rural and provincial areas.[2] The settlements are treated as virtually invariant, and are indiscriminately labeled as *barriadas, favelas, callampas,* etc., which are the local equivalents of slums.

Actually, squatter settlements represent a wide range of conditions. The pioneering work of such people as John Turner, principally in Lima, and Guillermo Rosenblüth in Santiago introduces some typologies of settlement which differentiate vastly variant human conditions.[3] For example, Turner has distinguished two types of squatter settlements, the bridgehead and the consolidation. The bridgehead houses, the poorest of the city's lower class, are located near the urban center's sources of employment. Here, crowding is extremely high and conditions generally very poor. These areas' living standards are declining and thus they can be considered real slums. The consolidation, on the other hand, represents an attempt by the more organized and effective (but not, generally, the wealthier) segments of the lower class to attain economic and psychological independence.

They seek better dwelling conditions—meaning primarily proprietorship and space, within their economic limits—and these motivations find an outlet only in the organized invasion of peripheral, unoccupied land. These settlements thus represent a considerable investment and continuously improving living standards. The residents consider them to be permanent, incipient communities, or "towns in formation." (Another type discussed by Turner is the mixed settlement, with combinations of the above sets of characteristics, but these will not be considered here.) Three of the four research communities are of the latter, permanent type. The fourth is also permanent, but is one of the new Chilean government settlements. Despite its obvious differences from the others in its relations with government—the receipt of dwellings and substantial urban services from the government, and original title to seized lands—as a public housing project composed partly of invaders, it shares the depreciated status of the other settlements and the condition of being a community in formation. Politically these areas are virtually an unknown quantity.

These towns in formation present some important experiences and characteristics with respect to the whole complex of development. While it is useful to keep in mind the questionable romanticism of "community development" mythology, this should not preclude recognition of what these towns in formation demonstrate. If the preindustrial mode of lower-class orientation is resignation before an immutable world, the invaders represent a significant departure from that tradition, having successfully manipulated an important part of their environment. They have shown initiative and future orientation (the capacity to waive immediate gratification in pursuit of long-range goals); many have persevered in the face of a hostile state, including armed attack on the provisional encampments. One of the more elusive capacities in the underdeveloped world is the capacity for organization, but many of these communities were carefully planned, and their successful establishment reflects a rather high level of organization regarding land allotment, provision for basic services, representation before the public and the state, etc. The capacity for organization seems not to derive from any mystical ancestral communalism,[4] but rather to be a creative response on the part of a highly selected, self-recruited set of people to an environment otherwise foreclosing opportunity. Theirs has been a major achievement, for independence in dwelling and land is the major way to economic and psychic security for the lower class,[5] when industrialization lags far behind urbanization and population growth, and ways out of national poverty remain unknown even to highly educated planners and intellectuals. In the face of their reputation for social disorganization, these settlers reveal remarkably little of it; crime, promiscuity, broken homes occur infrequently, particularly in comparison with the bridgehead settlements and traditional city slums. Furthermore, although they were born as illegal invasions, these communities display a prevailing orientation toward law and order.[6]

The Four Research Communities

The two barriadas on Lima's outskirts had their origin in organized invasions of undeveloped state-owned land in the arid, rocky slopes and valleys of the Andean foothills. Pampa Seca was thus begun in 1958; its invasion was met by relatively passive hostility on the part of the government. Today, it is a settlement of about 30,000 people, with well-defined, relatively broad, unpaved streets, lined with houses mostly of brick and adobe. The original shacks of reed matting have been largely replaced by permanent structures in various stages of improvement and elaboration. The government has agreed to install water facilities, but despite some substantial installation of pipes, water is not yet "normally" available, and must still be individually purchased from private trucks that pass by regularly.

El Espíritu was invaded in 1962, an act met by the government with both police harassment and army attacks on the squatters' huts. After protracted confrontations of this sort, involving some death and destruction, the invaders were allowed to stay. A second invasion resulted in overcrowding and diminutive lot assignments. This time, the government interceded to reduce the serious internal conflict and to rationalize the settlement, promising services and the acquisition of adjacent private lands to permit more decent individual plots, in return for the settlers' commitment to abide by government plans and to agree to a payment schedule resulting in final individual titles to the land. El Espíritu had about 10,000 residents at the time of this study. Great changes had taken place since the invasion, most obviously in home construction and improvements, although water and electricity were still lacking. At the time of this study, the government had just made available the expropriated adjacent lands, and many of the residents were moving down into their new homesites. The level of construction activity on weekends was furious, and work continued into the night.

3 de Mayo is a callampa established apparently with little public notice about 1960 on the Santiago periphery, the location and layout of which have been deemed appropriate by the Housing Corporation for "radication." This means that the settlement has won a

Table 1
BACKGROUND DATA ON THE FOUR SETTLEMENTS

	Lima		Santiago			
	Pampa Seca	El Espíritu	Santo Domingo	S.D. Applicants	S.D. Invaders	3 de Mayo
Age of settlement (years)	7	3	4			4
Size of settlement (thousands)	30	10	12			1
Born in capital metropolitan area*	%9	%12	%41	%35	%51	%24
Length of residence in capital:						
less than 3 years	6	6	1	1	0	4
less than 5 years	11	18	3	1	0	12
12 years or more	61	56	80	81	86	64
Education:						
illiteracy	1	2	7	8	7	10
completed 5 or 6 primary years	48	41	35	35	29	30
some secondary or more	19	17	17	10	20	9
Family size:						
3 people or less	8	18	6	5	7	14
6 people or more	65	47	65	77	52	53
Age: 39 years or older	43	28	28	43	15	39
"How far do you think your children can really go in school?":						
primary	17	22	40			46
secondary-tech./commercial	17	21	12			8
secondary-liberal arts	39	34	41			38
university	26	15	5			6
"How much opportunity has a child of this area to attain the position he deserves in society?":						
good opportunity	28	21	34			24
not very good	61	47	50			60
none	10	29	14			15

* Herein after, the data reported are from the survey. For each group, N is as follows: Pampa Seca, 127; El Espíritu, 119; Santo Domingo, 191; Santo Domingo Applicants, 79; Santo Domingo Invaders, 59; 3 de Mayo, 98.

presumption of legal permanence from the government. The government began to negotiate with the private owners of the hitherto unused invasion site a few years ago for purchase. This was supposed to be followed by large-scale government assistance in home construction and the installation of urban facilities. In the meantime, water is obtained from standpipes located intermittently along the muddy streets, and electricity is available. 3 de Mayo has a population of about 1,000.

Santo Domingo is one of the new Chilean government housing projects located along the periphery of the capital's working-class districts. At an early stage of site development in 1961, a massive invasion occurred. The police surrounded the area and political tensions rose. The Chilean Left supported the invaders, and the Right was shocked by the seizure of public land designed to meet the housing needs of those who had registered at the Housing Corporation and patiently proceeded to qualify for housing under construction. A compromise was reached, so that those invaders who could qualify by "normal" criteria for project housing would receive it, but the remainder would be moved to vacant government lands, where minimal assistance in settlement would be provided. There are two major recruitment patterns in Santo Domingo. About 40 percent of the residents were successful applicants, having approached the government or been approached as residents of callampas by government social workers and become enrolled, qualifying through a point system based on number of children, prospects for meeting the (relatively low) monthly quota payments consistently, etc. About 30 percent were either direct invaders of the project site or invaders of other government projects who won recognition of their desperate housing situation and were transferred into Santo Domingo. The remaining residents included those who had qualified through negotiations between the Housing Corporation and labor union or company committees, and relatives of those who were otherwise qualified. Our analysis of Santo Domingo will treat the community sample as a whole, and the "normal" applicants and invaders separately. (The people who were otherwise recruited, as described above, will not be considered separately because of their small number in the sample, and because we want to focus on the extreme cases represented by normal application and invasion.) Today Santo

Domingo has about 12,000 residents. They are housed predominantly in single-story dwellings on individual plots. The original housing in that area was minimal. It is currently being replaced by more substantial brick structures. Water, electricity and sanitary facilities are provided for each dwelling. The size of the lots, though small, allows for gardens and such activities as chicken raising. As in the case of the two barriadas, and as projected for 3 de Mayo, the residents are proprietors, who are to receive legal title upon completion of monthly quota payments amounting to a long-term mortgage.

There is a great deal of variation among the four communities in terms of demographic background and socioeconomic indicators, but there is also much that confirms the generalizations made above about permanent squatter settlements. On the basis of our survey data, for example, the majority of the adult male residents are migrants from provincial and rural backgrounds, the proportion ranging from about 90 percent in the two barriadas to 76 percent in 3 de Mayo and 59 percent in Santo Domingo. These are not extremely recent, awestruck arrivals in the metropolis. Only 6 percent or less have resided in the capital less than three years, and less than 20 percent fewer than five years, while a majority ranging up to 80 percent have lived there twelve years or more.[7] In countries where, even in the capital cities, large proportions of the lower class fail to pass beyond the first few years of primary education, these samples seem to range from somewhere above the bottom to a relatively high level of education. For example, a recent field study published by the Economic Commission for Latin America on Santiago's callampas found that 29 percent of the sample was illiterate.[8] Illiteracy occurred in 10 percent of the cases in 3 de Mayo and only 7 percent in Santo Domingo, while 39 percent had completed five years of primary schooling or more in 3 de Mayo and 52 percent had done so in Santo Domingo. Educational attainment was even higher in the two Lima barriadas (though in general Chilean educational levels substantially exceed Peru's), where 67 and 58 percent of the samples had completed five primary grades or beyond. The residents can thus be distinguished mainly as migrants, but they are also experienced in urban life and relatively educated in their lower-class metropolitan context.

Prevailing family sizes are large: from about half to two-thirds of the samples indicate households of six people or more, while small families (three persons or less) are uncommon. Since the great majority of the respondents are young men (less than 39 years of age), this means young children and probably more to come, so that the importance of opportunities for the next generation is apparent. These are high-achieving people, with large families and relatively high expectations for their children (if we accept educational expectations as a good measure of parental ambition in general). Asked how much education they really believed their children could attain, from 53 to 82 percent indicated some secondary schooling or more, referring usually to a liberal arts education, traditionally a middle-class curriculum, and not merely technical or commercial training.[9] Meeting this expectation will require a very large-scale expansion and improvement of the two nations' higher educational facilities, both secondary and university. Along with these ambitions, however, there exists an overwhelmingly widespread sense of deprivation in opportunity for the young. Asked what opportunity a child in this area has to achieve his deserved place in society, the preponderant response was negative, though relatively few—aside from the El Espíritu sample—replied, "no opportunity."

This sets up the context for the inquiry into the degree of political integration of the settlers.

Local Associations

Latin American politics has been characterized by extreme underdevelopment of an infrastructure, or organizations that function to integrate rulers and ruled, to articulate the interests of sectors of the citizenry and to convey to the latter the interests of the political elite. This organizational underdevelopment is associated with low levels of national integration. Despite the existence for many decades of labor unions in the Latin American metropolitan areas, this condition has largely persisted, with the qualified exception of the few situations bordering on the totalitarian (Perón's Argentina, Castro's Cuba), where the elite organized the society to an unusually high degree.

In this relative void, one of the potentially significant characteristics of the new settlements is the organization of local associations

	Lima						Santiago			
	Pampa Seca	P.S. Orig. Invaders*	P.S. Latecomers	El Espíritu	El Esp. Orig. Invaders*	El Esp. Latecomers	Santo Domingo	S.D. Applicants	S.D. Invaders	3 de Mayo
Membership in local association	10%	13%	3%	22%	21%	8%	6%	1%	10%	21%
"How interested are you in what the (local association) does?":										
very much	8	13	3	8	8	12	28	23	40	36
substantially	13	13	12	21	21	19	15	13	14	26
a little/not at all ("there is no association")	76	70	85	68	68	62	54	64	46	39
Evaluation of extent of help given by local association:										
much	9	23	6	21	22	15	32	26	44	30
some	21	17	12	33	35	35	27	28	24	23
none/don't know	67	53	70	45	37	46	41	46	29	47
"How interested are you in what the municipality does?":										
very much	11									
substantially	17									
a little/not at all	71									
Evaluation of extent of help given by municipality:										
much	6									
some	28									
none/don't know	65									
Evaluation of extent of help given by Cooperación Popular (Lima/Promoción Popular (Sgo.)):										
much	20			10			35	34	36	18
some	18			17			28	32	24	24
none/don't know	62			73			37	34	40	58

* We have distinguished here between original invaders and a set of the most recent invaders in the two barriadas, omitting from analysis those of intermediate residence. The N for Pampa Seca original invaders is 30 and for the most recent group, 33; for original invaders in El Espíritu 76 and for the most recent ones, 26.

which invade, represent their interests before outsiders, and promote the internal development of the communities.[10]

The local associations of the new settlements help the settlers meet their needs through mobilizing their own efforts and those of government agencies. Potentially, other functions might also be performed, such as educating the government elite in the capabilities of the settlers and providing it with a means to explain its plans, priorities, and problems to the settlers, mobilizing them for the efforts necessary to implement such plans.

Our data indicate, however, that participation in the local association tends to atrophy as the settlement becomes established, a tendency which William Mangin has suggested is generally the case with barriadas.[11] Of the four, 3 de Mayo and El Espíritu have attained the distinctly lower level of completion of homes and installation of urban services, while the level of membership in the local association is markedly higher than in their more developed counterparts. Furthermore, within both the Santiago pair and the Lima pair, personal interest in the activities of the association is also higher in the less developed settlement; and personal evaluation of the association's helpfulness varies in the same way between the two barriadas. The only deviation is the slightly more positive evaluation of the association's helpfulness in (developed) Santo Domingo compared to (underdeveloped) 3 de Mayo.

The fact that higher interest and positive evaluations occur more frequently in both Santiago settlements than in both Lima settlements qualifies the relationship. It suggests that the local association may be becoming institutionalized in the two Santiago cases, not in regard to active participation, but as an output agency, perhaps mediating between the community leadership and the government hierarchy. There is evidence of this in the slightly more prevalent positive evaluation of, but lower participation in, the association in Santo Domingo compared to 3 de Mayo. This apparently reflects the recent government policy of allocating some services to the new projects through the association. This could reverse the tendency for its total atrophy with the increasing consolidation of the community and provide a new integrative mechanism between government and settlers. This would certainly be an important function, given the past lack of articulation between them, but the character of the relationship would appear to be paternalistic (participation *is* much lower in Santo Domingo than in 3 de Mayo), and as such, it would probably not involve some of the other highly significant political functions previously mentioned that would require a more active, contributory role on the part of the settlers.

Within the settlements, those who have taken the most risk in the endeavor are also those who most sustain the local association. Data are available on three of the four cases (excepting 3 de Mayo) that distinguish between original invaders and latecomers in the barriadas, and between invaders and "normal" applicants in Santo Domingo. It is clear that the most disparaged of the settlers, the original invaders in the barriadas and the invaders in Santo Domingo, provide most of the active participants in the associations. In two of the three cases, they are also more interested in the activities of the association (they are virtually equal to the latecomers in the third case, El Espíritu), and in all three cases, they more frequently evaluate the association as helpful. At this point, we cannot identify the substance of their activity, interest and appreciation. It may be merely personal interest, reflecting little of value for the communities as a whole. Equally conceivably, these may be people especially oriented to and capable of autonomous organizational behavior for community problem-solving, or as Weiner has put it, integrative behavior.[12] The latecomers to the barriadas, and those who gained entry into Santo Domingo by conformity to the bureaucratic rules of the game, are not less decent citizens, but they appear to be more passive with regard to the affairs of their community as it struggles for improvement, perhaps more oriented toward the traditional mode of dependence on paternal authorities.

"Municipalizing" the barriadas in Peru

One way in which the local problem-solving function has been structured for greater permanence is the creation of municipal districts in the established settlements. This has been done recently in the Lima area; Pampa Seca is one example. The data show that its residents are indeed more interested in municipal activities than in those of the local association, and they evaluate the municipality as

more helpful than the association, but the difference is small in both
cases. Furthermore, the municipality's helpfulness in the view of
Pampa Seca residents is markedly less than that of the association as
evaluated by those of El Espíritu, so that as the barriadas become
more established, the formalization of the local settlement's government structure may not be sufficient to reverse the normal decline in
relevance of local organizations. (On the other hand, the muni-
cipalization of barriadas is such a new policy in Peru that these
remarks cannot be considered more than provisional. It is surely
possible that the municipal government will become more politically
vital with time.)

Promoción Popular and Cooperación Popular

Perhaps the major organization to perform national integrative
functions in societies seeking to shake off poverty is the mass political
party. Such organizations have occurred infrequently in Latin
America, and there are very few cases of parties that have focused
their program or ideology directly on problems of urbanization and
the condition of the settler. (Though little had been done about
agrarian reform, it was much more common for "reform" parties to
symbolize the *peasant* as the forgotten citizen.) Our data show that,
despite the very substantial differences between the Chilean and
Peruvian party systems, political parties are evaluated as less personally helpful than the president, government officials, the municipality and the local association in every case among the four
settlements (see Tables 2 and 5). Thus, it appears that mass parties
have not yet developed in either country, with reference to the new
urban settlements.

However, in Chile and Peru the incumbent national administrations have developed plans for an agency that would incorporate
those mass sectors of the population which were previously politically
and socially alienated. These agencies, Promoción Popular and Cooperación Popular, respectively, *could* serve as important steps toward
the transformation of the governing parties—Christian Democracy in
Chile and Acción Popular in Peru—into mass parties of national
integration.

In both cases the agencies are seen as contributing technical assistance and initial leadership for community development. Both have important university branches through which students are recruited to participate in community development. This provides one of the few cases in either country where the highly privileged work directly with the highly underprivileged in the field, and the program could of course serve as a major agency of political socialization, broadening the scope of identification of both rich and poor in such a way as to nationalize both.

In Peru, Cooperación Popular had an auspicious beginning in rural areas with indigenous populations, the integration of which President Belaúnde saw as vital to national development. It is inactive in corresponding urban areas, however, because Belaúnde is not sympathetic to the invasion-established communities, which he apparently considers a blight. Publicity about Cooperación Popular has been plentiful, and despite the presidential exclusion of the barriadas, our data reveal a substantial minority in each barriada who evaluate the program as offering them at least some help. If the program were to acquire an urban direction, it might develop additional support-carrying capacity. The importance of this potential is underscored by the relatively low level of legitimacy accorded the political system by the settlers in our two barriadas. That this may remain only a potential is suggested by the cutting of the program's budget by the opposition majority Congressional coalition (composed of APRA, Peru's erstwhile radical reform party, and the personalist party of former dictator General Odría), while Belaúnde maintained silence.[13]

In Chile, Promoción Popular has been more elaborately planned by the brain trust of President Frei, and a major dimension is the incorporation of the callampa and new housing project populations. The link between Promoción Popular and the latter is the local association, thus building up community development into the structures created by the settlers themselves. Though the program has been barely initiated in 3 de Mayo, the respondents there were relatively evenly divided in evaluation as to whether or not it afforded any help. By contrast, in Santo Domingo, where there has been more activity, the evaluation was considerably more positive. Despite the relatively high support for the Marxist opposition coalition (FRAP) among the Santo Domingo invaders, they are just as enthusiastic about the program as

the more Christian Democracy-oriented applicants. This augurs especially well for the program, because of the invaders' high participation
and involvement in the local association. In turn, Promoción Popular
may contribute to the maintenance of the local association as a basic
mechanism for problem-solving in the settlement as well as communication between the government and this sector of citizens. In addition,
the substantially lower level of support accorded the political system by
the invaders than by the applicants may be counteracted by the
program.

Costs of Political Demand-Making:
Sanctions and Depoliticalization

Perhaps the most surprising aspect of recent Latin American politics to academic observers is, given its poverty and general deprivation, the relatively continuous apoliticalization or low politicalization
of the urban lower class. We have tried to account for this phenomenon elsewhere, citing the complex structure of the subculture of
poverty, the restricted conception of time and space, the perceived
immutability of the environment, the nature of lower-class occupations, the nonpolitical supports available, the effects of extreme deprivation and vulnerability to sanctions.[14]

One might expect a higher level of politicalization among the permanent squatter settlements and housing projects, because: the
residents have had to anticipate dealing with the government before
entry; the invasion preparations involve sophisticated planning with
regard to mobilizing political support and immobilizing agencies of
governmental repression; invasion itself is an illegal—and therefore
governmentally relevant—act; and the residents have thus been faced
with the problem of acquiring urban services.[15]

An opposing factor, however, is the lower class's particularly high
vulnerability to sanctions in preindustrial and transitional contexts.
Under such conditions actual repression or even the threat of it may be
sufficient to discourage any behavior that might antagonize the establishment. The tangible gain through land seizure, in the face of the
desperate need to find permanent, independent, economical housing,

may represent the extreme case where potentially costly political action is resorted to by lower-class people. If this were so, the level of politicalization might be low, even in the permanent settlements, and the political orientations and behavior associated with the invasion planning and occurrence (or even the application to the Housing Agency) might have been exceptional.

In what ways might such people be considered highly vulnerable to sanctions? First, their level of occupational skill is low, the labor market is glutted (unemployment and underemployment are severe in Latin America), and they have little countervailing power because of restrictions on or underdevelopment of unions. Second, the distance between social classes, particularly between the middle and lower classes, is so great that general social support for lower-class people in trouble with the government tends to be low. Awareness of this may also serve to deter political risk-taking on the part of those at the bottom. Third, the bureaucracy tends to be staffed with middle-class people, frequently unconcerned with service to the public, and skilled in the dispensation of subtle humiliations to "inferiors" seeking administrative adjustments. One such form of discouragement is to relegate them to endless waiting. Finally, a different kind of sanction is police harassment of "troublemakers" from the lower class. Although such activity is not directed only at lower-class representatives, they are probably the most deprived in this respect in all societies.

American political scientists have tended to focus theoretically and empirically on factors that dispose people to enter the political process to the relative exclusion of factors (other than information costs) that discourage their entry, such as sanctions.[16] Theoretically, such sanctions as those mentioned above, or the fear of them, may operate at any point in the political process, discouraging demand-making, the organization of support behind demands, or even the communication of wants to preclude their being transformed into the substance of demands. Furthermore, this can involve not only truncated politicalization, but also reversals. For example, if we take such a recent useful formulation as *The Civic Culture's* classification of political cultures according to the prevalence of parochial, subject and participant orientations of the citizens [17] and apply it to the development of politicalization of individuals,[18] we can project the possibility not only of shifts from parochial to more complex syndromes of political orientation, but also of sanction-induced parochialism on the part of formerly more highly politicized actors.

In the course of presenting the utility of learning theoretical concepts in political science, Frank Pinner has made some relevant suggestions.[19] He cites classic research holding that responses learned under reward conditions are less deeply internalized than those learned under conditions of punishment (positive responses tend toward extinction without frequent reinforcement, while negative responses persist with much less of it). He also suggests that the substance of politics is much more frequently anxiety-producing than rewarding, thereby inducing a variety of avoidance behaviors. Given the sanctionability of the lower class, particularly in the conditions described above (societies in transition from preindustrialism), and in view of the limited rewards allocated to the lower class in Chilean and Peruvian governmental processes, we suggest that where severe sanctions have occurred in relation to political activity, the sanctioned will exhibit an avoidance of politics. Thus the severely sanctioned will be severely depoliticized.

Among our four settlements, one—El Espíritu—contrasts sharply with the others in this regard. Though illegal invasions are the origin of all the settlements, and this illegality is a source of anxiety in all, the response by authorities has varied. The 3 de Mayo invasion occurred quietly, and the government has come to mediate the dispute between the legal owners and the invaders to the advantage of the latter. The invaders in Santo Domingo were subjected to close police surveillance and constraint, but not to violent suppression. Furthermore, they achieved their objective: the receipt of government housing. Pampa Seca also was invaded without provoking a violent government reaction. El Espíritu, on the other hand, was the scene of a series of pitched battles between troops and squatters, involving some loss of life and property. In addition, the armed forces ringed the area for some time after the initial invasion, so that the squatters lived under constant fear that attacks would be launched to drive them off the land. We have some survey evidence bearing on this matter for the two barriadas. The respondents were asked what problems they encountered in establishing themselves. Only 5 percent of the Pampa Seca sample referred to traumatic experiences with police or soldiers, but 41 percent of the El Espíritu sample mentioned the fighting, the encirclement, the necessity for posting night guard, etc. In the context of this kind of background and survey data on the four settlements, we conclude that El Espíritu suffered a distinctively severe sanction.

Following the invasions and settlement, major governmental relations toward the four communities varied in the following manner. Santo Domingo began to receive a relatively full complement of urban services. 3 de Mayo began negotiations with the government for public housing assistance. Pampa Seca gradually began to acquire urban services and was formally made a municipality. El Espíritu has received the least services at this point, but the Housing Agency has acquired additional land to relieve its overcrowding and has participated in the resolution of conflicts over lot boundaries. We conclude that the two Santiago settlements have had the most experience with government, while the two Lima barriadas have had less. In terms of gratifying postestablishment experience with the government, our speculative assessment is that Pampa Seca has had more of such benefits than El Espíritu, but in both cases less has been received than their Santiago counterparts. It should be remembered that El Espíritu has an educational level close to Pampa Seca's and substantially higher than that of the Santiago settlements. Thus, the effect of the severe sanction it experienced must overcome the politicalization resources nurtured by its population's relatively high educational level.

The data on politicalization reveal a pattern of high consistency, particularly those from El Espíritu, which are clearly in accord with the hypothesized relationship between sanctions and politicalization. El Espíritu respondents report the *least* interest in activities of the national government and the municipality, with the differences between them and the Santiago settlements in particular being extremely large. While only a minority in any of the four report that they have actually tried to get the government to do something or stop doing something, El Espíritu shows almost no such activity. A similar but even more pronounced pattern appears in the proportions of the samples who can imagine what they could do to instigate government assistance. There is not much difference among the settlements in their rate of political discussion with primary groups or in attendance at political meetings, though again, El Espíritu tends to be lowest. El Espíritu respondents also report the least dealing with a government agency regarding housing, despite the actual presence of government Housing Agency personnel engaged in activities previously described.

Table 3
POLITICALIZATION INDICATORS

	Lima		Santiago			
	Pampa Seca	El Espíritu	Santo Domingo	S.D. Applicants	S.D. Invaders	3 de Mayo
	%	%	%	%	%	%
"How interested are you in what the government is doing?":						
very	16	9	39	37	42	32
substantially	20	14	31	34	24	24
a little	44	37	25	24	27	38
not at all	20	35	5	5	7	5
"How interested are you in what the municipality is doing?":						
very	11	6	27	25	29	30
substantially	17	7	32	33	32	24
a little	37	25	31	34	32	36
not at all	34	50	9	6	7	9
Ever tried to get government to do (or stop doing) something: detailed affirmative response	14	2	11	11	15	20
Conception of how he can get government to do (or stop doing) something: detailed affirmative response	32	14	36	32	41	40
Discussion of Politics with: family:						
frequently	15	9	12	13	17	10
occasionally	23	35	33	25	36	33
never	57	56	55	62	48	57

friends and neighbors:						
frequently	17	9	15	14	24	18
occasionally	35	47	30	30	30	36
never	47	44	54	56	46	46
co-workers:						
frequently	13	10	18	16	22	22
occasionally	30	37	32	33	32	39
never	57	53	50	51	46	39
Meeting attendance or active part in a demonstration: indicates has done something	28	25	32	28	34	39
Has taken some step to get government agency to help solve his housing problem:	29	18	56	68	46	64
Has heard of and can evaluate Law of Barriada/Housing Plan	54	40	69	71	71	66
Makes some mention of what is "most important national problem"	87	69	88	89	93	88
Voted in both last presidential and congressional or municipal elections	82	78	81	81	80	66
Indicates elections and campaigns have personal significance	60	34	58	62	56	58

(It is conceivable, in view of their positive evaluation of the Housing Agency and their negative evaluation of the government generally, that they dissociate the two.) Fewer of them than among the Pampa Seca residents indicate they have heard of the Law of the Barriada or that they can evaluate it, although it has received substantial publicity and directly regulates much of the government's dealings with them. A much higher proportion of the Santiago samples report knowledge and evaluation of Plan Habitacional, the government housing program analogous to that organized under the Law of the Barriada. El Espíritu respondents rank far below those of the other settlements in their capacity to articulate some conception of the most important problems facing the nation. Although their voting participation is on a par with two of the other communities, the proportion who either see no personal significance in elections and campaigns or do not answer the item at all is a great deal higher among El Espíritu respondents than among any of their counterparts elsewhere.

Furthermore, if we distinguish the original invaders from those who came afterwards in El Espíritu, we find among these people—whom we know were sophisticated enough to accomplish the invasion against severe obstacles and who continue to be the main participants in the local association—indications of lower politicalization than among the others in the barriada sample. For example, fewer of them (13 percent) than the latecomers (19 percent) can imagine a way in which they could influence the government to act favorably, whereas there is a strong reverse relationship in the Pampa Seca sample (43 percent of the original invaders have such a conception, compared to 18 percent of the latecomers).

This seems strong evidence in support of our hypothesis. Despite their relatively high level of education, their politically sophisticated preparations for the invasion, and their close dealings with the housing agency after the invasion, the El Espíritu residents appear to have been powerfully depoliticized by their traumatic experience associated with the invasion.

Since El Espíritu's original invaders were those directly sanctioned, and since (as we indicated in the previous section) they tended to monopolize membership in the local association, it seems reasonable to assume that depoliticalized community leadership may be an important factor in the low level of politicalization throughout.

In certain obvious ways, this means that El Espíritu residents are not likely to add to the stress on the political system, since their potential for demand-making seems for the present to have been sharply curtailed. But it also means that these people, who have maintained a relatively strong nonpolitical organization in their community and who are working extremely hard to promote its consolidation, will not be participating as full citizens in the national polity—and this represents a waste of human resources. When we recall how few of these otherwise very effective people could formulate a national problem, how few recognized or could give an opinion on a national law objectively important to their lives and how few believed in the significance of the electoral process, the limitations of the civic responsibilities that can realistically be expected of them at this point become clear.

A particularly poignant segment of John Turner's film on the El Espíritu experience ("A Roof of My Own") expresses this lost opportunity for promoting national citizenship. A spokesman from among the original invaders describes the culminating moment of the invasion, when the first shacks of reed matting were thrown up, signifying the establishment of the barriada. Peruvian flags were run up on bamboo poles, and the spokesman, overcome by emotion, says, "For the first time we felt we were citizens of Peru." Then the troops attacked. While the barriada persisted, the promise of full, participatory citizenship was lost.

Politicalization:
A Continuous or Discontinuous Process?

The diffuse "revolution of rising expectations" concept, and our tendency to assume progress in human affairs, can lead to a logically constructed but empirically unsatisfactory model of the politicalization process. The rising expectations idea has an obvious connotation of automatic escalation. In its political aspect, it projects the image of an expanding government scope under increasing stress. The very expansion of government functions is seen as contributing to an increasing view of situations as problems requiring government action, and which in turn supposedly generates demands. Thus, because previous situations are converted into wants, and wants into demands more rapidly than political resources become available, this model suggests that the system undergoes increasing stress, and in the poorer countries, frequently collapses. At the individual level, the implicit assumption is that once one learns to make demands (or engage in other behaviors representing a relatively high level of politicalization), the capacity and disposition to make them is established. Demand-making may not become a constant activity, but a latent orientation to engage in this kind of behavior is in existence and can be easily triggered into operation.

We have been operating with a similar concept of the politicalization process. Although it has been obvious that the intermediate stages, indicated below, may actually occur in a variety of sequences, the general direction of development has seemed to be: nonawareness of government; awareness; a perception of its utility; a realization of its manipulability; the development of a political preference; an appraisal of one's probable effectiveness; a calculation of gains and costs of action; and the making of demands.

We have already suggested the manner in which sanctions can short-circuit or reverse the politicalization process. Here we want to assess the experience of our respondents in order to isolate other factors that may produce reversals or constraints.

At what point are we encountering these people? Possibly at that point in their lives where their politicalization is highest. They have all been dealing with the problem of housing. In a bad or extreme situation, they had a tangible alternative: seizure and settlement of unoccupied land or application for government housing. They could see the land, and they knew their own skills in home construction. The invasion itself represents at least an implicit demand that the government not enforce the letter of the law regarding illegal squatting, and for many of these people, there was explicit recognition and planning in terms of this demand. In any event, after the invasion (or application and receipt of public housing), there followed a period of protracted demand-making associated with negotiations for urban services (and, in the case of 3 de Mayo, for housing). A high level of politicalization was reached. The question is whether it became stabilized; in other words, whether the psychological underpinnings of demand capability were established.

It has been repeatedly found in American studies that those who feel personally effective in politics tend to participate more. Almond and Verba conclude that personal political efficacy provides a psychological reserve for maintaining the civic culture.[20] They suggest that efficacy needs periodic exercise and testing in order to continue performing this function, but that demand-making need not and cannot be continuous.

Before assessing the psychological condition of the settlers, we need to make our limitations clear. We have data only from one survey taken at one point in time, and are therefore limited largely to analyses of associations. Comparative data using these same measures are not available. There are no well-defined criteria for distinguishing the person whose sense of political efficacy is stably internalized from the one whose sense of efficacy is unstable. Nor do we know how many stably effective people there must be in a collectivity in order to attain a threshold beyond which that demand-making is likely to be the response to a feeling of need.

Do past demand-making or high levels of politicalization instill a high sense of efficacy? Asked whether "people like you can only wait and accept government programs, or can have influence and make the government help you," a range from 32 to 46 percent of our sets of respondents opted for the more assertive, effective-seeming alternative. When asked their degree of agreement or disagreement with the proposition, "Only if things change very much will I be able to affect what the government does," a lower range of from 14 to 31 percent expressed disagreement. Furthermore, not only the internalization of a sense of efficacy, but also the very perception of the personal relevance of the government seems in doubt. Confronted with the proposition, "What any government does won't affect my life very much," the response was overwhelmingly affirmative in most cases, with rejection ranging from 23 to 56 percent. And only a fairly uniform minority of about one third rejected the proposition that, "One gains nothing with political activity." [21] Perhaps one would not expect a higher level of awareness and efficacy among a general cross-section of people, but it would seem more likely among a group that has been involved in demand-making concerning matters of great import. In this situation, it is questionable whether past political demand-making and effectiveness have been converted into a sense of political efficacy. On the basis of these data, therefore, we cannot conclude that an important element of demand capacity has been created.

The tangible alternatives available regarding the housing problem and the tangible gains represented by the acquisition of urban services

Table 4
POLITICAL EFFICACY, AWARENESS, UTILITY

	Lima		Santo Domingo %	Santiago		
	Pampa Seca %	El Espíritu %		S.D. Applicants %	S.D. Invaders %	3 de Mayo %
Can only wait and accept government programs	50	54	63	67	56	59
Can have influence and make government help	46	41	35	32	39	39
"Only if things change very much will I be able to affect what the government does":						
agree strongly	42	37	55	62	44	62
disagree slightly/strongly	31	23	20	16	25	14
"What any government does will not affect my life very much":						
agree strongly	21	30	42	48	34	46
disagree slightly/strongly	56	37	33	23	41	23
"One gains nothing with political activity":						
agree strongly	35	44	42	46	42	50
disagree slightly/strongly	36	32	36	32	39	37
Cite economic problems as most important national problems	74	55	73	68	78	62
Cite economic problems as matters they can take before the government	9	3	17	10	20	10

may not readily be repeated for other problem situations in which these people find themselves, with the result that previous high levels of politicalization will not so readily be reached again. For example, a very high proportion of the respondents in all communities mentioned economic problems as the most important ones facing the country. The responses to this open-ended item clustered around such matters as unemployment, the high cost of living (especially food staples), poverty, misery, etc. Another, multifaceted item asked (a) what one could do to get the government to do (or stop doing) something, and (b) what sorts of problems could be taken to the government in this regard. Although the proportion mentioning economic problems as "most important" ranged from 55 to 78 percent,[22] the proportion mentioning economic problems as the kind of matter they could take before the government was only one-tenth or less in most cases, ranging from 3 to 20 percent. If alternative solutions to these economic problems are not apparent, the formulation of related demands *would* probably be low. It should be noted here that, while there is rather broad agreement in these societies that economic problems, including those mentioned, are the most important, there have been few alternatives posed for their resolution. Moreover, the general lines of attack have been so couched in intellectual, abstract terminology that they have probably not elicited the settlers' interest.

The level of politicalization of this sector of the urban lower class may show considerable fluctuation. Depoliticalization may occur as a function of failure to develop a generalized sense of political efficacy or even a generalized sense of the personal relevance of government; and of failure to conceive or rely on political alternatives to outstanding problems.

It should not be simplistically argued that meeting the demands of people—even where it is vitally important to them—will only result in the generation of more demands from them, and in a situation of extreme scarcity and more stress on the system.

The case of the Santo Domingo invaders

Once again, the Santo Domingo invaders stand out as a highly politicalized group. Many more of them than any other of our sets can conceive of how to translate economic problems (those considered by all sets as "most important") into personal demands on government. While their levels of efficacy and awareness are not the highest among the various sets, they are relatively high. A series of factors can be proposed at this point that together may suggest the reasons for their demand capability. One factor is a relatively high level of education, in comparison with the other Santiago sets. Another is the relatively high degree of competition within the group between affiliates of Christian Democracy and those of FRAP, which may have defined economic problems in terms that are meaningful for the poor. Finally, the high demands these invaders made on the government (they invaded valuable public land designed for public housing, demanding not only their right to remain but to housing itself) *and* the successful outcome may have been a particularly potent political experience, establishing a high level of politicalization.

Patterns of Legitimacy and Projected Consequences

There has been a tendency to define problems of political legitimacy in societies emerging from preindustrialism in terms of possible political instability. We will now briefly assess the potential for instability in the patterns of legitimacy orientation found in the four settlements, and also treat other possible (and perhaps more common) consequences of lack of legitimacy. One of these is simply the absence of positive support. In other words, low legitimacy may involve the elite's inability to mobilize the citizens or to make policy that assumes their positive support. Another consequence of the failure to find personal significance in the political system may be social disorganization. In this situation, the society and polity must bear the costs of directly antisocial acts, widespread personal aimlessness, and personally destructive behavior.

The actual patterns of legitimacy orientation are quite distinct. Though there is considerable variation in support for the system between the two Santiago settlements, and within Santo Domingo between applicants and invaders, the greatest differences are between these Chilean respondents and the residents of the two Lima barriadas. The Santiago set respond much more positively than their Lima counterparts to the system as a whole. They evaluate the president, the municipality, government officials, and a political party as being much more helpful than do the Peruvians. Many more of them report affiliation with a major political party (indicating at least provisional acceptance of the parliamentary system). Many more of them than the barriada residents evaluate the government's method of selecting people for public housing as fair. A much higher proportion of them also endorse the proposition that people must make sacrifices to help the country develop (potentially a highly significant indicator of the elite's capacity for mobilizing the citizens to implement development policy). Finally, the Peruvians are considerably more disposed to condone violence as a means of settling political questions and to accept social disorder as a consequence of desired social change, which seem probable indicators of dissatisfaction with present political arrangements. Clearly, the Santiago respondents give much more support to and feel they derive much more support from the political system than do the Lima respondents.

The Chilean political system has a considerable cushion of legitimacy vis-à-vis the settlers. The government's housing program is a major element in this situation. The following seem to be some of the other significant aspects of this pattern.

Local government (the municipality) substantially contributes to the system's legitimacy. One reason for this is that it exercises some functions regarding urban services that are currently of particular importance to the settlers. Furthermore, in a situation of two-party competition (Christian Democracy and FRAP), where one party dominates the presidency and congress, the election of local councilmen permits another forum for the expression of opposition. However, we lack information in any depth on the local government as a political subsystem. In contrast to the widespread judgment that the municipality plays a small role in Chile, the data indicate the usefulness of a study of its place in the polity.

It is apparent that the political party and administrative bureaucracy are relatively weak integrative elements of the political system, so that despite the many elements of strong support for the Chilean system, the general Latin American political problem of an ineffective or underdeveloped organizational infrastructure remains. Previously we had mentioned the importance of the potential role of the Promoción Popular program in this context in light of the relatively high level of support it has.

Table 5
PATTERNS OF LEGITIMACY

	Lima		Santiago			
	Pampa Seca %	El Espiritu %	Santo Domingo %	S. D. Applicants %	S. D. Invaders %	3 de Mayo %
"In general our system of government and politics is good for the country":						
agree strongly	22	18	65	76	51	53
agree slightly	38	35	21	16	24	28
disagree slightly/strongly	38	42	11	6	19	15
Evaluation of extent of help given by President:						
much	10	14	50	60	36	33
some	18	24	20	15	24	22
none	50	50	17	10	27	33
don't know	20	11	13	14	10	12
Evaluation of extent of help given by municipality:						
much	6	8	35	38	32	41
some	28	14	24	19	27	24
none	55	66	28	30	32	28
don't know	10	11	12	11	7	7
Evaluation of extent of help given by government officials:						
much	5	7	27	38	14	21
some	17	24	26	20	37	24
none	57	51	31	24	37	42
don't know	17	11	16	16	7	12
Evaluation of extent of help given by a party:						
much	3	2	20	25	15	17
some	12	18	22	23	24	17
none	63	62	44	40	46	51
don't know	20	17	14	11	12	13

Affiliation to a party:						
none/independent	54	53	35	35	34	32
government *	21	18	43	49	37	44
opposition †	21	26	18	10	25	24
Evaluation of public housing selection process:						
fair	28	15	54	58	48	48
not very fair	32	49	31	32	34	34
very unfair	34	33	12	8	15	13
In agreement that people should sacrifice for national development	44	45	79	82	71	68
"Violence should never be the way to resolve political problems":						
agree strongly	46	44	75	84	61	69
agree slightly	20	15	12	2	22	14
disagree slightly/strongly	34	38	12	13	17	15
"Social change is acceptable only if it doesn't provoke disorder":						
agree strongly	49	40	80	85	75	76
agree slightly	26	26	15	13	17	16
disagree slightly/strongly	20	28	5	2	8	6
Change in ideas about politics:						
gov't. more helpful now/better	7	3	22	22	22	4
gov't. less helpful now/worse	11	14	2	1	3	2
Unable to mention anyone to count on for help	30	38	19			20
Finding someone to count on in case of need:						
harder now	37	38	34	35	22	24
same as ever	34	37	19	18	25	35
easier now	26	23	46	44	52	39
"Do you think people around here are":						
united strongly/slightly	35	50	48	48	46	56
disunited slightly/strongly	64	49	48	48	52	41

* *Note:* The government party is Acción Popular in Peru and Christian Democracy in Chile.

† The opposition coalition is APRA and Socialist and Communist (FRAP) in Chile.

Table 5, continued

Evaluation of extent of help given by rich:				
much	0	1	10	7
some	6	5	19	21
none	82	82	58	67
don't know	10	11	10	3
Evaluation of extent of help given by university students:				
much	20	13	46	34
some	30	39	15	15
none	27	27	10	19
don't know	21	21	28	30
Evaluation of extent of help given by priests:				
much	35	11	32	22
some	32	34	29	33
none	26	44	27	36
don't know	6	9	10	8
Evaluation of extent of help given by JNV (Housing Agency):				
much	40	28		
some	31	35		
none	18	29		
don't know	9	7		

The Santo Domingo invaders show considerably less support for the system than do the applicants in the same housing project. In some instances they accord more, and sometimes less, support than do the 3 de Mayo settlers. It is hard to derive a meaningful interpretation from a single cross-sectional survey. For example, it may indicate a continuing ambivalent disposition toward the system and its components; but in view of the recent threatening experiences these invaders have had with the government and the army (during the invasion experience itself), it may also represent a trend of growing support. An additional datum provides some evidence favoring the latter interpretation. We asked the respondents whether their political ideas had changed over the years, and if so, in what manner. The majority of responses dealt with acquiring more information, experience or understanding with maturation. But, in Santiago, a much larger proportion of Santo Domingo residents, both invaders and applicants, than 3 de Mayo residents mentioned that the government was more helpful now than in the past. Virtually no one in either Santiago settlement said that the government had become less helpful or more harmful, in substantial contrast to the barriada responses.

It should be investigated over time whether the more cautious or limited support of the system by the Santo Domingo invaders (plus their high politicalization relative to the applicants) stimulates more solicitous government action than if they were considered "safer" constituents, and tends to maintain the invaders as autonomous—as opposed to patron-oriented—dependent actors in the political system.

The Peruvian respondents show more opposition to the system and its components. Neither the president, government officials generally, the municipality, nor the parties stand out as positive elements. Furthermore, these people perceive less social support than do the Chileans. For example, a higher proportion of the barriada residents say they can count on no one for help when they need it, a distribution found again in response to a question asking whether help is harder or easier to find now than in the past. Moreover, the barriadas report virtually no help from the rich, whereas a minority of about 30 percent in the Chilean settlements say the rich give at least some help. This indicates a climate of somewhat less interclass hostility in Santiago than in Lima. Thus, conditions seem present in the Peruvian case that would oppose the continued development of the barriadas toward strong communities, with a respected place in polity and society. In fact, the four settlements' self-image regarding the degree of unity reveals that the more established settlements within each city (Santo Domingo in Santiago and Pampa Seca in Lima) perceive less unity. In the Santiago case, there are many countervailing forces promoting the integration of the residents into the nation. In the case of Lima, however, where the least unity is perceived, there is much less in the external environment to deter the tendency toward alienation over time.

Projected consequences

As has been clear throughout, the residents of the four settlements have experienced a great deal of change over a short period of time. The consolidation of these areas may represent a brief historical moment, for generations are short. Quite conceivably, what the settlers have achieved individually and collectively within the past few years may be dissipated tomorrow. Much depends on whether they find some support within the society, and on their integration into the national society. If they do not find support, if neither their achievements nor they themselves win recognition and respect somewhere in the larger society, then the following consequences seem likely in the near future. Children, raised with much parental ambition and sacrifice, may fail to find the means to get ahead or become embarrassed about living in such settlements. In either event, high intrafamilial tensions and a high level of frustration and self-hate among the youth may result. Thus, the next generation could greatly raise the costs to the nation of malintegration of the settlements, either by venting their frustrations in political opposition, across-the-board delinquency, or extreme privatization. Opposition would seem to be promoted to the extent that they are socialized in a home and community environment where the political system is regarded as bad. A second consequence might be that the frustrations and embarrassment of the children could impel many of the original settlers (and presumably community leaders) to relinquish their high hopes for a community and leave for less troubled areas.

Lack of support and its consequences would seem to promote the residents' loss of faith in the achievements of the past. Individual family dwellings once proudly erected through the entire family's effort could well be vacated for subdivision and renting at high rates to the even more enormous and desperate wave of lower-class urbanites of the future. This sort of shift in orientations toward exploitation would produce neighborhood decline, and soon, slums.

But if the recent achievements can be consolidated through a commensurate gain in social—or political—status, then it may be possible for the settlements to continue to develop into communities, and the "Watts stage" might be skipped. Even where social status is not forthcoming, political systems *can* deal with resistant societies by providing people with channels to national integration and by giving them political dignity. A partial example is the Puerto Rican experience under Muñoz Marin and the Popular Democratic Party, where the peasant was made the political hero. Tumin and Feldman suggest in their massive study of the island society that the high morale and sense of national integration of the lower class, in the face of a growing disparity between its material condition and that of the middle class, was a function of this political structure and support.[23] If the political system fails to provide this, and the society continues to be closed to the settlers and their children, then these human achievements and resources seem likely to be wasted. Not only would this involve a failure to integrate a substantial sector of potentially effective citizens, but it could also mean a considerable drain on the scarce development resources needed to maintain a minimum level of social control in the resultant slums and to contain the politically alienated.

Nonetheless, even in the more extreme case of Lima, there are potential bases for integration. A substantial proportion of the barriada samples perceive support from university students, priests (no doubt those operating constructive activities within the barriadas), and the Cooperación Popular program, though little has been done by any of these agents so far. All of them, however, have something to do with plans for community development and the integration of the barriadas into the society. (We have discussed this as a possible nexus of cross-class ties and ties between rulers and ruled in our analysis of the role of the local associations.) A further potential element in this situation is the Junta Nacional de la Vivienda, the Peruvian government housing agency, which has been very helpful and creative with regard to the barriadas, particularly with regard to other government agencies. This support and favorable experience are widely reflected in the evaluation by the settlers of the JNV, which stands in strong contrast to their other political evaluations. The JNV has been engaged in a home improvement loan and title program allowing a great deal of individual decision, responsibility and labor. The program is helping large numbers of settlers (that is, *lower-class people*), with little administrative overhead and very few cases of default on their part.[24] The JNV has thus depended on the strength of the settlers' experience and skills, as might the Cooperación Popular idea if permitted to operate in the barriadas. Though underdeveloped in this situation, this is clearly an extremely important potential and opportunity. A community development program capitalizing on these elements builds on demonstrated human organizational skills and orientations which are scarce and easily dissipated; it uses relatively little capital, which in this kind of development situation is extremely scarce; and it tends to promote political and social integration under political conditions generally extremely unfavorable toward such a process.

This research report has focused on the political integration of four new urban lower-class settlements in Santiago and Lima. The three squatter invasion settlements and a government housing project were surveyed at a time when they had considerable potential for becoming consolidated communities, with their inhabitants capable of contributing to the national development process.

The findings and conclusions are:

1. The highly significant local association tends to atrophy with time as the settlement consolidates. This threatens the loss of a potential channel of political elite-citizen integration in societies characterized by political organizational underdevelopment. A Chilean government program may contribute to the transformation of the association into a mediator between government and settlers, but the latter may become less autonomous in problem-solving and more dependent. A similar program of considerable potential in Peru was directed away from these urban settlements, and has now been seriously weakened by political opposition.

2. Sanctions were suggested as important factors retarding lower-class politicalization in transitional societies. The hypothesis

presented is that extreme depoliticalization will result from severe sanctions being levied against lower-class people relatively inexperienced in politics. Our data conform closely to the pattern predicted by the hypothesis. The effect can "help" a government by reducing demands and therefore stress, but there is also a loss in the capacity to mobilize support.

3. Politicalization may be a discontinuous process, contrary to prevailing theory. A high level of politicalization may not be established despite an important demand-making experience. One such experience may not establish the psychological basis for continuing demand-making. Furthermore, the general case regarding the Latin American urban lower class is one where alternative solutions to serious problems are not defined, and this retards politicalization. Consequently, meeting an important demand concerning housing and urban services, for example, does not necessarily trigger a chain of additional demands which would overwhelm governmental capacity in transitional societies.

4. Considerable variation in patterns of political legitimacy orientations exists between the Chilean and Peruvian settlements. The Santiago residents responded much more affirmatively than did those in Lima to their political system and its components. Since the settlers in Santiago also perceive much more social support than those in Lima, they appear to be much more integrated, although such major integrating agencies as the political parties and public bureaucracy appear to be weak links. Where political and social support is lacking to the settlers, as in Lima, internal stress in the barriadas seems likely to promote long-run decline and slum formation, involving social disorganization, personal ineffectiveness, and political alienation. The political costs of maintaining control under such circumstances, and the waste of potential citizenship are considerable for any society trying to move toward development.

NOTES

1. This term has been defined as "forcible preemption of land by landless and homeless people." Cf. Charles Abrams, *Man's Struggle for Shelter in an Urbanizing World* (Cambridge: M.I.T. Press, 1964), chapter 2, "Squatting and Squatters," p. 12.

2. See, for example, José Matos Mar, "The *Barriadas* of Lima: An Example of Integration into Urban Life," in *Urbanization in Latin America*, ed. P. Hauser (New York: International Documents Service, 1961), p. 171; James L. Payne, *Labor and Politics in Peru* (New Haven: Yale University Press, 1965), p. 15; and Tad Szulc, *The Winds of Revolution* (New York: Praeger, 1965), pp. 49–54.

3. John Turner's work is so far available in "Three Lectures on Housing in Peru," presented at the Athens Centre of Ekistics, November 1964 (mimeo); and in the special number edited by Turner, "Dwelling Resources in South America," *Architectural Design* (London), vol. 8 (August 1963), throughout. Rosenblüth's work is available in *Problemas socio-económicos de la marginalidad y la integración urbana; el caso de "las poblaciones callampas" en el Gran Santiago* (Santiago: Universidad de Chile, Escuela de Economía, 1963).

4. Matos Mar cites traditional communalism as operative in the barriadas, "The *Barriadas* of Lima," p. 176. Richard N. Adams presents a contrasting analysis in "The Community in Latin America: A Changing Myth," *The Centennial Review* 6 (Summer 1962): 409–434; as does Richard W. Patch, "How Communal are the Communities?" American Universities Field Staff Report, Lima, June 1959.

5. See Turner, "Three Lectures," and Richard Morse, "Recent Research on Latin American Urbanization," *Latin American Research Review* 1 (Fall 1965): 35–74. In a study of Lima industrial workers, it was found that ownership of a house was *the* major objective. See Guillermo Briones and José Mejía Valera, *El obrero industrial* (Lima: Universidad de San Marcos, Instituto de Investigaciones Sociológicas, 1964), p. 71.

6. Abrams fears that squatting will promote disrespect for law and government; *Man's Struggle*, p. 23. This does not appear to be a major problem in the Lima or Santiago cases, however.

7. These data conform closely to the general pattern observed in Lima by anthropologist William Mangin. See his "Mental Health and Migration to Cities: A Peruvian Case," reprinted in *Contemporary Cultures and Societies of Latin America*, ed. D. B. Heath and R. N. Adams (New York: Random House, 1965), p. 549.

8. Comisión Económica para América Latina, "La urbanización en América Latina . . .," E/CN.12/662/Rev. 1 (March 1963) 19.

9. See Mangin, "Mental Health," p. 548, for an appraisal of parental ambitions in the barriadas.

10. What we have termed the "local association" carries such varied titles as *junta de vecinos, comité de vecinos, asociación de la barriada*, etc.

11. Mangin, "Mental Health," pp. 549–550.

12. Myron Weiner, "Political Integration and Political Development," *The Annals of the American Academy of Political and Social Science* 358 (March 1965): 52–64.

13. Selden Rodman, "Peruvian Politics Stalls Belaúnde's Reforms," *The Reporter* 35 (July 14, 1966): 37–40.

14. D. Goldrich, "Toward the Comparative Study of Politicization in Latin

America," in *Contemporary Cultures*, ed. Heath and Adams, pp. 361–78; and *Sons of the Establishment: Elite Youth in Panama and Costa Rica* (Chicago: Rand McNally, 1966), chapter 1.

15. See the Mangin and Turner articles in *Architectural Design*.

16. For a very useful theoretical discussion of this, see Jerry F. Medler, "Negative Sanctions: Their Perception and Effect in the Political System," Ph.D. diss. University of Oregon, 1966. See also the treatment of sanctions in R. E. Agger, D. Goldrich and B. E. Swanson, *The Rulers and the Ruled* (New York: John Wiley, 1964).

17. G. Almond and S. Verba, *The Civic Culture* (Princeton: Princeton University Press, 1963).

18. Medler, "Negative Sanctions," pp. 111–133.

19. Frank A. Pinner, "Notes on Method in Social and Political Research," in *The Research Function of University Bureaus and Institutes for Government-Related Research*, ed. D. Waldo (Berkeley: Bureau of Public Administration, University of California, 1960), pp. 183–218. See also Henry Teune, "The Learning of Integrative Habits," in *The Integration of Political Communities*, ed. P. Jacob and J. Toscano (Philadelphia: Lippincott, 1964), pp. 247–82.

20. Almond and Verba, *Civic Culture*, "The Civic Culture and Democratic Stability."

21. Response set may be a problem regarding these items. On the other hand, it is quite possible that the acquiescent (those who tend to agree to such items, regardless of substance) are also those least oriented to political and environmental manipulation.

22. Economic problems were mentioned far more than any other type by the respondents.

23. M. Tumin and A. Feldman, *Social Class and Social Change in Puerto Rico* (Princeton: Princeton University Press, 1961).

24. John Turner discusses this JNV program in his third Lecture, "Popular Housing Policies and Projects in Peru," in Turner, "Three Lectures."

Sandra Powell*

Political Participation
5.   in the Barriadas:
A Case Study

Urbanization and increased social differentiation are associated with industrialization. Cities provide skilled workers for an increasingly interdependent and specialized labor market. Industrialization and urbanization, however, do not necessarily proceed at simultaneous rates. Indeed, the movement of people to the cities many times outstrips the system's capacity to provide jobs. Even if jobs are available for the skilled, much migrant labor is unskilled. Slums become the most salient testimonial to this economic and social incongruity.

Not all of the poor, however, are slum dwellers. Differentiation exists within the poverty stratum of urban areas as well as throughout the total society. This differentiation is saliently marked in the *barriadas* of Lima, Peru, where approximately 25 percent of the city's population lives in areas comparable to the *callampas* of Santiago and the *favelas* of Rio de Janeiro. These are areas where the urban poor are found. That, perhaps, is the only generalization applicable to all, for they are marked more by their diversity than by their similarity.

Most are squatter settlements, although land has been purchased in some cases. Some are slums, physically deteriorating areas where too many people live without water, sewage, or electricity. Others attest to the possibility of limited economic mobility within the urban environment. They have become an escape from the crowded slums of the inner city and are a place where people no longer pay rent. Compared to their first years in the city, life has improved for some of the barriada inhabitants. Nonetheless, all barriada dwellers comprise

* The author is grateful to the Social Science Research Council for a Study and Research Grant in Lima for the summer of 1967.

part of the most deprived sector of the society. What are the forces for social betterment and economic mobility in such areas? One potential force is political—participation by deprived groups in the political process. Presumably, participation can influence policy, equalizing benefits and deprivation. "Demand aggregation" is the term given to the process of communicating policy desires, or social needs, to the political system. The mechanisms for barriada demand aggregation, and their effectiveness in converting demands to policy, were the focus of this research.

Political Party Demand Aggregation

In democratic societies, political parties are the most important structures for performing demand aggregation functions. People cast a vote for many reasons—on the basis of habit, a candidate's personal appeal, a particular issue, the advice of friends. Thus, although it cannot be assumed that all votes for a particular candidate are cast because individuals believe one party will articulate their interests more forcefully than another, neither are party programs totally irrelevant to the vote decision. In some measure electoral support should reflect either how adequately political parties are aggregating demands, or which parties the voters believe will most effectively convert demands into policy once in power.

To study political party demand aggregation, three elections were selected—the presidential election of 1963 and the municipal elections of 1963 and 1966. The three-way presidential race in 1963 was contested among Fernando Belaúnde Terry (Acción Popular), Manuel Odría (Unión Nacional Odrista), and Raul Victor Haya de la Torre (Alianza Popular Revolucionara Americano, hereafter APRA; its adherents are Apristas). Belaúnde Terry won and held office until October 3, 1968, when he was deposed by a military coup. Following the presidential election, two coalitions were formed. The Acción Popular and Christian Democratic parties banded together in the Alianza (Alliance); and the Apristas and the Odristas formed the Coalición (Coalition). Congressional control rested with the Coalition and executive power with the Alliance. In the municipal elections of 1963 and 1966, the individual parties did not run separate candidates.

Instead, the Coalition and Alliance each presented one list to the voters.

Both coalitions became increasingly factionalized between 1963 and 1968. Luis Bedoya Reyes, mayor of Lima, broke with the Christian Democrats to form the Popular Christian party, and the National Social Democratic party, led by Senator Julio de la Piedra, was formed by dissident Odristas. Prior to the parliamentary elections of August 1968, to choose the presidents of the House and Senate, the APRA dissolved the Coalition.

Electoral returns from the 36 districts comprising Lima Province in Lima Department were analyzed to determine whether variations in electoral support for the various parties were systematically related to the population composition of a district (barriada-nonbarriada). It was reasoned that, if one party drew support almost exclusively from barriada districts and another from nonbarriada districts, it would be plausible to infer that both parties were strong aggregators of their particular interests. Whether or not the barriada party was successful in converting demands into policy would depend on other factors involved in the policy process, but demands would be aggregated. Also, strong differences in support would probably indicate considerable ideological and programatic differences between parties, reflective of the different interests of their major sources of electoral support.

Conversely, electoral support might be drawn from all areas, barriada and nonbarriada in approximately the same proportions. Within the barriadas all parties might receive some support because no party, either by action or campaign appeal, had been able to identify itself as the major representative of barriada interests.

In the first situation, that of different party support in barriada and nonbarriada areas, demand aggregation might exist without effective policy action on demands. If a party were heavily supported in the barriadas but had little national strength, policymakers could isolate and disregard its members. Conversely, similarity in electoral support from area to area might have two consequences. If political party leaders felt the increment of support they received from the barriadas was essential to their power maintenance, presumably they would seek to assure and augment that support by concrete policy concessions. Thus, demands would be both aggregated and satisfied. However, it is also possible that if support was divided among parties in the barriadas, barriada demands would be neither aggregated nor satisfied. No party would be wholly dependent on the barriadas for political power. Thus, division of support might be preferred by all parties over competing for increased support with policy benefits, since that would necessitate increasing the resources allocated to the barriadas. Divided electoral support, then, would undermine the potential political power of the barriadas in the electoral and policy processes.

In the discussion which follows, the three elections are analyzed on this dimension of cohesive-divided political party support in the barriadas. Secondly, an attempt is made to relate demand aggregation to policy promulgation.

The 1963 presidential election

To ascertain whether electoral support varied with a district's barriada population, it was necessary to categorize the 36 districts according to the percentage of the population classified as barriada dwellers living within each district.[1] Five divisions were made, as shown in Table 1. The districts of Category 1 have no barriada dwellers; those in Category 5 are the most heavily barriada populated, with barriada dwellers comprising either the entire district or 70.5 percent of it.

The voting statistics in Table 1, arranged to show differences in the distribution of candidate support within districts and population categories, indicate what percent of the district vote each candidate received. For example, in district 005, Belaúnde Terry received 39.9 percent of the votes cast in that district; Haya de la Torre, 27.2 percent; Odría, 31.4 percent; and Samone, 1.5 percent.[2]

To determine whether variations in support were systematically related to population type, plurality victories were compared first. Analysis of Table 1 shows that no systematic variation occurred between district type and winner of plurality victories. In the three districts with the highest barriada population (Category 5), two favored Odría and one Belaúnde Terry. All districts in Category 4 strongly preferred Belaúnde Terry over Odría. Haya de la Torre ran third in

Table 1
1963 PRESIDENTIAL ELECTION

Population Category	Percent of District Vote Received by Candidate[a]			
District (IBM code) [b]	Belaúnde Terry	Haya de la Torre	Orida	Samone
1. 0% Barriada Population				
001[b]	24.7	27.6	**47.0**[c]	.7
011	37.5	20.4	**41.1**	1.0
013	**45.1**	23.7	30.0	1.2
017	**51.3**	17.0	30.5	1.2
019	30.8	31.4	**35.2**	2.6
020	**47.9**	22.5	28.4	1.2
022	**43.1**	24.6	31.5	.8
023	31.1	30.3	**36.0**	2.6
025	37.7	20.3	**42.0**	0.0
026	**51.1**	16.2	31.6	1.1
030	**40.0**	27.1	31.7	1.1
031	14.4	3.6	32.0	**50.0**
032	39.6	26.4	30.5	3.5
015	**42.0**	23.6	33.5	.9
018	24.9	25.3	**48.3**	1.5
2. 1.0–3.6% B.P.				
016	**46.6**	21.7	30.5	1.2
003	**39.6**	29.3	30.1	1.0
012	**40.3**	26.1	32.6	1.0
034	**44.6**	21.1	33.4	.9
3. 8.3–12.8%B.P.				
007	37.7	20.1	**41.1**	1.1
002	36.8	25.2	**37.2**	.8
021	**39.5**	23.4	35.7	1.4
004	29.5	33.0	**35.9**	1.6
4. 17.1–27.0% B.P.				
006	**44.5**	21.7	32.6	1.2
027	**43.1**	18.9	37.2	.8
024	**36.7**	26.4	35.9	1.0
036	**41.9**	26.0	31.0	1.1
014	**40.4**	29.3	29.6	.7
5. 70.5–100.0% B.P.				
005	**39.9**	27.2	31.4	1.5
035	35.3	27.1	**36.6**	1.0
028	33.4	25.2	**40.5**	.9

Source: Jurado Nacional de Elecciones

[a] Vote by district totals 100%.

[b] The IBM code designations refer to the following districts: 001—Ancon, 002—Ate, 003—Brena, 004—Carabayllo, 005—Comas, 006—Chaclacayo, 007—Chorrillos, 008—El Augustino, *009—Independencia, *010—Jesus Maria, *011—La Molina, 012—La Victoria, 013—Lince, 014—Lurigancho, 015—Lurin, 016—Magdalena del Mar, 017—Miraflores, 018—Pachacamac, 019—Pucusana, 020—Pueblo Libre, 021—Puente

both groups of districts. Category 3 is made up of districts with a much smaller barriada population (between 8.3 and 12.8 percent of the total district population). There, as in Category 1, more districts favored Odría than Belaúnde Terry (three to one). In all but one district, Haya de la Torre ran third. In all four districts of Category 2, Belaúnde Terry was the preferred candidate, Odría the second, and Haya de la Torre the third. Support was evenly divided between Belaúnde Terry (eight districts) and Odría (six districts) in the largest category, 1, composed of districts without barriada populations.

If population—barriada or nonbarriada—were related to support, we would have expected one candidate to win his victories in districts with the same population type and the other to win his victories in districts with a different population composition. Instead, most plurality victories were won by Belaúnde Terry, regardless of area; and in the largest area (1), Belaúnde Terry and Odría showed almost equal strength.

This conclusion is strengthened by comparing differences in the average candidate electoral support by population category. The votes for every district in each of the five population categories were averaged to determine the average percent of the vote each candidate received in the five types.[3] Table 2 shows that Haya de la Torre was the least preferred candidate in all areas; Belaúnde Terry the most preferred in three (1, 2, 4), Odría in one (3), and in one (5), Belaúnde Terry and Odría received exactly the same average percent of the vote.

Finally, comparing support for each candidate separately fails to indicate that strength of support systematically varied with population category. Belaúnde Terry demonstrated his greatest strength in Categories 2 and 4, weakest in 3 and 5. Conversely, Odría's greatest support was in Categories 3 and 5, weakest in 2 and 4. The largest average percent vote was cast for Haya de la Torre in Categories 5 and 3, lowest in 1 and 4. For none of the candidates did support consistently increase or decrease in Categories 1 through 5.

Piedra, 022—Puenta Negra, 024—Rimac, 025—San Bartolo, 026—San Isidro, 027—San Jose de Surco, 028—San Martin de Porres, 029—San Juan de Miraflores, *030—San Miguel, 031—Santa Mira del Mar, 032—Santa Rosa, 033—Santiago de Surco, 034—Surquillo, 035—Villa Maria del Triumfo, 036—Lima. (Asterisks indicate those districts formed just prior to the 1966 municipal election.)

[c] The greatest percentage of the vote in each district is bold face.

Table 2
1963 PRESIDENTIAL ELECTION

Population Category	Belaúnde Terry	Haya de la Torre	Odría
	Average Percentage Vote Received by Candidates in Population Category		
1.	37.4 *	22.7	35.3
2.	42.8	24 6	31.7
3.	35.9	25 4	37.5
4.	41.3	24.5	33.3
5.	36.2	26.5	36.2
Average percent received in all districts	38.4	23.9	34.8
Range	6.9	3.8	5.8

* The greatest percentage of the vote in each district is boldface.

Moreover, the differences in magnitude of support from category to category were small. Table 2 shows that Belaúnde Terry's average in all districts was 38.4 percent of the district vote, Odría's 34.8 percent, and Haya de la Torre's 23.9 percent. Range variation from a candidate's strongest to weakest district was, respectively, only 6.9, 3.8 and 5.8 percent. All candidates received approximately the same percentage of support in all categories. Furthermore, the small differences in average percent of the vote from category to category were not associated with the percent of the population classified as barriada. No candidate depended primarily on the barriadas for his votes while another depended on nonbarriada areas. Did this divisiveness in support characterize the 1963 and 1966 municipal elections as well?

The 1963 municipal election

In municipal elections, the number of seats each party receives is based on a system of proportional representation. Voters select a list, not individual candidates. The person heading the list which receives the most votes becomes mayor. In 1963, List 2 was the Coalition list (Aprista-Odrista); List 4, the Alliance (Acción Popular and Christian Democratic); and List 6, the Independent list. Table 3 shows the percent of the district vote received by each list in that election.

Table 3
1963 MUNICIPAL ELECTIONS

Population Category District	Percent of District Vote Received by List:				
	2	4	6	N [a]	B [b]
1.					
001	29.5	**66.9***	0.0	.9	2.7
011	36.2	**49.0**	0.0	6.3	8.5
013	37.1	**49.6**	4.9	4.2	4.2
017	32.8	**59.8**	0.0	3.3	4.1
019	**44.8**	36.3	4.1	3.2	11.6
020	32.9	**49.1**	11.0	3.3	3.7
022	32.0	**53.7**	12.9	0.0	1.4
023	28.9	0.0	**63.9**	4.6	2.6
025	**49.8**	48.0	0.0	1.3	.9
026	33.5	**58.0**	0.0	3.1	5.4
030	39.8	**51.2**	0.0	3.9	5.1
031	23.2	34.9	**37.1**	3.1	1.7
032	0.0	0.0	0.0	**63.3**	36.4
015	24.6	**43.9**	18.3	7.5	5.7
018	**36.2**	20.2	30.9	4.0	8.7
2.					
016	32.1	**51.5**	7.7	4.9	3.8
003	**42.1**	40.7	8.9	3.9	4.4
012	42.9	**45.4**	.9	4.6	6.2
034	42.0	**42.4**	2.0	7.4	6.2
3.					
007	40.6	**41.0**	4.7	6.6	7.1
002	**44.5**	37.6	1.3	7.6	9.0
021	**46.4**	34.2	2.8	9.0	7.6
004	**39.1**	31.2	17.8	9.7	2.2
4.					
006	31.1	**38.1**	21.8	4.1	4.9
027	**43.9**	30.3	14.5	5.3	6.0
024	**45.9**	42.7	1.7	4.3	5.4
036	42.0	**46.1**	3.0	6.5	2.4
014	43.1	**44.0**	5.1	.7	7.1
5.					
005	**42.4**	37.9	4.8	7.7	7.2
035	**40.0**	30.0	3.1	21.4	5.5
028	**51.0**	33.7	3.0	6.1	6.2

[a] Void ballots.
[b] Blank ballots.
*The greatest percentage of the vote in each district is boldface.

Cursory inspection of this table suggests that the Alliance was considerably stronger in districts without barriada populations and the Coalition stronger in barriada areas. In districts with no barriada population (Category 1), List 4 won many more plurality victories than did List 2. List 4 captured the greatest proportion of votes in ten districts, whereas List 2 was most preferred in only three. In Category 2, also with a small barriada population, List 4 won three of the four districts. This trend of stronger preference for List 4 was reversed in Category 3, where List 2 captured three of the four districts. In Category 4, List 4 was again somewhat stronger than List 2; but in Category 5, districts with the largest barriada population, List 2 was preferred in all districts.

Table 4
1963 MUNICIPAL ELECTIONS

Population Category	Average Percent Vote Received by List in Population Category		
	2	4	6
1.	32.1	41.4*	12.2
2.	30 9	45.0	4.9
3.	42.7	36.0	6.7
4.	41.2	40.2	9.2
5.	44.5	33.9	3.6
Average percent received in all districts	37.1	40.2	9.2
Range	12.4	11.1	8.6

* The greatest percentage of the vote in each district is boldface.

Comparison of average support by areas also indicates a relationship between party strength and the population composition of the various districts. Table 4 shows that, whereas List 4 received a greater percent of the vote than List 2 in Categories 1 and 2, List 2 was stronger than List 4 in areas 3, 4 and 5. As expected, this table also indicates that as barriada population increased, support for List 2 increased. List 2 captured an average of 32.1 percent of the vote in districts without barriada populations. Support continued to increase with increasing barriada population in all but one (4) of the categories, and reached 44.5 percent in 5, the most heavily barriada-populated area.

For List 4, the converse relationship (increasing support with decreasing barriada population) was less strong, but nonetheless apparent. Average support for List 4 was stronger in districts with between 1.0 and 3.6 percent barriada populations than in districts with none. Likewise, support did not consistently decrease in categories 3, 4 or 5. But comparison between categories with the smallest barriada populations (1 and 2) and those with the largest (3, 4 and 5) shows that List 4 candidates received their strongest support in scarcely barriada-populated districts—41.4 and 45.0 percent of the vote, contrasted to 36.0, 40.2 and 33.9 percent of the vote in highly barriada-populated districts.

The preceding analysis has shown that, unlike the 1963 presidential race, support did vary with population type in the municipal election of the same year. Moreover, the differences in magnitude of support from area to area were considerably greater in the municipal elections. In the presidential election, Odría's average support varied only 5.8 percent between the area that most strongly supported him and the one that least strongly supported him, whereas the difference in average support for List 2 varied 12.4 percent from weakest to strongest area. Similarly, the range difference for Belaúnde Terry and List 4 was 6.9 and 11.1 percent, respectively. However, just as the direction of change was somewhat more consistent for List 2 than List 4, so was the magnitude of difference between areas greater for List 2, indicating that, of the two lists, the relationship between population type and voting preference was stronger for List 2.

Unlike support for the major parties, support for the Independent list was not related to population (see Table 4). The Independent list demonstrated its greatest strength in Categories 1—districts without barriada populations—and 4—districts with a high concentration of barriadas. Similarly, weakest support was not found predominantly in one type of area; the Independent list received the smallest average percent of the vote in Categories 5 and 2.

The 1966 municipal election

As in 1963, results of the 1966 municipal election showed that most districts with small barriada populations, in Categories 1 and 2, voted

Table 5
1966 MUNICIPAL ELECTIONS

Population Category District	Percent of District Vote Received by List:				
	2	4	6 c	N a	B b
1.					
001	**40.8**	14.9	40.2	2.3	1.8
010	35.4	**55.8**	0.0	4.6	4.2
011	40.0	**41.0**	8.7	4.4	5.9
013	27.2	**45.2**	22.3	2.4	2.9
017	11.9	**45.3**	38.6	2.1	2.1
019	43.1	**48.5**	0.0	4.3	4.1
020	27.1	**53.2**	14.4	2.6	2.7
022	0.0	**53.9**	43.8	1.3	1.0
023	0.0	32.6	**60.9**	3.8	2.7
025	32.2	30.4	**34.7**	1.2	1.5
026	24.1	**55.9**	14.3	2.6	3.1
030	42.5	**50.2**	0.0	3.8	3.5
031	0.0	0.0	**88.2**	8.2	3.6
032	0.0	33.7	**62.0**	3.1	1.2
015	**63.0**	6.3	20.5	6.0	4.2
018	**31.7**	23.4	38.0	3.1	3.8
2.					
016	27.9	**50.1**	17.3	1.9	2.8
003	**32.9**	30.6	31.9	2.2	2.4
012	37.7	**40.5**	15.0	2.5	4.3
034	40.0	**41.9**	12.0	2.4	3.7
3.					
007	28.2	**43.1**	23.0	2.5	3.2
002	**47.8**	24.3	16.7	4.3	6.9
021	28.7	22.4	**40.0**	3.9	5.0
004	17.6	26.9	**46.9**	4.1	4.5
4.					
006	**43.7**	39.1	8.4	4.6	4.2
027	28.7	**38.7**	27.8	2.0	2.8
024	**41.5**	37.6	14.7	2.3	3.9
036	42.1	**49.3**	4.2	2.5	1.9
014	28.2	**32.7**	29.7	3.9	5.5
5.					
005	**41.5**	25.7	22.6	4.2	6.0
008	**42.5**	28.8	21.4	3.3	4.0
009	**37.8**	22.0	29.7	4.8	5.7
035	**36.9**	33.5	22.1	2.3	5.2
029	**37.2**	36.3	19.2	2.5	4.8
028	30.7	20.0	41.5	3.4	4.4

Source: Jurado Nacional de Elecciones

a Void ballots.

b Blank ballots.

c The percentage figure under List 6, in most cases, is not a vote for one list but rather the summary score for all independent lists running in a particular district. The independent list is underlined only if one independent list received a greater proportion of the district vote than either List 2 or 4.

predominately for List 4 (see Table 5). Support in Categories 3 and 4 was not related to population. In Category 3, each list won two plurality victories; and in Category 4, List 4 captured three districts and List 2, two. Prior to the 1966 election three new districts, composed almost entirely of barriadas, were formed, increasing the number of districts in Category 5 from three to six. In all but one of these districts, plurality victories were won by List 2. Only in three categories (1, 2 and 5), then, was support, as measured by plurality victories, related to population. This suggests that the relationship between the two variables had weakened between 1963 and 1966.

Table 6
1963 AND 1966 MUNICIPAL ELECTIONS

Population Category	Average Percent Vote Received by List in Population Category				Deviation From Average Percent			
	List 2		List 4		List 2		List 4	
	1963	1966	1963	1966	1963	1966	1963	1966
1.	32.1	26.2	41.1	36.9	– 5.0	– 5.0	+1.2	+1.6
2.	39.8	34.6	45.0	40.8	+2.7	+3.4	+4.8	+5.5
3.	42.7	30.6	36.0	29.2	+5.6	– .6	– 4.2	– 6.1
4.	41.2	36.8	40.2	39.5	+4.1	+5.6	0.	+4.2
5.	44.5	37.8	33.9	27.7	+7.4	+6.6	– 6.3	– 7.6
Average percent of deviation	37.1	31.2	40.2	35.3	5.0	4.2	3.3	5.0

This conclusion is reinforced by examining Table 6, which compares average support by category for lists in both of these election years. In both years, support for List 2 increased with barriada population in all but one category (4 in 1963, and 3 in 1966). However, differences between areas were greater in 1963 than in 1966, as the average deviation from the mean shows (5.0 percent in 1963, compared to 4.2 percent in 1966). Thus, although support continued to vary with population, the magnitude of difference was not so great in the more recent election. In 1966, List 2's support was less strongly related to population area.

In 1963, support for List 4 also was associated with population, but more weakly than for List 2. Support for List 4 was strongest in areas with small barriada populations and weakest in areas with large barriada populations. In 1966, plurality victories for List 4 were

Table 7
1963 AND 1966 MUNICIPAL ELECTIONS

| | Average Percent Vote Received by List in Population Category | | | | | | | | |
| | List 2 | | | List 4 | | | List 6 | | |
Population Category	1963	1966	Percent Decrease	1963	1966	Percent Decrease	1963	1966	Percent Increase
1	32.1	26.2	5.9	41.4	36.9	4.5	12.2	30.4	18.2
2	39.8	34.6	5.2	45.0	40.8	4.2	4.9	19.1	14.2
3	42.7	30.6	12.1	36.0	29.2	6.8	6.7	31.7	25.0
4	41.2	36.8	4.4	40.2	39.5	.7	9.2	17.0	7.8
5	44.5	37.8	6.7	33.9	27.7	6.2	3.6	26.1	22.5
Average of all districts			7.1			5.0			19.1

concentrated in nonbarriada Categories 1 and 2. However, Table 6 shows that List 4's magnitude of support was not greatest in those two areas. As expected, support was weakest in districts with high barriada concentrations (Category 5), but second strongest support also came from districts with large barriada populations (Category 4). In the third group, support weakened again. Strongest support came from Category 2, with a small barriada population, but in districts with no barriada population, List 4 received only third-ranking electoral support.

Thus, in 1966, List 4's support did not systematically vary with barriada population—if all categories are included. If Category 4 is disregarded, then average percent vote was high in nonbarriada Categories 1 and 2, and low in barriada Categories 3 and 5, but the relationship was extremely weak, more so in 1966 than in 1963. Although differences in the magnitude of the vote among categories were greater for List 4 in 1966 (as indicated by an average deviation from the mean of 5.0 percent in 1966, compared to 3.3 percent in 1963), this is not an important dimension unless differences are systematically related, which, as we have just shown, they were not.

One of the more salient aspects of the 1966 municipal election was the markedly decreased support for both List 2 and List 4, and the concomitant increased support for Independent lists. As Table 7 shows, both List 2 and 4 had higher average percentage votes in 1963. The average decrease in strength for List 2 was 7.1 percent, and for List 4, 5.0 percent. More striking yet was the average increase for

Independent lists, of 19.1 percent. This increase, however, was not related to district population type.

Summary

Political support for the major candidates in the 1963 presidential election was divided similarly in barriada and nonbarriada districts. No candidate received significantly stronger or weaker support in one or the other type of area. But this was not true for the municipal elections of the same year. In that election, List 2 obtained noticeably greater support in districts with either no or small barriada populations. The relationship was stronger for List 2 than for List 4. Although the same trend was discernible for List 2 in 1966, it was weaker, and the relationship was either nonexistent or weakly apparent for List 4 in the latter election.

Although we have no way of determining a causal relationship between type of demand aggregation, measured by electoral divisiveness or cohesion, and demand satisfaction, indexed by barriada policies promulgated by the national government, it is possible that the two are empirically related. Except for the 1963 municipal election, support for parties in different areas was more divided than strongly associated with one candidate or list. Earlier it was suggested that, given this type of demand aggregation, demands would be satisfied only if political party leadership, weighing the three variables of support, resources and power, believed that barriada electoral support was crucial to party power maintenance. Electoral divisiveness, then, depending on party response, could either place the barriadas in a position of power or undermine their influence on policy formulation.[4]

A review of barriada policies during this period suggests that these areas have not been able to exert pressure on the national system, through either political parties or other structures of demand aggregation. Further, it can at least be suggested that electoral divisiveness is one important factor hindering the barriadas' effective exercise of political power; and the increased strength for Independent lists may reflect voter disenchantment with those parties wielding policymaking powers.

Demand Aggregation and Barriada Policies

At the end of the Odría administration in 1956, the Law of the Barriadas (Law 13517) was passed.[5] Article 1 of this law recognized the need for: remodeling existing barriadas; providing sanitation facilities; and granting legal title to the land held by barriada dwellers. Article 2 prohibited the formation of new barriadas after the passage of the law, and excluded barriadas formed after September 20, 1960, from the benefits of the law. The Junta Nacional de la Vivienda (JNV), a government agency, was made responsible for executing the law.

The first task facing the JNV was to identify existing barriadas. By 1961, the JNV had mapped and named 155 barriadas within metropolitan Lima. A six-type categorization scheme was developed to differentiate these barriadas according to type of home construction (straw matting or some more durable material), location (flat land or hills), density of population and regularity of physical layout.

Most people living in the barriadas have no legal title to their land, and one of the functions assumed by the JNV was to decide to whom the land belonged, and then to grant legal title. In many barriadas, huts of straw or stone are built one on top of another up a hillside with no space for sidewalks or streets or areas for laying water or sewage lines. The JNV reasoned that, if title were once granted in the existing disarray, future change and improvements would be extremely difficult, if not impossible. Thus, the JNV's operating procedure has been first to draw up a plan for the community—with rectangular streets, ample lots for houses, and free spaces for parks, schools, a post office, and other community services—before attempting to grant legal title.

In actuality, this decision has meant that the JNV has not attempted to work in three of the six types of barriadas, classified as D, E and F. Type D barriadas are those with too many families occupying a land space that cannot be expanded. For example, a highway may set a definite boundary, or contingent land may be privately owned. Because the homes in Type D are built of *estera* (cane matting), it would be possible to tear them down, rebuild and move the excess people elsewhere. However, since the people are living in close proximity to their employment, they usually do not want to move. Also, attempts by the JNV to acquire additional land have failed. Congress quickly halted the JNV's proposal to obtain private land by forceable expropriation (with compensation).

Type E barriadas are like Type D, except that the homes are built of stone or concrete instead of cane. Consequently, renovation would be impossible without vast expenditures of money.

Barriadas classified as Type F are those that the JNV feels will be eradicated at some future date for technical reasons—for example, a barriada situated along a highway which someday will be widened. The 82 barriadas of these three types, which have not received any benefits from the law, because renovation is too difficult and too expensive, comprise 52.9 percent of the total 155 barriadas.

The first three types of barriadas—A, B and C—do not present such great problems. Type A barriadas are those with rectangular streets, free spaces, sufficient land and ample lots. The JNV's work in these has consisted in regularizing the existing situation. Type B corresponds to A, except that Type A barriadas are located on flat land and Type B on hills. In Type C barriadas, land is limited and lots are small. Because land cannot be expanded, the JNV has had to subdivide lots to find room for everyone. The 72 barriadas of these three types represent 47.1 percent of the remaining barriadas.

By the summer of 1967, the JNV had completed the first phase of renovation—remodeling or the drawing of proposed plans for land use—in 43 barriadas. "Sanitation" refers to the installation of water and sewage pipes and electric power lines. Almost none of the barriadas have electricity or plumbing. People buy their water from trucks and, in many cases, carry it up steep hills bucketful by bucketful. With the JNV's aid, seven barriadas had acquired water and sewage pipes and four had electric power lines.

It is also the JNV's responsibility both to settle conflicts arising over land ownership, and to find another location for the dispossessed party. Although exact figures were not available, almost no land titles had been granted by 1967. It was not until July 19, 1968, that the Council of Ministers, using extraordinary powers, passed a decree calling for the immediate dispensation of titles under the auspices of the JNV. According to the Minister of Development, Pablo Carriquiry, 8,000 titles were to be granted in Comas (a Type A barriada on the outskirts of the city, with a population of approximately 150,000), 2,000 in Arequipa, and 800 in Tacna, both outside the city.[6]

Certainly, in the seven years of its operation, the JNV has not been able to remake the face of barriada Lima, or to significantly improve social conditions for the people living there. Because the socio-economic problems that give rise to the barriadas remain, new barriadas continually appear, despite the regulation in the law prohibiting the formation of new barriadas (as of summer 1967, nearly 60 new barriadas had been formed). Nor is it the JNV's fault that so little has been accomplished. The agency does not have funds to actually pay for installing water, sewage and electrical facilities. It only serves a technical-advisory function. It is not an agency to allocate and administer funds, provided by the government, for social improvements in the barriadas. The people living in the barriadas must raise the money themselves. At that time, the JNV will help them contract with a private agency to do the work. Given the meager resources of these people, it is not surprising that extensive change has not occurred.

Alleviation of barriada poverty would require massive expenditures by the national government. Yet, far from initiating a direct and forceful attack on urban social problems, the Belaúnde government hoped to solve the "barriada problem" by forestalling future barriada formation.[7] This was to be accomplished through a program known as Cooperación Popular, a plan for the social and economic development of the rural sierra. It was reasoned that, if opportunities are created and living conditions improved in the rural areas people now leave, the flow of migrants to the city can be greatly reduced. Creating an economic infrastructure to connect the hinterlands with the market economy of the urban centers formed one segment of this regional development program. In addition, agrarian reorganization, improved agricultural techniques and educational and medical facilities were considered essential to make the interior an economically viable region, capable of fulfilling the social needs of the people living there and of making a positive contribution to the total gross national product.

But because resources are scarce, more were concentrated on the infrastructure and fewer on actually changing the social fabric. Developmental resources were overwhelmingly allocated to a highway construction program—perhaps an essential element for long-range development, but one with little immediate impact on peoples' lives.

Meanwhile, migration to the cities continues, new barriadas emerge, and the population of existing barriadas increases. Although mortality rates in the barriadas are estimated to be considerably greater than 50 percent, family size averages 5.2. Yet, as the population of the barriadas continues to increase, almost nothing is being done by the national government to assuage present living conditions, or to provide channels of economic and social mobility out of the barriadas for the children of the present residents.

Political parties certainly have not been effective aggregators of barriada demands. Although aggregate data do not yield any conclusive hypotheses concerning voter motivation, the great increase in independent voting apparent in the municipal elections of 1966 may reflect a realistic evaluation on the part of the residents of what has not been done for them by the major political parties. Yet, just as electoral divisiveness may undermine the potential power of the barriadas to influence policy, divisiveness among Independent lists likewise undercuts the barriadas' power to recruit individuals, perhaps more sympathetic to their needs, into policy roles. Again potential power is neutralized because many Independent lists exist, and not just one.

This is not to say, however, that no efforts are being exerted for change. The barriadas attempt to achieve satisfaction of demands within the context of the social community, not the larger political system. Instead of organizing the barriadas to force policy concessions through political action, attempts are being made to organize the community itself for social action without aid from the political system.[8] Customarily, such organizations begin at the block level. People are asked to save a certain amount of money each month to eventually finance some type of community improvement, such as a school, a medical center, or perhaps even the laying of water pipes. Efforts are made to extend the organization block by block. To the extent that demand aggregation occurs, it takes the form of requesting an appropriate ministry to provide a teacher for a school that the people have financed and built. Rarely, however, are these organizational attempts successful on a large scale.

One problem is organizational divisiveness, another, resources. While some areas are without organizations, the more prevalent situation seems to be a complex of many small organizations. Because they are small, it is difficult to finance through them projects that must be resolved on a community-wide basis. For example, water pipes cannot be laid for one block. Moreover, these small groups seem incapable of combining and working with one another. In part, the people seem fearful of contributing money that may not bring them immediate benefits. ("Where will the first power lines go? If not on my block, then I won't contribute.")

Furthermore, political party leaders seem to foster this community divisiveness. Most community leaders make a point of excluding political leaders from the organization.[9] Ironically many of the barriadas were formed by invasion, a type of action that required a high degree of organization. However, research tends to indicate that these organizations atrophy after the seizure of land is accomplished. Likewise, the barriada must designate a group of leaders before the JNV will work in the area, but this has not been a viable focus for large-scale organization either. As a consequence, very few barriadas have been successful in bringing public services into their communities.

Conclusions

The model guiding this research was based on the premise that urbanization is often associated with economic deprivation, and concomitantly creates a living situation conducive to attitudinal change. Because organizational potential is greater in the urban setting than in rural areas, some form of radical political behavior may be expected if economic deprivation is perceived. This behavior may take the form of demand aggregation by ideologically leftist parties, or by strong political organizations acting independently of political parties and using either the electoral process or tactics of limited violence. The research has shown that neither of these forms of behavior exists in the Lima barriadas to any great degree.

There is no reason, of course, to assume that some dynamic historical force for change will deterministically assure social betterment. Nor must social change necessarily depend on political action. Yet, if social scientists, from a value perspective, hope for social change, today they seem to be faced with the necessity of explaining the nonexistence of sociopolitical phenomena previously believed to accompany urbanization. At least, this seems to be the case in Lima. It is the belief of this writer that social change will depend on action directed toward the national political system, simply because the resources required are so massive that they will, of necessity, have to be reallocated through the policy process. Illustrative of this point is one community that successfully carried through a major project. Three years were spent building a medical clinic. The clinic was entirely financed and constructed by the residents themselves. But from where will the money come for equipment and staff? This is beyond the resource capability of the barriada.

It is conceivable that if enduring community organizations emerged on a community-wide basis, in time these could acquire a political orientation, the strength of which could be reflected in both voting cohesion and tactics of direct political action. Consequently, if we are interested in the prospects for sociopolitical change, it seems important to ask what explains this political divisiveness, as well as the lack of success, when people try to organize their communities socially to bring about change?

Theory suggests a number of attitudinal variables that may deter organizational efforts. G. A. Almond and S. Verba [10] have stated that distrust may be a cultural characteristic inhibiting group formation. Also, if attitudes are in part culturally derived, it may be that poorer people in Hispanic cultures accept their lower status without question. For them, status is a matter of birth, not achievement; therefore, there is nothing to be done. Third, *fatalismo,* associated with religion, may further reinforce this attitude that man has very little ability or right to direct the course of his own life. If these attitudes, associated with culture, do explain divisiveness within the barriadas and failure to organize on a large scale, then the prospects for future change are indeed dismal, since such ingrained attitudes would be difficult to change.

Alternatively, other attitudes not intrinsically tied to culture, but simply associated with lower socioeconomic status, may account for this organizational weakness. Feelings of inefficacy or of cynicism are illustrative. These attitudes, however, would not necessarily be *explained* by low socioeconomic status. Instead, they may reflect the experience of people who have tried and failed. One success may be the key to further organizational effort. Also, because the barriada people have had to fight so hard for the little they do have, they may have a very low risk-potential level. Alternatively, those who have achieved something may be relatively satisfied and believe that future economic mobility is possible.

A third category of possible factors are nonattitudinal. Of these, potentially the most important are time and leadership skills. People living in poverty consume many hours in such tasks as washing clothes, buying and preparing food, traveling to and from work. Wage-earners work long hours, and leisure time to spend in organizational efforts is limited. Meetings attended by this writer customarily began at 10:00 PM. Skills to make people devote time, energy and money—to make them feel a sense of purpose and part of a group that can be effective—are rare. However, if these, and not attitudes, are the important factors, then the likelihood for change becomes much greater.

Because the barriadas differ so greatly, it would be possible to determine, by systematic interviewing, the possible relevance of these three categories of factors as explanations of nonbehavior. Two potentially important differences between the barriadas are economic and cultural ones. Some barriadas are slums, especially those surrounding the central market place in an area known as El Augustino. Many, but not all, of the people living there have come directly from the sierra. They still speak Quechua and have not been assimilated into the Spanish culture of the Lima coastal region. A markedly different area is Comas. Most of these barriadas have been formed by invasion by people who first had acquired job security and then wanted land to assure themselves a permanent home. They are poor communities, but not slums.

What are the attitudes of people who have been culturally assimilated and have experienced some economic mobility, compared to those of the recent Indian migrant living in slum conditions without a stable source of income? If neither group expresses beliefs reflective of culture, that category of attitudes can be dismissed as an explanation for noninvolvement in organizational efforts.

It is likely that many of the inhabitants of Comas are proud of what they have achieved. Is this sense of achievement related to satisfaction with things as they are, or to a desire for more? If the latter, does their belief in their own ability to achieve vary with prior experience, or are their attitudes uniformly expressed suggesting feelings of inefficacy, cynicism and distrust? How do the attitudes of the new migrants compare? I would hypothesize that neither group is satisfied, and that experience accounts for the attitudinal variations within the first group. The new migrant is too busy with the problems of day-to-day existence to set future goals; and he still lacks sufficient information about the environment he now inhabits to conceptualize future possibilities. Perhaps some economic security and cultural assimilation are necessary for organizational involvement.

Finally, do attitudes vary with generation? People instrumental in an invasion effort may feel a sense of accomplishment; but do their children feel the same? Because this younger generation is not being given the opportunity to acquire the skills necessary for economic and social mobility out of the barriada, they may feel frustration in contrast to their parents' sense of achievement. The outlet for such frustration could be social or political activity, but criminal activity to satisfy material needs is just as likely, as the preceding chapter illustrates.

Four structural variables differentiate the barriadas. These are: type of origin (by invasion or by some other means), time of origin, type of construction materials used in dwelling units (straw or some more durable material), and location (flat land or hills). In part, these structural differences reflect the differences discussed above. People living in brick homes are better off economically than those living in straw huts. The date the barriada was formed gives some insight into what has been achieved over time. People instrumental in an invasion effort have first lived in the inner city and probably have succeeded in their assimilation efforts. They are now *mestizos*, unlike the Indian from the sierra who settle in a slum barriada immediately upon arriving in the city.

As previously suggested, systematic probing of individual attitudes in these different types of barriadas could tell us something about the relative importance of experience in shaping attitudes, in contrast to attitudes which somehow are intrinsically a part of culture or irrevocably associated with lower socioeconomic status. If attitudes regarding self-capabilities, future improvement possibilities, efficacy and the like do vary with experience, then, perhaps, with the right kind of leadership skills, social-political change may occur after all.

NOTES

1. Source: Junta Nacional de la Vivienda and Dirección de Estadística y Censos. These data are estimated figures only, indicating relative, not absolute, differences between districts. They were derived by taking the number of barriada families in each district and multiplying by five, the average barriada family size. Total district population figures were taken from the official 1961 Population Census.

2. Because the vote received by Samone was so small, it is excluded from the following analysis.

3. For example, Belaúnde received 39.9, 35.3 and 33.4 percent of the vote in the districts of Category 5. His average vote in Category 5 was thus 36.2 percent.

4. These are definitional statements only, not presumed empirical relationships.

5. Information contained in this section was obtained from interviews with officials at the Junta Nacional de la Vivienda.

6. *La Prensa,* July 20 and 22, 1968, p. 1.

7. Interview with an official of Cooperación Popular.

8. The only exception known to the author was the March of the Barriadas, planned for July 24, 1968. The march did not occur because the law granting land titles, previously discussed, was decreed on July 19.

9. Students at the Escuela de Servicio Social are required to spend time working in the barriadas. This point was reiterated many times in the reports they wrote on barriada community organizations.

10. G. A. Almond and S. Verba, *The Civic Culture: Political Attitudes and Democracy in Five Nations* (Princeton: Princeton University Press, 1963).

David Collier

6.

The Politics of
Squatter Settlement
Formation in Peru*

The formation of squatter settlements [1] around major cities in the rapidly urbanizing countries of the Third World has been recognized as an important mechanism for easing the plight of large numbers of cityward migrants. It is argued that these settlements substantially reduce the shortage of low-cost housing, provide rent-free housing for many poor families, and offer opportunities for improvement of housing by the residents and for community projects that both improve the community physically and contribute to a sense of identification with the community.[2] However, the political significance of this aspect of settlements and settlement formation has not been adequately assessed.

The present research is concerned with exploring the political significance of settlement formation on the basis of data from Lima, Peru. The argument is that previous writings on Lima settlements have given only scant attention to one of the most important political facts regarding the settlements: namely, that their formation has in considerable measure been promoted by the Peruvian government, and that settlement formation became a large-scale movement in Lima with the support of a conservative military government that sought to substitute a paternalistic style of elite-mass relations for the pattern of class politics that was emerging in Peru during the late 1940s. This research examines the history of the government's role in the settlements on the basis of data collected by the author on settlement formation. Following the analysis of settlement formation, the kinds of paternalistic political relationships that have formed around the government's role are examined.

* This is revised from a paper presented at the 1971 Annual Meeting of the American Political Science Association in Chicago. The research was carried out while the author

In exploring the policy of the Peruvian government toward squatter settlements, we seek to contribute to a growing literature that attempts to give public policy serious attention as a variable in studies of political development. Following a period during which social science research on the political consequences of modernization focused rather narrowly on the political consequences of social and economic change,[3] more recent research has adopted an increasingly complex view of these consequences. It has begun to emphasize the fact that public policy itself can influence both the direction of social and economic change and the types of political relationships that emerge as a consequence of social and economic change.[4]

This chapter offers a clear example of the way in which public policy can influence the kinds of political relationships that emerge within a context of rapid social change. Since it has been widely argued that settlements in Lima ease the transition to urban life for low-income migrants, and since the government is in considerable measure responsible for the appearance of settlements, it appears that public policy has had an important influence on the consequences of urbanization —including, as we shall see, the political consequences. It is clearly impossible to analyze the consequences of rapid urbanization in Peru without considering the role of public policy.

Sources of Data

The analysis of settlement formation in Lima is based on data covering the period through 1972. Detailed information was collected on the formation of 84 settlements by means of a questionnaire prepared by the author, as well as from published and archival sources.[5] The questionnaire was applied to 92 settlement leaders who were familiar with the history of particular settlements, using both closed and open-ended questions to discover in the greatest possible detail how each of the settlements was formed. Additional information

was a Latin American Teaching Fellow at the Instituto de Estudios Peruanos, Lima. The Latin American Studies Program of Indiana University supported a brief return trip to Peru in 1972. Sinesio López, Jorge Reyes, Fernando Calderón and Dale Nelson provided indispensable assistance with the survey of settlement leaders.

was collected on 52 other settlements from the records of two government housing offices.[6] These data are less complete, and are not used extensively, but give at least some idea of what was involved in many of the remaining cases of settlement formation. The smaller sample of 84 settlements includes 40 percent of the settlements and 82 percent of the settlement population of greater Lima. The 136 settlements in the larger, total sample that includes the cases of less complete information represent 65 percent of the settlements and 90 percent of their population. [7]

Squatter Settlements in Lima

Lima offers a highly favorable geographical and climatic setting for squatter settlements. The virtual absence of rain means that the minimal straw mat houses that first appear when settlements form are far more adequate than they would be in less favorable climates. The absence of rain also simplifies the basic drainage problems of these communities. The disaster of settlements being washed down hillsides after heavy rains is unlikely to occur in Lima. Likewise, the climate does not present the hardships of cold winters found in cities such as Santiago or Buenos Aires. Finally, the fact that Lima is surrounded largely by unused desert means that large areas of land are available for the formation of new settlements.

For the poor of Lima, these settlements offer an important alternative to the more crowded slums of the inner city. One of the major advantages is that settlement residents generally do not pay rent, though there are some cases of subletting. This is a great help to poor families, particularly in periods of unemployment or sickness of the wage-earner, and in old age. Though migrants lack the skills needed for many urban occupations, one skill that they often bring with them is the ability to build their own houses. The settlements provide an environment in which this ability is important. Also, in most settlements, the residents have space to keep a few animals—chickens,

* The "straw" (estera) houses are more correctly wicker matting sections usually made from split bamboo tied to a pole framework.

ducks and perhaps a pig—which provide a source of food that may help a family to make it through periods of little or no income.

Because groups of relatives, friends or people from the same province often join together in the formation of settlements, and because new arrivals often come to join relatives or friends in the settlement after its initial formation, the settlement resident tends to be surrounded by a network of friends and both real and ritual kinsmen, forming a supportive social environment. The existence of this environment, and the presence of many opportunities for community improvement through self-help—improvement both of individual houses and community facilities—leads to a high degree of cooperation among neighbors, and to an ideology of self-improvement which is commonly expressed by leaders of settlements and actively encouraged by the government and private agencies that work in settlements. This ideology emphasizes the ways in which settlements are a world where people can get ahead through cooperation among neighbors and self-help, and perhaps diverts attention from some of the more basic problems of Lima's poor—such as underemployment and low income.

Basic Types of Settlement Formation

Our assessment of the government's role in Lima's settlements will begin with an examination of three basic types of settlement formation: invasions, government authorization and gradual formation.[8]

Invasions. The literature on Lima settlements has devoted a great deal of attention to invasions.[9] Invasions commonly occur at night, and are typically planned with great care. The leaders often organize well before the invasion occurs and meet many times to recruit members, choose a site and plan the occupation itself. In the more elaborately planned invasions, there are systems of delegates who are responsible for recruiting members from given areas of the city, and are in charge of the families from their area when the invasion takes place.

Police reaction to invasions ranges from not appearing at all to the violent eviction of the invaders from the site. The police are usually aware of invasions before they occur, and during at least one period they gave the government housing agency that deals with settlements information about when invasions would occur, who was leading them and what land would be occupied. The police have often evicted invaders when the land involved has unquestionably been private property. Their reaction when land of ambiguous title was involved depends on the political influence of the claimants, and on the government under which the invasion occurs. There is apt to be less police interference when there is no claimant whatsoever.

Government Authorization. Settlement formation that receives some form of government authorization is the second major type. The literature on Lima's settlements has largely neglected this type of formation, although some instances of political involvement in the formation of settlements have been mentioned. For example, William Mangin notes that in one period the government showed considerable leniency toward invasions [10] and suggests that the support of a sympathetic political leader or journalist may be sought by the invading group to provide protection from police intervention.[11] John F. C. Turner describes a case in which a city-wide settlement organization provided important support for an invasion,[12] and Henry Dietz describes a case in which a government housing agency relocated families in a squatter settlement.[13]

These observations on the role of political groups represent a useful step toward recognizing the importance of political support in the formation of settlements. However, in the past we have not had sufficient evidence about settlement formation to permit an assessment of either how important political support has been, or the types of governments or groups that have most actively given it.

In general, political support has taken the form of government authorization. In one type of authorization, the formation of the settlement resembles the basic invasion pattern except that there is an informal suggestion from a government official, often a representative of the president, that a particular piece of land is available for occupation and that the police will not interfere if it is occupied. This type of government involvement may be motivated by the desire to gain popular support, but it is also used as a way of facilitating the eviction of tenants from inner-city slums in order to permit wealthy landowners to develop the land for other purposes.

In other cases of government authorization, there is a more formal and public approval of the occupation of the land, occasionally through a special decree or law. In such cases, the occupation of the land does not occur at night, and often government or army trucks carry the families to their new home sites, simply leaving them in the desert to build their new community. Such authorizations are usually accompanied by promises of title to the land, although until recently these have rarely been supplied, and settlements that are formed with this type of authorization often end up being indistinguishable from those formed without government authorization. This type of government involvement occurs in a variety of situations. It may occur when the dispute over an eviction has become public and the government wishes to intervene dramatically in a way that gives the impression that it is concerned with the plight of the poor. In other cases, it may be used to aid families who have been left homeless by a flood, earthquake or fire. Such authorizations have also been used systematically as a means of gaining political support from the poor.

The government has also intervened in many cases after the initial formation of the settlement in order to prevent the police from evicting invasion groups.

Gradual Formation. The third type of settlement formation, gradual formation,[14] differs from both invasions and government authorization in that there is not a well-defined moment at which a substantial group of families occupies the land. This type of formation may occur in a semirural area where one or a few families are living in shacks on land which they are cultivating or quarrying, and are joined over the years by other families who build houses nearby, thus producing a pattern of gradual growth of the community without any well-defined starting point. Cases of gradual formation have also occurred within the city, in situations where construction workers build temporary houses on vacant land near the construction sites where they are working and, rather than leave when the construction is over, they stay on and are joined over the years by other families.

Government Role in Settlement Formation

An examination of the data on settlements suggests that, of these three basic types of formation, the one involving government authorization is far more important than has previously been realized. In the larger sample of 136 settlements referred to earlier, the three basic types of settlement formation are of approximately equal importance, with 30 percent of the cases involving government authorization, 37 percent invasions, and 30 percent gradual occupation (see Table 1). The remaining settlements did not fall clearly into any of these categories.

Because settlements vary greatly in size, it is useful to examine not only the number of settlements in each category, but also the proportion of the settlement population that lives in each type of settlement. This allows us to assess the importance of each type of formation in terms of the number of families to whom it has offered a chance to find better housing.[15] From this point of view, government authorization is by far the most important type of settlement formation—61 percent of the residents of settlements in the larger sample live in settlements formed by government authorization, as opposed to 27 percent in those formed by invasion, and 11 percent by gradual occupation.

Since the government role in settlement formation has involved not only outright authorization, but also intervention after the occupation of land (in cases which we have been treating as invasions), the figures that have been presented so far clearly underestimate the importance of the government's role. The smaller sample of 84 cases on which there is more complete information may be used to examine this government involvement more closely. It is important to note that a somewhat larger proportion of the cases in the smaller sample involve government authorization—42 percent, as opposed to 30 percent in the larger sample (see Table 1).[16]

Looking more closely at the cases of formation previously classified either as government authorization or as invasions, we may distinguish the following types of political involvement in settlement formation: (1) informal intervention by some branch of the national executive before the actual invasion, to encourage the formation of the invasion group and indicate that land is available; (2) public authorization by some branch of the national executive before the occupation of the land; (3) informal intervention by the national executive after the occupation of the land, to limit police intervention; (4) involvement of a political party other than that of the president; (5) possible government involvement, but lack of full information; and (6) no apparent political involvement.

Table 1
TYPES OF SQUATTER SETTLEMENT FORMATION *

Type of Formation	Larger Sample				Smaller Sample			
	Number of Settlements	%	Population	%	Number of Settlements	%	Population	%
Government Authorization	41	30.1	465,169	61.3	35	41.7	460,495	67.0
Invasion	50	36.8	205,762	27.1	37	44.0	177,539	25.8
Gradual Occupation	41	30.1	85,008	11.2	11	13.1	48,702	7.1
Other	4	2.9	3,079	0.4	1	1.2	580	0.1
Total	136	99.9	759,018	100.0	84	100.0	687,316	100.0

* This and the following tables cover the period through 1972.

Table 2 shows that, among the cases in the smaller sample that were classified earlier as government authorization, most involved either informal intervention by the government before the occupation of the land or public authorization before the occupation. In the remaining four cases, occupation was authorized by a nonpresidential political party. In these last four, all of which occurred during the 1960s, the settlement appeared in a municipal district that was controlled by a nonpresidential political party, and thus involved authorization by a municipal government, rather than the national government. Among the cases that were originally classified as invasions, ten involved informal intervention by the government after the occupation of the land. Five involved some role of a nonpresidential party (though in none of these could this be said to have been crucial in the formation of the settlement); seven involved some evidence of a government role, but not enough to permit assigning the cases to another category; and in 15 cases there is no evidence at all of either government or party involvement.

We may assess the overall importance of government involvement by indicating the number of settlements in which the support of the government may be said to have been crucial. It was certainly crucial in cases of government authorization (see the first column of Table 2), and

Table 2
TYPE OF SQUATTER SETTLEMENT FORMATION BY ROLE OF
POLITICAL GROUPS
(Government Authorizations and Invasions from Smaller Sample)

Role of Political Group	Type of Formation		
	Government Authorization	Invasion	Total
Informal government intervention, preoccupation	15	—	15
Public authorization, preoccupation	16	—	16
Informal government intervention, postoccupation	—	10	10
Intervention by nonpresidential party	4	5	9
Possible government involvement, but ambiguity or insufficient information	—	7	7
No apparent political involvement	—	15	15
Total	35	37	72

it may be argued that it was also crucial in the ten instances of informal government intervention after the occupation (in column two), since, failing this intervention, the police would probably have evicted the invaders. In addition, we may somewhat arbitrarily say that half (rounded to four out of seven) of the cases in row five involve a crucial government role. We thus get a total of 49 cases out of 72, or 68 percent, in which the government's role is crucial. Since this sample was biased toward cases of government involvement, this impressive figure is obviously too large. We would not wish to infer from it that the government's role was crucial in 68 percent of all cases of settlement formation in Lima. However, we may come closer to estimating the overall percentage by adding to these 49 cases in the smaller sample the six cases of government authorization from the larger sample which were not included in the smaller sample (see Table 1). This gives us 55 cases out of 136, or 40 percent of the larger sample, in which the government's role may be said to be crucial. If we consider the entire universe of squatter settlements to be 208 (see footnote 7), we may still argue that the government's role was crucial in the formation of more than a quarter (55 out of 208 cases, or 26 percent) of the settlements in Lima—at the very least. This is obviously an overly modest estimate of the importance of the government's role, since there are certainly additional cases of government involvement in part of the larger sample about which there was less complete information, as well as among the settlements which were not included in either sample. Thus, the real percentage is certainly somewhat higher.

If the findings are presented in terms of the percentage of the residents who live in these settlements, the finding is even more impressive. These 55 settlements have a population of 563,169, or 67 percent of the settlement universe. This leads to the startling conclusion that at the very *least,* over half a million people—that is, over a sixth of the total population of metropolitan Lima—live in settlements in whose formation the government played a crucial role.

Periods of Formation

In order to gain an understanding of the political meaning of settlement formation, we must go beyond the frequency of each type of formation to examine the major periods during which settlements have been formed and the most important periods of government support for their formation. We may begin by examining the number and the population of the settlements that were formed under each of the presidents of Peru since 1930. In terms of the number of settlements formed, the first major period was that of Odría, with the second government of Prado also being extremely important (see Table 3). In terms of present population, the first major period was again that of Odría, with the settlements formed under the present government of Velasco also having a very large population, in spite of their recent formation.[17] If the massive growth of settlements since 1972 (the date of the population estimates in Table 3) is considered, the Velasco period is clearly the most important.

Since these presidents were in office for unequal periods, it is also useful to calculate the *rate* of formation under each president (not

Table 3
NUMBER AND POPULATION OF SQUATTER SETTLEMENTS FORMED
UNDER EACH PRESIDENT
(Larger Sample)

President	Number of Cases	%	Population (1972)‡	%
Pre-Sánchez Cero (1900–30)	2	1.5	2,712	0.4
Sánchez Cero (1930–31, 1931–33)	3	2.2	12,975	1.7
Benavides (1933–39)	8	5.9	18,888	2.5
Prado (1939–45)	8	5.9	6,930	0.9
1945—ambiguous *	5	3.7	24,335	3.2
Bustamante (1945–48)	16	11.8	38,545	5.1
Odría (1948–56)	30	22.1	203,877	26.9
1956—ambiguous *	2	1.5	11,890	1.6
Prado (1956–62)	30	22.1	93,249	12.3
1962—ambiguous *	2	1.5	22,377	2.9
Pérez Godoy (1962–63)	2	1.5	1,737	0.2
Lindley (1963)	3	2.2	11,046	1.5
Belaúnde (1963–68)	15	11.0	93,407	12.3
Velasco (1968–1972 only)	10	7.4	217,050	28.6
Total	136	100.3	759,018	100.1

* One major source of data for the larger sample indicated the year, but not the month, of formation. Hence, for a few settlements, it was not possible to be certain whether they were formed under the outgoing or the incoming president.

‡ See footnotes 7 and 17.

shown in table). The highest rates were under the government of Bustamante, with an average of 5.1 settlements being formed per year, and the second government of Prado, with 5.0 per year. This was followed by Odría, with 3.9 per year, Belaúnde with 2.9 and Velasco with 2.8. The rates prior to 1945 were far lower: 1.4 under the first government of Prado, and 1.2 under Benavides. It thus appears that the periods before 1945 were of little importance. There was a sharp increase in the rate of settlement formation in that year, and the following periods, involving the governments of Bustamante, Odría and the second government of Prado, were the most important periods of settlement formation.

We may also examine the types of settlement formation which occurred during each of these periods. Looking first at the three basic types of formation for the cases in the larger sample (see Table 4), it appears that 17 of the 26 cases formed prior to and including the 1945-ambiguous category involved gradual formation. Five of the nine remaining settlements are instances of invasions, and there are just two authorizations. Under Bustamante, between 1945 and 1948, there is an abrupt increase in the proportion of invasions, and the Odría period is clearly the starting point for extensive government authorizations,

Table 4
TYPE OF FORMATION BY PRESIDENT
(Larger Sample)

PRESIDENT	Government Authoriza- tion	Type of Formation			Total
		Invasion	Gradual Occupation	Other	
Pre-Sánchez Cerro (1900–30)	–	1	1	–	2
Sánchez Cerro (1930–31, 1931–33)	1	1	1	–	3
Benavides (1933–39)	1	3	4	–	8
Prado (1939–45)	–	–	6	2	8
1945–ambiguous	–	–	5	–	5
Bustamante (1945–48)	1	6	8	1	16
Odría (1948–56)	11	11	8	–	30
1956–ambiguous	–	2	–	–	2
Prado (1956–62)	11	11	7	1	30
1962–ambiguous	–	1	1	–	2
Pérez Godoy (1962–63)	–	2	–	–	2
Lindley (1963)	1	2	–	–	3
Belaúnde (1963–68)	12	3	–	–	15
Velasco (1968–72 only)	3	7	–	–	10
Total	41	50	41	4	136

being also a period of many invasions. The second Prado government, like that of Odría, is a period of many invasions and authorizations, and under Belaúnde there were many more authorizations than invasions, with no cases of gradual occupation. It appears that there is a clear trend toward greater government involvement, beginning in 1948.

Table 5
ROLE OF POLITICAL GROUPS BY PRESIDENT
(Smaller Sample)

President	Informal government intervention, pre-occupation	Public authorization preoccupation	Informal government intervention, post-occupation	Intervention by non-presidential party	Possible government involvment but am-biguous or insufficient information	No apparent political involvement	Total
Sánchez Cerro	1	–	–	–	1	–	2
Benavides	1	–	–	–	–	–	1
Prado–I	–	–	–	–	–	–	0
Bustamante	–	–	5	–	–	1	6
Odría	6	4	2	1	2	3	18
Prado–II	5	2	3	1	2	3	16
Pérez Godoy	–	–	–	–	1	–	1
Lindley	–	1	–	2	–	–	3
Belaúnde	2	6	–	5	1	1	15
Velasco (to 1972)	–	3	–	–	–	7	10
Total	15	16	10	9	7	15	72

Turning to the more detailed classification of types of political involvement in the smaller sample (see Table 5), we find that many of the cases under Bustamante that were previously listed as invasions are actually settlements in which the government became involved after the initial occupation of the land. Under Odría, in addition to the 11 cases previously identified as involving government authorization, there were two instances of informal government intervention after the invasion, two cases of incomplete information with some suggestion of a government role, and only three cases for which there was no evidence of political involvement. This was a period of extensive government involvement in settlement formation. The other two main periods of settlement formation—the second government of

Prado, and the Belaúnde government—likewise show a variety of kinds of government involvement, and few cases in which political groups had no role at all.

The Emergence of Settlement Formation
as a Large-Scale Movement

It is clear from the data that we have examined that there was a sharp increase in the rate of settlement formation and in the government's involvement in settlement formation beginning in 1945. How can we explain this increase? We know that this was a period of rapid population growth in Lima. In the period between the national censuses of 1940 and 1961, metropolitan Lima's average annual rate of population growth was 5.4 percent.[18] However, the rapid rate of growth over this 21-year period is not sufficient to explain the sudden increase in the rate of squatter settlement formation starting in 1945.

Within this context of rapid urbanization, the more immediate causes of the increase in the rate of settlement formation must be sought in the political situation in Peru.[19] The end of President Prado's first term, which lasted from 1939 to 1945, was a period when the APRA party (Alianza Popular Revolucionaria Americana) was emerging from a period of illegality and preparing to enter the 1945 elections. APRA, a middle-class party with a strong base in the labor movement, had been perceived for many years by Peru's traditional political forces as a serious threat to the established political order.With the reemergence of APRA, this became a period of more active, competitive party politics—a period in which APRA was actively building its party base at the local and national levels. It was also a period of active labor organizing on the part of APRA, and of greater government tolerance of labor unions.

APRA entered the 1945 national elections as part of the National Democratic Front, winning the presidency for the non-APRA presidential candidate of the coalition, and gaining an APRA majority in the Congress. Having thus achieved substantial access to government resources, APRA became even more active in building its party and union bases. It is within this context that we must view the sudden increase in the rate of squatter settlement formation in Lima.

Fragments of information about the invasions that took place during this period suggest that individuals from various political parties, including the Communist party, and perhaps others connected with APRA, were involved. There is even clearer evidence that the man who was Minister of Government during part of this period, General Manuel Odría, was also involved in the invasions, intervening on at least three occasions and ordering police not to evict invaders once they had occupied the land. The circumstances of Odría's rise to his position in this ministry must be understood in order to interpret his role in the squatter settlements.

The period between 1945 and 1948 was a time of considerable political unrest and violence, much of which APRA appeared to have caused. Following the assassination of Graña, a leading conservative newspaper editor, Odría was appointed Minister of Government (hence he was in charge of the police)—with the job of investigating the assassination and other violence that was occurring. As head of the ministry, he became the center of anti-APRA sentiment in the cabinet, believing that a government coalition with APRA was impossible, and that the party would have to be outlawed. Odría was therefore interested in finding ways of competing with APRA's popular appeal, and it seems that his intervention on behalf of poor families who had formed settlements and were threatened by police eviction was one of the ways in which he sought to do this.

The data available on this period make it difficult to present an exact assessment of the relative importance of newly mobilized party groups, as opposed to Odría, in encouraging the sudden increase in the rate of settlement formation that occurred at this time. It is clear that both were involved, and also clear that Odría's appeal to the settlements was made neccessary and relevant by the fact that the reemergence of APRA had made this a period in which military leaders who wished to gain political power had to make some attempt to get popular support. Hence, the APRA's reemergence is a crucial, immediate cause of the increase in settlement formation, regardless of the exact proportion of the invasions in which they were involved.

In early October of 1948, a faction of APRA attempted a military coup, which was quickly suppressed. Three weeks after this revolt, Odría toppled the coalition government in a coup of his own, enjoying the strong support of the Peruvian Right as he assumed the presidency. Bustamante had already outlawed APRA, and Odría actively sought to destroy its power and the union and party groups that it had formed. Large numbers of APRA members were arrested, others went into exile, and unions linked to APRA were destroyed or taken over by leaders sympathetic to Odría. However, Odría's campaign against APRA was not based solely on repression, but equally on a strong appeal that he made to the working and poorer classes, in which he tried to offer an alternative to the kind of popular mobilization that APRA was promoting. As James L. Payne put it, Odría

> was antiunion but not antiworker. While on one hand he gave employers what amounted to complete liberty to destroy the unions in their shops, he would give startling wage and social benefits to the workers. He decreed, for example, seven blanket wage increases while in power. Odría [left] power with many people convinced that he had done more for the worker than anyone in the history of Peru. Odría's labor policy was, in an elephantine manner, paternalistic.[20]

Odría's effort to establish a more paternalistic relationship between the government and Lima's poorer classes was not restricted to the area of labor relations. He placed tremendous emphasis on charity and on gifts to the poor. In this way he sought to provide an alternative to the political arrangement that APRA had been trying to promote, in which government benefits were made available in response to the mobilization and articulation of the interests of the poorer sectors. Odría's wife, María, in imitation of Eva Perón, played an important role in this show of paternalism, making frequent charitable visits to the poor, visits which were extensively publicized by pictures on the front page of the government newspaper.

One of the most important aspects of Odría's effort to reestablish a more paternalistic kind of politics was his extensive promotion of settlement formation. The most spectacular case of government involvement during the Odría period was the formation of the settlement called "27th of October," named after the day of Odría's coup. A special law established a new political district with this name, and gave an association made up of Odría's supporters the power to enroll members to settle in the district and develop it into an immense authorized settlement, which is now the second largest in Peru. The headquarters of the association had large pictures of Odría and his wife in the main room and, interestingly enough, of Juan and Eva Perón as well. The residents of the settlement were periodically marched to Lima's central plaza in massive demonstrations of support for Odría on occasions such as the anniversary of the coup, his birthday, and his wife's birthday.

Other settlements formed during this period were named after Odría, his wife, his home province and the wife of one of his close associates; one was also formed on Odría's birthday. The naming of settlements after things associated with Odría, the demonstrations in the central plaza, the idea of the president intervening when the poor needed help and offering them land to form settlements—these and many other devices were used to build the idea that the poor had a special relationship with Odría. They were all part of Odría's attempt to substitute a paternalistic relationship between the president and the poor for the more drastic kind of political change that APRA had been promoting.

It is interesting to note that, in spite of the extensive and public involvement of the Odría government in promoting settlement formation, and in spite of its promises to grant land titles to the residents in certain cases, the Odría government in fact rarely granted land titles in the settlements. When viewed in terms of Odría's concern with reestablishing a paternalistic relationship between the government and the popular classes, this failure is quite understandable. If the squatters were simply located on public land, their security of tenure on that land appeared to depend on the willingness of the state, and particularly that of the president, to let them stay there. If they received title, their security of tenure would have had a formal, legal basis that was independent of the goodwill of the president. This failure to give land titles thus reinforced the idea that the squatters were dependent on having a special connection with the president of Peru.

Another way in which Odría's policies tended to increase dependency of the poor on the government can be seen in his relation to political groups. Though Odría attempted to control political mobilization by destroying the strong party organization and aggressive labor unions that APRA had been promoting, he did not try to eliminate all political groups. Indeed, through his support of settlement formation, Odría also promoted the formation of the dwellers' associations that typically appear when a settlement is formed. These associations played an important role in Odría's relation to the settlements, for they formed the organizational basis for the numerous demonstrations in the central plaza, and later for a political party through which Odría hoped to perpetuate himself in power. In a sense, community associations that "mobilize" people to participate in mass demonstrations seem to differ little from the political groups that APRA had been forming. However, the type of participation that Odría promoted only served to express political support that was unrelated to demand-making, and therefore quite distinct from the APRA movement.

In general, these settlement associations have not made significant demands on the political system; rather they channel outputs and express support. The associations exist largely for the purpose of carrying out community projects and for cooperating with any government or other aid programs that are available, often changing their leadership at the beginning of a new national president's term in order to maximize such cooperation. In promoting settlement formation, Odría was thus creating a new world of benign associational linkages for poor people in order to insulate them from radical appeals.

Settlement Formation and the
Opposition to Odría

Odría used squatter settlements so successfully in building popular support [21] that any politician who wished to oppose him not only had to concern himself with problems of housing, but was inevitably tempted to get directly involved with settlement formation as well. In this sense, it would seem that Odría had defined one of the major ways in which the problem of urban poverty would be treated as an issue in Peruvian politics—that is, as a problem of housing. This was a desirable way for the problem of poverty to be treated from the point of view of the political Right—far more desirable than the more radical terms in which APRA had raised the problem, and one that lent itself to inexpensive solutions, such as settlement formation. It is therefore not surprising to find that Odría's political opponents—even those on the Right—made a calculated appeal to the settlements for political support.

As the end of Odría's term of office approached, a group of conservative leaders who wanted to be sure that Odría did not stay on as president began to prepare for the 1956 presidential elections. They were interested in competing with him for political support, and establishing their own credibility with the masses in the area where Odría had won the most popular support, such as the settlements. It is the overwhelming opinion of most Peruvians who have had long experience with the settlements that people closely associated with this conservative group—most prominently the conservative newspaper publisher Pedro Beltrán—were intimately involved in sponsoring one of the largest settlement invasions ever to take place in Peru, that of the Ciudad de Dios (City of God) settlement, formed on Christmas Eve, 1954.

The involvement of this conservative group was not restricted to this invasion. Another aspect of their competition for support involved a case of settlement formation on land which was claimed by a landowner associated with them who was also a leading figure in the Asociación Nacional de Propietarios (ANP), an association of landowners in urban areas. The government newspaper, *La Nación,* covered the dispute with a series of front-page stories accompanied by headlines printed in red ink. Every effort was made to present the ANP leader as an enemy of the people. Counterstories appeared in Beltrán's *La Prensa,* a newspaper associated with ANP, defending the man who claimed the land and the rights of private property. At one point the claimant decided to sell the disputed land to the squatters who were occupying it for a symbolic price, and *La Prensa* hailed him as a friend of the people, while *La Nación* attacked him as a fraud for pretending to sell land that he did not own.

In order to present themselves as sympathetic to the housing needs of the poor, *La Prensa* and the ANP conducted a campaign to promote new housing policies that would ease Lima's housing crisis and at the same time protect private property. A central feature of their program was the abolition of rent-control laws, which they claimed had destroyed the incentive to invest in new housing. *La Prensa* carried numerous editorials on this subject, and in 1954 donated a full page of space to a periodic "Bulletin" of the ANP, which deplored the growth of squatter settlements and urged the repeal of rent control. This campaign also emphasized the idea that every Peruvian should have his *casa propia,* his own house. Peruvians interviewed by the author who were knowledgeable about the history of housing policy in Peru felt that one of the main reasons for this emphasis was the belief of the conservatives that—if the poor possess their own house and even just a tiny plot of land, it gives them a feeling of being tied into the system, increases their respect for private property, and makes them less susceptible to radical appeals. This line of reasoning has an inherent plausibility, and is in fact reminiscent of Marx's famous characterization of the nineteenth-century small-holding peasants in France as resembling "potatoes in a sack," because of their inability to join together in a common political effort.[22]

The thinking of this group of conservatives is expressed with surprising clarity in the *Report on Housing in Peru* prepared by the Commission on Agrarian Reform and Housing, which was set up under the second government of Prado and headed by Pedro Beltrán.[23] In a chapter that outlines overall goals of housing policy, the *Report* discusses the advantages of

> a healthy and normal family life within a propitious environment, consisting primarily of the home, the neighborhood, and the local community. . . . Family life under these circumstances not only strengthens the moral fiber of the members . . . but is conducive to emotional stability, . . . and minimizes social conflict. . . . All these factors contribute to the country's security and stability. . . .[24]

A related idea is expressed in another section of the *Report* concerned with the role of the state in constructing housing. In discussing the advantages of the "decent and healthful" houses that the state will offer, the *Report* emphasizes that

> [S]tate housing not only should seek to place a decent dwelling at the disposal of families who cannot afford one but to provide a social education as well. . . . [T]he educational effort should inculcate in the people the conviction that only through their own efforts to raise their economic level will they be able to . . . achieve a better life.[25]

There is a striking similarity between the self-help tone of this document and Nun's description of the way in which the Victorian bourgeoisie in England

> skillfully exploited the deferential attitudes that persisted in the working class; . . . tirelessly diffused the values of its capitalist, liberal, and Christian ethic; . . . [and] enthusiastically promoted adhesion to a complex of institutions 'devoted to self-improvement and self-help' . . . .[26]

It thus appears that by making a popular appeal on the issues of housing and squatter settlements, this group of conservatives, like Odría, sought to control the poor politically.

Settlement Formation after Odría

A variety of other types of government involvement in settlements and settlement formation have appeared since Odría first gave the settlements their great political importance. Government policy has fluctuated widely, including a less active role in authorization under the second government of Prado, a period of rigid prohibition of invasions during the early sixties and a 1961 squatter settlement law that set up a procedure through which the government could legally be involved in the formation of new settlements. However, due to a failure of the Congress to appropriate funds and to a variety of other reasons, the government housing agency empowered to carry out the law had returned by the mid-1960s to a relatively informal and unplanned pattern of authorization that differed little from what had occurred before.

The period since Odría has been marked by the appearance of several kinds of involvement in settlement formation, apart from that of the national government, and these too reflect the impact of the Odría period. The second Prado government was the heyday of the *traficante,* the man who made a living working as an invasion leader and an advisor to settlements on legal and other problems. Though these leaders made use of party and government linkages, they were usually quite ready to shift their political loyalties as the situation dictated. Apparently some of these *traficantes* got their original experience with settlement formation in government-sponsored invasions during the Odría period. This is another example of how settlement formation as a large-scale movement got started under Odría. The four cases from the Belaúnde period that involved the sponsorship of settlements by opposition parties which controlled municipal governments have already been mentioned in the discussion of Table 2. Less complete information is available on a number of other cases of party involvement in invasions, including one spectacular case in 1968 in which APRA arranged an invasion of some land which was thought to belong to a prominent political opponent of APRA, the purpose being to force the owner to call the police to evict the invaders, thereby discrediting him as a friend of the poor.

The period since 1968—that of Velasco's reformist military government—has been characterized by an attempt to institutionalize government involvement in settlement formation within the framework of property law, under the terms of the 1961 law referred to above.* The government does not appear to be sponsoring invasions, and when invasions occur, it has not permitted the invasion groups to remain on the invaded land. Instead, the government has offered the families lots in government-sponsored settlements, most importantly a new settlement established by this government called Villa el Salvador. Though founded in mid-1971, by late 1972 this settlement

---

* For an extended discussion of settlement policy since 1968, see Collier, *Squatters and Oligarchs: Authoritarian Rule and Policy Change in Peru* (Baltimore: The John Hopkins University Press, 1976), ch. 7.

already had a population well over 100,000, with sufficient space for a far greater number of residents. The active granting of land titles in the settlement is also a central feature of the new settlement policy. [27]

The government has also experimented with a program of offering lots in government-sponsored settlements to any family which applies for one through the government housing office. However, for fear of stimulating a massive demand for new lots, this program has received little publicity, and hence has operated only on a very small scale. The most reliable way to get a lot, therefore, is to participate in an invasion and then get moved to a government-sponsored settlement. In addition, thousands of families were acquiring lots by occupying land at the edge of already established settlements.

Discussion of the Policy

We have seen that the Peruvian government's role in settlement formation in Lima has been far more extensive than was previously recognized, and that during certain periods, beginning with the period of Odría, the government has been extensively involved in promoting the formation of settlements in Lima. This government involvement first appeared as part of a broader attempt to reassert a paternalistic style of politics in the midst of a period of great political stress—stress due to the growing power of APRA.

The pattern of government involvement in settlements that has been described here contradicts common suppositions about the policies that are apt to be adopted by different types of governments toward settlement formation. It is often assumed that the willingness of governing groups to be less strict about protecting land from invasions by squatters is a function of their liberality, the more liberal governments being more concerned with the benefits that the poor can derive from settlement formation than with a rigid interpretation of property law. William Mangin and Carlos Delgado have used the term "liberal" to describe the quality of the political climate of the 1960s in Peru that made it possible for settlement formation to occur relatively freely. [28] Similarly, Talton F. Ray describes as "permissive" and "lenient" the attitudes toward the poor of the Acción Democrática governments of 1945 to 1948 and of 1959 in Venezuela that led them to tolerate extensive settlement formation.[29] By contrast, the Venezuelan military ruler Pérez Jiménez (1952 to 1958) was "dedicated to maintaining order, . . . and staunchly defended government and private property. . . . The image-conscious dictator thought [the squatter settlements] spoiled the new look of the capital, which he was remodeling, and bulldozed them off their sites. . . ." [30]

On the basis of these descriptions, one might imagine that liberal governments would generally be more flexible about permitting squatter invasions, and that military and conservative governments, taking a more legalistic view of the protection of property, would systematically oppose them. However, this does not fit the Peruvian case. Comparing the governments of Odría, Prado and Belaúnde, Odría's government, concerned as it was with the systematic repression of APRA, was certainly the least liberal, and yet settlement formation first became a large-scale movement with Odría's support.[31]

Although the major role of leaders such as Odría in settlement formation contradicts the assumptions of previous writings on squatter settlements, their role was entirely consistent with the general pattern of paternalistic politics that emerged at that time—a pattern in which aid programs were offered to new social sectors in a way that tended to limit or weaken their capacity to organize for independent demand-making. Aid programs and other public policies that tend to weaken the capacity of new political and social groups for independent demand-making are increasingly being recognized as an important part of Latin American politics.

A variety of terms have recently been applied to Latin America to identify these types of political relationships. Corporatism in labor relations, the practice of using government sponsorship and official recognition of unions as a means for controlling the development of organized labor, is an example of the use of public policy as a means of controlling a whole economic sector.[32] The expression "clientelism" has been applied to Latin America to describe political relationships that are initiated from above—in which programs of aid tend to establish or reinforce certain kinds of political control.[33] The term is applied in much the same way that "paternalistic" was used to describe Odría's policies toward the poor, and sheds particular light on the reason why, in spite of his extensive authorization of settlement formation, it made sense that Odría never actually legalized the settlements. John Duncan Powell has written that the

contract between patron and client ... is a private unwritten, informal agreement, and highly personalistic in content. There is no public scrutiny of the terms of such agreements. ... This stands in sharp contrast to the relationship ... in modern systems of political transactions. In essence, the patron-client pattern occurs in the realm of private accountability, the modern pattern in the realm of public accountability.[34]

In the clientelist relationship, the lack of public accountability obviously works to the disadvantage of the client, because of

the degree of power asymmetry between superior and subordinate. Superiors in a clientele system are relatively free to behave in an arbitrary and highly personalistic manner in dealing with their subordinates. Subordinates in a clientele system have relatively little recourse in such a situation.[35]

From this point of view, it might be argued that Odría's neglect of formal land titles gave him more power over the poor.

The more legalistic emphasis of the military government that came to power in 1968 clearly departs from this tradition of informality. An important source of this change appears to lie in the belief of this government that ambiguous property law may be a source of political instability. The land invasions and unrest in the Peruvian highlands during the 1960s were largely produced by serious ambiguities regarding landownership, and the government is anxious to end the widespread ambiguity of landownership in both rural and urban areas, as a means of preventing future instability. The empirical problem of distinguishing between the conditions under which informal land tenure arrangements may increase political control and the conditions under which they will produce instability is beyond the scope of the present discussion. What is clear is that the beliefs and policies of the present military government regarding the importance of property law differ notably from those that guided policy under Odría.

Still another expression that has been used to describe the type of aid programs that we are considering is "segmentary incorporation."[36] This term refers to a process similar to corporatism, in which

the most organized parts of a new social sector—such as the strongest
unions within the working class—receive substantial aid from the state
in a way that makes them more interested in seeking further immediate
benefits for themselves than in broadening and strengthening the labor
movement. Cotler has written that

> though the basic problem underdeveloped societies confront is that of
> creating ways and means for new population sectors to gain access to social
> and political resources—it might be added that to the extent that such
> incorporation is partial or in progressive steps [i.e., segmentary] it favors
> the maintenance of the system of domination as it expands, neutralizing
> the activities of those promoted by alienating them from the marginal
> sectors.[37]

In the case of the policy under consideration here, those who are
"promoted" are those who have moved into settlements. After
experiencing this improvement in their life situation, they may feel
less interest in defending the class interests of the poor in general, and
more concerned with protecting their own, more narrow interests.

It thus appears that the tendency for government policy to limit or
destroy the capacity of new social sectors to organize for demand-
making is not uniquely characteristic of policy toward settlements in
Peru. Rather, it is a tendency that has been widely noted. Hence, even
if the development of squatter settlements in Lima is atypical because
of the unusual extent to which the settlements offer a desirable
residential environment, and of the unusual degree of government
involvement in settlement formation, it appears that the type of political relationships that have developed around settlement formation
in Lima are in no way atypical for Latin America.

We have argued that an important policy response to the stress of
social and economic change in Peru—the involvement of the government in settlement formation—has played a significant role in
influencing the type of politics that has emerged in a context of rapid
urbanization. There has been a clear need for this policy perspective
in studies of urbanization and politics in developing countries. A
considerable body of research has appeared that attempts to explain
why it is that the urban poor in rapidly urbanizing countries are more

passive politically than had been anticipated by many early writers on urbanization.[38] This literature has devoted careful attention to explanatory factors—such as the nature of migration, the social and economic experiences of migrants in cities and the political characteristics and orientations of impoverished groups, and has largely neglected the political context in which urbanization occurs.[39] The data on Lima suggest that the government's policy of involvement in settlement formation has been an important part of this political context, and that it may have contributed significantly to the political passivity of marginal urban groups. The data thus suggest that public policy is a significant factor in explaining the political consequences of urbanization in Peru.

NOTES

1. Following roughly the current use of the term *pueblo joven* in Lima, the expression "squatter settlement" is used in this research to refer to residential communities formed by low-income families in which the houses are constructed mainly by the residents themselves, and which are formed with the anticipation that the residents will eventually become owners of their lots. This definition appears to neglect an important feature of settlements, namely, the illegality of squatting. This element has been excluded from the definition to permit the inclusion of the full range of degrees of illegality that are present among these communities in Lima. The definition thus includes communities such as the huge Villa el Salvador, which has been formed with the full authorization of the present military government. Since this authorization is simply the culmination of a long tradition of varying degrees of government support for settlement formation, it is clearly appropriate to include it in the definition. The criterion that the residents anticipate eventually becoming owners of their lots is intended to exclude certain communities which resemble settlements in some ways but which were formed through the renting either of houses or of lots on which the renters built houses.

2. See John F. C. Turner, "Barriers and Channels for Housing Development in Modernizing Countries," *Journal of the American Institute of Planners* 32, no. 3 (May 1967): 167-181, and "Uncontrolled Urban Settlement: Problems and Policies," *International Social Development Review*, no. 1 (1968): 107-130; William Mangin, "Latin American Squatter Settlements: A Problem and a Solution," *Latin American Research Review* 2, no. 3 (Summer 1967): 65-98, and "Squatter Settlements," *Scientific American* 217, no. 4 (October 1967): 21-29; Joan M. Nelson, "Urban Growth and Politics in Developing Nations: Prospects for the 1970's," Conference on Economic Development, Columbia University, 1970; Daniel M. Goldrich, et al., "The Political Integration of Lower-Class Urban Settlements in Chile and Peru," Chapter 4 of this volume; and Sandra Powell, "Political Participation in the Barriadas: A Case Study," Chapter 5 of this volume.

3. Daniel Lerner, *The Passing of Traditional Society* (New York: The Free Press, 1958), and Seymour M. Lipset, "Some Social Requisites of Democracy: Economic Development and Political Legitimacy," *American Political Science Review* 53 (March 1959): 69-105, were two of the most important statements within this perspective.

4. The failure to emphasize political factors in much political analysis has been interestingly discussed in Glenn D. Paige, "The Rediscovery of Politics," in *Approaches to Development: Politics, Administration, and Change*, ed. John D. Montgomery and William J. Siffin (New York: McGraw-Hill, 1966). The appearance of Albert O. Hirschman, *Journeys Toward Progress* (New York: Doubleday and Company, 1965) and Charles W. Anderson, *Politics and Economic Change in Latin America* (Princeton: D. Van Nostrand Co., 1967) represented a major shift toward recognizing policy as an important factor in Latin American development. Philippe C. Schmitter, *Interest Conflict and Political Change in Brazil* (Stanford: Stanford University Press, 1971), is an example of a more explicit focus on policy as an intervening variable between social and economic change and major political outcomes.

5. These additional sources included newspaper archives, archives in government housing offices, interviews with government administrators who had long experience

with settlements, and the following published sources: José Matos Mar, *Estudio de las barriadas limeñas* (Lima: Departmento de Antropología, Universidad Nacional Mayor de San Marcos, 1966); Carlos Enrique Paz Soldán, *Lima y sus suburbios* (Lima: Universidad Nacional Mayor de San Marcos, Biblioteca de Cultura Sanitaria, Instituto de Medicina Social, 1957); Fondo Nacional de Salud y Bienestar Social, *Barriadas de Lima metropolitana*, 1958-59 (Lima: 1960); William Mangin, "Urbanization Case History in Peru," in *Peasants in Cities*, ed. William Mangin (Boston: Houghton Mifflin Co., 1970), pp. 47-54; and Turner, "Barriers and Channels for Housing Development." These sources served as a check on the quality of the information obtained in the interviews with community leaders. Aside from assuring greater accuracy in the tabulations of various types of settlement formation, this information also served to provide confirmation from at least two or three sources of virtually all of the most important or dramatic cases of government involvement in settlement formation. Since different versions of what happened are sometimes offered by people who have different interests to promote or protect, this cross-checking is important.

6. The Oficina de Barrios Marginales of the Junta Nacional de la Vivienda allowed me to spend several weeks copying material from their files on Lima squatter settlements. Marcia Koth de Paredes of Plan Metropolitana de Lima generously provided other data on the formation of settlements.

7. The estimate of the universe was derived from the results of a 1970 census of Lima settlements which reported the existence of 273 settlements with a population of 761,755 (Oficina Nacional de Desarrollo de Pueblos Jóvenes, *Censo de población y vivienda de pueblos jóvenes* [Lima: 1971]). Several modifications had to be made in these figures. First, there have been ten cases of settlement formation or attempted formation since 1970. Second, 23 older communities were added which were considered settlements for the purposes of this research but have been excluded from government lists. Third, 45 communities were subtracted that had come to be considered settlements under the terms of a 1961 squatter settlement law that included in its definition of settlements communities that were formed through the renting of lots to families who built their own houses on the lots (see *Ley de barriadas* [Lima: Distribuidora Bendezu, 1965]). These communities were included in 1961 for political reasons, and do not really involve squatting.

This leaves a total of 261 settlements. An additional problem with this figure is that it includes a number of communities that had been studied by a government housing office in a survey carried out in 1961 and declared not to be settlements on the basis of criteria that corresponded closely to those used in this research. It is impossible to estimate the exact proportion, but an estimate was made on the following basis. In addition to the 136 settlements in the larger sample, 21 additional communities were known from my survey to be settlements, even though no detailed historical data were collected on them, giving a total of 156 known settlements. Of the remaining 105 settlements—the difference between 156 and 261—we may make the conservative assumption that half were communities that had been excluded in the 1961 survey and therefore should not be considered to be settlements. This would leave a total of 208 settlements, with a population of 841,075. The estimate of half is obviously a very rough guess, but even if the correct proportion that should be excluded is considerably smaller, it makes little difference in terms of the population of the communities involved, since they are all very small.

It should be noted that the sample overrepresents cases in which some political support for the formation was suspected, since, in addition to estimating the proportion of cases of settlement formation that involved political support, it was also a purpose of the research to discover what this support consists of when it occurs. This bias in the sample must be kept in mind. The sample also overrepresented large settlements on the assumption that they are more important, since they provide improved housing for far more poor families than do small settlements.

8. As was indicated in footnote 7, a number of communities that were formed by the renting of lots to families who built their own houses on them have been included in some definitions of squatter settlements, but are excluded here because they do not involve squatting in terms of any usual meaning of the term.

9. See Mangin, "Urbanization Case History in Peru," "Latin American Squatter Settlements," and "Squatter Settlements"; Goldrich, "The Political Integration of Lower-Class Settlements"—Chapter 4 of this book, and Turner, "Barriers and Channels for Housing Development."

10. Mangin, "Urbanization Case History in Peru," p. 50.

11. Mangin, "Squatter Settlements," p. 23.

12. Turner, "Barriers and Channels for Housing Development," p. 171.

13. Henry Dietz, "Urban Squatter Settlements in Peru: A Case History and Analysis," *Journal of Inter-American Studies* 11, no. 3 (1969): 364.

14. Mangin, "Latin American Squatter Settlements," p. 69.

15. Some caution is appropriate in dealing with the population data on squatter settlements. The number of families that actually participates in the initial formation of the settlement is usually small compared to the population of the settlement when it reaches its full size, often after many years of growth. In looking at the present population of the settlements, I do not intend to imply in the cases of government authorization that the government authorized the arrival of all of the families that arrived later on. Rather, one must think of the initial invasion or authorization as defining a particular area as being available for the formation of a new settlement, and one should note the present population of the settlement simply as a way of assessing how important a particular settlement (or period of formation) is in terms of the number of families to which it offered a new housing opportunity.

16. This results from a bias in the sample, mentioned in footnote 7, toward getting the best information on the cases that seemed most likely to be instances of government involvement.

17. Because of the pattern of gradual growth of settlements referred to in footnote 15, many of the present-day residents of settlements formed in the earlier periods actually arrived more recently. The relative importance that one assigns the different periods of formation thus depends on whether one emphasizes the period in which the land was defined as a settlement, or the period when the residents arrived. If one emphasizes the latter criterion, the periods of Belaúnde and the second government of Prado are more important than is implied in Table 3. The period of Odría is undeniably important in any case. I would like to thank Marcia Koth de Paredes for emphasizing this problem of interpreting population data in a discussion of these findings.

18. These population figures are taken from Dirección Nacional de Estadística y Censos, *Censo nacional de población de 1940*, vol. 5 (Lima: N.D.), p. 5, and Dirección Nacional de Estadística y Censos, *Sexto censo nacional de población*, vol. 3 (Lima: 1966), p. 187. Criteria for defining metropolitan Lima and the formula for calculating the rate of growth were supplied by Carl Herbold.

19. The following account draws heavily on information from interviews with party leaders, specialists in housing and retired army and police officers. The published sources which have been consulted include Frederick B. Pike, *The Modern History of*

Peru (New York: Praeger, 1967); James L. Payne, *Labor and Politics in Peru* (New Haven: Yale University Press, 1965); José Luis Bustamante y Rivero, *Tres años de lucha por la democracia en el Perú* (Buenos Aires: Barolomé U. Chisino, 1949); Víctor Villanueva, *El militarismo en el Perú* (Lima: Empresa Gráfica T. Scheuch, 1962); and Percy MacLean y Estensós, *Historia de una revolución* (Buenos Aires: Editorial EAPAL, 1953).

20. Payne, *Labor and Politics in Peru,* p. 51. See also David Chaplin, "Blue-Collar Workers in Peru," Chapter 7 of this book.

21. François Bourricaud, "Lima en la vida política peruana," *América Latina* 7, no. 4 (October-December 1964): 90, notes the surprising level of support that Ōdría enjoyed in one area of squatter settlements whose formation he sponsored as late as the 1962 presidential election.

22. See Karl Marx, *The 18th Brumaire of Louis Bonaparte* (New York: International Publishers, 1963), p. 124.

23. Comisión Para La Reforma Agraria y La Vivienda, *Report on Housing in Peru* (Mexico: Regional Technical Aids Center, International Cooperation Administration, 1959).

24. Ibid., p. 33.

25. Ibid., p. 77.

26. José Nun, *Latin America: The Hegemonic Crisis and the Military Coup,* Politics of Modernization Series no. 7 (Berkeley: Institute of International Studies, University of California at Berkeley, 1969), p. 43.

27. The rationale behind this emphasis on granting titles is discussed below.

28. Mangin, "Squatter Settlements," p. 23, and Carlos Delgado, *Tres planteamientos en torno a problemas de urbanización acelerada en areas metropolitanas: El caso de Lima* (Lima: Cuadernos Plandemet, Serie Anaranjada, Asuntos Sociales, no. 1, 1968), p. 25.

29. Talton F. Ray, *The Politics of the Barrios of Venezuela* (Berkeley and Los Angeles: University of California Press, 1969), pp. 31 and 33.

30. Ibid., pp. 32-33.

31. The need to avoid simplified conceptions concerning the liberality of regimes may also be seen in the striking contrast between the patterns of involvement of Peruvian governments in supporting settlement formation and their permissiveness toward labor union formation. Payne's interesting table summarizing government policy toward union formation under different presidents *(Labor and Politics in Peru,* p. 54) suggests a tendency for the governments that have lenient policies toward union formation to have more restrictive policies toward settlement formation. This is most notably the case for the comparison of Odría and the second government of Prado.

32. See Schmitter, *Interest Conflict and Political Change in Brazil,* Chapter 5; Howard J. Wiarda, "Toward a Framework for the Study of Political Change in the Iberic-Latin Tradition: The Corporative Model," *World Politics* 24, no. 2 (January 1973): 206-235; and David Scott Palmer and Kevin Jay Middleton, "Corporatist Participation Under Military Rule in Peru," Chapter 16 in this volume.

33. See John Duncan Powell, "Peasant Society and Clientelist Politics," *American Political Science Review* 64, no. 2 (June 1970): 411-425, and Julio Cotler, "The Mechanics of Internal Domination and Social Change in Peru," Chapter 2 in this volume.

34. Powell, "Peasant Society and Clientelist Politics," pp. 423-24.

35. Ibid., p. 424.

36. Cotler, "The Mechanics of Internal Domination," Chapter 2 in this volume.

37. Ibid.

38. For excellent summaries of these early predictions and the subsequent revisionist position, see Joan M. Nelson, *Migrants, Urban Poverty and Instability in Developing Nations* (Cambridge: Center for International Affairs, Harvard University, Occasional Papers in International Affairs, no. 22, 1969), and Wayne A. Cornelius, Jr., "The Political Sociology of Cityward Migration in Latin America: Toward Empirical Theory," in *Latin American Urban Research*, vol. 1, ed. Francine F. Rabinovitz and Felicity M. Trueblood (Beverly Hills: Sage Publications, 1971).

39. See Nelson, *Migrants, Urban Poverty and Instability in Developing Nations*, p. 69, and Cornelius, "The Political Sociology of Cityward Migration," pp. 115–116.

David Chaplin

Blue-Collar Workers
in Peru

7.

The Peruvian industrial labor force is not only unlike its counterpart in currently developed nations, but it also differs from that of developed areas at a similar period in their own growth. Unlike most Western countries at a comparable stage, Peru's small percentage of industrial workers (5.02 percent) [1] are highly organized and receive elaborate and effective welfare and working condition benefits. Their real income has risen since 1945 absolutely, and even relatively, compared to that of white-collar workers.[2] As a result, they are not the vanguard of radical social progress, but rather they have become—"prematurely"—a part of the current power structure of Peruvian society.[3] Thus the search for a segment of society to serve as the base for a revolutionary movement passed beyond the urban industrial proletariat, to a combination of university students and peasant-guerrilla organizations.[4] Between 1940 and 1961 (the dates of Peru's first twentieth-century censuses), the industrial sector of the labor force actually declined. This relative stagnation is common throughout Latin America and arises basically from an increasingly capital-intensive type of investment in industry. In addition, not only the entire labor force, but especially the secondary sector has also become increasingly masculine (see Table 1). Another distinctive feature of Peru's industrial labor force is that the more highly organized factories, which are largely in the Lima-Callao area, are characterized by an extremely low level of labor turnover.

Before examining these patterns, a word must be said about relevant studies. There are very few reports available on Peruvian industrial workers.[5] Industrial relations as an academic discipline has yet to develop in Peru, and departments of sociology have been established only recently. There are, however, other bodies of literature which

overlap somewhat with this subject—namely studies on the APRA,*
and on Lima's slums. The former help to explain the favored position
of the small body of organized workers. (James L. Payne estimates that
197,000 workers in Lima-Callao were organized in 1961, which would
constitute 29 percent of the labor force in this area.) [6] The latter studies,
by now quite numerous,[7] deal with a much larger lower-class category,
of whom the factory workers are the elite. Most of these studies are by
anthropologists who tend to focus more on the disorganized, marginal
slum dweller than the established factory worker.

The Political Climate

The privileged status and nonrevolutionary character of the organized urban blue-collar workers in Latin America are characteristics about which observers of all ideological persuasions agree. An
earlier interpretation of organized Latin American labor [8]
characterized it as "revolutionary," but today the organized urban
unions are definitely part of the contemporary Peruvian power system
and, as such, strive to improve their situation within it rather than by
overthrowing it.

One could explain a nonrevolutionary stance on the part of the
unions simply as a rational reaction to their own weakness. The labor
union movement in Peru and throughout Latin America is certainly
weak in comparison with that of the more developed Western countries. The labor market is saturated with surplus workers in all areas
except those of modern skills. (However, the most highly organized
workers are not necessarily the most skilled. Many "classic" skilled
crafts, such as printing, are still poorly organized in Peru.) Weakness, as
indicated by recent guerrilla tactics, seems to result in desperate
revolutionary action,[9] whereas relative union strength—facing a
divided "oligarchical" elite—tends to result in appreciable gains
through nonrevolutionary pressure.

* The APRA (Alianza Popular Revolucionaria Americana) has long been Peru's best-
organized middle-class reformist political party. For many years it dominated most of
Peru's labor unions—especially in textiles and on sugar plantations. Up to 1968, it had
drifted so far to the Right that it was the best hope of conservatives feeling the
development of newer parties on the Left,

Henry Landsberger notes that "revolutionary fervor and ideological sensitivity have declined over the years." [10] This is yet another respect in which Latin America is precocious. At a comparable level of industrialization in currently developed countries, radicalization was still increasing. A stage of reradicalization should not, however, be ruled out. The low labor productivity of the most strongly organized Peruvian factories represents past concessions by presidents of Peru who bought labor peace at the expense of still-marginal industrial entrepreneurs. A productivity showdown has thus only been postponed. Today many no-longer-infant industries in Peru have costs so high (or at least charge such high prices) that they cannot export to other Latin American countries, and are even failing to fully penetrate their own markets.

Whether such a showdown would elicit a leftist or rightist response from the privileged workers is not easy to predict. It could more easily occur under a military regime but, on the other hand, in the past, such governments have awarded substantial benefits to organized workers, in order to wean them away from the APRA. The current military junta has yet to face up to the productivity issue—except, apparently, in terms of the fishing industry. Since Payne's study of Peruvian labor politics focuses mainly on "political bargaining" by unions through the threat of violence against the president during democratic eras, it de-emphasizes the fact that most of Peru's very progressive labor and welfare legislation was enacted by military dictators.[11] Their objective was clearly to bypass the union, by linking the individual worker directly to the government. So far as unions were concerned, the dictators' policy was to suppress reformists—the APRA, in Peru—favoring instead Communist infiltration of the union movement.[12] At the managerial level, "sweetheart" contracts between factory owners and union leaders were found in a few factories in the mountainous town of Cuzco, which has long been a Communist stronghold. The owners in this case obtained labor peace at the expense of relying on the Communist labor leader as their de facto foreman and personnel manager.

Corruption must also be considered in explaining Peruvian labor docility—even though extensive data on such an issue is virtually unobtainable. Landsberger characterizes Mexico, Brazil and Argentina as having had "major problems of corruption over critical periods of their histories." [13] In Peru, the APRA's moderation over the years and its extraordinary coalition with its former archenemy, the military dictator General Manuel Odría, have led many observers to assume that a high-level payoff must be involved. The party has strained its relations considerably with its unions, especially the sugar workers in the modern plantations along the northern coast, by counseling moderation in their demands made of management. The APRA also singled out the land of these plantations for exemption from all of the land reform laws passed before the 1968 junta came to power. One could also explain such policies in terms of an aging leadership and a desire for respectability. The conservatism of Peru's urban factory unions must also be viewed in the light of United States efforts to encourage such a "responsible" business-union orientation. There are various U.S. programs for training Peruvian labor leaders in Peru and Puerto Rico, to be followed by trips to the U.S. The U.S. is, of course, as involved as are the other cold war adversaries in trying to influence Latin labor politics on a less overt level.[14] However, to attribute the nonrevolutionary stance of Latin America's manufacturing unions, or the fascistic tendencies in Latin America, primarily to U.S. influence, is to give such efforts more credit than they deserve. There are very substantial local roots for both these tendencies.

Many writers indict the entire Latin American intelligentsia for not giving the workers more consistent leadership. Frank Bonilla, Luis Ratinoff, Landsberger and others confirm William C. Thiesenhusen in observing "an unseemly willingness of the liberal-minded university-trained in Latin America to be co-opted by the establishment." [15] Certainly, agents and leaders of lower-class movements were corrupted during Western industrialization, but this problem appears to be more serious today in Latin America. In one of the agonizing reappraisals of the failure of the 1965 guerrilla uprising in Peru, not only the competence, but also the virtue of the guerrilla leaders was attacked. One hears anguished cries from the left that:

> The Latin American revolutionary movement is profoundly demoralized ... hunted down by the U.S.-supported and trained counterinsurgency forces, or as is more usually the case, bought out by the lure of middle-class careerism. Despite the growing economic stagnation of Latin America, there is greater opportunity today for middle-class individuals than ever before, especially if they are university educated. As the social distance

between the middle and bottom has widened, the older "popular front" reform alliances are becoming less feasible—the old partners no longer share common interests and outlooks. Many of the former revolutionary middle-class intellectuals, because of recent openings in the new international institutions, the research foundations or the new U.S.-sponsored planning agencies, have become inactive or have cut themselves off from radical political movements.[16]

James Petras then proceeds to list case after case of such coopted "careerists," many of them Peruvians.

The fact is that, while violent repression has been a major pillar of rural order throughout both the colonial and republican eras, urban dissent has been and is increasingly handled in a more subtle manner. Revolutionaries of middle- and upper-class backgrounds have characteristically been exiled—some in style, as ambassadors or subsidized students. For example, the famous Peruvian Marxist writer, Jose Carlos Mariátegui, was removed from Peru by the dictator Leguia (1919–30) by being awarded a fellowship to study in Europe.

The expectation that the growing middle classes in Latin America's "primate" capitals would at once lead the way to liberal reform and mediate the extremes of rich and poor to establish political stability, is misplaced. As Petras notes, "The 'middle classes,' unable to push their countries into sustained economic growth, have opted for military hegemony in a desperate attempt to maintain their status and class positions against the restless and growing mass of the poor." [17] It would be more accurate to view their political perspective as a new variety of fascism, than as liberal socialism in the European tradition.

Labor and welfare laws

In order to fully understand the striking differences between Peru's current urban proletariat and political situation, and that of Western countries at a comparable period, Peru's labor and welfare laws must be examined. The outstanding facts about labor and welfare legislation and development in Peru and throughout Latin America are the following:

1. The more "modernized" countries, in terms of literacy, political participation and urbanization, have "social" legislation in advance

of what their economies could support if fully enforced and, in many cases, in advance of many developed Western societies.[18]

The result, or at least a correlated fact—especially visible in Chile, Argentina and Uruguay—has been economic stagnation which could generate a fascistic as well as a Communistic reaction. These countries enjoyed considerable growth in all respects during the first half of the twentieth century, but now appear to have created an impasse which may be harder to break out of than the semifeudal situation from which the modernization process originally began in Latin America. Peru has yet to approach this stage of economic development, although its manufacturing sector has already stabilized in terms of its proportion of the labor force.

Walter Galenson, while conceding that, "at the bottom of the developmental ladder, [one finds] a low return to investment in human capital . . . nations which are approaching economic maturity [such as Italy, Japan and Spain in his sample], but in which per capita income is still relatively low, are the ones likely to benefit most from investments in human capital." [19] Peru, in terms of Galenson's sample, is clearly among the underdeveloped countries for which "social security exprnditures represent consumption rather than investment," and as such are likely to slow down economic development.[20]

2. The political origins of this social legislation are: a desire on the part of Latin Americans to reassert their membership in Western civilization—shaken by the post-World War II lumping together of Latin America with Africa and Asia as underdeveloped; and the fact that in Latin America the market mechanism as a basis for wages and working conditions is rejected as a just or effective economic institution by most segments of the population, for various reasons. For example, both Catholic and Marxist idealists take the position that it is immoral and exploitative. In discussing "the market," some focus more on international trade—where one can find domestic fascists talking like Marxists about "capitalist imperialists"—while others are more concerned with the domestic economy. The "paranoid cynics," on the other hand, deny the reality of a free competitive market in any part of the economy. If they find themselves the losers in business, they assume that a clique of enemies has used political influence, fraud, etc., in order to destroy them. In reasoning this way they are projecting onto others their own motives and tactics. Their business policies involve the

extensive use of cartels, fraud, bribery, etc., so they cannot accept anyone else's defense of a price or wage as "just what the market allows." In international trade, they find the constant U.S. reference to the "law of supply and demand" a shallow ruse to cover up "obvious exploitation." Needless to say, this position has considerable empirical support. However, this perspective operates as a fixed set of beliefs, so that even those situations which are actually influenced by market factors are not recognized as such. Also, military dictators often try to legitimize their dubious authority by creating new mass support, while at the same time forestalling the radicalization of the growing urban proletariat through decreeing populist social legislation.

3. One of the primary consequences of all this is the "pre-structuring" of the legal context within which new participants in the polity must operate. These laws and their administration tend to coopt the most aggressive minority, while dividing the majority. In general, the more generous the benefits, the greater is the control over protest organizations at the blue-collar level. Governments wish to give these benefits in a noblesse oblige fashion—thus retaining their initiative in deciding when, and to whom, they will be given. (Female suffrage was doled out in Chile and Peru in the same fashion by a relatively conservative and a dictatorial regime respectively, in order to conservatize the electorate.)

Given the Catholic tradition of authoritarian charity, one is tempted to interpret this progressive legislation as simply a natural application of historical social ideals to twentieth-century legal expectations. Actually, there was a constant struggle between the Creole (born in Latin America) aristocracy and the crown and church, over the issue of the treatment of Indians throughout the colonial period. The famous Law of the Indies was imposed on the colonies as a result of the wholesale slaughter of the aboriginal inhabitants of the West Indies by the first colonists. The Creole tradition of "obeying but not complying" is usually cited to describe the actual enforcement of this protective legislation.

After independence, when the ineffective protective influence of the crown was removed, the abuse of the Indians, Negroes and later of Chinese coolies, worsened. After the government forced the church to sell much of its land, Indian communities were also exposed to a laissez-faire real estate market, which resulted in the loss of most of the land they had retained or been "given" during the colonial era. Nineteenth-century legal reform in Latin America then took the form of the removal of governmental control over many areas of life, especially the economic ones. This had the advantage of separating church and state in many countries, but greatly worsened the situation facing the lower class. The early passage of labor and welfare laws in the twentieth century cannot be explained as the legal expression of local traditional upper-class ideals, nor as the extension of a nineteenth-century style of detailed government control of the economy or protection of individuals. Traditional class relations, at best, were based on personal charity. Wealthy individuals took care of their own servants and workers on an ad hoc basis, thus enhancing their own disciplinary control. Beyond this, some families would patronize "public" charitable institutions, such as orphanages and hospitals, always as a family monopoly with religious legitimation. Progress took the form of "nationalization," with the government expropriating some church institutions and building others according to the structure of its welfare laws—usually involving a separate hospital system for each category of worker. There was no intervening stage of impersonal voluntary public support for nongovernmental charitable institutions.

The enactment of this legislation, then, must be explained in terms of twentieth-century populist politics and foreign models, as explained above. (Foreign influence is certainly not passive. The Western labor and management—in manufacturing—representatives to the International Labor Organization's conventions have a common interest in eliminating "unfair competition" from cheap labor countries. Other U.S. interests, to be sure, benefit from cheap labor in some raw material-exporting countries.)

There is, of course, some generic similarity between traditional and welfare state paternalism, thus tempting one to explain the current system as a natural extension of traditional noblesse oblige. However, in principle, the operation of state welfare undercuts the power of private wealth holders. One reason it was not more vigorously opposed by the early twentieth-century "power elite" is that they find that they can more effectively protect themselves privately, through personal influence over the administration of laws. (In the context of populist mass politics, it is no longer feasible—or necessary—to hold the line on issues of principle. In Machiavelli's zoology we are dealing with foxes not lions.) Furthermore, the enforcement of these laws has been largely at the expense of large foreign firms and the larger organized local manufacturing plants. The latter group of industrial entrepreneurs are not yet powerful enough, or cohesive enough, to effectively defend their interests in the area of labor and welfare laws. Faced with this situation—of growing labor costs and obstacles to improvements in labor productivity—they protect themselves largely by corruption in other areas of business, namely taxation, government contracts, evading import tariffs, etc. An additional basis for such legislation is that unions, faced with constant inflation, naturally favor the "flexible price asset" of nonwage fringe benefits, since these benefits are available only to the employed and in practice only to workers in unionized factories.

The immediate historical model for Peru's legal system is a consistent comprehensive code in the Napoleonic tradition. Such rationalization is, however, notably lacking in the area of Peruvian labor and welfare legislation. Current developmental-reformist regimes are therefore faced with a hodgepodge of laws, special executive decrees and a tradition of highly inconsistent and limited enforcement. Laws "revolutionary" in implication are merely superimposed on standing legislation. Some Peruvians have considered trying to rationalize this body of laws into a Labor and Welfare Code, but with little success as yet.

Whether such a codification would be desirable from the point of view of industrialization, welfare or political development is doubtful. The benefits actually enjoyed by workers depend overwhelmingly on their political strength. The function of the law is mainly to place limits on their legitimate aims and on means to these ends. However, even here new benefits are constantly being awarded to special sectors, areas, or even specific firms—depending on effective political power.

Pending more research on the matter in other Latin American countries, it is my impression that those regimes preferring a systematized labor code are military dictatorships, while the more or less democratic governments prefer the "mixed" system. The latter system leaves more legitimate options open to governments, since for almost any labor dispute there are precedents, laws or decrees for whatever type of action may be politically most feasible at the moment.

The issue of law enforcement differs greatly between labor and welfare legislation. In the former case, there are two main types of laws: those which benefit workers as individuals—i.e., minimum wages, fringe benefits to be provided by employers, etc.; and those designed to control unions as protest organizations. In the first case, the official expectation is that labor inspectors and labor courts will look after the workers' interests. As could be expected, labor inspectors are some of the most notoriously corrupt government officials. They are in an ideal situation to extort protection money from managers. Smaller firms tend to defend themselves at this level, while larger firms often maintain a correct posture toward such men, preferring to operate directly at the top level of labor courts or the labor ministry. There is also a middle range of corruption, in which minor government officials work part-time (in an open and accepted pattern of half-day government employment), in the firms with which they deal in their public office. Enforcement here is clearly poor and highly dependent on the political party affiliation of the union in question. A street demonstration of physical force uncomplemented by support from middle-class political influentials is likely to be simply repressed. In fact, the initiative in ordering such public action usually comes from the party—which is often more useful for its own program than the immediate interests of the workers. Enforcement, then, is initiated from below. (Original enactment of labor laws, however, generally preceded effective labor protest.) In the second case, the government initiates control over unions—if already affiliated with an out-party—or it may even use the mechanism of control to foster unionization—using labor inspectors as organizers where a mass base is sought.

Welfare legislation, on the other hand, is largely oriented toward a middle-class clientele of white-collar workers, especially in government employment. There are lower but similar benefits for blue-collar workers, but, in fact, only a very small percentage of them actually enjoy these benefits by virtue of working for large unionized firms. In the case of the white-collar welfare benefits, the clientele are highly organized to defend their interests, with the result that they often enjoy *more* benefits than the law officially provides (dubious disability allowances, pensions while still fully employed, etc.).

There are also regional differentials in enforcement. To begin with, welfare benefits are available only in the larger cities and a few large foreign mining camps and modern plantations. Another factor is the

Table 1
THE PERUVIAN LABOR FORCE, 1940-61 *

	1940	1961	Sector	% of all workers 1940	% of all workers 1961	% male 1940	% male 1961
Agriculture	62.4	50.3				68.5	86.2
			Primary	64.4	52.5		
Extractive	1.8	2.2				97.3	97.3
Manufacturing	15.4	13.3				43.5	71.8
			Secondary	17.2	16.7		
Construction	1.9	3.4				98.0	99.0
Commerce	4.6	9.1				67.8	72.1
Transportation & Communication	2.1	3.0	Tertiary	16.8	27.5	95.3	95.1
Services	10.2	15.2				50.9	50.8
Other	1.6	3.3		1.6	3.3	80.1	72.9
Total	100	100		100	100	64.6	78.4

Percent Economically Active
of the Various Base Populations

	1940 Total	1961 Total
Total	38.8	31.5
Male	52.1	49.6
Female	27.9	13.6

* Dirección Nacional de Estadística, *Censo Nacional de Población y Ocupación, 1940* (Lima: 1944), vol. 1, pp. 69, 370, 606-607. *Censo Nacional de Población, Características Económicas, 1961,* Tables 81 and 84 and p. 15. In order to increase comparability with 1940, those looking for work for the first time "aspirantes a trabajador" (added in 1961) were deducted from the 1961 enumeration.

appointment or election of mayors. Where appointed, enforcement is weakened, but where locally elected and where unions already exist, enforcement is more common. Peru has periodically resorted to appointed rather than elected mayors (they were elected from 1963-68), so this factor is highly variable. The widely observed pattern of central authority being more "progressive" still holds—but mainly at the center.

The Structure of the Industrial Labor Force

The most outstanding and problematic aspect of Peru's current socioeconomic structure is that the flood of rural migrants to the larger cities cannot find employment in secondary occupations. They are therefore forced into marginal service occupations which, in the face of the absence of any functioning system of unemployment compensation, can be fractionalized to provide a minimal level of subsistence. Politically, most of these activities are virtually impossible to unionize, so that the apparently increasing misery of this category of workers does not result in effective collective action—except in the area of squatter invasions to obtain housing. Even these actions seem to give rise only to many short-lived associations which fade away once these areas are stabilized. This is especially the case when the squatters are given title to their holdings. Such a policy seems to be the urban counterpart of agrarian reform in deflecting lower-class action from collective to individualistic ends.

One of the basic reasons for the stagnation of industrial employment [21] is the capital intensive investment politics pursued by private owners and encouraged (not necessarily intentionally) by governmental policies. Through exchange controls and development loans for machinery (but not for working capital), manufacturers have been lured into buying the latest labor-saving equipment. Government policy acceding to middle-class consumption aspirations has also fostered the development of durable consumer goods, such as automobiles, as well as other products whose manufacture is much more capital intensive than the food and fiber processing plants which still employ the bulk of the manufacturing labor force. In addition, "social charges"—or fringe benefits amounting to over 40 percent of the wage bill,[22] and the other disadvantages of a unionized factory's political visibility have persuaded factory owners to regard "cheap" labor as too expensive. Their reaction has been to become more capital intensive, or to keep their plants below the minimum size at which these regulations apply, or to rely more on political influence than internal rationalization as the best way of maximizing profits. In the latter two cases this may take the form of elaborate subterfuges involving the separate incorporation of each section of a single plant—or even the physical dispersion of stages of processing in spite of the transportation costs thus created.[23]

The remedies for the employment problem (regardless of the type of ownership system involved—capitalistic or Communist) would seem to be a combination of fertility reduction policies and labor intensive types of investments. In rural areas, land reform might offer some promise of "bottling up" the redundant rural labor force until needed in the urban labor market—as did the family farm in the U.S. outside of the South.[24] Unfortunately, it seems that this function of land reform will be more short-lived in Peru than it was in Mexico, since suddenly improving the economic opportunities of peasants is likely to bring about an increase in their fertility through a reduction in their age of marriage and an increase in the percent married. However, other types of rural overhead projects—such as dams, highway construction projects, etc.—which separate the sexes for prolonged periods and which do not make childbearing apparently economically advantageous, as on a subsistence farm, might be more effective in lowering fertility.

Another approach to the problem of labor absorption would be to reduce the cost of fringe benefits for employers. The latter are already working in this direction by eliminating female employees—as will be more fully explained below. In view of the political unfeasibility of directly attacking the privileges of organized workers in a more or less democratic society, several other approaches would be desirable. The funding and organization of some welfare benefits could be restructured to weigh more heavily on the government and less on the employer's payroll. (Attempts to decentralize industry, for instance, are frustrated by requirements that isolated factories establish schools, hospitals and housing for their workers.) On the other hand, holding workers or unions primarily responsible for high labor costs overlooks the extremely inefficient organization of Peruvian industry.[25] It would seem more just to require a drastic rationalization of manufacturing in order to reduce labor costs, before asking workers prematurely to adopt a nonpolitical technocratic policy of development-oriented restraint. However, such an industrial reform would only create more

Table 2
THE PERUVIAN MANUFACTURING LABOR FORCE, 1963 [26] WORKERS,
PLANTS AND PRODUCTION BY SIZE OF PLANT

	Manufac-turing Estab-lishments %	Number of Workers	Average Workers per Plant	Annual Gross Value of Production in Soles		
				%	Per Worker	Per Plant
Less than 5 Workers	83.4	18.3	1.7	2.1	19,187	33,442
5 or more Workers	16.6	81.7	39.3	97.9	199,984	7,858,999
5-19 Workers	10.8	12.9	9.5	5.8	75,018	714,923
20-49 Workers	3.1	12.0	30.8	7.9	110,092	3,391,508
50 or More Workers	2.7	56.8	170.5	84.2	247,344	42,169,643
Total percent	100	100		100		
Total Number	25,321	201,751	8.0		166,914	1,329,924

Distributions of Plants by
Size and Location

	5 or More Workers Percent	Less Than 5 Workers Percent
Lima-Callao	67.0	27.4
Arequipa	5.3	5.9
Rest of Peru	27.7	66.7
Total Peru Percent	100.0	100.0
Number	4,195	21,126

employment as a long-run multiplier effect of a larger sale of lower-priced goods, since the immediate effect would be even lower factory employment.

Peruvian industrial workers are not only a very small proportion of the labor force, but they are also highly concentrated in one city—the Lima-Callao metropolitan area—which contains 67 percent of them (see Table 2). Arequipa, the next-largest city (only one tenth the size of Lima), runs a very poor second, with 5.3 percent of Peru's manufacturing workers in plants with over five employees. Table 2 also reveals the small average (mean) size of even the "large" plants—170 workers in the 672 plants with over 50 workers. The low productivity of the smaller plants is also roughly measured by the per worker and per plant production averages. The absolute level of these figures is certainly too low, but their relative differences are sufficiently reliable to reveal gross differences in productivity. Only 2.7 percent of the plants account for 84.2 percent of gross production.

Readers who rely on such international sources as the U.N. Demographic Yearbook's reprinting of the 1961 census figures on the Peruvian labor force are thus cautioned to note that only about a quarter of the manufacturing labor force are actually factory workers. The inflation of such developmental indices, aside from the problematic quality of published data, requires that investigators invest considerable time in "cross-examining" such data. The percent of urban workers in Peru, for instance, is almost doubled—relative to an arbitrary definition of 2,500 as urban, by the inclusion of the capitals of all political units—no matter how small they may be.

Another of the major issues relating to blue-collar workers in developing countries is their adjustment and commitment to factory life. It now seems that the earlier works on this topic, which emphasized the clash of cultures and the inevitable era of high turnover and absenteeism, were either mistaken in blaming labor for what was as much a managerial responsibility, or were referring to mines and plantations. These employers had gone to rural areas, rather than benefiting from an urban milieu and the favorable self-selected traits of migrants. A sample of 4,000 textile factory workers in 1959, and Briones and Mejia Valera's survey of 1,096 factory workers in 1962, found a very low level of turnover.[27] It is lower, in fact, than that of European workers which, in turn, is lower than the turnover rate in the United States. Briones and Mejia Valera also noted a high level of expressed satisfaction with the workers' current employment, similar to that found in the United States by Robert Blauner.[28] In the Briones and Mejia Valera study, the adjustment to city life was judged to be more difficult than the adjustment to factory work. The ease of the latter adjustment, however, also represents an adjustment of factory organization to both labor and management "inefficiency," as the above cited studies by the U.N., Clague and Chaplin indicate.

The final distinctive aspect of the Peruvian blue-collar labor force to be considered is the reduction in female employment.[29] As Table 1 indicates, there has been a reduction in female employment—not only within agriculture, owing to mechanization and because agricultural employment is declining—but also within manufacturing itself. In fact, it has experienced its sharpest decline in female employment owing to the enforcement of expensive general welfare and maternity and other special female benefits. It was observed in the textile worker study that most employers had sharply curtailed hiring women after 1955 (the end of the Odría dictatorship). Interviews with factory owners on this point made it clear that they were very conscious of these costs and that the elimination of female workers was a deliberate policy—even in textiles, which tends to be a heavily female-dominated industry in most countries. The union leaders were not at all opposed to this policy, since female workers are harder to organize and control and are no longer likely to be their own wives or close relatives.

These female benefits apply to plants with over 25 workers and include equal pay, limitations on night work and daily hours similar to those on minors, a 25 percent surcharge for industrial accidents, 42 days off before and after childbirth at 70 percent of full pay, indemnization equal to three months' pay for a discharged woman who will have or has had a child within 90 days; a day nursery, an hour off daily at full pay to nurse and a two-hour rest period at mid-day (although increasingly factories are adopting the one-hour lunch break).[30] The overall effect of these and other laws has been to make women more expensive to employ than men at the blue-collar level. Women are still moving into the labor market at the white-collar level (but not, of course, the same women who could not find employment in manual work). Since white-collar workers have a considerably lower fertility rate than blue-collar workers,[31] the former do not impose so many of these costs on their employers.

An ironic aspect of this situation is that many of these laws are "pronatalist," that is, designed to promote childbearing by protecting working mothers. They have, in fact, had this result (since the fertility of women not in the labor force, as well as those working in agriculture and artisan shops, is still high)—by pushing lower-class women out of this one potentially fertility-reducing occupation. The "disemployed" mothers then probably bear many children, but without the maternity benefits which are available only to some of those employed.

The Military Junta

The current junta's policy with respect to industrial workers has been as improvised as its other reforms. The major elements in its labor policy are: its persistent stance against Aprista and far-left political "sabotage" of workers' organizations;[32] and its commitment to worker cooperatives and industrial communities as a device for eliminating unions and playing down class conflict. (These issues are discussed at length by Palmer and Middlebrook in Chapter 17 and by Cotler in Chapter 3.)

Productivity reform has been largely ignored—along with the issue of the Andean Common Market. Many of Peru's manufacturing industries—notably, textiles—are even less efficient than their counterparts in Colombia, Ecuador, Bolivia or Chile. The only major effort at technical reform has been made in the fishing industry—and this effort was encouraged by several factors. For one thing, the fishing industry was already in a state of extreme disorganization, owing to overfishing, dependence on export markets and the proliferation of underscale firms, resulting in bankruptcies and takeovers by foreign creditors. Furthermore, this industry "belonged" to the more technically oriented Ministry of Fisheries, rather than the Ministry of Industry and Development—which controls most manufacturing operations. In addition, the junta closed down some of the notoriously inefficient auto assembly plants which had been widely touted as a symbol of Peru's high level of industrial development.

The major labor-related junta reform is the Industrial Community Law of July 1971. While it contains many provisions designed to promote the establishment and expansion of Peruvian-owned firms (thus affirming a procapitalist stance), this probusiness effort is potentially undercut by a policy of facilitating worker ownership.

Industrial Communities, or Worker Coops, including all workers, white- and blue-collar, are to be formed by allocating 15 percent of the annual profits for the purchase of company stock from the initial owners in favor of the industrial community. When the community owns 51 percent, it will then take over full control of the firm. Many foreign observers found this reform especially significant, reading into it a Yugoslav social model. In fact, worker control was a last-minute improvisation added to the final version of the industrial development law. Only belatedly (in January 1972) was the Yugoslav prototype fully explained to the junta, by Jaroslav Vanek on a visit to Lima.

Since this provision has not yet been fully implemented, no discernible effect can be described so far as labor-management relations are concerned. Union leaders were quite conscious of the absence of any role for themselves in the sugar mill version of this reform. The only relevant worker opinion studied on this issue was a survey taken in Lima in 1970 by Mejia Valera, just before the publication of the industrial community law.[33] The respondents were asked, "Which goals should the Peruvian Union movement promote during the current year?" and "which during the next 10 years?" To the first question, 45 percent of the workers responded "economic goals"; 17 percent said "labor and social justice"; with "cooperativization of the enterprise" running a poor third at 6 percent. State ownership was even less favored, at .4 percent. Over a ten-year period, "cooperativization" rose to 13 percent and state ownership to 2 percent, but nearly 40 percent were unwilling to respond to such a long-range conjecture—24 percent answered "don't knows" to the first question.

Given the sharp decline in domestic and foreign investment in manufacturing, rising urban unemployment and the military's unwillingness to tolerate serious mass participation in any sector, this reform seems an unlikely one. The abortive effort of the junta's left-wing supporters to organize a mass movement in the form of Committees for the Defense of the Revolution was suppressed by the junta when it began to generate serious dissention. The regime's response was the establishment of a "Social Mobilization System" (SINAMOS) which, in spite of its inclusion of left-wing members, appears to be aimed at *forestalling* any positive mass intervention in national policy. The most likely outcome will probably be the Chilean model where, as Strasma (Chapter 13) notes, "The main concern appears to be to give the sensation of participation in state enterprises without creating any new mechanism that would actually inconvenience the central planners." Thus one can only speculate on some of the implications of the industrial community reform, were it to be pursued. Two possible results would be: an aggravation of low labor turnover, by further enhancing workers' "rights in their jobs"; and shifting the arena of class conflict, rather than suppressing it. The apparent military-technocratic hope of engineering a facile elimination of labor-management conflict is at best naive. The owners and workers could reach agreements on specific issues, such as tariffs, but this would probably be done at the expense of national welfare. This "abuse" of the cooperative ideal fits the Spanish and Italian fascist syndicalist ideal of vertical societal organization. It is thus not surprising that neither the Castro nor the Allende regime is in favor of full worker control of industry. Also, since the unit to be owned is only the single manufacturing plant, rather than all of the highly interdependent enterprises belonging to the original owner, these worker communities are destined to acquire badly organized, underscale enterprises, whose previous survival depended on their vertical and horizontal integration with the owners' other investments. Torn loose from these financially profitable, but technically and commercially irrational "conglomerates," few could stand on their own feet.[34]

Political factors have been more important than the market in structuring Peru's small factory labor force. The result is a privileged proletarian elite facing an already saturated labor market and a capital intensive industrial development policy. Their reaction has therefore not been to make common cause with the mass of marginal urban workers, or the peasants, but rather to work through the system to hold on to their current position.

Structurally, this stagnation has resulted in a "premature" foreclosure of industrial employment opportunities for women, which, in turn, may help explain Peru's persistently high rate of fertility. The extremely low turnover of Peru's factory workers is also clearly related to the absence of alternative opportunities, and to their favored status.

These blue-collar workers are thus not only unlike their counterparts in currently developed countries, they are also not recapitulating the Western pattern of development. They represent a new mixture of the latest machinery and social welfare legislation, with a political regime as yet unwilling to face up to the problems of either technological reform within industry or increasing employment throughout the nation.

NOTES

1. The 1961 Peruvian Census (see Table 1) does not state how many of the 410,980 workers in the "manufacturing" sector are factory workers, as opposed to handicraft artisans. However, a 1963 census of manufacturing (Primer Censo Nacional de Estadística y Censos, Lima, August 1966) reveals that there were only 164,930 employees in firms with five or more workers (or 131,020 blue-collar workers). The first figure is 5.02 percent of the total 1963 labor force, if one assumes it grew 2.5 percent annually between 1961 and 1963.

2. James L. Payne, *Labor and Politics in Peru* (New Haven: Yale University Press, 1965), p. 20; U.N., Economic Commission for Latin America, *Analysis and Projection of Economic Development* 6: *The Industrial Development of Peru* (Mexico City, 1959), p. 43.

3. Henry Landsberger, "The Labor Elite: Is It Revolutionary?" in S. M. Lipset and Aldo Solari, *Elites in Latin America* (New York: Oxford University Press, 1967).

4. David Chaplin, "Peru's Postponed Revolution," *World Politics* 20, no. 3 (April 1968): 393–420.

5. David Chaplin, *The Peruvian Industrial Labor Force* (Princeton: Princeton University Press, 1967); Payne, *Labor and Politics;* U.N. Economic Commission for Latin America, *Analysis and Projection;* Guillermo Briones and José Mejia Valera, *El Obrero Industrial* (Lima: Instituto de Investigaciones Sociológicas, Universidad Nacional Mayor de San Marcos, 1964).

6. A 1967 survey found that 39 percent of the blue-collar and 20 percent of the white-collar workers in Lima-Callao were organized. By industry, the blue-collar percentages were: transportation, 51; manufacturing, 23; commerce, 18; services, 17. C. Andrew Lininger, *Union Membership in the Lima-Callao Area* (Lima: Servicio del Empleo, Ministerio de Trabajo, 1968), p. 11.

7. William Mangin, "Latin American Squatter Settlement: A Problem and a Solution," *Latin American Research Review* 2, no. 3 (Summer 1967): 65–98. Richard W. Patch, "La Parada, Lima's Market," American Universities Field Staff Report, vol. 14, nos. 1, 2 and 3 (February 1967).

8. Robert J. Alexander, *Organized Labor in Latin America* (New York: Free Press, 1965), p. 12.

9. Landsberger, "The Labor Elite," p. 265.

10. David Chaplin, "Peru's Postponed Revolution."

11. Payne, *Labor and Politics*, pp. 44, 46, 51.

12. Alexander, *Organized Labor*, p. 116.

13. Landsberger, "The Labor Elite," p. 283.

14. See William J. McIntire, "U.S. Labor Policy," and William A. Douglas, "U.S. Labor Policy in Peru—Past and Future" in *U.S. Foreign Policy and Peru*, ed. Dan. A. Sharp (Austin: University of Texas Press, 1972).

15. William C. Thiesenhusen, "How Big is the Brain Drain?", Land Tenure Center Paper no. 29, University of Wisconsin, January 1967, pp. 20–22; also Landsberger, "The Labor Elite," Frank Bonilla, "Cultural Elites," and Luis Ratinoff, "The New Urban Groups: The Middle Classes," in *Elites in Latin America*, ed. Lipset and Solari.

16. James Petras, "Making South American Safe for U.S. Tourists," *Ramparts* (December 1966): 44.

17. Ibid., p. 50. See also José Nun, "The Middle Class Military Coup," in *Latin America, Reform or Revolution?*, ed. J. Petras and M. Zeitlin (New York: Fawcett, 1968).

18. Jorge Ramirez Otarola, *Codificación de la legislación del trabajo y de previsión social del Peru* (Lima, 1963). An English summary of some of these laws and others affecting business: *A Statement of the Laws of Peru in Matters Affecting Business*, Washington: Pan American Union, 1962, and its supplement by Hernando de Lavalle, published in 1965.

19. Walter Galenson, "Social Security and Economic Development," *Industrial and Labor Relations Review* 21, no. 4 (July 1968): 566-7.

20. Ibid., p. 559.

21. See Section 3 in David Chaplin, *Population Policies and Growth in Latin America* (Lexington, Mass.: Heath Lexington, 1971), for further discussion of the interrelations between popular growth and employment.

22. Romulo A. Ferrero and Arthur J. Altmeyer, *Estudio económico de la legislación social peruana y sugerencias para su mejoramiento* (Lima, 1957), p. 118.

23. See Appendix A, David Chaplin, *The Peruvian Industrial Labor Force*, especially pp. 245, 250.

24. See Thiesenhusen, p. 252, in Chaplin, *Population Policies*.

25. See Chapter 4 in Chaplin, *The Peruvian Industrial Labor Force*, and Christopher Clague, "Economic Efficiency in Peru and the U.S.," Ph.D. diss. Harvard University, 1966.

26. Dirección Nacional de Estadística y Censos, *Primer Censo Nacional Económico 1963, Industria Manufacturera* (Lima, August 1966), pp. xi, xiii.

27. David Chaplin, "Labour Turnover in the Peruvian Textile Industry," *British Journal of Industrial Relations* 6, no. 1 (March 1968); Briones and Mejia Valera, *Obrera Industrial*, pp. 41-42.

28. Robert Blauner, "Work Satisfaction and Industrial Trends in Modern Society," in *Labor and Trade Unions*, ed. Walter Galenson and Seymour M. Lipset (New York: John Wiley, 1960), pp. 339-60.

29. Other manpower aspects of the textile labor force in Peru are analyzed by the present author in "Industrial Labor Recruitment in Peru," *America Latina* (Oct.-Dec. 1966), año 9, no. 4, pp. 22-40; and "Labour Turnover."

30. Ramirez Otarola, *Codificación*, pp. 105-6.

31. J. Mayone Stycos, "Female Employment and Fertility in Lima, Peru," *Milbank Memorial Fund Quarterly* 53, no. 1 (January 1965): 43.

32. Jaime Castro Conteras, "Peru: Implicancia política del conflicto bancario de 1964," *Aportes*, no. 24 (April 1972): 98. Castro Conteras is a sociologist, and a professor at the Centro de Altos Estudios Militares C.A.E.M.—the postgraduate training center which was so widely cited as the intellectual basis for the junta's radical programs.

33. José Mejia Valera, "El Comportamiento del Obrero Peruano," *Aportes*, no. 24 (April 1972).

34. See David Chaplin, *The Peruvian Industrial Labor Force*, p. 102.

David L. Bayer

8. Urban Peru: Political Action as Sellout

The military government that has ruled Peru since October 1968 has posed something of a puzzle to the managers of American foreign policy, and something of a threat to the managers of the heavy American investments in that Latin American country. On the one hand, the generals in Peru have been making distressingly Castro-like noises about United States imperialism; on the other hand, they have actually done rather little harm to American interests there, apart from staking out a fairly grandiose sweep of the Pacific for their tuna fishermen, at the expense of ours.

The dilemma exists, of course, only for those who reflexively equate a political stance against American imperialism with an enthusiasm for Cuban communism. Certainly, no such enthusiasm stirs the hearts of the generals who now govern Peru. Quite the contrary. But to understand what has happened in that country, one has to go back a little in time to trace the history of those civilian governments that have been in power since the end of General Manuel Odría's dictatorial regime in 1956. The continuous failure of the social and economic policies of those governments lies behind the October 1968 takeover by the military, led by General Juan Velasco Alvarado.

This was particularly true of the government of Fernando Belaúnde Terry, which remained in power from July 1963 to October 1968. Behind an apparently high rate of economic growth of 3 to 5 percent per year was the increasing impoverishment of the peasants and marginal urban sectors of the population and the concentration of wealth in the hands of the upper classes, especially those connected with foreign export-import and manufacturing activities. The guerrilla movement of 1965, which the Peruvian Army crushed with the aid of United States advisers, and the splintering of Belaúnde's Popular Action Party and the Christian Democrats, pointed to two possible outcomes. Either there would be increasing leftist agitation and possibly a Cuban-style revolution, or else APRA (Popular American Revolutionary Alliance) would win the 1969 elections. Both of these possibilities were abhorrent to the armed forces.

What follows is a case study of the failure of populism and electoral politics in one urban center of Peru, the provincial city of Ica; it provides, I believe, at least an indirect explanation for the fall of the Belaúnde government and the rise of the military rulers.

The city of Ica lies south of Lima on the semiarid coast of Peru. The paving of the Pan-American highway in 1930 cut down the two-day trip between Ica and Lima to about four hours by car or truck, and has led to the development of a transportation industry. But the city emerged from and is still dependent upon cotton and grapes grown in the fertile Ica Valley and the industries derived from these crops, such as wine, cottonseed oil, cloth and animal feed.

Beginning with this century, the agricultural economy upon which the city depends has passed through major transformations. People with a large supply of capital have introduced technological improvements and increased their relative land supply and wealth. Since World War I, cotton production has increased nine times, but the initial expansion from 1900 to 1940 was labor intensive, whereas the cotton boom following World War II and the Korean War depended on capital and machinery.

Barriadas and Bosses

A series of social changes were brought about by the consolidation of land and the rationalization of agriculture. First, the old landed aristocracy has shifted its center of activity from the hacienda to the city, not for the purpose of enjoying the comforts of town houses in Ica and Lima as in the past, but with an eye to participating in new investments in trade and finance. Since less labor is required to operate the capital-intensive agriculture of the hacienda and since trained agricultural engineers are capable of administrating the daily work, the hacienda elites have been freed to act in other economic spheres. Moreover, the old aristocracy has found it important to gain a foothold in the capital markets of the city in order to rationalize hacienda operations; thus it has been forced to open its ranks to the new banking and financial elites who manage the inputs of national and foreign capital. In addition, the demand for technical and white-collar workers has given rise to a new middle class. Third, since 1940 approximately 26,000 immigrants from the rural areas of the Ica Valley and the surrounding Andean mountains have entered the city and settled in the marginal areas, called *barriadas,* along the Ica River.

In the course of these developments, national and local politics have interacted in such a way as to promote the interests of the rising middle class, the hacendados, the landlords of the city and the financial elites, by manipulating the people in the marginal barriada society and depriving them of their share in the city's economic growth.

The families who live in adobe and *quincha* houses in the barriadas can be divided into three distinct groups. First are the old members, those who have lived in the barriadas since before 1940. Having been born, schooled and employed in the city, they are completely acculturated to the urban style of life. People from this group are literate, have voting cards and have become affiliated with the APRA political party by way of their participation in trade unions and public employee associations. Between 1924 (when Victor Raul Haya de la Torre founded the party) and 1956, the Apristas (as members of APRA are called) championed the goals of the rural and urban poor and gained control over the Peruvian trade unions. Old members are blue-collar workers in factories, white-collar workers in public and private institutions, chauffeurs, skilled mechanics, builders, carpenters and wholesale merchants. Since these are the best-paying jobs available to the barriada people, the old members generally have the highest income and socioeconomic status, compared to the other groups.

The *campesinos* are those who have come from the rural areas of Ica and the Peruvian coast since 1940. Before settling in the barriadas, they had periodic contact with the city by buying and selling products there. Those few who could read received city newspapers, and many communicated with city merchants who traded in the rural areas. In some cases the campesinos sent their children to schools in the city, making use of the cars and buses that traveled daily between the countryside and the urban center. Many campesinos have been displaced from agriculture by the processes of land consolidation and mechanization, but a certain proportion still retain their identification with rural Ica through agricultural jobs and related occupations. Although the campesinos are less acculturated to the city than the old members, they have better-paying occupations, more education and higher socioeconomic status than the *serranos.* Since some campesinos lived and worked on rural haciendas unionized by the Aprista party, their main political affiliation is with the latter.

The serranos are people who have migrated to the barriadas from the Andean highlands (i.e., the sierra) since 1940. Compared to the old members and campesinos, the serranos are generally less educated, less acculturated to the city and less involved in the politics of the barriadas and formal political parties. They came to the city speaking Quechua, or Quechua and Spanish, the latter being a second language learned later in life and spoken with a peculiar highland accent. Moreover, the process of acculturation to the city has been inhibited by the fact that serranos migrated in groups and settled near people from their hometowns, called *paisanos,* establishing in this manner cultural enclaves within the barriadas. The paisano enclaves help maintain the serrano's identification with his native highland culture, his home community and his maternal tongue. Serranos work at the lowest-paying jobs, such as unskilled construction work, street-sweeping, waiters, cooks and vendors of agricultural products and small manufactured goods in the market at the fringe of the barriadas. Due to their low socioeconomic status, Indian dress, accented Spanish and paisano associations, serranos are sometimes discriminated against by the old members and campesinos who, in such cases, view them as outcasts. Although unemployment and underemployment are basic features of barriada life, the serrano group suffers more from its cyclical effects than do the other groups.

Each of Ica's nine barriadas has been governed by a barriada committee made up of residents from the time of its foundation, and since 1960 the election of committeemen has been held once a year. Old members and campesinos almost always win the elections, and often the same people serve year after year by rotating the post of president, vice-president, secretary and so forth among themselves. In this way the committees become microcosms that mirror the characteristics of APRA on the national level. At its inception in the early 1930s, APRA had been a radical, anticlerical, antimilitary, antiimperialist party, but by 1945 the party had become friendlier toward foreign, and therefore United States', investment, and operated through a rigid, authoritarian, bureaucratic hierarchy with Haya de la Torre acting as a *caudillo*. (Students and young militants who opposed Haya's collaboration with United States imperialism and looked toward the Cuban Revolution as a model for change were expelled from the Party in 1959. They formed APRA Rebelde, and in 1961 changed their name to the Peruvian Movement of the Revolutionary Left [MIR]. In June 1965, MIR, led by Luis de la Puente and Guillermo Lobatón, carried out its first armed action, for which de la Puente paid with his life.)

On November 15, 1960, the Aprista committeemen united the nine barriadas into a Central Barriada Association (CBA), and joined forces with local and national Aprista leaders to get the National Barriada Law, designed to resolve housing problems in marginal urban areas of the Peruvian coast, applied to Ica. In 1961, the Ica barriadas were officially recognized and brought under the provisions of the law, and a branch office of the National Housing Corporation (junta) was set up in the city of Ica.

The junta began its work by taking a barriada census and by assigning plots of land to each family, thereby legalizing the family's right to participate in the low-cost housing program. Barriada families were recognized under this act of *empadronamiento* and issued a "ticket." Migrants who came to the barriadas after 1961 (henceforth called *newcomers)* were not permitted to participate in the junta program.

Law as an Instrument of Populism

The local and national Aprista leaders of Ica attempted to capitalize on the rising aspirations of the barriada people by exchanging the Barriada Law for political support in the national elections that were coming up in June of 1962. The low-cost housing guaranteed by the law was held up as a symbol of progress and used by the Apristas to mobilize the barriada masses against the upper-class candidates offered by Ica's elites. They were able to do this because the functionaries of the junta were new to the city of Ica and did not know the people of the barriadas, while the Aprista committeemen were well organized in the Central Barriada Association. Thus the National Barriada Law had the latent effect of putting more power in the hands of the latter.

For example, even though the empadronamiento had left many people (especially the newcomers) unsatisfied, the Aprista committeemen were able to seize the opportunity to use the housing law as an organizing tool and to raise their prestige vis-à-vis the masses. They began selling tickets of empadronamiento to newcomers who were willing to give them political support, and punished those who refused to grant such support by claiming before the junta that certain families had or had not lived in the barriadas before 1961. The Apristas transformed the barriada committees from advocates on behalf of all the marginal people before the junta, into political bases of power from which they could look forward to moving up within the ranks of the Aprista party. The position of barriada president, and posts in the CBA, raised one's status in an environment where status symbols were scarce. Some committeemen jealously coveted their positions and acted like *caciques,* demanding that all barriada people bring their problems to them.

The Aprista political strategy paid off when their leaders from Ica were elected to the National Congress in 1962 and returned to it in 1963, after the annulment of the 1962 elections by the military. But, for those who looked beyond politics and to new houses, the situation in the barriadas in 1963 became worse. With the election of President Fernando Belaúnde Terry, the Aprista committees had to contend with a junta which now came under the control of Acción Popular, a party bitterly opposed to APRA. Belaúndistas (as members of Acción Popular were called) distrusted APRA for several reasons: APRA and General Manuel Odría's party both supported ex-President Prado in the 1956 elections, thereby helping defeat Belaúnde; in the 1963 elections APRA went a step further to the Right by forming the Coalition with Odristas; and the fact that APRA could join with Odría, who oppressed and outlawed APRA from 1948 to 1956 during his dictatorial reign, demonstrated that the Apristas had become corrupted by their hunger for political power.

Two other events occurred in 1963 that made the barriada housing program more precarious and political: first, the city was flooded by the Ica River on March 8 and second, an Aprista was elected in December to be mayor of Ica in the first municipal elections in the city's history.

After the flood, a Corporation for the Development and Reconstruction of Ica (CRYDI) was created by the national government with an appropriation of close to $6 million. At the beginning, the CRYDI was administered by relatively neutral functionaries, but the Apristas in the National Congress who owed political debts to party workers in Ica and were in the majority while combined with Odristas, succeeded in "democratizing" the CRYDI with the passage of Law 15045 on June 5, 1964, which designated the mayor of Ica as its president. In effect, the CRYDI became loaded with Apristas and stood in opposition to the Belaúndista junta.

Caritas and Peace Corps

Two other organizations, the Catholic Relief Service (Caritas) and the United States Peace Corps, joined the already complicated political arena with the ostensible purpose of providing free food and medicine for the barriadas, which had been hit hardest by the flood. Initially Caritas and the Peace Corps volunteers worked together, since the material aid was coming from the United States through the Food for Peace program and was channeled through the local priest who headed Caritas. Later, however, a split developed between the 20 Peace Corps volunteers and the Peruvians of Caritas. One of the politically oriented volunteers managed to make it appear as though he was "the boss" of all the Ica volunteers. He also chose to identify the organization with the Aprista leaders in the barriadas, who were opposed to the priest.

Although the Peace Corps volunteers did not appear to know it, the priest was closely linked with the Christian Democrats, a political party that had united with the Belaúndistas in an alliance against the

Apristas, and he sold food to and through barriada people who supported the Christian Democrats.

Many observers in many different countries have noted that middle-class political candidates get into office on the backs of the
working-class vote, but then proceed to adopt ruling-class norms and
conservative tendencies, thereby selling out their followers in the
popular organizations. R. E. Scott of the University of Illinois has
further observed that "the followers accept this symbolic participation in the political process with little protest, despite the lack of any
practical payoff for them." For that small proportion of barriada
followers who became leaders of the committees, one might argue
that the power and prestige that the barriada law put into their hands
was a sufficient reward for their political support of middle-class
candidates. But the masses in the barriadas gained nothing but frustration from their symbolic participation in the political process.

Political Conflict and Alienation in the Barriadas

One must bear in mind that, relative to all other areas in the city,
the living conditions in the barriadas did not improve; they grew
worse. Population growth and crowding plagued the barriadas. The
1963 flood destroyed the improvements that some inhabitants had
made in their houses. The promises from the junta raised aspirations
and kept people waiting, but finally led to nothing.

By 1966, five years after the junta-led housing program was initiated, not one house had been constructed in the barriadas. Indeed,
the junta now began deviating from its mandate to construct low-cost
housing, and shifted its plans to middle-class housing to be built near
an upper-class neighborhood in the southern part of the city. There
were a number of reasons for this change in the junta's program, most
of which are political.

First, the junta was forced to bargain with the city landlords and
the landowning aristocracy, many of whom came from the hacendado class and who owned land in the barriadas, land that had to be
expropriated for the housing program. Long legal disputes about its
true value were arbitrated by the Peruvian Taxation Board in Lima.

The final price fixed for the land was generally higher than its true market value, leading to a substantial profit for the landlords, the absorption of too high a proportion of the junta's budget and the passing on of the extra costs to the barriada people. The legal manipulations were carried on behind closed doors without the participation of the barriada residents, thereby leading to increased mistrust between the junta and the Aprista committeemen. The latter insisted that the junta was selling them out, that it worked in collusion with the city landlords, and that the interests of the landlords and the junta functionaries were identical (i.e., to make money from the housing program). The Aprista leaders argued that the barriada people themselves knew the true value of the land, that they had improved it and raised its value, and that they should not have to pay the additional costs. The fact that no time limits were set for the construction projects or the expropriation of land allowed the arguments and legal manipulations to drag on for months.

Second, the junta decided to construct houses in San Joaquin, an area outside the barriadas, for those who were *empadronado* and displaced from the barriada by the 1963 flood. This housing project absorbed more time and money than the junta had anticipated. By late 1964 and early 1965, the junta's budget from the national government was being cut, since the United States Agency for International Development had held back funds for the Belaúnde administration in an attempt to force it to reach an agreement with the International Petroleum Company. Rumors spread that the junta was bankrupt, a situation that was not helped by the fact that between 1961 and 1966, Ica administrators of the junta were changed five times.

Third, the Belaúndistas who controlled the junta had mixed feelings about working with barriada Apristas who had won most of the barriada voters to their side and might turn a successful housing program into an Aprista electoral victory. The junta took the offensive and began to foster division among the barriada people in an effort to destroy the Aprista strongholds. Committeemen from San Joaquín who favored Acción Popular were treated with more respect than the Apristas, and urged to recruit more families from the barriadas with the aim of expanding the housing project. The success of the first stage of the San Joaquín project can be largely attributed to the fact that leaders of residents there did not follow the Aprista party line.

Then in 1964, in a further effort to undermine the Apristas, the junta began to support a new social movement, spearheaded by newcomers and serranos. Called the Frente Cívico, the movement claimed to back Belaúnde and accused the Central Barriada Association of corruption. Conflict flared up between the CBA and the Frente, leading to the resignation of the Aprista boss of the San Carlos barriada. But as the resources of the junta decreased and as it met increased resistance from the CBA, the junta backed off from its support of the lower-class Frente and saw an opportunity to gain a political victory by appealing to the middle class, which also wanted housing and had more votes to offer relative to the barriadas.

Finally, the junta shift to the middle-class constituency indicated the degree of conflict and outright sabotage between the Belaúndista junta and the Aprista CRYDI. Instead of funds and technical resources being applied through sincere program coordination and being allocated more democratically among the barriadas and other areas of the city, there tended to be economic waste through the duplication of technical studies and functions. Rather than waste energy trying to fight barriada Apristas and risk losing the middle-class vote to the CRYDI, the junta cancelled the barriada program and secured a loan from the Cooperative Housing Bank to build middle-class houses.

The policy of state paternalism practiced by the junta failed in the barriadas. It attempted to replace the hacendado as the new patron and to appeal to the authoritarian values brought into the barriadas by the rural migrants, values inculcated by the church and reinforced by the existing political parties. In line with this strategy, the junta program called for minimum participation by the barriada people and maximum control by its own bureaucracy. The people should have committees, but these must act as mere communications centers, passing on decisions coming down from the junta hierarchy. When the Central Barriada Association took the initiative in suggesting modifications in the housing program, the administrators of the junta claimed that all changes would have to be approved in Lima. Thus the fate of the people in Ica depended on the decision-makers in the capital. Three of the last five junta administrators from 1965 to 1966 were strangers to Ica and had no vested interest in the future of its barriadas. The junta administrators hoped to climb the hierarchy of the National Housing Corporation and secure political hegemony for their party, and this meant subjecting the wishes of the people to their own concepts of efficiency, building houses regardless of their quality and demonstrating their capacity to control the lower classes. Some administrators went to barriada meetings, though very infrequently, while others kept their distance and never attended any. At times the junta avoided direct confrontations with the committeemen by closing its doors just before they arrived at the office or by having its functionaries "called" to Lima.

Nor did the Aprista-controlled CRYDI offer aid to the people in the marginal society. The Central Barriada Association, although made up of members of the same party, was not represented in the CRYDI board of directors, although many other urban and rural associations were members. The CRYDI appropriated large sums of money for reconstruction of the city plaza, with the aim of winning the middle-class votes, but it did virtually nothing for the barriadas. Almost all of the CRYDI's loans for the repair of houses damaged by the flood of 1963 and for the construction of new houses went to people of the upper classes. Although the president of the CRYDI was the mayor of Ica and an Aprista who had been supported by the CBA in the municipal elections of 1963, he did little for the barriadas. The CRYDI was as far removed from the barriadas as the junta and it began competing openly with the latter in 1966 when it drew up plans for housing designed to be sold to middle-class Apristas and Aprista-dominated housing cooperatives.

One might wonder why the university students of Ica did not enter the political battles between the junta and the CRYDI, or between the junta and the CBA. Some barriada leaders attended the university and participated in militant protest movements, but they were a minority within the CBA and could not mobilize it for confrontation politics. Moreover, since roughly half of the students came from outside Ica and largely from the middle classes, they did not identify with the problems of the barriadas. In addition, competing political parties vied for control of the university; the Aprista and Belaúndista students had less power than the Communists and most of the student energy was expended on the internal politics of the institution.

If student militants had opted for a strategy of political agitation in the barriadas, it is likely that they would have met with strong resistance. First, the barriadas were controlled by Apristas and student militants would most likely come from the Peking-oriented faction of the Communist party which APRA opposed. Second, the Peace Corps volunteers offered the barriada people an alternative, nonmilitant strategy of change—a program completely dissociated from university politics. None of the volunteers was capable of forming a strong base of communications with the militant elements of the university. They were not trusted by Peruvian students and were seen as an extension of Yankee imperialism. Peace Corps training did not prepare the volunteers for Peruvian politics, and the central Peace Corps office in Lima discouraged political activism.

The community development strategy of the Peace Corps was based on the consensus model, which aimed at peaceful change by agreements among competing factions. But this strategy was doomed to failure; it did not face up to the fact that people without their own source of political power are helpless before those who have such power. The barriada people depended on Aprista political power, but its control was not in their hands. It was located in the hierarchy of the party structure emanating from Lima and held tightly in the hands of middle-class elites who were making deals with the traditional elites. For example, in one case the middle-class functionaires in the CRYDI financed a feasibility study worth more than $5,000 for the introduction of a new species of grapes primarily for the benefit of the Ica Valley's richest hacendado. In another case, the president of the CBA was appointed inspector of municipal taxes in 1968 by the Aprista mayor of Ica. By identifying with the Aprista committeemen, the Peace Corps volunteers encouraged greater dependency on the party structure, rather than independent action. The volunteers, in effect, substituted their own brand of paternalism for that of the junta and angered the latter by taking the Aprista side. The Peace Corps did work that should have been executed by the barriada leaders. They visited influentials in the local and national institutions on their own, instead of bringing committeemen with them or inviting outsiders into the barriadas.

Furthermore, there was a basic inconsistency in the Peace Corps program: on the one hand, they insisted that the barriada people work with existing institutional structures such as the junta and the CRYDI, while on the other hand they encouraged the people to initiate their own programs based on resources that were virtually nonexistent. Not until late 1965 did the volunteers come to grips with the fundamental problem of scarce resources. Thus they encouraged the formation of housing cooperatives in the barriadas of Acomayo and Alfonso Ugarte. But this was a small effort that came too late. The Peace Corps failed in the barriadas, and because its goal was essentially the reform of existing institutions, the Ica volunteers, like the junta and the CRYDI, turned away from the barriadas to work with the middle-class groups.

In short, the people in the barriadas were mobilized for political power in 1960 by their own Aprista leaders and those from the middle class, but by 1966, although Apristas dominated the politics of the city and controlled the development corporation (i.e., CRYDI), not one house had been constructed in the barriadas. Middle-class Apristas, together with Belaúndistas, representing the new and old financial elites, have used the state institutions to serve their own ends and increased their relative share of the wealth by controlling state funds. This outcome was supported fully by the activities of the Peace Corps in Ica. Needless to say, it is only a question of time until the urban masses realize what is going on and seek means that go beyond legitimate political parties to change things. As was pointed out in the beginning, the fact that the marginal sectors of the urban population might well support a revolution from the Left (e.g., like the one started by MIR in 1965) must be taken into account when we try to explain the military takeover of October 1968.

Rural
Politics

William F. Whyte

9. Rural Peru: Peasants as Activists

*The guerrillas' presence tends to alter the situation in which
peasants, sharecroppers, squatters, peons and Indians live. These
people are condemned to an existence which follows the same
unchanging routine from year to year, from decade to decade,
from generation to generation, until it assumes in their minds the
proportions of an immutable natural order.*

Carlos Romeo

The writer of those lines is a follower of Fidel Castro and a theore-
tician of the revolutionary potential of the peoples of Latin America.
My point in citing him is that his sentiments about the rural peasantry
sum up the feelings of an extraordinarily wide range of observers of
the Latin American scene, whatever their political views or goals.

For revolutionaries or reformers, for Fidelistas or rhetoricians of
the Alliance for Progress, the peasants are mired in "an immutable
natural order." They are seen as an ignorant lot, tradition-bound and
incapable of change even when that change might substantially
improve their earthly condition. As such they cannot be brought to
share in their country's wealth without the intervention of more
enlightened outsiders who will point the way.

Of course, reformers and revolutionaries have radically different
notions of what form their intervention should take. The former,
generally speaking, embrace a theory of community development
according to which strategies have to be devised so that the peasantry
will be "involved" in discussions of possible changes and their traditional conservatism overcome through the "participation process."
Revolutionaries tend to assume—sometimes at the cost of their
lives—that the agents of change will be their own guerrilla bands

operating in the countryside, where they will serve as catalysts of the dormant revolutionary impulses of the peasants.

I would argue the contrary proposition, that far from being dull pawns in an immutable natural order, the peasants are caught up in constant processes of change, and that many of these changes are initiated by themselves without benefit of outside guidance. I will try to demonstrate this proposition from studies of the Peruvian countryside, but I believe that this general conclusion would apply throughout Latin America and, indeed, in most of the Third World. It should be borne in mind, however, that I am not arguing against outside intervention, whether by reformists or revolutionaries. I am simply suggesting that, before any self-appointed agents do intervene, they would do well to find out where the ball is and in what direction it is rolling. Then they will be able to give it a well-directed push, rather than falling flat on their faces, as so many "development projects" have done, or being killed, as so many guerrillas have been.

For the purposes of this argument, there is one segment of Peruvian rural society that presents the toughest challenge to my contention. This is the sierra hacienda or large landed estate, which would seem to offer peasants a minimum of opportunity to change their lot. Here, if anywhere, one would assume that change could come only from the outside, and that it would probably have to be effected by violent force.

The Sierra Hacienda

In Peru the word "hacienda" is used to refer to two quite different types of social and economic units. In the coastal hacienda (sometimes referred to in English as a "plantation"), workers generally live in houses built by the company, are paid regular wages, and their children have access to at least elementary schooling. Many of the haciendas are unionized. Many of them also can best be described as agroindustrial complexes, since they run from cultivation to manufacture (of paper, chemicals and rum, for example). Many of the commercial haciendas are operated at a high level of technology and agricultural sciences, with agronomists serving either as managers or consultants.

The traditional sierra hacienda is drastically different. It has been likened to the feudal manor because of the extreme domination exercised by the hacendado over the peasants. The owner or renter of the hacienda retains the best lands for himself while each peasant family, in return for the right to occupy and cultivate a small plot of land, generally in the most undesirable areas, is required to provide from three to six man-days of work per week, either on the hacendado's lands or on projects for which he hires out his laborers and for which he himself pockets the wages. Furthermore, the women of the peasant families usually have obligations in the household of the hacendado. In general, the hacendado has good connections with the political and economic power figures in his area; the peasants traditionally have lacked these connections and are subjected to various forms of exploitation and denial of opportunity. Because he normally received only a token payment—perhaps a penny or two a day, plus a supply of coca to chew on—he was unable to accumulate capital to become a landowner himself. In fact, the only major difference between the traditional Peruvian hacienda and the manor at the height of the middle ages is that the Peruvian peasant is free to leave the land. If he does, however, he loses any claim to the land he has cultivated and on which he built his home. This is the situation that has prevailed through much of the Peruvian sierra, where over half of the population lives. We are therefore talking about a situation of extreme inequality of power and resources, where it is natural to raise the question as to whether any basic change is possible without outside intervention or violent revolution. Let us examine several cases in the light of this question.

Twenty years ago the Yanamarca Valley, north of Jauja in the central highlands, was almost entirely made up of haciendas. In the past two decades, five communities have emerged out of serfdom, and the only two remaining haciendas in the area are organized and operated in a manner far different from the traditional style.

I shall tell the story in terms of one community, whose history seems broadly representative of the process of liberation throughout the valley. To maintain the anonymity of the principal actors, I shall use pseudonyms for personal names and call the community "Pueblito," but the facts are carefully documented by our associates carrying out the field work.

The liberation of Pueblito began in 1952. The first initiative came from Arturo Sánchez, a young man from the highlands who had gone to Lima for a medical education and had become involved in APRA Party activities. As a student leader, he had to go underground when General Manuel Odría took over the government in 1948 and began his repressions of APRA (Popular American Revolutionary Alliance), which he regarded as a leftist organization because it was then actively seeking the support of workers and peasants. Some time later, Sánchez turned up in Pueblito, settled down to work the land, and married a Pueblito girl.

Organizing Peasants

Sánchez's first organizational step centered on a project for establishing a school in Pueblito. Although Peruvian legislation requires the hacendado to provide some schooling for the peasants, most landlords in the past have ignored this obligation altogether, or have complied in a token fashion, providing one dilapidated room and an occasional teacher. Like many other landlords, José Marimba sought to discourage the school project, arguing with the peasants that school would be of no value to their children. Under Sánchez's leadership, however, the peasants succeeded in interesting the Ministry of Education in their project, so that there was the beginning of a school, despite the landlord's opposition.

As the peasants began to organize themselves around the school project, Marimba got into difficulties on another front. In the first place, he had only won control of the land through fighting a bitter court battle. His father had divided several haciendas and a power plant in Jauja among his children, with Pueblito going to one of José's sisters. At great expense to himself, Marimba carried through litigation that won him Pueblito in exchange for other properties that he gave up. Marimba thus started his operation of Pueblito in somewhat tight financial straits. This was unfortunate for Marimba, since he was a man of expensive tastes. From 1942 to 1952 he had secured large loans from the Agricultural Development Bank, ostensibly to improve Pueblito, but he had spent most of his money on international travel and gracious living in Jauja and Lima.

Until 1952, Marimba spent very little time in Pueblito, leaving everything in the hands of an administrator. When the bank began to press for repayments on its loans, Marimba turned his concentrated attention on Pueblito and sought to squeeze more work out of the people. When some men proved unresponsive to his urgings, he expelled them from the land. The first time he did this, there was no overt response from the other peasants. Therefore, some time later, when he found two of the community leaders not applying themselves as diligently as he wished, he promptly ordered them and their families to leave the property at once. At this point, all the peasants rallied around and vowed that if these two men were to be thrown out, Marimba would have to throw them all out. At the same time, they flatly refused to do any further work for him. Marimba appealed to the authorities in Jauja, but this did not break the unity of the community.

When the peasant challenge came, José Marimba found himself in a deteriorating position. The legal struggle for Pueblito against his brothers and sisters had been expensive and had destroyed family solidarity. While the Marimba family had held unquestioned social and political preeminence in Juaja in the days of his father, José now found himself in acrimonious competition for prestige and influence with a rising businessman-farmer who actually worked in his various enterprises. Furthermore, José's arrogant manner had made him unpopular with both his peers and his social inferiors.

Marimba's response to the peasant challenge was typical of the old order in rural Peru. In Jauja and Huancayo, the departmental (state) capital, he lavishly entertained members of the local and national elite—thus further depleting his resources. As the bank pressed for repayment of the loan, he sought to cultivate the officials of the Huancayo office, two recent graduates of the Agrarian University. He urged on them the following arguments: "We are friends," "We are gentlemen," "We are fellow white men."

When the officials persisted in their unfriendly, ungentlemanly and unwhite demands, José went to Lima to call on the president of the bank, whom he considered to be a friend of the family. The president went through the motions of telephoning Huancayo and asking information on the case. When the Huancayo officials submitted a written report that documented in detail Marimba's incompetent and irresponsible management of Pueblito, the bank president took no further action, and the Huancayo office renewed its pressures on the landlord.

By the time of the strike against Marimba, the community leaders had already been in touch with lawyers in Jauja and with union leaders in Jauja and Huancayo. Through these contacts they learned that the title of José Marimba to Pueblito was in doubt and that another family claimed to own the property. On the advice of their lawyer, they made a deal with the other claimant to buy Pueblito from him. At the same time, they made a deal with the Agricultural Development Bank to take over the mortgage on which Marimba had been defaulting.

Marimba has not given up yet. At this writing, he is still fighting in the courts to get Pueblito back, but now that the peasants have the bank, lawyers, union leaders and relatives and friends of the other presumed former owner on their side, it seems hardly likely that Marimba will ever make a comeback. Meanwhile, Pueblito is developing as an independent community. The villagers have started building new homes and vigorously developing their own economy.

If change in rural Peru is as widespread as I claim it to be, how do we account for the fact that so many Latin American intellectuals, whether radicals or reformers, persist in seeing the countryside as an area of social and economic stagnation? They do this by applying the exception principle. Whenever a case of change comes to their attention—and the Convención Valley movement has received wide public attention in Peru—they explain it away as an exceptional situation that has risen out of peculiar conditions. But they do not then go on to ask whether there may not be other instances of change, that are less well publicized. For example, the transformation of the Yanamarca Valley was completely unknown in intellectual circles in Lima until our field workers happened upon this less dramatic peasant movement. The unionization movement throughout rural Cuzco was indeed publicly noticed at the time, but it seems to have been forgotten soon after the government roundup of union leaders. It was as if intellectuals assumed that the Cuzco haciendas had returned to their former status quo, which was definitely not the case.

Underlying the application of the exception principle is the intellectual's inclination to view reality through moralistic and ideological filters. The moralistic filter is supplied by the concept of "exploitation." The Peruvian constitution, the United Nations Declaration of the Rights of Man, and any number of other such statements of principle, decree that no man shall be forced to work for another or to work without adequate compensation. When in hacienda Chawaytiri the *condición* of work-day obligations is cut by more than a third, and when the daily payment is raised by 200 percent, intellectual reformers or revolutionaries see no change at all because the Indians are still being exploited.

The ideological filter is the intellectual's mental model of the way major structural changes take place. If revolutionary, he has an image of a dramatic nationwide confrontation of reactionary and radical forces, culminating in a radical capture of power in the capital city. The community and area level changes I have described clearly have no place in this model, and so they are not allowed to disturb the myth of the passive peasant.

When faced with the realities of events in the Yanamarca Valley, one Peruvian social scientist made this comment:

> You can't say that those communities have become independent. They continue to be under the domination of the national oligarchy, and that oligarchy continues to be under the domination of Yankee imperialism.

By that logic, no change will take place until the millennium.

While the approach presented here differs from that of the ideological revolutionaries, it is important to recognize that it differs in an equally fundamental way from the usual line of community development theorizing. While the radical ideologists are fixated on the concept of power, the community developers avoid the power issue altogether. For them the secret of change and progress on the countryside is "participation." If the peasants can be involved in solving the problems of their community together, progress will result. Furthermore, community development theorists tend to treat the community as if it existed in a vacuum, thus neglecting the crucially important relations it has with the outside world.

Power is a central issue in our approach, but I am undertaking to dispel the mysticism that tends to cloud the power issue in an ideological argument. By getting down to cases, I seek to show how power is exercised and how shifts in power actually take place.

What explains the changes I have described in the Yanamarca and Convención Valleys and in rural Cuzco? In order to provide a systematic explanation, we need to think in terms of the transformation of the structure of power.

The hacendado is at the apex of the triangle. Peasants are clustered at the bottom of each side of the triangle. The absence of a line connecting them depicts their unorganized state. The hacendado deals with the peasants and their families strictly on an individual basis, holding out special favors for those "loyal" to him and threatening dire penalties for those who are not submissive. The hacendado himself has strong horizontal ties—family, social and political connections with people at roughly the same status in the society. The hacendado also has links upward in the society with important politicians and judges, with bank officials and other figures of economic significance. The peasants do not have these ties. To gain favors from any of these superior power figures, they must go through the hacendado himself, which means that he is in a position of monopoly, both political and economic.

How do the peasants break this monopoly? They do it basically in two ways: by closing the base of the triangle, and by establishing upward ties in the society, independent of the hacendado.

We have seen that the peasants may close the base of the triangle through coordinated efforts to found a school on the hacienda, through organizing against repressive landlords or through an extensive unionization movement, as in the Convención Valley. The peasants' upward ties can be forged with the Ministry of Education, with the Ministry of Labor or with the Agricultural Development Bank. In the case of the peasants of the Convención Valley, upward ties were not established until the growth of the coffee industry created middlemen in the towns whose interests were allied with those of the peasant growers.

Part of the drama was played by lawyers in the courts. When the peasants laid claim to the land or stopped working for the hacendado, he would typically appeal to the political authorities to get the police or troops sent in. Sometimes this worked, but sometimes it did not. If he was unsuccessful in this direct appeal for force, he would go to court to get a legal order requiring the peasants to comply with his interpretation of their obligations. In that event, the peasants would get their own lawyer (for various reasons, there is a buyers' market for legal services in rural Peru) and he would sue the owner on their behalf for 30 years of back pay. The legal justification for this claim is clear, for the Peruvian constitution outlaws the traditional hacendado-peasant relationship, in which the peasant is forced to work without wages (other than a token payment) in order to cultivate a plot of land. Where the hacendado's power is unchallenged, this constitutional provision remains a dead letter, as does the law requiring him to provide a school, but when the peasants can organize themselves to make the challenge, they create a very awkward situation for the hacendado, his lawyer and the courts, since they are claiming rights that are unequivocally guaranteed them.

There are also forces at work that tend to make the old ways increasingly unsatisfactory to the hacendado. The traditional style of farm management does not yield increasing economic returns over the years. The hacendado does not care to spend much time on his hacienda, where the cost of living is relatively low. He is a city-oriented man, and with each passing generation this orientation becomes more pronounced. The hacendado and his family are committed to the "good things" of modern urban living, from education to entertainment and travel, and the price of those "good things" is constantly increasing.

When the hacienda no longer yields the income necessary to maintain the status and style of life to which he has become accustomed, what can the hacendado do? He has just three alternatives: he can try to squeeze more work out of the campesinos; he can sell the hacienda and invest the money in something else; or he can invest money in the hacienda to reorganize it in terms of "modern" scientific agriculture and "modern" farm management methods.

As José Marimba's experience suggests, the first strategy is more likely to yield increased peasant resistance than increased farm output. If he decides upon the second strategy, to whom can he sell? For reasons that should be abundantly clear by now, the demand for land on the part of current and potential hacendados does not begin to meet the supply of purchasable haciendas. Poor as they are, the peasants are emotionally attached to the land and are likely to be willing to pay the hacendado more for it than any other potential purchaser, given the threats of peasant unrest and agrarian reform and overpopulation. If the hacendado sells out to them, the transformation of hacienda into community is thereby accomplished.

We are just beginning to find hacendados who have successfully pursued the third strategy. It is too early to make any definitive statements, but so far we are inclined to assume that very few current sierra hacendados have the will, ability, knowledge and psychological orientation required to transform their properties into "modern" farm enterprises. And those few who successfully carry out the third strategy thereby build a social system that is drastically different from the traditional hacienda.

The Need for Revolution

What does this approach tell us about the probability of a violent social revolution in Peru? On the one hand, it knocks one of the props out from under the argument for the inevitability of violence: a violent revolution is inevitable, it is said, because those holding power will not yield it voluntarily. José Marimba, the hacendado of Pueblito, did not yield power voluntarily, but he lost it nevertheless. And so it was with the other hacendados in the Yanamarca and Convención Valleys.

On the other hand, nothing written here provides grounds for optimism to those who would like to prevent a violent revolution in Peru. I have demonstrated that sweeping changes in social structure have come about in certain rural areas, but generalizations from these cases must be made with the following reservations in mind:

First, I have carried the cases only to the point of the power shift and slightly beyond it. It must not be assumed that, after overthrowing the hacendados, the campesinos live happily ever after. They continue to face very serious economic and political problems, which I shall not discuss here, as we are just beginning to study postindependence developments.

Second, in the countryside, avoidance of a revolutionary situation probably depends upon the geographical extent and the rapidity of movements such as those examined here. Neither the data we have nor the behavioral science theories available permit us to make any predictions as to the probability that widespread changes will come fast enough to relieve the severe tensions now prevalent throughout rural Peru.

Third, until Fidel Castro, it was generally assumed that revolutions started in cities. The smashing defeats of those who tried to apply his rural model in Peru and Bolivia suggest that students of revolution would be well advised not to neglect the urban front. And I have ventured no statements about the state of Peruvian cities.

Finally, the present military government of Peru is committed to preventing a violent revolution through carrying out its own model of revolution, imposed from the top down. If and when the Agrarian Reform Law promulgated in June of 1969 is fully implemented, it will mean a transformation of the countryside far more extensive and drastic than any change we have yet observed in Peru. Indeed, the government's efforts to carry out a peaceful revolution without popular participation are being closely watched by politicians, military men and social scientists throughout Latin America. We hope to study this next stage of the development of Peru, but that story must await some future report.

This essay grows out of a joint collaborative research program between the Instituto de Estudios Peruanos in Lima and Cornell University, José Matos Mar being coprincipal investigator for IEP and William F. Whyte and Lawrence K. Williams being coprincipal investigators for Cornell. The program was launched in 1964 with surveys of 26 rural communities in five areas of Peru. Fourteen of these were resurveyed in 1969. In the course of these five years, more intensive anthropological studies were carried out in a number of these communities, and additional field projects were carried out in other areas as new opportunities arose.

In this joint program, Julio Cotler serves as coordinator of research for the IEP. J. Oscar Alers served as coordinator for Cornell in Lima from 1965 to 1967. Giorgio Alberti is now serving in that capacity.

Discussion of the Yanamarca Valley is based upon the work of Giorgio Alberti, La Mond Tullis, Rodrigo Sánchez and Luis Deustua. The interpretation of developments in rural Cuzco is based upon studies carried out under the general direction of Oscar Nuñez del Prado.

Financial support for the program has come primarily from the National Science Foundation and the National Institute of Mental Health.

Giorgio Alberti

10. Peasant Movements in the Yanamarca Valley

A variety of explanations of peasant movements have been advanced in recent literature.[1] Many of these explanations involve processes of change that are considered important because of their direct influence on the experience of the peasants. These include: the effects of rapid population growth; the impoverishment of the peasantry, produced by the impact of commerce and industry; the proletarization of the peasantry; urban exposure, urban political agitation, and the diffusion of new aspirations and the concomitant changes in the peasants' values, attitudes and behavior.

The present study, however, following in the tradition of Barrington Moore and Eric Wolf,[2] focuses on the way in which the uneven impact of modernization produces changes in the power of traditional ruling elites, thus creating the structural conditions necessary for the development of peasant movements. Hence this study concentrates, not on the direct impact of modernization on the peasants, but rather on its indirect impact, as mediated through changes in the dominant class structure. This approach requires historical data on the transformation that occurred within the class structure, rather than the types of cross-sectional data on peasant attitudes and peasant community characteristics that have generally been collected.[3]

In this chapter, we shall describe the transformation of a regional power structure and the origins and development of a peasant movement which swept the Yanamarca Valley, an intermontane valley in the Peruvian central sierra. We shall also present certain generalizations which are relevant to the development of a theory of

This chapter grew out of a research project directed by the author, with the collaboration of Rodrigo Sánchez. His contribution is thankfully acknowledged.

political peasant movements. Anibal Quijano defines a political peasant movement in these terms: "The notion of politicalization is used here to describe the behavior of all social movements whose objectives, ideological models, organization forms, leadership and strategies of action, are mainly directed toward fundamental economic, social and political change in the society." [4] In this chapter, the term "political" is used in a much narrower sense. That is, a peasant movement is political when it attempts to alter the existing power structure, whether local, regional or national. I would argue that a peasant movement per se never attempts "to question the basic aspects of the dominant social order," unless by "social order" we mean the peasants' order rather than the national one.

The term "peasant" as used here refers to landless peons, sharecroppers and small landowners living in indigenous communities. We shall use the terms "Indian" and "peasant" interchangeably, even though the two words are not synonymous. While Indians are almost exclusively also peasants, all peasants are not necessarily Indians. (For a detailed answer to the question, "Who is Indian in Peru?" see Fernando Fuenzalida, et al.[5])

The historical development of Peru since the days of the Republic has been characterized by two interrelated social processes: foreign dependency and unequal regional development. Their specific mode of interaction has produced a widening gap between the modernizing coast and the backward, stagnant sierra. Yet, rather than moving along parallel and unconnected lines, these two regions have been integrated by various mechanisms of "internal domination," as Cotler's chapter illustrates. This system of domination has operated at two levels: through the domination of the national power structure—centered in the coast—over the sierra, and through the domination of the sierra's urban elite over the local rural population.

The traditional expression of this system of internal domination was always the sierra hacienda. And, despite repeated attempts at rebellion on the part of the dominated peasantry, the system's essential features persisted until the 1950s. While changes in the structure of both the economy and the society had been intensifying since the turn of the century, their impact on the rural population had been limited by the tight control that the hacendado class maintained over its peasants. Beginning in the 1950s, the traditional system of internal domination entered a period of crisis due to a process of societal differentiation that was produced by certain changes in the nation's dependency structure, and the rapid development of the society's dependent capitalist sectors. The emergence of new social forces—such as new economic groups and political parties; the decay of traditional elites; the opening of new occupational opportunities; the intensification of internal migration; the spread of education and the diffusion of antioligarchical ideologies—all these changes caused the peasant populations of the dominated sierra to embark on a process of political mobilization that would give the final blow to an already crumbling social order. The specific form in which this process was manifested varied from one sierra region to another. There were, however, three primary types of manifestations: union formation and struggle; land invasions; and petition for the legal recognition of the indigenous community—particularly the groups of peons who were being held captive within the confines of the hacienda system.

The peasant movement that occurred in the Yanamarca Valley belongs to this generalized process of rural political mobilization. It started in 1945, when a group of peons presented their first list of complaints to their *patrón*; it developed through the formation of a union during the following years; it continued with various forms of conflict with the hacendado; and it ended with his bankruptcy and the takeover of the hacienda by the peasants.

The strains and tensions that gave rise to the peasant movement had their roots in the structural transformation that occurred in the Yanamarca and Mantaro Valleys during the course of the last few decades. This transformation developed through four different stages, involving:

1. an initial period in which the hacendado class ruled the valley;
2. the appearance of a competing center of power, due to changes in the valley's economy;
3. the displacement of the traditional hacendado class by a new regional elite; and
4. the successful emergence of a peasant movement in the context of these new power relationships.

The Traditional Regional Social Structure
of the Yanamarca Valley

An examination of the social structure of this valley around the year 1850 provides a baseline against which one can appreciate the magnitude of the changes that have transformed the region since that time.

In 1850, the Yanamarca Valley was part of a much larger area known as the Jauja province, which extended over a territory of approximately one hundred square miles in the central highlands at an altitude of about twelve thousand feet.

The capital of the entire region was Jauja, a city of some 3,000 people, and the residence of the regional power elite. At the next level of the administrative hierarchy were four district capitals whose municipal authorities were appointed by, and who were directly responsible to, the provincial authorities. Each of these four districts directly controlled a number of indigenous communities which had the administrative status of *anexos*. While these communities had their own traditional authorities, their respective district capitals appointed a number of representatives of the municipal administration, who in fact also controlled local government. The case of Muquiyauyo, an anexo of Huaripampa, as described by Richard N. Adams, clearly illustrates this situation.

Between the establishment of independence in 1821 and the establishment of Muquiyauyo as a separate district in 1886, the general political structure of Muquiyauyo was completely subordinate to Huaripampa. The municipal officials were all men of Huaripampa, and the Muquiyauyinos had little to say in municipal government. In Muquiyauyo itself were a few *mestizo* officials, a lieutenant governor and a municipal agent, appointed by the governor, and the *alcalde* in Huaripampa as their agents in Muquiyauyo. There was also a justice of the peace, but it is not clear whether he was appointed in Huaripampa or Jauja. At the same time, the Indian community continued and retained its own officials. During the first fifty years of the republic, however, the Indian's positions declined in importance, and many of the posts were dropped. By 1886, the position of *cacique* had disappeared entirely and with it the last vestige of Inca officialdom; only the posts of the Spanish colonial hierarchy survived.[6]

In addition to the indigenous communities, there were six haciendas in the Yanamarca region whose owners or renters lived most of the time in Jauja, and who were important members of its power elite. Like other sierra regions in Peru, the Jauja province was controlled by a local mestizo elite, who maintained a relative political autonomy until the beginning of this century.

When describing the nonwhite population of Peru, three racial and sociocultural terms are commonly used: mestizo, cholo and Indian. Up to the last decade of the nineteenth century, the distinction between "mestizo" and "Indian" was clear-cut. Adams describes the caste system of Muquiyauyo, in which a particular series of traits served to distinguish one group in the community from the other:

> Characteristic Indian clothing was worn by Indian men and women, and European clothing was worn by the *mestizos*. Only Indians had usufruct of communal lands, and these lands were owned by the Indian community; this land was under neither the authority nor the control of the *mestizos*. All Indians spoke the Quechua language, and some spoke Spanish; all *mestizos* spoke Spanish although many also knew Quechua. Certain family names were known to be carried only by Indian families, others only by *mestizos*; an individual's ancestry was the primary determinant as to whether he belonged to one caste or the other. Indians were said to have physical features by which they could easily be distinguished from *mestizos*. Only Indians could hold office in the Indian community organization; only *mestizos* could hold office in the district government. While everyone was a Catholic, some of the *fiestas* were sponsored by the Indian caste and other social factors. Intermarriage between the castes was theoretically prohibited. In addition to these traits, others frequently mentioned by informants were these: Indians owned very little private land; Indians seldom traveled; Indians were poorly educated or had no formal education at all; Indians were never invited to the homes of the *mestizos* for *fiestas* except in a subordinate capacity; Indians lived "much lower" than did the *mestizos*; and so forth.[7]

Through the years, due to a generalized process of modernization—with its correlates of rural-urban migration, urbanization, exposure to mass media, expansion of the political market, etc.—a new sociocultural category has emerged: that of the cholo, who, while racially closer to the Indian, follows the sociocultural behavior and attitudes of the mestizo population. Since the cholo speaks Spanish, wears European-style clothes, has some education and "participates" in local activities more than the Indian, he is hard to distinguish from the mestizo. Perhaps the best single indicator of the cholo status is occupation: cholos are organized blue-collar workers, mechanics, "small-time" tailors, street vendors, small-town shopkeepers, artisans, chauffeurs, noncommissioned military officers, policemen and the like.[8] The second-best indicator of the cholo status is a person's mobility. In fact, cholos are so mobile—both socially and physically—that they often change their status and become mestizos. While occupation and mobility are the general indicators of cholo status, an individual's immediate social context is also quite important in determining his sociocultural status. For example, a mestizo in a sierra community would almost surely be considered a cholo in Lima.

Within this context of relative regional autonomy, the domination of the local elites over the indigenous rural population was indeed all pervasive. This was the period during which the defenseless Indian communities were subjected to systematic assault by white and mestizo landowners who established a much harsher system of domination over the Indians than that which had existed during colonial times.[9]

The specific manifestations of this pattern of domination in the Yanamarca Valley varied according to the types of settlements in which the indigenous population lived. In the haciendas, the domination of the mestizo elite reached its greatest intensity; Indians lived under quasi-feudal conditions, as will be described later. In the indigenous communities, the structure of domination took a different form. While the hacienda's peons depended on the patrón for their means of subsistence, the Indians of the communities owned communal lands for grazing and individual plots for agriculture. Thus, in a sense, they controlled their means of production. Yet, because of their social and cultural colonial heritage, this was not sufficient for them to escape mestizo exploitation. For example, Indians residing in communities were still required to pay the personal tribute imposed on them by the Spanish crown, while Spaniards and Creoles were exempted. Furthermore, they were forced to perform various tasks in the urban center—such as street cleaning, public works and road construction, etc.—for the exclusive benefit of the dominant group. The Indians were also forced to furnish building materials for the city's public works.

In addition to these direct mechanisms of domination, the regional power elite had at its disposal the entire national institutional structure, which clearly discriminated against the Indians. For example, Indians were economically marginalized by mestizo intermediaries, who forced the Indians to sell them their products at the prices established by the mestizos. Indians were excluded from voting through literacy requirements; they were also virtually excluded from educational facilities, and were discriminated against culturally. Thus, social interaction in the valley took place within the context of a class structure in which the dominant mestizo class monopolized authority, power, institutional and economic resources, while the dependent Indian class was excluded from political, social and economic participation. The distinctiveness of these two classes was further reinforced by their racial and cultural differences.

Changes in the Political-Administrative and Economic Structure

The monolithic control exercised by Jauja's elite over this region was first challenged in 1864, when Huancayo, now the fastest-growing and most dynamic center of the Peruvian sierra, became the capital of the new province. This meant that the southern part of the Mantaro Valley was now separated from the Jauja province, and thereby removed from its control. Various political, social and economic factors brought about this situation. Huancayo occupied a geographically strategic position, which converted it into a natural frontier town connecting the central sierra to the southern departments of the country. This geographical location was utilized for political purposes by the military *caudillos* of the Republic's early years. For example, Gamarra * camped in Huancayo where, after convening a national assembly, he established the constitution of 1839. In 1854, one of the most important political figures of the nineteenth century—Ramón Castilla—† during his civil war against Echenique,‡ established his headquarters in Huancayo, because he

* General Agustín Gamarra was Peru's president from 1831-33 and from 1839-41.
† General Ramón Castilla was Peru's president from 1845-51 and from 1855-62.
‡ José Rufino Echenique was president from 1851-54.

needed the support of the Indian masses in the Huancayo area. Castilla rewarded the Indians for their military contribution to his campaign by abolishing the Indian tribute and raising the administrative status of some of the villages of the southern part of the Mantaro valley, including Huancayo.

Economically, Huancayo was developing into an important commercial center, a place where the merchants who traveled south from Jauja found it convenient to stop overnight before continuing their trip. Furthermore, Huancayo enjoyed a strategic position in terms of communications. At least six dirt roads converged there; among them, the road to the mines of Cercapuquio and Huancavelica was particularly important. As mining activities and commerce increased in importance, a new group associated with these activities was emerging in the valley. By 1860, Huancayo's population equaled Jauja's. With the establishment of a new province and the development of a new city—characterized by a more homogeneous and integrated social structure, and already prepared to take advantage of the important changes coming to the valley—the era of Jauja's elite domination in the valley was over. When the war of the Pacific broke out in 1879, the position of the landowning class in Jauja was further weakened. Apart from the material damage caused by the war and the disruption of normal agricultural activities, most of the expenses for the defense and the preparation of Cáceres's* army were met by the "notables" of Jauja. The richest ladies of the city offered their jewelry to finance the campaigns against the Chileans.

In the years following the war with Chile, however, Jauja enjoyed something of a comeback. This was primarily due to the incursion, in 1893, of a group of foreign businessmen who, taking advantage of the construction of railways from Lima to La Oroya—located at about 60 kilometers from Jauja—ten years earlier, started to bring in merchandise from Lima and Europe.

Both the immigration of foreigners and the commercial exchanges with the coast intensified during the first decade of this century—since, in 1908, the railway reached the valley, rapidly transforming Jauja's social and economic profile.

* Andrés A. Cáceres, an important national figure during the war against Chile (1879–83), was president of Peru from 1886–90.

During the first years of the twentieth century, the commerce between Jauja and the Peruvian coast was controlled by eight families, all of them foreigners or migrants from the coast. They operated in a situation of quasi-monopoly and rapid business expansion. For example, one of the most important businessmen was an immigrant of Italian origin who controlled eight stores, a pharmacy and a hotel. The same people who imported from Europe, taking advantage of their personal contacts, soon managed to monopolize the valley's exports as well, due to their superior buying capacity. For example, another immigrant of French origin monopolized the commerce of wool during the same period. These changes in the economic structure of Jauja had an important impact on the composition of its dominant group, and above all opened up the possibilities for new social forces to participate in the political control of the city. In fact, if before 1880 the *"principales,"* or "notables"—those who controlled the city politically, were the landowners—in this new stage, political power was shared between the old families from Jauja and the new group of businessmen. There were, however, no manifestations of conflict between this new emerging elite and the traditional landowning class. Alliances and agreements among them were quickly established, particularly through social and family interconnections.

Yet, while this process of differentiation and social recomposition within the dominant group of Jauja was taking place, not much was happening in the rural areas.

Perhaps the single, most important factor that upset the valley's total social organization was the massive intrusion of modern capitalism. The Cerro de Pasco Corporation, Peru's largest copper producer, established its operations for the exploitation of the Peruvian central sierra's rich mining zone in 1902.

The beginning of this new type of economy meant the alteration of archaic forms of production and the social relations associated with them. Most of the working force had traditionally been recruited directly from the surrounding peasant population, through the mechanism of *enganche* (indentured labor). This concentration of a working population of peasants under a single economic regime, characterized by salary exchange relationships and the depersonalization of the system of domination, encouraged the appearance of various processes of politization and unionization on the part of the peasant proletarian mass, who for the first time clashed in an organized way with the capitalist class. These experiences were particularly important for their socializing effects, since they favored the development of new attitudes and organization abilities, which were used later on by the peasant-miners in their communities of origin.[10] At the same time, work in the mines provided an increase in the buying power of that part of the peasant population that survived the hard conditions of such labor; this allowed them to modernize their agricultural activities, or invest their savings in the modernization of their small industry.

Since the introduction of Cerro de Pasco and its labor recruitment policy had a direct impact on the people of the countryside, new forces of modernization were added to the already changing situation.

Two large enterprises for cattle raising were formed: *La Sociedad Ganadera Junín* (1906) and *La Sociedad Ganadera del Centro* (1910). The former was particularly important, because it meant the incursion of financial groups from Lima who, in combination with some large landowners from Jauja, established more rationalized and technologically more advanced enterprises. The most immediate consequence of the formation of the *Sociedad Ganadera Junín,* from the point of view of the local power structure, was that the old owners of the haciendas incorporated in the new enterprise left Jauja and moved their residences to Lima, leaving the administration of the enterprise to professional workers. Thus the hacendado group lost some of its most powerful members.

At the same time, new antioligarchical ideologies originating in Lima began to spread to the areas affected by the first wave of the modernization process. Members of the urban working class in Jauja also participated in the change process and formed their first organization in 1913. It brought together mainly small artisans—such as tailors, carpenters, small shopkeepers, etc.—who attempted to follow anarcosindicalist ideology.

Emergence of a New Regional Elite

By the beginning of the 1920s, the regional social structure had already undergone radical transformations. In the rural areas, new district capitals and legally recognized indigenous communities proliferated, thereby acquiring new channels of direct communications with the central government and weakening the rural areas' dependency relationship with the urban centers. Although indigenous communities had been abolished at the beginning of the Republic, they were legally recognized again in 1919, as soon as they met the following criteria: communal ownership of lands and pasture, and the tradition of communal work. Through their legal representative, the *personero,* they had direct access to the offices of the Ministry of Labor and Indigenous Affairs. Jauja's old elite had lost its traditional dominant position both internally and valleywide, where Huancayo, capitalizing on the breakup of the previous monolithic structure of rural control, was emerging as the new dominant center of the valley, with an economy based mainly on commerce.

Two additional factors intervened to definitely end one historical period and begin a new one, in which the Mantaro Valley entered completely into a process of urban expansion and rural urbanization exemplified by the explosion of Huancayo, as shown in the figures in Table 1, taken from the national censuses of 1876, 1940 and 1961 which illustrate the differential development followed by Jauja and Huancayo. First, in 1929, due to the international financial crisis, the commerce that the foreign immigrants had established between Jauja and both Lima and Europe collapsed. This meant the economic and social bankruptcy of one important faction of Jauja's power elite. Second, the election of Sanchez Cerro (as president of Peru) in 1931 brought about the overt political defeat of the landowning Jauja elites who had aligned themselves with the conservative forces which were defeated by a populist leader. The electoral process of 1931 also meant an effective expansion of the national political market: both *Sanchezcerristas* and *Apristas,* members of the nation's two largest competing political parties, attempted to establish clientelist politics [11] in the more modernized rural areas of Peru. In the Yanamarca and Montaro Valleys, electoral committees were established in rural districts for the first time.

Jauja's decay was officially confirmed in the same year (1931) when the capital of the department of Junín, including both the provinces of Jauja and Huancayo, was moved from Cerro de Pasco to Huancayo.

Table 1
THE POPULATION OF JAUJA AND HUANCAYO

	Jauja	Huancayo
1876	2,773	4,053
1940	12,280	26,729
1961	14,298	64,153

A precensus estimate for 1972 indicates that Huancayo's population is around 120,000, while Jauja's is approximately 15,000.

All these converging processes produced an opening in the regional social structure, setting the stage for the peasant movements of the Yanamarca valley which broke out in the following years.

Peasant Mobilization in the Yanamarca Valley

While these structural transformations were taking place in the area that constituted the Jauja province of 1850, life in the haciendas of the Yanamarca Valley continued practically unchanged until the early 1930s. Of the six haciendas in that area, we will concentrate on one, hacienda Yanamarca, to describe the process of peasant mobilization.

The hacienda of Yanamarca had maintained the closest contacts with the outside world, due to the fact that it bordered on Acolla, an independent indigenous community, which was the educational and commercial center of a microregion. The hacienda, located only a few miles away from Jauja, belonged to a Spanish captain during the last years of the colonial period. With the establishment of the Republic, it passed over to the control of the state, which rented it to private individuals. The hacienda, with peons as its labor force, passed from one renter to another. It consisted of 3296 hectares (about 8,240 acres) of which only 540 were cultivable. Its main products were barley, potatoes, quinua (an especially nutritious Peruvian type of wheat) and more recently, onions.

The internal social organization was simple, and social relationships were extremely hierarchical. The renter, commonly referred to as the patrón, was at the top of the organization, but he resided in the city during most of the year. An administrator had the immediate

264 GIORGIO ALBERTI

responsibility for the hacienda's functioning. He counted on the help of a *mayordomo* (general supervisor), one white-collar employee and two foremen. The true labor force was made up of approximately 120 peons, subdivided into two categories: full-time and half-time peons.

The arrangements governing the exchange relationships between the hacendado (in the present context, synonymous with "patrón") and his peons were like those prevalent in other parts of the sierra.[12] In exchange for the right to cultivate a small plot of land for his own subsistence and that of his family, the resident peon had to work for the hacendado an average of three days a week. Furthermore, the peon had to use his own tools, manure the lands with his animals and furnish the hacienda house with water and wood. Women were also subjected to a number of personal obligations in the hacienda house.

The peons did not form a homogeneous group. Rather, they were characterized by significant internal differences in terms of the amount of land received and the number of days worked for the hacendado, as can be seen in Table 2.

Table 2
THE LABOR SYSTEM OF A YANAMARCA HACIENDA

Status within the hacienda	No.	No. of week days of work	Extension of assigned plot (in hectares)
Peons with help (of kin)	51	4	2.9
Peons without help (of kin)	17	4	1.9
Recently married	29	2	1.1
Women	5	2	1.1
Peons with plots	23	1	.80
"Landless" Peons	11	1	Allowed to continue living on hacienda lands.

Source: José Matos Mar, *El Valle de Yanámarca* (Lima: Universidad Nacional Mayor de San Marcos, 1964).

In addition to the peons, there were a number of day laborers who usually joined the hacienda work force during the period of highest labor demand, such as harvest time. They received wages in exchange for their work. For example, in 1960, Matos Mar reports that peons recruited outside the hacienda earned 15 *soles* * a day without food,

* At that time, the rate of exchange was 26 soles to the U.S. dollar.

and 12 soles a day with food. Women received 8.50 soles without food and 7 soles with food, while children received 6 soles without food and 5 with food.[13]

The system of social control was maintained through two different mechanisms. The hacendado or his administrator used a differential reward system in an attempt to ensure the peons' loyalty. First, those who behaved in the prescribed way received personal favors which could be withdrawn any time they ceased to obey their superior's orders. Second, a complex system of sanctions was utilized to punish those who did not comply with the regulations. The most extreme of these sanctions was actual expulsion from the hacienda's lands.

The hacienda system of social organization rested on two additional features. First, as we noted earlier, the hacendado was a prominent member of the provincial power structure. He controlled the system of public administration, either by occupying important positions himself or by establishing close personal relationships with the holders of public offices. The hacendado and his associates—the head of the local police force, the judge, the priest and a few lawyers—constituted a closed power elite which safeguarded primarily their own interests. Second, the peons had no chance to establish effective contacts outside the hacienda.

Furthermore, the type of cultural orientation produced by these overall structural conditions favored intragroup hostility, which functioned as a displacement mechanism to compensate for the frustration inherent in the patrón-peon relationship.

This regime continued, with only insignificant changes, until the 1930s. Yet by that time, some of the peons had already gained new experiences in the mining centers. Their first timid attempt to introduce changes into the hacienda system was an effort by the peons to establish a school. They invited a private teacher from the nearby community of Acolla to give classes to their children. Next, they established connections with the Ministry of Education, in order to demand support for the local teacher's activity. This support was achieved at the beginning of 1940. Meanwhile, the children of the wealthier peons received their first years of instruction in the hacienda, and later continued their schooling in Acolla, which was only three kilometers away.

Some of these young men, after receiving their initial education, went on to work in the mines. They were in a privileged position, because they could take advantage of regional opportunities from which their fathers were excluded. In fact, they could choose between working in the hacienda as day laborers or leaving it to look for work in the mines or the urban centers. They could always go back to the hacienda and take over their father's positions, while if their fathers left the hacienda, they would lose their rights to the plots of land allotted them by the hacendado. At the beginning of the 1940s, some of the peons' sons were working in La Oroya and in Casapalca, both important mining centers of the Cerro de Pasco complex. There they learned about union activities, and some of them became directly involved in the conflicts that characterized labor-management relationships in the mining industry during those years. At the same time, they established contacts with political leaders and were exposed to antioligarchical ideologies. Some of them returned to the hacienda and were incorporated into the local labor force, either as peons or as helpers. All this occurred before 1945. Later on, a series of important national events would help speed up the process of change in Yanamarca. For the first time, APRA, a populist party, was allowed to come out into the open—after many years of persecution and underground activities; many of its members held posts in parliament and occupied offices in provincial public administrations.

These changes in personnel occupying positions of authority, in addition to the political activities of parties representing the emerging social forces, caused an immediate reaction in many rural areas of the country.[14] With the direct participation of APRA members in positions of regional and national power, the process of unionization spread not only among the urban proletariat, but also throughout the rural areas of the coast, where for the first time groups of peons formed their unions. The winds of change also blew over the lands of hacienda Yanamarca. Jauja's mayor at that time was a well-known local Aprista who participated in APRA's early attempts to penetrate the countryside during the election of 1931. It was during his term of office that a group of young ex-miners, under the leadership of an Aprista schoolteacher from Acolla, managed to mobilize a large segment of the peon population. After a series of general-assembly meetings, held at night in order to avoid the hacendado, they decided to present their first series of complaints to the hacendado. Their aim, at first, was to improve their exchange rate with their patrón. In the presence of an official from the Ministry of Labor and Indigenous Affairs, representatives of the peons and the hacendado reached an agreement signed by both parties, according to which the patrón agreed to abolish some of the peon's obligations and the peons promised to comply regularly with their tasks. However, very soon after the agreement had been signed, the peons filed a complaint with the Ministry of Justice, accusing the patrón of breaking the pact. Later on, the peons established contacts in the Ministry of Labor and Indigenous Affairs, to whom they sent a memorandum about their case. It was the beginning of a long struggle in both the national and the department capital. At one point, the prefect of Huancayo intervened, following the denunciation of a patrón who had accused the peasant movement's leaders of being Communists and social agitators. The peons immediately sent an angry written statement to the Minister of the Interior but, in spite of all their efforts, the Ministry ordered the expulsion of the peasant leaders who had constituted the backbone of the movement. This order, however, was not carried out, since the leaders reached an agreement with the hacendado, in which they promised not to participate in any subversive activities, to obey their superior's orders, and to drop all the demands they had previously presented. This might have meant the end of the peasant movement, but the peasants gathered in a general assembly, repudiated their leaders, and a new leadership emerged. This leadership turnover clearly indicates that the necessity for change and the willingness to act in order to effect such change was felt throughout the peons' group. At this stage of the conflict, the peons decided to get in touch with the deputy for the province of Jauja. After many trips to Lima, they finally obtained an interview with him, and enumerated all the details of their long conflict with the hacendado. Just when it seemed that the peasants were likely to win the deputy's support, events of national importance brought about their temporary defeat. In 1948, with the change in the national government brought about by the establishment of the Odría military dictatorship and the disbanding of the national parliament, the peasants' connections with the Jauja deputy became irrelevant. As a result of this chaotic situation, Yanamarca temporarily returned to the same styles of life and work that had been prevalent during the days before the conflict.

Yet a lasting transformation had occurred among the peons of

Yanamarca: they had become class conscious. In fact, they had broken down their social and cultural isolation; disrupted local and vertical solidarity and loyalty; perceived that their individual interests were not opposed to group interests; developed new intragroup systems of communication; defined their overall situation more realistically, both in terms of their enemy and their potential allies; and finally, they had devised a strategy of action designed to attain their newly defined objectives.[15]

In 1950 an important change occurred at the top of the hacienda social organization. The renter could no longer arrange for the extension of his leave, and so he was replaced by the ex-deputy who had previously established contacts with the peons. The new renter, who was already aware of the unequal relationships which had existed in the hacienda, wanted to introduce a more rational system, which would clearly specify, in the form of a written contract, the rights and obligations of both parties. He accorded the peons a few concessions, and in exchange he received a written statement in which they assumed the full responsibility for their work obligations. For a few years there were no further instances of overt conflict. Meanwhile the organizational activity of the peons, which had been centered around their conflicts with the previous renter, became directed toward other endeavors. It was then that the parent-teachers' association acquired importance. The functions of this organization went beyond simple educational matters and the relationships between parents and teachers. Rather, this organization extended its activities to many aspects of life in the hacienda. For example, the leaders of the parent-teachers' association persuaded the hacendado to provide a small plot of land whose production would go toward the running costs of a school. After obtaining the land, the association built the school.

Meanwhile, seasonal migration to the mines of the central sierra continued, as did the education of young men in the nearby schools. One of the most prominent figures in the new conflict, after completing primary education in the hacienda school, continued his education in a secondary school at Acolla. Afterwards he worked as a miner in La Oroya, where he participated actively in the union movement. When his father died, he went back to the hacienda and assumed the obligations which went along with the role of peon. Like many others who had had similar experiences, this young man was anxious to share what he learned in the mines with those who had never left the hacienda. He encountered a very receptive audience. While the ferment he engendered was continuing among the peasants, the patrón made a number of changes in the production process, with the introduction of new machinery, insecticide and new crops such as onions. After a few years during which the hacienda produced good profits, the hacendado had to face a serious economic crisis—due to the fact that bad weather during two consecutive harvests had nearly destroyed the crop. The patrón's first reaction was to squeeze more work out of the peons. In order to do this, he depended on the help of those peasants who already occupied privileged positions, such as the mayordomo and the foremen, to whom he gave more land and higher wages, in the hope that they would be stricter in making the peons comply with their obligations.

This rigid control of the hacendado turned out to be counterproductive, however; it ultimately caused the peons to react and defend their own positions. On the night of April 20, 1961, the peons gathered in a general-assembly meeting and decided to form a union in order to face the patrón's new demands in a united and organized way. During the following days, they established connections with a lawyer from Huancayo in order to have the legal advice needed for the recognition of their union. Their first effort failed. They were informed by labor officials that they could not form a union, because their working conditions did not meet the legal requirements. This did not dishearten the peons, who were finally supported by the leaders of a leftist union which was attempting to expand its base. Two years after the initial founding of their union, the peons of Yanamarca succeeded in obtaining legal recognition, and registered their organization with the subregional office of the Ministry of Labor in Huancayo.

After achieving its new legal position, the union presented the patrón with a list of complaints, including all those presented in 1945. In addition, they asked for wages instead of payment for labor in usufruct rights in land. Upon the refusal of the hacendado to satisfy the peasants' demands, the union called a strike. The hacendado reacted by calling for the intervention of the prefect of Huancayo, rather than appealing to labor officials.

Higher-level regional officials attempted to persuade the peons to stop the strike as a precondition for establishing discussions between the two parties. However, agreements were not reached because the peasants insisted on their right to wages, while the hacendado refused, claiming that the peons were given remuneration for their services in the form of the small plot of land which he let them use for their own subsistence.

When the situation had reached a standstill, national events once again had a direct impact on the local situation at the hacienda Yanamarca. In 1963, Fernando Belaúnde was elected president, after a much-disputed election campaign during which agrarian reform was promised by all parties. Upon taking office, President Belaúnde announced a program of vast reforms and the formation of a community development agency called Cooperación Popular, whose main task would be to assist the peasants. Political ferment spread to many rural parts of the country, including Yanamarca. The peons, encouraged by the president's promises, radicalized their goals. They sent a petition to the president, in which they presented their case and asked to be allowed to rent the hacienda directly from the state, thereby bypassing the patrón. The answer from the Office of the President was long delayed; they finally were told that their request had been taken into consideration, but that they should wait for the institution of an agrarian reform law which was then being prepared.

The two years of union struggle were particularly harsh on the hacendado. In fact, in a situation like that of hacienda Yanamarca, where agricultural laborers kept a plot of land for their subsistence, the strike is a very effective conflict mechanism. It damages only one party; while the patrón loses his labor force, the peons can continue working the plot of land assigned to them. Of course this is true only where the hacendado lacks the power to expel them from his land. The result of these years of conflict was a new financial crisis for the hacendado-renter who could not pay for the renewal of his lease. Under these circumstances, the peasants finally achieved success and received permission to rent the hacienda directly, so long as they formed a cooperative.

Similar processes of mobilization took place in some of the remaining five haciendas of the Yanamarca valley.[16] The only one in which peasants did not organize and rebel against their patrón was run in a completely different fashion. In this case, the hacendado introduced many technological changes, eliminated the "feudal" obligations attached to the traditional role of peon, paid the peasants a salary and offered them his advice on marketing the crops produced in the plot of land assigned to them, thus facilitating their participation in the changing situation.

Theoretical Considerations

From a theoretical point of view, the empirical material presented in this chapter suggests a four-stage model of regional transformation and the origin of peasant movements. At stage one, the hacendado is at the heart of the regional power structure and has full control over the peons' environment. The unequal distribution of power is reinforced by cultural and ethnic differentiation in Peru, between the subordinated Indian and the dominant mestizo. At stage two, a regional power contender appears as the result of changes in the economic structure of the valley. The power domain of the hacendado is reduced, but his hold on his peons is still strong.

By stage three, a new regional elite has displaced the traditional hacendado class. By the time this shift in regional power relations occurs, the social structure of the region has already undergone important transformations. Not only has there been a regional "revolution" in the seat of power, but also the economic structure and the social relations associated with it have changed their quasi-feudal nature and taken on a more capitalist orientation. This stage is also characterized by the opening up of new alternatives and the entrance of national politics into the rural areas. Yet at the local, provincial level, the hacendado class, because of personal connections and the weight of tradition, still manages to control the situation by sharing its power with the newly emerging groups. Given this set of conditions, while the autonomously organized Indian committees can take advantage of changing regional opportunities, social relations within the hacienda tend to persist and the peons continue their exploited existence as if nothing has happened around them. But things have changed. Some of these same peons have themselves been actors in the change process. For example, they have participated in union activities away from the hacienda, in the mining centers; they have built up new client relationships with political figures; they have gained other usable allies and, fundamental to their subsequent behavior, they have acquired a new consciousness of their position. Stage four represents the total bankruptcy of the hacendado class. By now it has completely lost local political control: new forces, such as merchants, politicians, professionals and national bureaucrats, now occupy local seats of power. For example, lawyers who have antioligarchical ideologies, or who are simply interested in making money, are now willing to help the peons with their court cases. This has been particularly true in the Jauja region, where—as the importance of education as a status symbol increased, its elite produced a surplus of lawyers who soon discovered that the peasants were a good source of potential clients. At the same time, the hacendado class faces serious financial problems, mainly due to mismanagement, bad relations with its labor force and lack of modernization in its technology of land exploitation. The hacendado class commonly reacts to these problems by attempting to squeeze more work out of its peons. This often serves to precipitate the peasants' reaction. The important thing is that, at this stage, the peons are no longer isolated. New, emerging social actors—such as politicians, union leaders and national bureaucrats—are willing to listen to their demands. At this point, the direct confrontation between peasant and landlord is inevitable. The success of the peasant movement will lead to the elimination of quasi-feudal working relationships within a capitalist regional structure.

On the basis of the empirical material at hand, and the preceding theoretical considerations, we propose three general propositions about the origins of peasant movements and their role in developing countries:

1. A peasant movement is the outcome of three interrelated social processes: 1. the persistence of an exploitative relationship between landlord and peasant; 2. long-range structural transformations that bring about the loss of power of the hacendado class; and 3. increased bargaining power on the part of the peasantry.

2. While these conditions create a structural situation conducive to peasant movements, precipitating factors [17] must also be present. The identification of the nature of these precipitating

factors requires a close examination of specific peasant movements. Our material suggests a number of factors—including the sudden worsening of exchange relationships experienced by the peasantry; population pressures due to natural causes and/or the closing of alternative occupational opportunities; the sudden decrease of peasant buying capacity as a consequence of national inflation, etc. *The important point to be made here is that the precipitating factors must not be taken to be the cause of peasant movements.*

3. A peasant movement, when successful in countries like Peru, serves to remove the vestiges of archaic systems of production and the social relations associated with them. That is, it brings a "backward" social sector into line with the dominant mode of production and the social relations prevalent in a given region or country. In this sense, a successful peasant movement, from the point of view of significant national social change, can become a conservative force.

The widely held belief that peasant movements are a potentially revolutionary force can be misleading. This is because peasant movements are strictly dependent upon the regional transformations that alter the local class structure of which they are a part. That is, peasant movements are ultimately the product of unequal development in which the modernization process has brought about the emergence of new groups and the decay of traditional elites. They occur in pockets of modernization where the traditional relationship between hacendado and peasant has varied little through the process of regional change, and has become obsolete in terms of the regional social structure. It is inherent in the dynamics of uneven development to create structural conditions conducive to peasant movements at *different points in time and space.* The purpose of the movement is to remove the hacendado, perceived as the major obstacle to the peasant's new aspirations of direct participation in the changing regional context. Since these pockets of modernization are brought about *unevenly* within the national context, the peasant response is also uneven and their success in obtaining their goals creates even more peasant class fragmentation, rather than promoting peasant class solidarity and consciousness. That is, the "classlike" behavior of some segments of the peasantry is not a sufficient indicator of the beginning of the change of the peasantry from a situation of "class in itself," to that of a "class for itself."

This point is clearly illustrated by what happened in Convención Valley, the site of the most widely known and best-publicized Peruvian peasant movement in recent years. Many observers thought that it was the birth of a general sense of peasant class consciousness. Yet, as the peasants of La Convención achieved their goal, which was mainly land ownership, they became rather conservative in the defense of their newly established interests.[19] The success of peasant movements must be analyzed in terms of both a local and a national perspective. And within the national perspective, particular attention must be given to the conditions under which peasant movements can merge with urban-based protest movements, and thus become an integral part of a total national transformation.

NOTES

1. For a discussion of these alternative explanations, see my "Los Movimientos Campesinos," in Robert G. Keith, et al., *La Hacienda, la Comunidad y el Campesino en el Peru* (Lima: Francisco Moncloa Editores, 1970).

2. Barrington Moore, *Social Origins of Dictatorship and Democracy* (Boston: Beacon Press, 1966); Eric Wolf, *Peasant Wars of the Twentieth Century* (New York: Harper and Row, 1969).

3. Howard Handelman, *Struggle in the Andes: Peasant Political Mobilization in Peru.*, Ph.D. diss., University of Wisconsin, 1971.

4. Anibal Quijano Obregon, "Contemporary Peasant Movements," in *Elites in Latin America*, ed. S.M. Lipset and A. Solari (New York: Oxford University Press, 1967), p. 306.

5. Fernando Fuenzalida, Enrique Mayer, Gabriel Escobar, François Bourricaud and José Matos Mar, *El Indio y el Poder en el Peru* (Lima: Francisco Moncloa Editores S.A., 1970).

6. Richard N. Adams, *A Community in the Andes. Problems and Progress in Muquiyauyo* (Seattle: University of Washington Press, 1959), p. 31.

7. Ibid., p. 82.

8. Carlos Astiz, *Pressure Groups and Power Elites in Peruvian Politics* (Ithaca: Cornell University Press, 1969), p. 73.

9. Frederick B. Pike, *The Modern History of Peru* (London: Weidenfeld and Nicolson, 1967), p. 67.

10. Petras and Zeitlin present interesting data on the relationship between mining centers and agrarian radicalism. They show that "Chilean mining municipalities are centers from which political radicalism is diffused into surrounding non-mining agricultural areas." See James Petras and Maurice Zeitlin, "Agrarian Radicalism in Chile," in *Latin America, Reform or Revolution?*, ed. Petras and Zeitlin (New York: Fawcett Publications, 1968), p. 235.

11. John Duncan Powell, "Peasant Society and Clientelist Politics," *American Political Science Review* 64, no. 2 (1970).

12. For a detailed description of the types of traditional haciendas in the Peruvian sierra, see Mario Vasquez, *Hacienda, Peonaje y Servidumbre en los Andes Peruandos* (Lima: Editorial Estudios Andinos, 1961).

13. José Matos Mar, *El Valle de Yanamarca* (Lima: Universidad Nacional Mayor de San Marcos, 1964), p. 174.

14. Julio Cotler and Felipe Portocarrero, "Peru: Peasant Organizations," in *Latin American Peasant Movements*, ed. H.A. Landsberger (Ithaca: Cornell University Press, 1969).

15. Quijano, "Contemporary Peasant Movements," p. 328.

16. Other works that have dealt with the peasant movements of the Yanamarca Valley are: Giorgio Alberti, *Intervillage Systems and Development: A Study of Social Change in Highland Peru* (Ithaca: Cornell University, Latin American Studies Program; Dissertation Series, no. 18, 1970); Rodrigo Sánchez, *Movilización Campesina y Cambio Social en Yanamarca* (Lima: Instituto des Estudios Peruanos [Manuscript],

1969); F. La Mond Tullis, *Lord and Peasant: A Paradigm of Political and Social Change* (Cambridge: Harvard University Press, 1970); William Foote Whyte, Chapter 9 of this book.

17. For a general theory of collective behavior which uses the concepts of structural and conduciveness and precipitating factors, but which is based on a different methodological framework than the one presented here, see Neil J. Smelser, *Theory of Collective Behavior* (New York: The Free Press, 1962).

18. Wesley Craig, "The Peasant Movement in La Convención Valley," in *Latin American Peasant Movements* ed. H.A. Landsberger (Ithaca: Cornell University Press, 1969).

David Chaplin

11.   La Convención Valley and the 1962–65 Guerrilla Uprising

The example of Castro's revolution found a new generation of students in Peru thoroughly disillusioned with the APRA after its flirtation with the oligarchy from 1956 to 1962. However, it appears that the major influence that Cuba and other foreign Communist nations have enjoyed is still largely in the universities. The unsuccessful guerrilla actions of 1965, although largely rural in locale, were urban in membership, since they were not able to enlist the support of a significant number of the local population. In fact, the following example of a successful peasant uprising is explicable by its spontaneous local leadership and its basically conservative goals, as well as by the willingness of the Lima-based power elite to buy peace in the sierra at the expense of local *gamonales*.

The outstanding example of this type of movement is the Federación de Sindicatos de Campesinos (Federation of Peasant Unions) of la Convención y Lares.[1] The conditions underlying its origin make it rather unusual, and hence one could conclude that more typical Indian communities would not be likely to follow suit. However, as Whyte and Alberti have shown, less publicized changes had already occurred elsewhere.

The change leading to the establishment of the federation began in a valley some 90 miles north of Cuzco, on the edge of the Amazonian jungle. Although this area was settled by Creoles in the sixteenth century, the distaste of the sierra (Inca) Indians for life in the jungle and the scarcity and intractability of local tribal Indians resulted in a shortage of labor that has never been fully relieved. The major system of labor recruitment relied on was similar to that employed in the sierra—i.e., a sharecropping "contract" under which the tenant also owed additional amounts of free labor to his landlord. The major differences between this area and the sierra were that here there were hardly any independent peasant communities as holdovers from the *reducciones* (concentrated regroupings of Indians) of the colonial era. In addition, the landlords here enjoyed an extreme degree of geographic isolation that enabled them to resist governmental attempts even to set up taxing units to support provincial capitals.[2]

Contact was finally established with the outside world and change commenced with the construction in 1933 of both a railroad and a dirt road to substitute for the traditional mule train. Simultaneously a malaria epidemic depopulated the valley. It was not until the late 1940s that the epidemic was conquered and a new wave of migrants recruited. Craig estimates that by 1965 two-thirds of the residents of the valley had come from nearby sierra provinces.

Previously, production had consisted largely of subsistence crops, since transportation had been inadequate for a cash crop. During the 1950s, however, coffee was introduced, not primarily by the landlords on their own land, but by their tenants on their marginal plots, which, circumstantially, were more appropriate to this crop. At the same time the price of coffee in this region enjoyed a sharp increase from an index of 100 in 1945 to one of 1,221 in 1954.[3] Production apparently increased over four times during the same period. The added income enjoyed by the tenants was used in part to hire more recent migrants *(allegados)* to take care of their labor obligations to the landowners.

Finally the landlords awoke to the opportunities demonstrated from below and began planting their own land in coffee and trying to recover the plots "leased" to their tenants. Both policies gave rise to an immediate reaction, the latter for obvious reasons and the former because the labor obligations created by the landlords' new coffee areas naturally coincided with the tenants' busiest season. The response of the tenants was to form local unions on each hacienda, starting at least as early as 1952. By 1958, these unions had combined into a federation. Wesley W. Craig's research reveals that the founders of these unions had the following characteristics: they were local peasants, not organizers from the city; they were largely recent migrants from the sierra who were relatively more educated, more nearly bilingual and more acculturated than their followers; and a disproportionately high percentage were from the small group of converts to Protestantism in Peru.[4]

Several outside groups were, however, of crucial importance to the federation's development and early success. One group consisted of a number of lawyers in the city of Cuzco, who, although landowners themselves, were willing in this case to side with the Indians against the jungle oligarchs. Gabriel Escobar offers the following explanation of this phenomenon: "The lawyer-hacendados of Cuzco do not own very large haciendas nor belong to the traditional 'sixty families of Cuzco.' In general, they belong to the provincial aristocracies and are of lower-class *(cholo)* extraction who have come very recently into possession of haciendas by sending their children to study law and get haciendas by litigation. As such they feel some insecurity in their position and are frequently stopped in their social mobility by a series of discriminatory practices. I view their adoption of Communistic ideology not as enlightenment but as part of the traditional mechanics of class struggle in Cuzco, something that already was happening in colonial times and reached its peak during the twenties." [5]

Cuzco had long been the stronghold of Communist unions in Peru, even after years of intermittent Aprista efforts to move in under government protection. A major reason for this is that the University of Cuzco, staffed in many fields largely by local professionals with legal training, had been alienated from Aprismo since the university's reconstruction in the 1920s.[6]

The Communist labor movement in the city of Cuzco was another group of great assistance to the peasant federation in one of the first and still very rare cases of true urban and rural proletariat cooperation. However, this "help" is described by James Payne and others as an example of revolutionary bungling.[7] After reaching its high point in April 1958, when it seized complete control of the city, the Communist labor federation had lost strength. The decision of the Trotskyites and Hugo Blanco, the leader of the 1962 sharecroppers' strike in La Convención, to go to the peasants was made from a position of weakness, since they were not even the dominant faction in the city of Cuzco.

During the 1950s the peasant federation's efforts consisted largely of defending itself—by means of legal grievances presented to the Ministry of Labor—against the incursions of the landlords. The Ministry, under Prado, was not effective in meeting their demands, so when Hugo Blanco joined the federation and suggested more forceful measures, he met with considerable success. One strike had already been carried out in 1960, without harsh repression. In fact, a government commission sent to the area in response to the strike recommended that the traditional free labor obligations be abolished, but the Prado regime decided to suppress this report. By 1962, Blanco had built up enough support to win election as secretary-general of the federation. (He was the son-in-law of one of the lawyers in Cuzco who had already represented the peasant union in an appeal to the Ministry of Labor.) However, as a self-confessed Trotskyite, dedicated, in his own words, to "putschist violence," he had already alienated the by now old-guard founders of the peasant federation as well as its "Stalinist" adviser, Huamantico, the long-time head of the Cuzco Workers' Federation.[8] As a result, most of the founding leaders quit after Blanco's electoral victory, taking 20 unions with them. Simultaneously, the police, under the military junta, were ordered to arrest Blanco, which they finally succeeded in doing nine months later (owing partly to the confession of some inept, amateur, Trotskyite bank robbers determined to finance their own revolutionary program). The problems of the police in finding him were due much more to geographical obstacles than to local support, of which Blanco enjoyed relatively little at that point.[9]

Blanco's capture did not, however, prevent the two factions of the peasant federation from cooperating on a labor boycott of all haciendas during 1962. This passive strike was encouraged by a final gesture on the part of the Prado government (a gesture made primarily to embarrass the subsequent regime), which legitimated the strikers' action by abolishing on April 24, 1962, their labor obligations (condiciones). The president still insisted, however, that the peasants make up for this concession by paying rent. The military junta that took over that July reaffirmed this abolition, but provided that payments be made for the purchase, not just rental, of the land. This success for the peasants was bolstered by the subsequent land reform agency's efforts in the less dramatic area of establishing cooperatives and securing titles—efforts accompanied by some repression (including an alleged massacre of 42 peasants in November 1962 and a roundup of local union leaders) [10] and internal dissension. Following this success, however, the radicalism and strength of the federation began to wane.

Subsequently, when Luis de la Puente (one of the leaders of the 1965 wave of guerrilla uprisings) returned to La Convención in 1965, he did not find the local support he had so glibly predicted.[11] The Ministry of War's account of these events and their historical background, while overlooking a number of relevant factors,[12] appears to be quite accurate in demonstrating the lack of popular support for the 1965 guerrilla uprisings.

In La Convención, then, we have a clear example of so-called revolutionary peasants turned kulaks by a land reform program. There are still intransigent conservatives who view agrarian reform as "Communistic," but it should be clear that it can produce one of the most conservative types of rural proletariat—the petty, but tolerably well-off, peasant.* Certainly such a consequence was, or should have been, one of the conscious goals of the bourgeois liberals who have promoted this program against the interests of both the far Left and the far Right.

We can also draw from this case the observation that peasants can be radicalized more easily by the threat of losing acquired gains than by simply raising their aspirations beyond their achievements. At the same time, it must not be overlooked that these peasants were always pursuing their own goals, namely, secure land titles. If they had met an intransigent urban elite determined to defend the isolated landowners, the situation would perhaps have polarized in the fashion de la Puente hoped for. (On the other hand, as he and others have observed, severe repressions can simply numb and depoliticize a whole generation of workers, especially in the context of a culture one of whose traditional themes has been fatalism.)

Land invasions in Peru have not by any means been limited to this region, although the movement here is still the most successful early case to receive such official recognition. Elsewhere in Peru, especially since Belaúnde took office in 1963 with military support, more or less successful invasions have been spreading. Under Belaúnde, very

* Karl Marx, *The Eighteenth Brumaire of Louis Bonaparte* (London 1943), pp. 135-37. Marx also observed that the benefits to the peasantry of the division of land had to be transitory—lasting only long enough to buy support and time for one regime—and that subsequently equally great poverty would result. Latin American land reformers should not expect this conservatizing effect to last indefinitely. An increase in fertility from the earlier marriages that such ready land makes possible can alone undermine the benefits of such a reform.

little land was distributed through the official and very conservative agrarian reform law, but many thousands of hectares were taken over by peasants and given de facto recognition by a government no longer willing or able to stem the tide of land invasion in the sierra. (The government, however, stopped such invasions among the modern plantations on the coast.)

Revolutionary Strategy

In the light of the foregoing discussion of factors unfavorable to revolution in Peru, it is interesting to look at the public discussion of strategy carried on among Hugo Blanco, Luis de la Puente, the military and other interested parties. The prime issue seems to be the relevance of the Chinese and Cuban examples. This position includes concentrating on the peasantry and relying on terror either to demoralize the military or to tease it into carrying out an indiscriminate massacre of peasants which would inevitably alienate the survivors.* (However, to the extent that so-called Fidelistas expose their "Communistic" goals *before* winning power, they are not following Castro's tactic of representing himself—perhaps sincerely as of 1959—as merely a reformer.)

The first issue to be taken up in that series of public discussions was the revolutionary potential of the urban proletariat. It is difficult to challenge de la Puente's assertion that "the city-centered scheme of the October Revolution does not apply to our reality, since the oli-

---

* On this latter point, *Caretas,* Peru's leading popular illustrated magazine, spoke effectively to the military in an issue published during the summer of 1965. It reminded them of this now-classic tactic in an article entitled, "No es una simple operación militar" (August 19–30, 1965), p. 13. The guerrillas could hope to prosper only if supported by the local peasantry. The crucial program to win such support away from the guerrillas would be agrarian reform, to which the military had already committed itself. In addition, the Peruvian army was already committed, if only half-heartedly, to a program of civic action in the sierra, consisting largely of road building.

† Luis de la Puente Uceda, "The Peruvian Revolution," p. 24. Horowtiz feels that "the movement of the peasantry from the rural to urban centers in countries such as Brazil, Mexico and Peru has clearly served to reduce the revolutionary discontent of these nations." See Irving Louis Horowitz, "Electoral Politics, Urbanization, and Social Development in Latin America," in *The Urban Explosion in Latin America,* ed. G. H. Beyer (Ithaca: Cornell University Press, 1967), pp. 215–253.

garchic power here is too strong." † The editors of the *Monthly Review* added that "no considerable section of the [largely urban] bourgeoisie, especially after the experience of the Cuban Revolution, is going to support [the revolution], still less fight. . . . The Latin American bourgeoisie are not interested in any kind of revolution; they prefer to throw in *their* lot with the imperialist defenders of the status quo." [13] The editors added, however, that the Russian urban model might still apply, as in the case of the Dominican Republic, if there were a split in the armed forces. But again the Cuban experience is unfavorable. Castro's elimination of the caste privileges of the military and, in fact, the military's complete replacement by a militia, have alienated at least the careerist professionals among military groups.

This deradicalizing effect of urbanization deserves further discussion, since it may appear to contradict Western industrial experience. The classic Marxist view of class conflict required that the lower class be proletarianized by factory work, presumably in cities. However, the most extreme cases of labor-management conflict have occurred in isolated mill towns rather than in factories located in large cities.[14] In Peru there have been many bitter strikes in the Cerro de Pasco mines, but the isolation of the mines has made such unrest easy for the military to contain. We might predict that once countries like Peru begin to develop a substantial amount of concentrated heavy industry in large cities, the urban working class would be radicalized. There are, however, several countervailing factors. First, Peru has already established a generous set of labor and welfare laws that tend to be applied at least to organized workers. Second, such industries are likely to be more capital-intensive than their counterparts in Western historical development—thus permitting higher wages and keeping their workers always a small proportion of Peru's total labor force. Peru's tertiary service sector is likely to bulge indefinitely, thus leaving the manufacturing sector a smaller proportion of the economy than it was at comparable stages of Western industrialization.[15]

The public debate then turned to the Marxist view of Indian society. Traditionally (and currently by ideologues seeking to radicalize the Indian masses), Indian society is viewed either as a communal ideal or more realistically as a *Lumpenproletariat* dominated by a "false consciousness" inculcated by the priests hired by their patróns. Martínez de la Torre epitomized this latter view in his attack on the Apristas'

success in championing the cause of the Indians in the 1920s: "They...
foment the vain cretinism of the enslaved feudal latifundist Sierra. ...
This tactic of dissipating in the provinces the exemplary effort demonstrated by the proletariat of the capital ... is one of the many means by
which the spiteful opportunism of the petty bourgeoisie ... reveals
itself. It is dyed with the false reformism and treacherous uneasiness of
recently arrived, twisted nationalist demagogues."[16] (It is not easy to
idealize the Peruvian *serrano.* He is not a "noble savage," but a
demoralized human being showing personality and character evidence
of hundreds of years of exploitation. Thus he is in many respects his
own worst enemy.)

The next stage of "the revolution" was heralded by the extremely
explicit article by de la Puente cited above and written shortly before
he took to the mountains for open warfare. He began the article by
disavowing bourgeois reform in favor of radical revolution.* He

This view, referring to events of the twenties and thirties, contrasts
with that of Hugo Blanco who, even from jail, still preferred peasant
unions to the urban-recruited guerrilla bands that replaced them.
While Blanco did note a tendency for such unions "to reconcile
themselves to small ... victories" because they are "susceptible to local
pressures" and "might turn towards syndicalism," [17] he still felt that
"the [campesino] masses understand the necessity of open struggle and
[will] create the militia. ... The campesinos have already agreed to
organize defense committees." In letters Blanco wrote from jail in April
of 1964 to one Rosendo in Lima (who, in turn, was preparing the
ideological groundwork for the 1965 guerrilla warfare), he admitted
that one reason the revolutionaries failed is that they were swallowed
up by the union movement, rather than operating from the base of a
centralized disciplined party. He even cited the case of Manco II
(named after an Inca hero), "who surrounded Cuzco ready to crush it[!]
and was abandoned by his troops because the time for planting and
harvesting had come. ...." However, in an interview with Craig on May
8, 1965, Blanco admitted that "the campesinos of La Convención are
too petit bourgeois; any future uprising of Indians will take place in the
highlands, not in La Convención."[18] Blanco conceded away his
position in these letters, yet ended by restating it.

The next stage of "the revolution" was heralded by the extremely
explicit article by de la Puente cited above and written shortly before
he took to the mountains for open warfare. He began the article by
disavowing bourgeois reform in favor of radical revolution.* He

---

* In view of de la Puente's guerrilla leadership, it is interesting to note his program for
agrarian reform published a year after he was killed: *La reforma del agro peruano* (Lima,

credited the Kennedy-Belaúnde program of peaceful revolution through representative democracy with having had excellent prospects until Kennedy's death, and he stated that the APRA-Odría coalition was organized to thwart Belaúnde's efforts in the Peruvian Congress. De la Puente then went on to take issue with "some people who, though calling themselves members of leftist, revolutionary, and Marxist parties, maintain that the objective and subjective conditions for starting an insurrection are not present in Peru.... The objective conditions ... have always been ripe.... If such subjective conditions have not attained their necessary ripeness this is partly due to the inability of the leftist parties ... to foster and cultivate the ground." [19] While subsequent events proved that the time was still not ripe, de la Puente made a telling criticism of the still largely urban-oriented revolutionaries by asking where they were when, on July 28, 1963, the day of Belaúnde's inauguration, a wave of land invasions took place all over the country without Communist support—or that of any outside political party. Belaúnde's campaign had promised a land reform program, and so the invaders were, in effect, responding to his campaign propaganda. These invasions soon "got out of hand" by spreading to coastal areas, and so they were eventually put down by an effective combination of selective repression and concession. The invasion tactic of picking an appropriate occasion had previously worked with great success in Lima. On Christmas Eve in 1954, 10,000 slum dwellers had moved all their belongings and building materials to construct on the eastern edge of the city a shantytown they called Ciudad de Dios—the City of God. The government did not expel them.

De la Puente went on to label the urban bourgeoisie and most of the factory workers as puppets of the oligarchy. In his view, the university students remained the revolution's best hope: "It deserves to be stressed that 12 of the 16 universities in the country are totally con-

---

1966). It was his thesis at the University of Trujillo, presented in 1957 while he was still an Aprista. In it, he took a moderate evolutionary position advocating that, with proper payment and no violence, the feudal latifundia should be transformed into efficient capitalist enterprises, while Indian communities, with their [supposedly] still-active cooperative spirit, should be encouraged to develop as peasant cooperatives (pp. 192–93). He warned against "leftist infantilism" or "Marxist intoxication," which would lead to the violent confiscation of all large landholders. He showed himself anxious to avoid "exhausting national energy on sporadic and ephemeral conquests" (p. 191).

trolled by the left." [20] On this base, then, de la Puente hoped to prove false "the assertion that the objective and subjective conditions are not ripe in Peru for beginning an insurrection." Such a position, he asserted, was "only a pretense to block the revolution." He still felt obliged to deal more considerately with some people who "still maintain dogmatically the traditional schemes of the October Revolution with proletarian leadership and the center of operations in the cities. On the other side there are Trotskyists such as the Frente Izquierdista Revolucionaria, formerly led by Hugo Blanco, who uphold the thesis of dual power, with peasant organizations taking over, one by one, the functions of oligarchic power. . . . This movement, following a process of growing radicalization, would undertake the creation of its own armed militia, and would culminate in the seizure of power as an essentially mass phenomenon." [21] De la Puente felt, on the other hand, that the way "to lift the veil of deceit, dread and skepticism" of the peasants was to bring in guerrillas. "Armed action radicalizes the masses and the same applies to the repression which it evokes." [22] (The latter statement is as close as de la Puente would come to admitting the tactic of provoking brutal reprisals by the army in order to stir up the "vain cretinism of the enslaved . . . Sierra," as Martínez de la Torre put it. Terror was a prime element in the strategy against the Guardia Civil, as well as against *amarillos* [informers] among the Indians.) De la Puente then went on to list the different guerrilla bands and describe the general plan of action that was shortly to be followed. (The military could not have benefited from this article, since it was published just after the last of the guerrilla bands was conquered and de la Puente was killed.)

There are a number of misjudgments in his program—which, since it was carried out, can be taken as more than propaganda. The prime mistake is undoubtedly the failure to realize that, more so than in most areas, political power in Latin America is overwhelmingly urban. Unlike the settlement of North America, Latin America colonialism was always urban based.[23] Moreover, *la violencia* in Colombia should demonstrate that Latin American governments can lose effective control over much of their countryside for over a decade—losing from 150,000 to 300,000 dead—and still survive.

De la Puente also was so naive as to think that peasant-based armies would not be willing to shoot down peasant land invaders. The fact is that the Peruvian army has long succeeded in converting Indians into soldiers to such an extent that, as the white foreman of a Cerro de Pasco mine once told the author, in the face of rumors of a miners' invasion of the foreman's walled compound, "I'm not worried about the local regiment joining the miners; I'm just worried that that trigger-happy sergeant is going to kill off my best miners. They may be Communists, but they are good skilled workers. It would take me years to replace them." One of the aspects of Peruvian social reality most disillusioning to a foreigner aware of the *Indigenista* (Indigenist) literature is the extent to which those who raise themselves out of the Indian category can so despise their antecedents. The *cholo* is a very different person from the Indian, even if he is actually the same person at an older age. *Cholos* have freed themselves from the brutalized lethargy of Indian existence without compromising the expression of their emotions or interests by having taken on middle-class pretensions. In their climb upward, however, they rarely make common cause with the Indian mass, but rather are as likely to take advantage of Indian ignorance as are the large landowners. If Peru practiced racial segregation as it exists in the United States, then the more acculturated Indians would be forced to improve their situation through leading "their people" in a "Brown Power" movement against such barriers. The different political posture of educated Africans in former French, as opposed to British, colonies is another example of this point. Racial tolerance, however desirable in itself, functions to deprive the submerged group of its own leaders.

We have yet another reappraisal made of the guerrilla movement following its collapse.[24] This analysis, however, does not offer a specific or optimistic plan of action for the next stage. Henri Edme felt that the new urban bourgeoisie in Latin America, epitomized by Belaúnde in Peru and Frei in Chile, were pursuing a policy of real economic development and palliative rural reforms sufficient to prevent a Communist revolution. He agreed with de la Puente that the urban proletariat cannot be counted on by the revolutionaries. "These slums, populated by the most enterprising elements from the countryside, who have come there in hope of finding work first, then individual advancement, are difficult areas for revolutionary activity despite their extreme poverty." Moreover, as landless peasants flee to the city, "the guerrillas are losing part of their base." As for rural areas, "for the capitalist in the large cities, the menaced big landowner is no longer a reliable ally whom one can allow to manipulate and dominate the rural masses as in the past. A process of dissociation is going on within the ruling classes at the expense of the feudal sector." [25]

Here we have a French Marxist writer who seems to see the conservative implications of agrarian reform very clearly. He notes that under pressure from its neighboring Indian communities, the Cerro de Pasco Corporation in Peru's central highlands "is proposing to redistribute lands. . . . Social tension will be reduced. . . . A new stratum of small landowners will be stabilized and it will disrupt the traditional collective cohesion of the rural world. The most intelligent members of this world will be encouraged to improve themselves. In a word, a protective ring of individualistic small proprietors will be encouraged who will have nothing in common with the landless mass and will keep them at bay." [26] This was an excessively complimentary assessment of the effectiveness of Belaúnde's agrarian reform efforts. Edme's only "reassuring" observation on rural agitation is that the benefits of agrarian reform, in the face of a high rate of population growth, can be of only temporary utility.

Edme concludes by condeming the Castroite reliance on guerrilla warfare. Without the cities ("the world of the cities does not belong to the guerrillas"), without the support of peasant unions, and without a simultaneous effort at all levels, "the revolution in Latin America is not inevitable either from within or without. . . . Imperialism has done a superb job—at least temporarily—of almost completely integrating all social classes whose existence depends on capitalist development in South America." [27]

NOTES

1. The major sources utilized for this description and analysis, aside from personal observation, are: Wesley W. Craig, Jr., "The Peasant Movement of La Convención, Peru: Dynamics of Rural Organization," a paper read at the meeting of the Rural

Sociological Association, Miami, August 27, 1966; Hugo Neira, *Cuzco: Tierra y muerte, problemas de hoy* (Lima, 1964); Livio Maitan, "The Revolt of the Peruvian Campesinos," *International Socialist Review* 26 (Spring 1965): 38–41, the "Hugo Blanco Correspondence," ibid., pp. 41–46; Ministerio de Guerra, *Las guerrillas en el Perú y su represión* (Lima, 1966); Luis de la Puente Uceda, "The Peruvian Revolution: Concepts and Perspectives," *Monthly Review* 17 (November 1965): 23; Anibal Quijano, "El movimiento campesino del Perú y sus líderes," *América Latina* 8 (October-December 1965): 43–65; Sebastian Salazar Bondy, "Andes and the Sierra Maestra," in Carlos Fuentes, et al., *Whither Latin America?* (New York, 1963), esp. p. 117; Gerrit Huizer, "On Peasant Unrest in Latin America," report to the International Labor Organization and the Comité Interamericana de Desarrollo Agrícola, Pan American Union (Washington, June 1967): 161–75; Ricardo Letts Colmenares, "Breve historia contemporánea de la lucha por la reforma agraria en el Perú," *Economía y agricultura* 1 (December 1963-February 1964): 121–30.

2. Craig, "The Peasant Movement of La Convención," p. 80.

3. Ibid., p. 11.

4. Ibid., pp. 15–16.

5. A personal communication, January 27, 1967.

6. In the southern mountainous region around Cuzco (in 1959), "workers' organizations are, . . . considering their [small] size, remarkably vocal. Their outlook is nearly always Marxist, if not Communistic and their affiliations with the professional group . . . especially the scholastic one . . . are traditionally close" (Southern Peru Regional Development Project, Vol. 5, *Human Resources in the Department of Puno* [Lima 1959], p. 17, mimeo).

7. James Payne, *Labor and Politics in Peru* (New Haven: Yale University Press, 1965), pp. 110–112.

8. See the "Hugo Blanco correspondence" written from jail in the spring of 1964. In this reappraisal, Blanco attempts to defend his strategic failure. He confesses to having had "heavy putchist vapors . . . floating in [his] brain" (p. 46).

9. *Las guerrillas en el Perú y su represión* (pp. 20–21). The text notes that "it is practically impossible to traverse the road without being seen by lookouts, and therefore the possibility of capturing any refugee from justice is very remote in those areas since he can be alerted and flee hours ahead [of one's arrival]."

10. Letts, "Breve historia," p. 128.

11. De la Puente, "The Peruvian Revolution," p. 23.

12. Such as the inappropriate diversion of perhaps a third of the Peruvian army to the Ecuadorian border in the spring of 1965, and the considerable assistance rendered the Communists by the two twentieth-century military dictators, Benavides (1936–1939) and Odría (1949–1956).

13. (November 1965) op cit, p. 11.

14. Clark Kerr and Abraham Siegel, "The Interindustry Propensity to Strike—An International Comparison," ed. Arthur Kornhauser, et al., *Industrial Conflict* (New York, 1954), chap. 14.

15. In fact, between 1940 and 1961 the percentage of workers in manufacturing fell from 15.4 to 13.1 in spite of considerable economic development. See David Chaplin, *The Peruvian Industrial Labor Force* (Princeton, 1967), pp. 168–73.

16. Ricardo Martínez de la Torre, *Apuntes para una interpretación marxista de la historia social del Perú*, vol. I (Lima, 1947): 35.

17. Ibid., p. 45.
18. Craig, "The Peasant Movement of La Convención," p. 33.
19. de la Puente, p. 21.
20. Ibid., p. 22.
21. Ibid., p. 23.
22. Ibid., pp. 25–26.
23. Richard Morse, "Latin American Cities," *Comparative Studies in Society and History* 4 (July 1962): 473–93.
24. Henri Edme, "Damping the Fires of Revolution," *Les Temps Modernes* (May 1966), reprinted in translation in *Atlas* (September 1966): 10–15.
25. Ibid., pp. 14, 13.
26. Ibid., p. 14.
27. Ibid., pp. 15, 13.

John Strasma

12.

Agrarian Reform *

In just a few years and without bloodshed, the Revolutionary Military Government has expropriated all of Peru's large sugar plantations and many of its larger sheep ranches. Output rose, even during the first year, on most of the expropriated properties. And, after a transition period averaging about one year, the government turned over legal title to the plantations and to many of the ranches, to production cooperatives representing the respective workers and the neighboring indigenous communities.

These are spectacular accomplishments, which leave no doubt that a genuine agrarian reform has taken place.[1] Even so, some urgent problems remain unresolved, and certain new areas of stress have appeared. Including the beneficiaries of previous laws, 439,000 families have land already, and 65,000 more are supposed to get land each year until the basic land reform is completed in 1975.[2] However, under the present law another half-million families will remain landless and frustrated with aspirations raised from seeing their neighbors receive land. Up in the highland sierra, land reform in certain critical provinces has succeeded in defusing one of Latin America's largest peasant movements several times during the last decade. Now, however, a new movement may be arising in the coastal valleys.

The economic objectives of Peru's land reform program include increased production and higher incomes for beneficiaries, both of which seem to have been attained in many but not all reform projects. As reform programs move to poorer and more remote areas, they will

* The views expressed in this chapter are entirely personal, and may or may not coincide with those of the Peruvian government or the Ford Foundation, which provided the author's services in 1970, as well as consultancies more recently, for a staff training program in the Ministry of Economy and Finance.

require ever-larger credits and infrastructure investments, and this may strain the nation's fiscal resources. The production cooperatives have unresolved internal tensions, especially in the sugar plantations, and the state has only recently relaxed its close control. Politically and economically, however, Peru's land reform program has already accomplished a great deal. Its principal problems have to do with the government of the cooperatives, the design and financing of the consolidation phase investments, and the question of whether or not the redistribution pace can be maintained until the project's completion, which is scheduled for 1975.

Background

Peru, in 1968, was still a "classic" case of an unjust and stifling rural economy. On the coast, export-oriented plantation enclaves held much of the irrigated land; in the highland sierra, minifundia intermingled with haciendas, while traditional Indian communities still clung to the poorest land.

This landownership pattern came from the Colonial period. The Spanish Conquest was disastrous for both people and land,[3] since complex irrigation systems and mountain terraces disintegrated, and the descendants of their builders were reduced to abject poverty. On the hacienda, laborers were bound to the land through arrangements that discouraged productivity and produced human relations reminiscent of the age of serfdom;[4] workers could not leave voluntarily until they repaid loans and advances, and the owner or manager kept the books. The supply of cheap, docile labor was regarded as an asset until after the Bolivian Revolution of 1953; before then deeds sometimes transferred specified quantitites of both land and Indians to the new landowner.

Population

The population pressure in Peru has appalled economists for years; the country's population grew at an average rate of 3.1 percent per year during the last decade.[5] About half of Peru's 13.6 million people now live in cities, but the remainder are crowded together at the rate of 2.2 persons per cultivated hectare, or about one per acre.[6] However, that figure exaggerates the problem somewhat, since the agriculture of the sierra is largely based on grazing and thus there are another six hectares or so of natural pasture per person.[7]

Unfortunately, this natural pasture is pretty poor, and the Indian communities had only the worst of it, the part not coveted by the hacendados. In much of the sierra, the grass is killed every three years or so by frost; this happened again in mid-1972. Each freeze leads to actual starvation for hundreds of Indian families, and another surge of migration toward the coastal cities.

Productivity and land tenure

In Peru, as in much of Latin America, traditional agriculture failed to keep pace with the 3.1 percent rate of annual population growth. In fact, the 1969 output was barely equal to that of 1962. Comprising half of the country's population, this sector produces less than 15 percent of its gross domestic product. Imports of food, much of which could be produced more economically in Peru, consumed some $135 million yearly in foreign exchange, about 22 percent of all imports.[8] The main items imported in 1969 were wheat ($51 million), meat and livestock ($28 million) and oil and fats ($15 million).

Yields of many crops were unsatisfactory, compared to those of other countries, and they were improving only very slowly. For example, potatoes are native to Peru, but yields in 1967 averaged 6,700 kilos per hectare, whereas the world average was 12,700 kilos per hectare.[9] After the traditional landowners, usually absentees, took out their shares, the cash income of the sierra rural population was too low to make them a mass market for domestic manufactures.

On the other hand, seven sugar plantations, occupying about half of the irrigated land in two northern coastal provinces, paid relatively good wages, had effective unions and generated substantial foreign exchange and tax revenues for Peru. The technology and yields on some of these plantations were among the world's best; it was there that W.R. Grace developed techniques in the 1930s for making paper out of bagasse, the residue left after sugar and molasses are extracted from cane.

The operation levels of these sugar plantations and of several commercial farms in the sierra showed that modern farming techniques and inputs were both known and available in Peru, at least to some people. As has happened in many countries, concerned local professionals and sympathetic foreigners assumed at first that the problem was primarily one of communication—of imparting to the peasants information about what to do to get better crops. But, as in many other countries, the efforts made to try and communicate this knowledge all too often were blocked by the stubborn fact of land tenure and other rural institutions that inhibited productivity, either removing incentive by denying the peasants the fruit of greater yields, or by denying them access to the necessary working capital and markets.

Much of the land of the sierra was owned by absentee landlords, who were unable to manage or finance modern farming operations. Large estates were typically owned by churches, schools or other nonprofit institutions, including government hospitals. Their trustees were not capitalists who invested in the land for profit, nor were they agriculturalists eager to become involved in intensive farming operations. Rather, they had received the land by bequest or legacy, or had invested in it to protect their wealth against inflation, and were hoping to receive a modest but dependable annual income from it without managerial effort. Such owners typically hired managers to run their lands, or else they rented their entire estates for several years at a time—they seldom agreed to longer contracts, for fear the manager would cheat them, or the tenant might not pay his rent on time. This tenure system essentially obliged the manager or tenant to exploit both land and workers ruthlessly, to make what he could before the contract ran out. He certainly had no incentive to invest in long-term projects, such as building soil fertility, pedigreed flocks, or improved pastures, since they would only benefit someone else.

The apparently logical solution of selling or renting the land on a long-term basis to the workers who lived on it and worked it was never applied in this "free market" economy, because the parties were so unequal. The owner lived far away and so wanted to deal with one manager or rent it in a single transaction with one tenant. Also, it simply may never have occurred to the owners, or to the Indians, that the racial gulf could be bridged and the two parties enter into a contract. When Cornell University Professor Allan Holmberg and his Peruvian colleagues suggested that an Indian community at Vicos lease itself the hacienda which a series of outside renters had mismanaged badly, the elitist trustees of the charitable institution that owned the land refused even to consider the idea. Only persistent political pressure in Lima from various interested parties (including a young visitor from Boston named Edward Kennedy, who helped persuade President Prado) succeeded in getting their land free from this unproductive form of landownership. Even then, the Beneficiencia refused to deal with the Indians; the government had to buy the land itself and resell it to the community. Once this precedent was established, however, various nearby land conflicts were settled by the direct sale of land by the absentee owner to the peasants.[10]

Even where the owners or managers were resident and competent, however, they still fell far short of full utilization of their lands. As early as 1953, aware of the Bolivian Revolution, they were afraid of the rising self-confidence and aggressiveness of the neighboring Indians and hence unwilling to invest new capital in the area. Even the owners of outstanding ranches, such as Algolan and Cerro de Pasco, were only willing to expand their livestock numbers through natural growth, rather than invest new cash. This meant that part of their land remained idle, leaving them a weak moral case for keeping off the neighboring Indians who had to try and feed their emaciated sheep on overgrazed hills. The Indians had suffered at the hands of the hacendados in this manner for centuries, but finally the political situation was beginning to change. The boundary markers were still moved during the night, but now it was the hacienda owners who complained to the courts and police. Even though they received more official support than the Indians ever did, the haciendas usually had disputes pending on their boundaries, and thus they were unable to end cattle rustling and the mixing of stray Indian sheep with their purebred animals.[11]

Something of the same sort happened with cultivated land in both the sierra and the coast; by declarations of the owners in the 1961 census, 1.3 million hectares of arable land were not cultivated that year. Part of this could be excused as land left fallow as part of the normal cycle of crop rotation, but this traditional method, while cheaper than fertilizing, is hardly appropriate for the labor-abundant

Peruvian rural economy. And so, with examples like these, even conservative economists and politicians–those who didn't own rural land–gradually came to accept the need for land tenure reform as a means to higher productivity, whether or not they shared the related goals of greater social and political freedom for the peasants.

Earlier attempts at reform

APRA had been calling for land reform ever since its founding in the 1930s, and even its sworn enemy, the Odría government, had promulgated a decree in 1949 asserting the right of the state to expropriate idle lands. This decree was never implemented, however, nor were provisions in the constitution calling for the expropriation and redistribution of land to "promote the diffusion of small and medium-sized rural property," and to aid Indian communities.

By 1958 Indian uprisings had begun, centered around seizing certain large estates in the Cuzco area, for reasons that were not entirely clear. Perhaps the abuses were the worst there, perhaps Indian pride and energy were at their highest level near the seat of the ancient Inca Empire, or perhaps the Indians were made desperate by a massive drought that afflicted that area in 1956. In any case, the government's reaction to these uprisings was to appoint a commission to study the problem and draft legislation to help remedy it. The landowner-dominated Congress rejected the $22,000 budgeted for this commission, but its chairman, Pedro Beltrán, obtained a small grant from the Rockefeller Foundation and for technical advice the commission obtained the services of Dr. Thomas F. Carroll, an American land reform expert then employed by the Food and Agricultural Organization of the United Nations (FAO). The opposition to the study also permeated parts of the government, and functionaries sympathetic to the landowners even tried to sabotage the commission's work by denying Carroll a reentry visa after a routine trip on business for the FAO.

Although it was never acted upon, the commission's report and recommendations were nonetheless a comprehensive proposal which influenced the legislators who drafted the reform laws of 1964 and 1969.[12] While it stressed measures designed to raise productivity and bring more land into cultivation, the commission bill also included provisions for land redistribution and the improvement of unsatisfactory forms of tenancy. The scope of this reform was also severely limited—as any such reform had to be—by the requirement that all expropriated land be paid for at a "just price" in cash.

During the 1962 election campaign, all the candidates, affected by the Kennedy rhetoric and the influence of the Bolivian and Cuban revolutions, promised agrarian reform of some sort. The outcome, which was very close, was clouded by many accusations of wholesale fraud, and a military junta took over and governed Peru for nearly a year. In August 1962, that junta decreed that all unirrigated and unexploited land claims would revert forthwith to the state, without compensation. In January 1963, it issued a decree-law setting forth certain "bases" or norms for future action and legislation on land reform. With more stress on social justice than the Beltrán Commission bill, this decree announced the junta's intention to legislate for the expropriation of inefficiently farmed land, articulating the doctrine that "the land belongs to the tiller." The junta also purchased and redistributed some land, especially in La Convención, near Cuzco. In fact, this was an ex post facto legitimization of land seizures, highly successful both in raising output and in inducing the beneficiaries to abandon their Trotskyite leader, Hugo Blanco, who was captured by the police and only recently freed by the Revolutionary Military Government.[13]

The Belaúnde regime

New elections held in 1963 produced a strong popular mandate for Fernando Belaúnde Terry, but not a sympathetic majority in Congress. Immediately, a new wave of land occupations far larger than those that had occurred during the Prado regime swept over Pasco, Junin, Cuzco and the sierra portions of Lima and Cajamarca. According to a study by the Interamerican Committee for Agricultural Development (CIDA), some 350 to 450 communities and 300,000 persons were involved.[14] These land "recoveries" were accompanied by peasant union movements at the local level, and in

Puno, Cuzco, Ayacucho, Pasco and Junin, there were federations of unions as well. These movements did not materialize overnight, nor were they the work of "outside agitators." Most of the villages involved had been trying unsuccessfully for years to regain their lands through the courts and the Ministry of Labor and Peasant Affairs. With the election of Belaúnde and the introduction of a land reform bill, they felt that it was all right to simply take back their ancestral lands.

Invoking "law and order," the opposition majority in Congress forced Belaúnde to order the police to dislodge some of the squatters. In other cases, the invading peasants agreed to withdraw temporarily, and wait for expropriation. Police repression of the invaders was effective in Cuzco, Ayacucho and Pasco, but in central Peru the peasant protest movement was ended by simply giving the communities title to much of the land they had claimed. When would-be revolutionary leaders left Lima for the hills in 1965, their potential followers either already had land or feared the police, and so the infant guerrilla movement quickly collapsed.

A month after his inauguration, Belaúnde introduced an agrarian reform bill; it was weakened in Congress but passed, and became law in 1964. While the Congress stalled, President Belaúnde borrowed $5 million from two U.S. banks to buy the strife-ridden Algolan Ranch, thus encouraging his supporters by taking some concrete action in the area of reform.[15]

The 1964 law was more radical than earlier proposals, because it provided that compensation could be paid largely in bonds. On APRA's insistence it completely excluded sugar plantations, efficient ranches and other agroindustrial operations from expropriation. Along with numerous provisions appropriate for a massive land reform, it provided checks and safeguards that enabled determined landowners to stall expropriation for years—for example, various steps in the paperwork required official approval from Lima. Land valuations were to be set as an average of three values: the tax value (generally grossly underdeclared), the market price and its potential income under good management, capitalized at 9 percent. However, Belaúnde's law also contained an original Peruvian contribution to agrarian legislation: the value so determined was to be divided: only 70 percent of it was to be paid to the owners, on grounds that since the underpaid labor of the workers was the source of the other 30 percent of the estate's value, they should not be obligated to pay for that as well.

Since the ex-owners were to be paid in bonds and the beneficiaries were to pay similar amounts to the state on a long-term basis, theoretically the state merely needed to finance the transaction as an intermediary, through a subsidized interest rate, as a grace period was also provided to the beneficiaries. Still, any massive reform would have required substantial sums for the cash down payments. The 1964 law specified that land reform's budget should be not less than 3 percent of the total central government budget. However, a fiscal crisis began and the average land reform budget for 1964–67 was closer to .6 percent, a third of which went into colonization programs instead of reform.[16]

Belaúnde's government seldom budgeted much cash for down payments, and its actual expropriations ran far behind the amount of eligible land that was ready for legal action. Furthermore, once the National Office of Agrarian Reform (ONRA) had established that a particular hacienda was eligible, neither the owner nor his workers farmed it very well during the long wait for the transfer to take place. Between May 1964 and September 1968, only 61 properties (a total of 651,419 hectares) were expropriated. Of these lands, 313,972 hectares were redistributed to 9,224 families, and the rest was supposedly in preparatory stages for redistribution.[17]

Another 324 properties including 47,132 hectares of land were affected by so-called "Title XV" actions. Under this legislation, resident laborers and small sharecroppers could obtain title to the tiny plots they had been allowed to till in exchange for working on the estate, free or for wages far below the "market" wage. Title XV required fewer formalities than formal expropriation, and it provided for repayment by beneficiaries on a long-term basis. Some 128,000 of these workers had applied for such titles by the end of 1966, and 54,800 of them had received provisional occupancy rights certificates by that time.[18] This, of course, greatly increased the number of families the government could claim as land reform beneficiaries; it also leads to confusing differences in the official statistics on the progress of reform. In addition, the Title XV program was legitimately criticized for "freezing" sub-subsistence minifundia that should have been combined instead. Also, many workers who demanded their Title XV rights got their plots but lost their small cash income from part-time employment on the estate—since the owners, in reprisal, substituted new full-time laborers who earned cash wages but did not have cultivation or grazing rights to estate lands.

Agrarian Reform Under the Revolutionary Military Government

For the first nine months of the Revolutionary Military Government's rule, little occurred on the agrarian front. The IPC affair and subsequent U.S. sputtering, and the seizure of California tuna boats fishing without Peruvian licenses, monopolized journalistic interest in Lima and abroad. However, the bureaucratic machinery continued to grind out Title XV and other modest actions under the 1964 law, and the generals gave agrarian reform more budget resources than it had ever had under Belaúnde.

In January 1969, the Cerro de Pasco mine gave up its farmland and livestock, long coveted by the surrounding Indian communities, for reasons which I have described elsewhere.[19] Sensing strong popular approval of this step, the Revolutionary Military Government decided to accelerate land reform. President Velasco dismissed his first Minister of Agriculture, General José Benavides, who was known to be on cordial terms with landowner association leaders, and who had expressed doubts about the wisdom of expropriating large and efficient plantations. Velasco then appointed a radical and energetic minister, General Jorge Barandiaran Pagador, who guided the draft of the new law through a careful, in-depth review by the president's advisors and the chiefs of the armed forces.

The new law

In proclaiming this law on June 24, 1969, President Velasco stressed the government's major goal: to replace both latifundia and minifundia with a new structure ensuring social justice, increased output, higher productivity and a secure income for those who till the soil. Specifically, the government's plan involved the expropriation of all large haciendas by 1975, in order to raise production, productivity and real incomes, thus creating an effective demand for domestic manufactures among the very large fraction of the rural population that had not been part of the market economy. Plantations and other efficient units were not exempt, but in law and in practice the government would promote their continued operation as a unit, while stressing producer cooperatives and community organization as the desired forms of farming and of obtaining social services.

The new law maintains the general structure of the 1964 law, but goes further in most respects, and attempts to resolve the problems that arose from trying to enforce the earlier law.[20] For example, Title XV of the 1964 law "froze" minifundia by granting laborers title to the small plots they had been allowed to till in exchange for labor on the estate, but the new law provides that other lands belonging to the same owner must also be distributed, in order to give each Title XV beneficiary at least a family farm unit. Clearly recognizing the shortage of technical staff in the reform agency, the law obliged owners to turn over the extra land themselves by June 30, 1970, without waiting for official action, on pain of a fine of half the value of the added land required.

The Belaúnde law had allowed corporations to own land, provided the amount per stockholder did not exceed the permissible holdings for individuals (Cerro Corporation had 23,048 stockholders in 1969, and so could legally have owned a great deal of the sierra). Under the new law, corporations were given just six months to get rid of all their agricultural land, or convert themselves into unlimited liability partnerships. The penalty for noncompliance was expropriation of the land and a fine of 50 percent of its value. The 1969 law also closed a loophole, by adding together the land of spouses, regardless of the legal formalities concerning their separate and "community" property.

The limit for land worked directly by its owner was reduced to 150 hectares of irrigated land on the coast, or its agricultural equivalent in other qualities of land and in other regions. This is still a substantial farm: imagine 375 acres in California. However, the exempt land may be decreased whenever labor laws have been violated—which could be proved for almost every hacienda in the sierra[21]—or if the land had been occupied by squatters for at least five years. Owners must supply maps and titles to the reform agency, or the cost of preparing them will be deducted from their compensation.

All the legal formalities involved have been accelerated, and the valuation will usually be based on the self-assessments required of owners in a 1968 real estate tax reform. If no declaration was made at that time, the value recorded when the land was purchased or inherited will be the basis for compensation. (The use of values already in public records and sworn to by the owner is much simpler than other methods, and it is morally awkward for ex-owners to justify demands that the government pay compensation at values higher than those they swore to, in fulfilling their own duty to pay taxes to support the government.)

The new land reform law was accompanied by a water reform law, the effect of which will be even more drastic, if it is ever applied. Existing water allocations, many dating from the colonial period, were declared void without indemnization, and a "new, rational and just" pattern is to be ordained. Specifically, everyone with 10 hectares of land or less is to get water before the larger owners get any more. When and if this law is implemented, it could lead to a drastic change in power, as well as a real redistribution of income.

Another significant provision moved "indigenous affairs" from the Ministry of Labor—where strikes seem a normal means of expression—to the new General Directorate of Agrarian Reform and Resettlement. The Revolutionary Military Government wants to emphasize production and technology, not protest. Indians are henceforth to be called *campesinos,* or peasants, which are deemed more dignified terms than "Indians." This move also appears to reflect the government's desire to integrate the indigenous population and prevent any tendency toward separatist movements by the Quechua- and Aymara-speaking peoples of the Andes.[22]

Another major legal innovation was the organization of separate Agrarian Tribunals, facilitating prompt and definitive court adjudication of all matters concerning rural land, water and labor. Rulings by local tribunals can only be appealed to the Agrarian Tribunal in Lima, whose verdict is unappealable.

The 1969 law provides that cash down payments for the land taken may not exceed S/100,000 ($2,400) for land, and S/1,000,000 for improvements. As before, the down payment, interest rate and bond maturity depend on the reason for expropriation, with absentee owners of unused land receiving the least remuneration.

Finally, the 1969 law contains drastic penalties for sabotage, with jail sentences and fines equal to the full value of expropriated land for owners who dispossess tenants, delay harvests, burn crops, etc. Saboteurs are tried before military courts, and held without bail. Originally aimed at landowners, these provisions were also extended to others in March 1970, with the establishment of another decree-law providing jail terms for persons who voiced unfounded criticism or other false statements about the reform, or who were troublemakers in general. (This measure was used at once to jail several APRA leaders who had tried to organize a work stoppage when a reform administrator forbade the party to conduct a rally at a sugar plantation.)

Early steps in implementing the new law

Moving quickly to prevent sabotage or loss of production, senior officers flew to nine major sugar plantations and refineries in the coastal valleys north of Lima. In two days, the operations were completely under government control, including their bank accounts, and a basic point had been made: no one, however distinguished his surname, was exempt from these measures of social reform, and implementation could begin just a few hours after the official promulgation of a law. By seizing the plantations, the new government had carried agrarian reform to the very heartland of APRA, the party which had so long advocated land reform—for others, but not for the sugar mills and cane fields—since they were the sources of the old union leaders' own livelihood, as well as their political power. Clearly, the new government did not respect the tacit truce between the sugar barons and APRA, nor did it share the APRA concern about whether or not the mills could be run without their owners.

Table 1 lists the major plantations. W.R. Grace was not the biggest plantation landowner, nor was it high on the "hate list" of the most revolutionary-minded reformer. That distinction went to the Gildemeisters, whose German and other high-level technicians lived behind a high wall which the Peruvian workers knocked down one month after the expropriation. The Gildemeisters had 11,714 hectares of cane; Grace was second, with 9,504 *ha*. Unlike Gildemeister, Grace had trained and promoted Peruvian technicians and managers, and its operations produced paper, chemicals and rum

Table 1
NINE LARGE PLANTATIONS EXPROPRIATED UNDER
DECREE-LAW 17,716: BASELINE DATA

Names			Plantation Labor Force				Total Area	Total Under Cultivation in 1968	Area Under Cultivation in Cane, 1968	% of Total Area in Cane in Peru *	Area Harvested in Cane 1970	Sugar Produced 1970
Plantation	Company	Principal Owners	Full Time	Seasonal	Feuda-tarios *	Total			Hectares			Metric Tons
Tuman	Neg. Tuman S.A.	Pardo	1,380	920	0	2,300	15,034	6,241	4,759	6.0	5,960	106,031
Pomalca	Soc. Ag Pomalca Ltd.	de la Piedra	3,200	1,000	630	4,830	143,010	13,035	9,000	11.0	4,771	92,267
Patapo, y Pucalá	Soc. Ag. Pucalá Ltd.	Izaga, Pardo	2,200	300	60	2,560	33,938	8,325	6,154	7.5	5,110	98,424
Cayalti	Aspillaga Anderson Hnos. S.A.	Aspillaga Anderson	2,200	300	353	2,853	31,673	5,205	2,991	4.0	4,163	46,934
Casa Grande	Emp. Ag Chicama S.A.	Gildemeister	4,600	N/A	5,930	10,530	125,325	34,298	9,800	12.0	11,472	178,913
Laredo	Neg. Ag Laredo Ltd.	Gildemeister	1,500	N/A	557	2,057+	N/A	5,079	1,914	2.5	2,200	46,363
Cartavio	Soc. Cartavio S.A.	Grace & Co.	2,000	N/A	595	2,595+	9,265	8,209	5,328	6.0	5,660	93,280
Para-monga	Soc. Paramonga Ltd.	Grace & Co.	3,000	N/A	667	3,667+	7,930	5,980	4,176	5.5	2,605	58,528
San Jacinto	Neg. Ag. Nepeña S.A.	González	N/A	N/A	N/A	N/A	13,615	5,402	3,458	4.5	1,701	19,338

*Feudatarios are permanent resident laborers who receive part of their wages in the form of use rights to a small amount of land and/or grazing rights for a few animals. The average area assigned was less than one hectare apiece, except at Laredo, where it averaged three hectares.

Sources: Carroll (18), p. 37, Alberti and Cotler (24), p. 7.

instead of merely growing and refining sugar for export. This integration, a goal for industrial planners and an important source of high wages, tax revenue, exports and modern technology, caused a headache for the promoters of land reform. Foreign-owned plantations could hardly be exempted, but the government had no desire to expropriate Grace's paper mill. Yet there are social and practical problems involved when only part of a factory is expropriated—in this case, the sugar refinery, which is next door and supplies the raw materials for paper.[23] For example, if the refinery and the mill have different owners, there is the problem of determining the price the paper mill should pay for the bagasse it obtains from the sugar refinery, its sole supplier, and the price the paper mill should charge the refinery for the steam it supplies. The solution Grace seeks, of selling the paper mill to the government, does not solve the accounting problem, because the two units have separate labor forces who live together in the former company town, but who are quite aware that their share of the profits will reflect the arbitrary prices set between the inseparable units. Even at the other plantations, similar allocation problems could arise between the workers who grow and cut the cane, and others— traditionally more highly trained and thus better paid—who refine it. The former owners paid what they had to for the skills needed in each job to be done, but the plantations and refineries became one-man-one-vote producer cooperatives in 1972, and the more numerous field workers may want to set their wages on a different basis. As an example of the salary range, Cotler and Alberti report the average monthly earnings (in U.S. dollars) for three levels of work at one plantation in 1970 (See Table 1).[24] There are also significant, although diminishing, differences in the quality of the workers' housing and other basic needs. Yet the technicians, if leveled downward, are the ones who can most readily find jobs in other countries, and who will be the hardest to replace. Perhaps this explains "grapevine" comments, not yet vouched for in print, to the effect that the technicians and white-collar employees did all right financially in 1970 and 1971, increasing their own real incomes more rapidly than those of the field and refinery manual laborers. If true, this would reflect in part the powerful position conceded to these groups in the interest of maintaining a high level of production. On the other hand, this may simply be a misunderstanding. When a high-level technician or manager did leave, in 1969 or

1970, his post was usually filled by promoting his assistant. Under the rules then in effect, the replacement automatically received his predecessor's salary. This "ripple" of promotions gave large-percentage increases to almost all the technical and administrative people at Paramonga, for instance, and a bitter poster soon appeared on the wall telling manual laborers that this was unfair to them, and hence that the union was still needed—to defend the interests of the majority against the elite. This brings us to the primary organizational problem involved.

Table 2

Group	Average/month	% of Labor Force
1	$ 38.50	53
2	89.17	30
3	547.49	17

Plantation organization

Most observers agree that one reason the army moved so far and so fast in land reform was to break up any incipient rural guerrilla movements in Peru. Another goal was to shatter the APRA party stronghold in the sugar plantation labor unions. Nonetheless, the government has steadfastly pledged effective peasant participation in the reform process and in management of the reform cooperatives. Unfortunately, the ideal mechanism for this participation seems to elude both the agency and the beneficiaries. (This problem and several representative cases are analyzed by Palmer and Middlebrook in Chapter 17 of this volume.)

Within the sugar cooperatives, the internal government initially established by the land reform was strongly oriented toward production and toward maintaining the hierarchy of technicians within the enterprise. Rather than one-man-one-vote representation, therefore, the Councils originally provided seats for each major category—technicians, white-collar and blue-collar workers—plus a substantial number of seats for workers appointed by the reform agency, in proportion to the debt owed the government for the expropriated assets given to the cooperative. A reform official at one estate told me in July 1970 that this was used solely to reward workers who complete the voluntary night course in cooperatives; skeptics suggested that it looked more like another means of maintaining control. Even the reform functionaries were not above criticism: by February 1970, a leftist magazine *(Oiga)* accused them of having come to enjoy the life of plantation managers, and hence to be dragging their feet on turning things over to the workers.

In 1972, however, the government showed its real self-confidence, as well as its comprehension of the fact that for the field hands, the new plantation management was almost as remote as the old. In April 1972, new elections were held without a government veto on candidates with past union or political activities, and with an unweighted, one-man-one-vote democracy. The government professed delight at the smooth turnover of operations to the newly elected committees, which were supposed to appoint all senior people to technical and managerial posts. Workers at some plantations appeared to respect knowledge and competence, electing lists of candidates that included the best technicians. In other cases, the old union officials made a clean sweep. They, too, may protect the technicians, if only out of enlightened self-interest; or they may pursue other goals, as Palmer and Middlebrook suggest.[25]

The government continues to appoint the general manager of each sugar complex, and strikes remain forbidden on grounds that the workers now own the plantations and therefore the only conceivable reason for a strike is to sabotage the agrarian reform. A few strikes occurred in any case, especially during 1971. Some leaders were jailed, but in other cases the government yielded, recognizing certain rights of the union stewards. In several plantations, APRA now appears to be almost as strong as it ever was.

Other peasant movements

One title in the 1969 law, as in the 1964 one, allowed landowners to divide their lands privately, provided the parcels not exceed a certain size, and provided they were sold to persons who would farm them directly (rather than being leased to tenants). In mid-1970, the workers on the coastal Huando hacienda struck over such a division of the enormous orange groves. The Graña family parceled out their estate among over 60 relatives and friends, largely professionals and businessmen residing in Lima. The workers protested that the true spirit of land reform requires that the land belong to those who get their hands dirty tilling it, and not to persons who merely make sure that somebody else does so. Eventually the government yielded, annulled the Huando division and modified the law to provide that future divisions must give preference to the workers, on payment terms similar to those of the land reform.

Similarly, in 1971, the quarters of the Piura chapter of the National Agrarian Society—along the Northern coast—were invaded in 1971 by peasants demanding membership, along with the traditional landowners. (In 1972, the Society was legally dissolved by the Revolutionary Military Government, which created a broader National Agrarian Confederation in its place.) In the sierra, as illustrated by Palmer and Middlebrook, the implementation of agrarian reform likewise often required some degree of pressure. One area of potential conflict is that of the livestock ranches in the sierra. In general, these have been turned over to the workers on the ranches, and the surrounding indigenous population receives only indirect benefits through a form of profit-sharing from the ranch to the communities. It may be only a matter of months until land disputes break out anew in this area.

The impact of reform on output

When the plantations were expropriated, many agrarian reform advocates feared for their output. Some of the skilled refinery technicians left for good jobs in other sugar-producing countries. Nonetheless, the rains were better than average and much better than in 1968 and 1969. Therefore, sugar exports in 1970 exceeded those of 1969 by 72 percent (all of it went to the United States). Total output for the 1970 calendar year was 780,000 metric tons of sugar, better than the 649,000 tons produced in 1969 although not quite up to the record 842,000 tons produced in 1966, another year of good rains. Total agricultural exports were $178 million, 17 percent more than in

1969, with a large part of the increase coming from sugar. Food imports were 124 million, down 9 percent from 1969.[26]

In the sierra, under interim management by state-appointed Special Committees, most of the expropriated sheep ranches also did well. In ceremonies turning over the ranches to the cooperatives in 1970 and 1971, the Minister of Agriculture stressed the profits, sometimes over 100 million soles, achieved under the interim management. (Most of these profits took the form of increased herds, and so increased the initial capital of the cooperative, which the beneficiaries are eventually supposed to repay.) While the minister did not say how much government credit and budget support went into the project, preventing the calculation of a rate of return, at least it wasn't negative. Nor did he say whether meat prices would be allowed to rise, to enable the ranches (called SAIS) to pay both better wages and the 7 percent interest, plus amortization, on their debt for cattle and working capital.

The increased output is significant, since many people—in Peru and elsewhere—still believe the myth that agrarian reform always causes output to fall in the short run. The Bolivian reform of 1953 is the most frequently cited example but erroneously so. Only in 1968 did scholars discover that Bolivian output actually rose after the reform, but that it was marketed through new channels and hence much of the production wasn't observed by statisticians for years.[27] Still, in Peru, reported output also rose in part because the rustling done by the Indian communities declined when they became part owners instead of aggrieved neighbors of a ranch which had been carved out of their ancestral lands. Some reform beneficiaries, formerly employees of the ranches, admit candidly that they habitually understated actual production in reports to the former absentee owners, to cover their own thefts.

Within the sugar units, the increased output is not only a result of good rains. Another major factor is labor peace: according to Alberti and Cotler, 1970 saw only one strike—at Pucala, and that only lasted seven days.[28] For many complexes, the first year of reform was the longest period in recent history without any days lost by strikes. This peace, in turn, apparently reflected a general expectation of great benefits.

The replacement of former owners did not markedly affect organization or output for another reason: in many cases, the owners were absentees and their technical staff agreed to stay on under the new management. When a few left, it was usually possible for their subalterns to take over. Grace had long trained and hired Peruvian technicians, and many of these had reached retirement but came back to responsible posts in the wake of the reform. Finally, in a few cases the former owners were part of the problem, and their removal helped to raise the output. In one case, the family was bankrupt and new capital was urgently needed; in another, the field manager and the refinery manager had a personal feud and reform provided the means to end a problem that the workers themselves perceived as preventing all rational planning of harvesting, milling and replanting.[29]

In the case of crops other than sugar, output has held up surprisingly well in view of an exchange rate which is somewhat overvalued (favoring imports) and other price policies which are obviously inspired more by a concern for the Index of Consumer Prices in Lima, than for production incentives. This affects land reform beneficiaries and other farmers alike, and presumably as the number of beneficiaries increases they will be more and more able to win better prices. Nonetheless, it is tempting for price controllers in Lima to suppose that the peasants are now owners and therefore receive profits, not wages, for their labor. The next step is to freeze prices, on the grounds that profits are always too high and so the "owners" should tighten their belts so that urban workers can escape paying higher prices. This policy could prevent the consolidation of peasant enterprises and in time could turn initial success of the reform to failure, at least for the SAIS ranches (Agrarian Societies of Social Interest).

One possible solution, of course, is for the state to interpose itself, paying more to producers and subsidizing consumers directly by selling at a loss. In November 1972, the Revolutionary Military Government published a new law bringing the production and marketing of all agricultural products officially under state control; like most Latin governments, Peru has long intervened in the area of essential foodstuffs, and the present government created an agency (EPSA) to take over much of this marketing.

Finally, just as favorable rains helped the output in 1970 and early 1971, the weather was a major factor in making 1972 a bad year, agriculturally. Heavy frosts at the end of 1971 and late, heavy rains in 1972 led to flooding in various valleys. Fearing food shortages, the

Minister of Agriculture announced the enforcement of an old law requiring all farms, plantations included, to put at least 40 percent of their land into foodstuffs for domestic needs. This, as well as the floods, hurt output of sugar and cotton in 1972 and 1973.

The impact of reform on incomes

There are only fragmentary data available at this point to show how the increased agricultural output is translated into incomes for the beneficiaries, but the results of some field studies have been tabulated. In one of these reports, just published by the University of Wisconsin's Land Tenure Center,[30] Douglas Horton has compared income by employment status in 1969 and 1972, for a sugar plantation (see Table 3).

Table 3

Category	Number	1969 Earnings *		1972 Earnings *	
		Per day	Per year	Per day	Per year
Owners	5	$136.15	$49,694	$	$
Technicians	30	10.97	4,004	14.73	5,378
White-Collar	354	2.31	845	2.95	1,079
Full-Time					
Laborers	2,854	1.20	377	1.98	662

* The "free" exchange rate in both years was S/.43.38 per dollar, but the cost of living for low-income families in the area is estimated to have risen 36 percent during the three-year period.

The Outlook for 1973: Problems
and Opportunities

We have already touched on the problems of organization and decision-making which exist in the sugar plantations. However, there are serious difficulties inherent in dividing the income of this sector among the beneficiaries and between them and the rest of the Peruvians, including the tax collector. In this section we will discuss that problem, the problem of the people who may be left out completely, the polemics over compensation to W.R. Grace and Co., and problems of staffing and financing the agrarian reform—all matters which are likely to be critical in 1973 and thereafter until the reform is completed.

Dividing up the "cake" among beneficiaries

The sugar complexes are fascinating, but they certainly are not representative of all Peruvian agriculture. Alberti and Cotler have estimated that the sugar plantation and mill workers, a proletariat accounting for only 1.5 percent of the rural population, produce some 13 percent of the value of agricultural outputs.[31] Therefore, turning the plantations into producer cooperatives could actually worsen the rural income distribution. Even before the reforms took effect, company towns were full of hangers-on who lived by petty commerce and by performing various services for the relatively well-paid sugar workers.

There are also questions involving the distribution of certain important resources between plantation complexes. Water flows vary in different valleys, directly affecting agricultural output. On Grace's plantations, aggressive unions had managed to win wage levels almost double those prevailing at Tumán: S/100/day compared to S/50/day for field work, with the wages for mill jobs proportionally higher. Except in years of heavy rains and high world sugar prices, Grace lost money on sugar (but not necessarily on paper), while Tumán could still be profitable. For the workers at Tumán, an obvious demand is an immediate raise to the wage levels paid on the Grace plantation: equal pay for equal work. Yet this would hardly be fair to the workers on another plantation, such as Cayaltí, where the former owner went bankrupt and the operation is less profitable by far than Tumán, even at its low level of wages.

The Finance Ministry is also interested in these questions: Tumán was one of the nation's top taxpayers, before reform. Thus, the government could hardly afford to allow Tumán's workers to vote themselves 100 percent wage increases, to Paramonga levels, if only because the resulting higher costs would greatly reduce the profits subject to taxes—since personal income tax exemptions are too high for revenues to be made up by taxing the workers directly.

For these reasons, as well as for political motives, it is obvious that the government will want to maintain its veto power over certain collective decisions—and that a mechanism is needed to make distributional adjustments between plantations, and between the sugar-producing sector and the rest of rural Peru.

Some of the same problems arise in terms of other crops where processing is important. Two vineyards (Ocuaje and Vista Alegre) were expropriated in September 1972, but by mid-December—in sharp contrast to the sugar plantations—no officials had arrived on the scene, so the owners continued work while awaiting developments. Another vineyard (Tacama) has apparently been found exempt, at least as far as 150 hectares of land and their wine-producing installations are concerned. Vineyard owners are investing on a large scale, but in terms of advertising and new brands, more than in fixed capital. In fact, the *Peruvian Times* recently reported that all vineyard owners are holding back and awaiting reform decisions.[32] If the state chooses to expropriate the entire processing facilities as well as the vineyards, then all of the problems of the sugar cooperatives will appear there as well. There is a further risk, in that the winemaker only knows if his work is good after six months to two years have passed—whereas incompetence is visible much more quickly in sugar processing. However, the rate of return on wine-making can be very attractive, and—like sugar refineries—the vineyards could possibly come to help finance some of the rest of the agrarian reform.

Those left out

Various official pronouncements made in 1969 and 1970 indicated that the Revolutionary Military Government intended to grant land to some 500,000 families over a five-year period (i.e., by June 29, 1974). This was plausible, in view of the 1966 CIDA estimates that almost one million rural families were potential land reform beneficiaries. On the other hand, many observers are dubious about whether such a goal is really attainable with the land, financing and reform agency staff that is currently available. Some skeptics envision rising discontent and new protest movements, if the government falls short of its goals—and in any case, they charge that the reform will fail to help another half million families in rural Peru. This focus on the postreform problem of rural poverty is certainly legitimate, but it is also like looking at a doughnut and seeing primarily the hole.

Goals and early accomplishments. A recent government publication specified Peru's redistribution goals for 1975, with indications of the extent to which they had already been achieved by late 1971.[33] According to this publication, there were approximately 650,000 farm families in the country in 1971, 333,909 of whom are expected to benefit directly from the reform process by 1975. By late 1971, 96,341 families had been identified as beneficiaries (since the reform program began in 1965), and 86 percent of these families had received their land from the present government.* In terms of livestock (mostly sheep), the national stock was estimated at 22,637,000 head, and by 1975 it was expected that 6,116,400 head would have been involved in land redistributions. By late 1971, 1,349,988 head of livestock had been counted in the course of land transfers—again, 87 percent of them under the present government. Land was broken down by types, as indicated in Table 4.

Table 4

	National Total	Goal for 1975	% of Total	Attained by 1971	% of Goal
Irrigated arable	1,117,594	793,888	71	284,540	36
Dry arable	1,775,061	1,264,868	71	358,077	28
Natural pasture	27,120,000	6,930,614	26	1,870,268	27

Unfortunately, this official document did not distinguish between the area expropriated by the present government and that expropriated by the Belaúnde administration. It is noteworthy, however, that the total goal for 1975 was more modest than the 11,427,378 *ha.* in seven area, that the Minister of Agriculture mentioned during a 1970 press conference.[34] In any event, the reader should beware of any single estimates of this type. For example, in his 1970 press conference the Minister of Agriculture announced that through June 1970, 3,439,361 hectares had been "affected," in the first legal step toward expropriation, but that only 1,235,759 *ha.* had been legally assigned to beneficiaries. Another analysis of "affectation" decrees published in the official gazette reveals that the expropriation process began for 1,362,021 *ha.* between June 1969 and August 1970.

* Title XV beneficiaries have obviously been excluded.

The other 2,000,000 *ha.* in the minister's statement must have been "affected" under Belaúnde, or during the first nine months of the present regime, under the rules of the 1964 law.

There are many stages in the reform process, from the first step toward expropriation to the final stage of transfer of title to some kind of cooperative, and even experts on the scene often have trouble determining whether official figures refer to land and people who have begun this process, are currently in it, or have completed it. It is also very difficult to credit reform actions to either the Belaúnde regime or the Revolutionary Military Government, since under Belaúnde a substantial number of large expropriations were initiated in a legal sense and then halted for lack of funds. I would assign credit for most such actions to the present government, which provided the funds and the will to complete these processes which had only been begun on paper.

When the figures are analyzed by zones, the relative priorities of the two governments become clearer. The recent push in the coastal zones of La Libertad and Lambayeque reflects the current regime's decision to incorporate plantations which were previously exempt. Although the hectares affected in Pasco-Junín and Puno are impressive, they probably reflect preliminary paperwork that had already been done for these sierra areas, where vast areas were affected under the previous law, and where the peasant movements were strongest throughout the last 20 years. More recent figures are not strictly comparable; they show continuing expropriations at significant levels in almost all areas (see Table 5).

Table 5

Zone	Old law, 1964–1969	June 1969– August 1970	% under new law
Piura	44,723 ha.	4,794 ha.	9.6
Lambayeque	152,682	78,753	34.0
La Libertad	67,940	266,061	79.6
Lima	188,404	23,131	10.9
Pasco-Junín	1,132,247	449,896	28.4
Cuzco	409,233	79,194	16.2
Puno	235,464	406,861	63.3
Total, seven zones	2,230,657	1,308,690	37.0

Source: Luis Pasara, *El primer año de vigencia de la ley de reforma asdfghjkl* (Lima: Centro de Estudios y promoción del Desarrollo, September 1970), p. 49.

Is there enough land? The conventional wisdom about Peruvian agriculture is that, due to the great population pressure, there can never be enough land for reform to benefit most of the rural population. The problem with this statement lies, as usual, at least in part in the definitions employed. The CIDA estimate of one million potential beneficiaries is larger than the government's 1971 estimate of 650,000. The government appears to be excluding some 300,000 salaried farm workers with regular jobs in agriculture—on plantations, which were expropriated and are to continue to be operated as units, or on acceptably modern medium and small farms that are not eligible for expropriation under the law.[35] There are another 300,000 tenant-laborers who have steady employment and less than one hectare of land; if we assume that they too are employed and not in line for sufficient additional land to make them independent small farmers, then it becomes possible to reconcile the CIDA estimate with the government's statement that the 1975 goal of 650,000 farm families would substantially complete the reform process, insofar as expropriation and land transfer is concerned. (We must also remember that the farm labor force continues to grow in absolute terms, by about 20,000 new farm families per year, despite the massive migration to the cities.)

One 1970 study by the Iowa Universities Mission to the Ministry of Agriculture was fairly optimistic about the availability of land in Peru.[36] It estimated that the number of eligible smallholders with insufficient land for a viable family unit was about 280,000 (230,000 in the sierra and 50,000 on the coast). Of another 350,000 family heads with no land at all, living under severely submarginal conditions, 300,000 live in the sierra and 50,000 on the coast. This gives a total theoretical goal of 630,000 families—100,000 on the coast and the rest in the sierra. Under the 1969 law, their minimum requirement for viable units would be 1.4 million cultivated hectares or its equivalent (natural pasture in the sierra is converted to cultivated hectares at a ratio of 15:1). According to the Iowa study, some 7,000 large farm units are subject to expropriation (excluding indigenous communities and other exempt units). They have the equivalent of 2.4 million hectares of cultivable land, about one million of which the owners may be allowed to retain, while some 1.4 million hectares will be available for redistribution—these are approximately the requirements of the potential beneficiaries identified by the Iowa group; they also coincide with the official goal of 650,000 families by 1975. What is less clear to me, however, is whether the 600,000 salaried farm workers and tenant-laborers with less than one hectare of land will be satisfied to remain in that landless status; nor is it certain that all their jobs will still exist if the 7,000 large farms are deprived of 60 percent of their present land. Such a move would require an intensification of production, and more employment per hectare, which is one possible reaction of the commercial farmowners. Another possible reaction, however, is a vigorous effort to reduce employment through mechanization, in the hope of diminishing future demands for land by their workers.

A particularly sticky question about land reforms, in Peru and elsewhere, is the role of the lower-status groups among the workers. As soon as the resident laborers of an expropriated farm have their status as beneficiaries confirmed, they try to exclude the seasonal, migrant and informal workers formerly associated with that farm, from any share in the reform benefits. At best, they will agree to hire these workers on an indefinite basis to do some of the hardest work. As novelists have known for centuries, a fellow peasant is a much harsher exploiter than the landed gentry—and agrarian reform thus tends to make the lot of the lowest classes worse, not better, than before. In Chile today, this fact has led to new waves of protest and land seizures by these irregular workers. The land they seized has included, not only privately held farms, but also parts of land reform projects from which they have effectively been excluded as legal beneficiaries.

Even if the land available in Peru could be sufficient, there is still a problem of varying population densities. In some Peruvian provinces, the pressure is so heavy that even denying owners any reserves at all will not provide enough land for all claimants; in others, however, the pressure is much lighter. It remains to be seen whether the government will decide to relocate thousands of families from one province to another. If it does, resistance can be expected from beneficiaries in the relatively underpopulated areas, who anticipate more than a mere subsistence share for themselves in the reform process and who will surely resist the bringing in of other families to share the available land.

The proposed "Grace amendment"

W.R. Grace and Company has not been happy about the $10 million value tentatively assigned to its expropriated plantations. The company claims that the Paramonga and Cartavio estates are worth approximately $24 million, and in lobbying before the U.S. Congress the company asked for a special clause in the sugar import quota laws. The version of these laws approved by the House Agricultural Committee authorized the president to levy $20 per ton against the payment made to sugar suppliers in any country that expropriates a U.S. company without mutually agreeing upon appropriate compensation.

Peruvian government officials naturally resented this effort to bypass the appeals process contemplated in the Peruvian agrarian reform laws. If such a clause were enacted and invoked, the net effect at first would be to oblige the land reform beneficiaries to pay Grace what it demands, by deduction from the price of sugar sold the U.S. under Peru's quota. (In 1971, the quota price was several cents above the world market price.)

Of course, the matter would undoubtedly not stop there. In order to compensate the reform beneficiaries, onlookers predicted that Peru would assess fines on other Grace Company assets in Peru, and if the U.S. retaliated, it would do so on other U.S. investment in general. All this evokes the bitter experience of Cuba in 1960. It also shows the risk inherent in the sugar quota system—an outright bribe to "friendly" countries leads to dependence on the subsidized price; then, any reduction in the quota or price appears as an unfriendly act, probably harming international relations far more than the quota ever helped them. 1973 might be a good year to abandon the whole system, since world prices are higher than U.S. quota prices, because of production problems in Cuba and Russia, so that the sugar producers, including Peru, would rather sell elsewhere.

The differences over valuation of the Grace properties should not be hard to settle in the Peruvian courts. Sources in Lima suggest that the $10.1 million figure understates assets, because the company took accelerated depreciation of capital assets under tax incentive laws. It probably also excludes the cane growing at the time of expropriation, because apparently Grace never carried growing cane as an asset on its books. One government official suggested that the company could expect to collect the cost of production of the standing cane and the "real" (or unaccelerated) depreciated value of equipment, but that it should also expect to have to pay the back profits taxes it had postponed through the use of these accounting methods.

At any rate, in early 1971 it appeared that Grace's top management—as opposed to company officials in Lima—was unwilling to abide by the appeals procedure established under Peruvian law. U.S. bank officers from New York, visiting in Lima, offered the opinion that Mr. J. Peter Grace wanted to sell all of "his" Peruvian assets now, that he would be angry if unable to do so at his own price, and that he simply did not care how all of this looked to the government and citizens of a country where Grace and Co. had long been considered the very model of a "good" foreign investor.

Grace has been divesting itself of its South American operations for some time now, trying to persuade investors to bid its stock up to the higher prices typical of chemical companies. It would like to have the Peruvian government buy up those operations which it has been unable to sell to anyone else. If this happened, Grace would no longer be doing business in Peru, and hence would not be able to use the land reform bonds for tax payments or for investments. Nonetheless, Peruvian dignity was understandably offended when the company's spokesman told a U.S. Congressional committee that to Grace, the bonds were virtually worthless. Fortunately, later in 1971 an agreement was signed in Lima concerning how Grace and the Peruvian government would move toward buying out the Grace paper mills, and toward resolution in the Peruvian courts of the valuation for the sugar plantations. As of late 1972, it appeared that both matters would be resolved by about June of 1973.[37] They weren't, but the current U.S. sugar price is not attractive and any punitive amendment would have no immediate effect, since Peru could sell its sugar at higher prices elsewhere. Negotiations are continuing in Lima, but the Grace proposal itself did no good for the image of U.S. companies abroad.

Human resources

Neither land availability, landowner opposition nor financial resources seems to be a serious impediment to the completion of the agrarian reform program sometime during the present decade. But the lack of sufficient human resources to carry out this project make it unlikely that the reforms will be completed until after 1975. The existing administrative apparatus of the Ministry of Agriculture has been geared toward more traditional and gradual development programs, and some functionaries are not convinced that reform is a good thing, or that the Indians deserve a more dignified place in society. The majority of government agency functionaries are of urban middle-class origins; according to Peruvian sociologists, these functionaries tend to deal with campesinos in a paternalistic way, and they are hardly prepared to deal at all with the lowlier Indians who are supposed to be their principal clients.

One possible solution is to try to retrain the present administrative staff; another, perhaps more promising solution is to make a special effort to recruit and train campesino leaders and technicians, with less formal education but far more empathy and ability to communicate with the people they are supposed to help. The training task has been assigned largely to an Agrarian Reform Research and Training Center (CENCIRA), sponsored by the government and FAO and patterned somewhat after the highly successful ICIRA in Chile, with modifications to suit Peruvian needs. The motivational task, and much more, is largely in the hands of the National System of Social Mobilization (SINAMOS), which is discussed in detail by other writers in this volume.

Financing

The Revolutionary Military Government has clearly channeled its resources into the area of highest priority—agrarian reform. Under Belaúnde, the Congress had rejected requests for funds for virtually everything beyond staff salaries. In 1969, even before promulgating the new law, the RMG gave the Ministry of Agriculture a substantial budget increase—to get things moving under the old law. This higher level of budget support has continued. The only question, really, is whether even the higher level will be enough to do the job, particularly since as reform action moves from the large but well-capitalized plantations and ranches, it takes in poorer lands and farm units which require long-term credit to create productive capital.

The government budget now includes sufficient funds for the needed expropriations and debt service, although the cash payment for livestock proved an unexpectedly large burden in 1970. In the future, however, the government may miss the taxes from the sugar estates (187 million soles in 1970); once free of tight control, the cooperatives are likely to vote higher wages, thus eliminating taxable profits. Similar things appear to be happening in the SAIS ranches of the sierra.

What would massive reform cost? Studies made during the 1963-68 period by an FAO/BID Mission provide a basis for rough "guestimates." [38] The taxpayers would not pay more than $8 million to landowners during the entire process; the balance of some $32 million more in compensation and interest would be recovered from land payments made by the beneficiaries. Cash payments for plantations, installations, construction and equipment would be about $2.3 million over 10 years, and the expropriation of 20 percent of the existing stock of cattle and sheep would take about $15 million. So total compensation for land, installations and livestock would come to about $67 million.

More important than these transfer costs are development outlays; but these are not really reform "costs," because they ought to be made regardless of who is the owner. The FAO/IDB Study on Reform Financing estimated the average cost per family at some $3,000 during the first four years of the total reform program; even if this cost could be cut to $1,000 (largely by putting more stress on low-cost sierra projects and by postponing some projects along the coast), the capital investment required to establish 500,000 families would come to $500 million. About 60 percent of this would be for agricultural credit, and the rest for administration and services to farmers. According to Dr. Thomas F. Carroll, an expert associated for many years with Peruvian land reform, this seems fairly realistic. [39] Total agricultural credit in

Peru in 1970 was estimated at about $120 million, divided about equally between the Agricultural Development Bank (BFA) and private commercial banks. The latter allocate about 12 percent of their loans to agriculture. If that amount could be raised to about 20 percent, it should cover the immediate credit needs for reform beneficiaries.

Overhead expenses, for administration and technical services, would require doubling the present Ministry of Agriculture's budget of $25 million. We must recognize, furthermore, that this merely establishes the beneficiary at an initial level. Consolidation into real development and market orientation requires heavier investments; on the coast, the farming is already rather capital intensive, and even current operations will require some replacement of private capital sources by state funding. In the sierra, the former owners invested so little that practically all new investment will be a net addition to the stock of productive capital. And, unfortunately, much of the necessary capital is not in the form of machinery or capital goods, for which export credit is available from many countries. Rather, a typical sierra project needs more and better breeding sheep *(corriedales)*, fenceposts and wire, and fertilizer.

The government has sought sources of external financing, but most loans for agriculture in the last decade went into long-term irrigation investments. However, USAID has provided some $17 million for a supervised credit program which is still the main low-cost source of credit for Peruvian smallholders, including many reform beneficiaries.[40] AID has continued this program, as well as training and advisory programs oriented to production planning and marketing, and additional help was provided in 1970 for the earthquake-stricken area.

FAO and the Interamerican Development Bank are the international institutions showing the most interest in Peru's efforts at land reform. The IDB loaned Peru $23 million in 1970 for small irrigation projects throughout the highlands; $10 million more for lending to individual borrowers through the Agro-pecuary Development bank is reportedly under negotiation. However, there are still no credits for the capital-deepening investments necessary to increase the number of families that can be included in the reform, at a decent income level, and there are relatively few sources of credit for the production cooperatives. There is also little hope in the short run, because U.S.

agencies and the international lenders seem unable to process new loans so long as a foreign investor thinks it has a claim against Peru. Some staff members at the World Bank expect to see a change in this policy soon, through the strong leadership of the bank's president, Robert McNamara. Such a change would be consistent with the progressive stance that McNamara presented at the UNCTAD meeting in May 1972; it also would show that the international agencies are not primarily "enforcers," and that one transnational company does not outvote the staff and all member countries in setting bank policies for a given country.

With external support or without it, Peru's agrarian reform program is well underway. It is massive, drastic and—compared to past effort—rapid, which is one of Chonchol's primary criteria for meaningful land reforms.[41] Whether it is completed by 1975 or over a somewhat longer time, it will clearly be one of the major accomplishments of President Velasco, the Revolutionary Military Government, and the Peruvian campesinos.

NOTES

1. By "agrarian reform," I mean the redistribution of land ownership in favor of those who actually till it, as well as greater social control over land and water resources. As compared with programs of colonization, rent control and labor legislation (leaving land ownership intact), agrarian reform tends to bring more radical increases in worker incomes, social mobility, equality before the law and human dignity. It is more effective, of course, when accompanied or followed by improved credit, extension and marketing services.

2. Unlike some published estimates, this includes Title 15 beneficiaries; see discussion in later part of this chapter.

3. See Thomas F. Carroll, "Agrarian Reform," in *Latin American Issues,* ed. Albert Hirschman (New York: Twentieth Century Fund, 1961).

4. See, for instance, Julio Cotler, "Traditional haciendas and communities in a context of political mobilization in Peru," in *Agrarian Problems & Peasant Movements in Latin America,* ed. Rodolfo Stavenhagen (New York: Doubleday-Anchor, 1970), pp. 543 ff.

5. Instituto Nacional de Planificación, *Plan Nacional de Desarrollo 1971-1975* (Lima, 1972).

6. Fred L. Mann, et al., "Preliminary Analysis of the Agrarian Reform Law" (Lima, Iowa Universities Mission Report T-4), 1970 (mimeographed).

7. Ibid.

8. U.S. Department of Agriculture, "Peru: Agricultural Situation, Annual Report," (Washington, USDA 1971, mimeographed).

9. Interamerican Committee for the Alliance for Progress (CIAP), unpublished 1970 country review for Peru. This report includes tables comparing the average yields for various crops in Peru, in certain tropical areas, and over the world.

10. I have discussed the history of land reform in Peru at some length, including the role played by American citizens and companies, in "The United States and Agrarian Reform in Peru," in *U.S. Foreign Policy and Peru,* ed. Daniel A. Sharp (Austin: University of Texas Press, 1972), pp. 156-205.

11. The basic source of land conflicts during the last two decades is Comité Interamericano de Desarrollo Agrícola (CIDA), Peru: *Tenencia de la Tierra y Desarrollo Socioeconómico del Sector Agrícola,* Washington, D.C., Pan American Union, 1966. See also Julio Cotler and Felipe Portocarrero, "Peru, Peasant Organizations," and Wesley W. Craig, Jr., "Peru: The Peasant Movement of La Convención," both in *Latin American Peasant Movements,* ed. Henry A. Landsberger (Ithaca: Cornell University Press, 1969). The Vicos Experiment was analyzed in many publications, but one of the best accounts is found in an anthology on Vicos: *Peasants, Power, and Applied Social Change: Vicos as a Model,* ed. Dobyns, Doughty and Lasswell (Beverly Hills: Sage Publications, 1971).

12. The Commission's report and draft law appeared as *La Reforma Agraria en el Perú. Exposición de Motivos y Proyecto de Ley* (Lima: Talleres Gráficos Villanueva, 1960).

13. See the sources cited in note 11, and David Chaplin, "La Convención," Chapter 11 of this volume.

14. CIDA, *Peru, Tenencia de la Tierra y Desarrollo Socioeconómico del Sector Agrícola.*

15. Gamalie Carrasco, *Algolán: Análisis Económico y Financiero de un Proyecto de Reforma Agraria en el Perú* (Washington, D.C.: CIDA, Trabajos de Investigación sobre Tenencia de la Tierra y Reforma Agraria, no. 2, 1968).

16. Gamaliel Carrasco, Arthur Domike, Jacques Kozub and John Strasma, *Movilización de Recursos Financieros y Económicos para la Reforma Agraria Peruana* (Washington, D.C.: CIDA, 1969).

17. Figures from a comparative study by the Dirección de Promoción y Difusión de la Reforma Agraria, "Ciento Veinte Días de la Reforma Agraria" (Lima, 1969).

18. Thomas F. Carroll, "Land Reform in Peru" (Washington, D.C.: USAID, 1970, mimeo).

19. John Strasma, "The United States and Agrarian Reform in Peru," in *U.S. Foreign Policy and Peru,* ed. Daniel A. Sharp (Austin: Institute of Latin American Studies and University of Texas Press, 1972), p. 183. See also CIDA, *Peru.*

20. The bases for expropriation and compensation in the 1964 and 1969 laws are compared in Carroll, "Land Reform in Peru," pp. 31-32. The original law of June 1969 was modified and extended by a host of further laws and regulations; my comments are based on the codification published by the government in August 1970.

21. The labor laws, enacted with an urban work force in mind but often not explicitly excluding farm workers, were until recently generally unenforced. Most land reform functionaries with whom I spoke in 1971 and 1972 were confident that every farm would be found to have broken enough regulations to make all of its land expropriable, if the agency so wished.

22. William P. Mangin, "The Indians," in *U.S. Foreign Policy,* ed. Sharp.

23. Based on fieldwork done by the author at one of the former Grace plantations, a year after its expropriation.

24. Giorgio Alberti and Julio Cotler, "La Reforma Agraria en las Haciendas Azucareras del Perú" (Lima: Instituto de Estudios Peruanos, 1971), p. 31.

25. David Scott Palmer and Kevin Jay Middlebrook, Chapter 17 herein.

26. U.S. Department of Agriculture, "Peru: Agricultural Situation."

27. See Ronald Clark, "Land Reform and Peasant Market Participation in Bolivia," *Land Economics* 44 (May 1965). Essentially, FAO observers in 1953 and 1954 counted only produce moving through the La Paz wholesale market—where the former landowners sold it—and overlooked large amounts of production bartered by reform beneficiaries on the altiplano, outside La Paz, directly with city merchants who came to the country when the former marketing channels dried up.

28. Alberti and Cotler, "La Reforma Agraria," p. 24.

29. Ibid., p. 25.

30. Douglas Horton, "The Effects of Land Reform on Four Haciendas in Peru," University of Wisconsin Land Tenure Center *Newsletter,* no. 38 (October-December 1972): 15-22.

31. Alberti and Cotler, Haciendas Azucareras.

32. *Peruvian Times,* December 22, 1972.

33. Ministerio de Agricultura, "El Marco Institucional: Aspectos Administrativos," document presented at the FAO/UNDP Seminar on Agrarian Reform, Chiclayo, Peru, November 29-December 5, 1971, as reproduced by Wayne Ringlien, in "Some Economic and Institutional Results of the Agrarian Reform in Peru," Land Tenure Center *Newsletter,* no. 38 (October-December 1972): 5-14.

34. Cited by Luis Pásara, *El primer año de vigencia de la ley de reforma agraria* (Lima, Centro de Estudios y Promoción del desarrollo, September 1970), p. 48.

35. Carroll, "Land Reform in Peru."

36. Fred L. Mann, John Huerta, Dennis Morrisey, et al., *A Preliminary Analysis of the Agrarian Reform Law* (Lima: Iowa Universities Peru Mission Program Report, January 1970).

37. Developments in the love-hate relationship between W.R. Grace and the Revolutionary Military Government are reported regularly in the *Peruvian Times*; the estimate that all would be settled about June 1973 appeared in the November 17, 1972 issue.

38. Carrasco, Kozub, Domike and Strasma, *Movilización*.

39. Carroll, "Land Reform in Peru," pp. 44–46.

40. Michael G. Finn, "Supervised Agricultural Credit in Peru: Technique Adoption, Productivity and Loan Delinquency in *Plan Costa*" (Madison, University of Wisconsin, Ph.D. diss., 1972).

41. Jacques Chonchol Ch., *El Desarrollo de América Latin y la Reforma Agraria* (Santiago: Editorial del Pacifico, 1964).

Economic

Growth

and

Development

John Strasma

13.
Some Economic Aspects of Nonviolent Revolution in Peru and Chile

In Peru since October 1968, and in Chile from November 1970 until mid-1973, imaginative and dynamic leaders attacked long-standing economic problems in the name of revolution at a pace that was never remotely approached by preceding "reformist" governments. In Peru, especially, these measures have enhanced national autonomy and dignity, while the economy has performed much better than critics predicted. In Chile, genuine success during the first year was followed by a confused situation in which sectarian politics and bureaucratic ineptness produced a completely unnecessary economic debacle that will take years to set right. In this chapter, however, I will concentrate on the Peruvian economy and refer to parallel or contrasting processes in Chile under Allende as aids to a clearer understanding of what is happening in Peru. Because the situation is unclear at the time of writing, there will be no analysis of the violent military coup that overthrew Allende in September 1973.

There are several important features common to revolutionary strategy and tactics in both Chile and Peru, although the details of the policies pursued differ as much as the two countries' economies and the ideologies of their leadership. The first common feature is the virtual absence of bloodshed and repression; neither government used a *paredón*, there are few forced political exiles and there are no camps or special jails full of political prisoners. (All of these, tragically, were to be imposed by the government that overthrew Allende.)

Second, both governments took office with programs similar in many respects to those of their predecessors, and indeed of most contemporary Third World governments: restore growth to a stagnating economy; redistribute incomes; plan economic growth, with a decisive role for public sector investment; recover national control of mineral and other basic resources; make educational opportunity available to more citizens; incorporate indigenous groups into the national market and society; and seek a way to give workers a sense of significant participation in decision-making.

A third common factor is the invention of a variety of sophisticated punctiliously legal means of avoiding or reducing the payment of compensation to those people whose assets were expropriated. This tactic removes one of the main economic constraints that had impeded action by previous governments in these countries; it also weakens the economic power of the displaced political forces, and hence lessens their ability to counterattack. There has been violence in Chile and Peru but, through 1972, at least, it hit balance sheets more than human lives, and in any case some of the accounting values that were wiped out were of dubious origin. The current situation has thus been an inversion of economic justice as it existed under previous regimes, wherein pickpockets and chicken thieves got jail sentences, while usurers and price-control evaders were merely given light fines.

In addition to these three basic similarities, there are important differences between the governments of Chile and Peru, in terms of style, priorities, goals and the road by which they came to power. President Allende was determined above all to "open the doors to Socialism," at the expense of short-term economic performance, if need be. President Velasco directs structural reforms aimed at modernization and national autonomy, but he also pursues economic growth and repeatedly stresses a "Third Way" ideology based on the rejection of both capitalism and communism. For example, Velasco actively woos both foreign and domestic capital investment, but subjects it to new "rules of the game." In Chile, however, many officials and Popular Unity (UP) party leaders professed no interest at all in new private investment; indeed, they spoke ill of businessmen as a class, blaming them for a wide range of problems. Such leaders explain the shortage of beef as the fault of farmers who "boycotted" by selling their breeding stock for slaughter in 1970 and 1971. More impartial observers might assign the blame in this case to the zealous land reform agency functionaries who publicly urged that cattle be expropriated, together with the land, with compensation (if any) to be given in the form of long-term bonds, instead of cash.

The political aspects of the Chilean and Peruvian scenes are fascinating, but they have been competently analyzed in other sources.[1] The present essay therefore centers on certain economic aspects, without thereby implying that political aspects are less important. They are, in fact, critical in making it possible to carry out the chosen economic strategy. In turn, the success or failure of the economic policies may affect to some degree the future (and longevity) of these governments. In what follows, I summarize the conditions under which each government took office, the constraints on its policymaking imposed by its constitutional situation, the stated economic objectives of the present governments and finally, the measures actually taken and the results obtained to date. Since agrarian reform has been analyzed separately, this essay will refer especially to two other critical sectors: mining and manufacturing.

Background

The Peruvian economy grew steadily from 1960 to 1967, at an average annual rate of 6.1 percent, thanks largely to export booms in fish meal and copper. Unlike most low-income countries, Peru's exports are diversified. They are all primary commodities but when sugar prices drop, copper or fish meal often go up in price, and vice versa. Other exports accounting for more than 10 percent of export earnings are iron ore, zinc and cotton. Even with diversification, however, fiscal deficits, fixed exchange rates and freedom of imports caused problems in 1966. It became obvious that devaluation was in order, but the Congress blocked action on this step for over a year. The familiar scenario ensued: exchange speculation, massive increases in imports, price inflation and credit restraint imposed to try to cope with these pressures, leading to general economic stagnation. When the *sol* was finally devalued in 1967, a recession was already under way. As often happens in Latin America, many journalists confused causes with symptoms, blaming the economic stagnation and price increases on the devaluation. In fact, the principal causes were the fiscal and structural factors of the two preceding years, which made devaluation inevitable and hence made exchange speculation and importing more profitable than productive investment.

The Chilean economy is much more dependent than Peru's on a single commodity for its export earnings—copper brings in 80 percent of Chile's earnings when the world price is 45 cents per pound, as it was in October 1971. On the other hand, the economy as a whole is much better developed than Peru's. Chile is really a semiindustrialized country, in which manufacturing employment accounts for 26 percent of the labor force.[2] Per capita incomes in Peru are around $246 per year, while Chile's per capita income is about $450.[3] Although copper dominates the exports, it is important to note that Chile also exports manufactured goods—such as newsprint, wood pulp and simple steel and copper products, canned peaches and superb wine. Neither country is self-sufficient in terms of food; Chile normally imports about $220 million a year in agricultural products and Peru only a little less.

Like Peru in 1968, Chile in 1970 presented its new government with a fiscal deficit and a stagnating economy; output (GDP) increased only 2.5 percent in 1970. Because the international trade terms worsened as copper prices fell, real income was up only 1.4 percent, insufficient to keep up with Chile's 2 percent net population growth rate.[4] Inflation, which has been a characteristic of the Chilean economy for more than a century, reached 35 percent in 1970. Like most incoming governments, the Frei administration had succeeded in slowing the inflation rate during its first years in office, but thereafter the annual rate rose again.

Reform efforts

Since 1963 and 1964, respectively, Peru and Chile had been governed by presidents who asserted that the very survival of democracy required modifications in the economic order. Both Belaúnde and Frei tried to change the internal and external relations that seemed to slow their countries' economic and social development—especially in agriculture and in minerals—and both were largely stymied. In negotiations with foreign-owned oil or copper companies, the national negotiators appeared, in retrospect, to have been outwitted by company bargainers.[5]

Agrarian reform laws were enacted and expropriation begun in both countries, but this process was stopped short of its stated goals by budget cutbacks and other restraints, imposed by an alliance of Left and Right in the respective congresses. In manufacturing, on the other hand, Belaúnde and Frei pursued "developmentalist" policies, providing incentives for domestic and foreign manufacturing investment, particularly the latter. Development outlays included the expansion of state-owned steel mills, plus several other large projects, but both governments relied primarily on the modern segment of the private sector to achieve growth in manufacturing.

The liberal democratic period ended in Peru when the armed forces hustled Belaúnde into exile in October 1968, giving as reasons his general ineffectiveness and, specifically, a scandal connected to recently concluded negotiations with the International Petroleum Company, a wholly-owned subsidiary of Exxon Corporation (formerly called Esso). In Chile, the drastic changes began with the November 4, 1970 inauguration of President Salvador Allende, elected on a Popular Unity coalition platform that stressed its socialistic aims. Allende only obtained a bare plurality, but that is sufficient according to the Chilean tradition, and his election was ratified by a substantial congressional majority that included the Christian Democratic Party.[6]

Objectives of the New Governments

Before analyzing some of the specific measures which characterize "the new economics" in Chile and Peru, we must summarize the objectives which the two governments announced upon taking power. The Peruvian military junta has at various times defined itself as "revolutionary" and "nationalistic," and President Velasco has taken pains to insist frequently that the armed forces seek a "different road" for Peru, neither capitalism nor communism. The monopolistic economic power of a few privileged families was reduced by state takeovers of sugar plantations, fish meal marketing, metal refining and marketing and a substantial part of the banking system. However, the government has not taken over mines that are in production, regardless of ownership, nor does it seek to nationalize all banks. At times, President Velasco even plays down the degree of state ownership in Peru. In agrarian reform, for instance, Velasco stresses that the land is to be owned by those who till it—although in the case of sugar plantations and mills, efficiency will be maintained (and taxes collected) by keeping the operation functioning as a single unit. Legally, then, these are not state farms. Yet their size and complexity make it hard to convince workers to regard themselves as self-employed, rather than as wage earners who work for and frequently fight with an employer. (See the chapters on agrarian reform in this book.)

In Chile, the People's Unity coalition of six parties and movements hammered out a common platform before the 1970 election campaign began. In the economic sphere the UP pledged a frontal attack on domestic "monopolies," on foreign ownership of natural resources, and on "economic oppression of the majority by the few." Elimination of these unacceptable structures was seen as the necessary and sufficient step to resolve more conventional economic problems, such as unemployment, unequal wealth and income distribution, inflation and a deficit in the balance of payments.

One goal both governments shared is that of consolidating and defending their power. The armed forces in Peru sought at the outset to weaken both the APRA political party and a dozen or so wealthy families who traditionally controlled much of the economic and political power in Peru. In Chile, UP leaders emphasized that the Left achieved control of government, but not of "Power" and that all other sources of power must be weakened, if not crushed, so the "People" can be secure.

Elections

In Chile, the use of the electoral road to power means that the government must pay attention to future elections—unless it is to abandon its constitutional and democratic postulates. Thus, the policies of the first six months were largely "populist," aimed at the municipal elections of April 1971. The UP won a slender majority, boosting the morale of supporters who remembered that Allende had won the presidency with less than 40 percent of the total vote. The

Opposition won the by-elections held to fill congressional vacancies in early 1972; the next regular elections were the congressional elections of April 1973. That date affected strategy planning by both UP and Opposition leaders, as did the possibility that a conflict between Allende and the Congress could lead to a plebiscite even sooner. Whatever the substantive issue which the people were asked to resolve, a plebiscite would constitute to some extent a vote of confidence in Allende and the UP. Even though he is not required to do so, after any such defeat the president might well feel obliged to resign, as de Gaulle did a few years ago in France.

In Peru, on the other hand, the government has not set a date for a return to elections of any kind. By late 1973, the armed forces will have been in power for five years—the target date a few officers hinted at back in 1969 and 1970. More recently, though, the stock answer has been that the government will return to parliamentary forms once the Revolutionary Military Junta has "substantially completed the Revolution." Civilian politicians discredited themselves in public opinion when they governed from 1963 to 1968, as they had done in many earlier periods. Political parties and leaders are so few and so weak that, even in 1973, there is very little pressure for a prompt return to party politics, elected legislatures and so forth. This situation could change, of course, if the government should lose the general confidence it has so far obtained from articulate Peruvians, and the tacit acceptance it has obtained from most of the rest of the populace. Even during President Velasco's critical illness in early 1973, speculation was focused on which other generals might take over, rather than on any plan to return the government to civilian hands, as was done in Argentina.

Restraints on the New Governments

Another fundamental difference between Chile and Peru was the set of rules which constitute due process for economic policymaking in each country. In Peru, where the present military government is merely the latest of many, the body of generally accepted law and procedure accepts as valid legislation given by *de facto* governments in the form of decree-laws. Subsequent civilian governments generated through elections have honored such legislation, as have the courts. The government meets for legislative purposes on Tuesdays and frequently on Fridays as well; members of the cabinet sit as quasi-legislators, free to say what they think about proposed laws, whether or not they fall into the area of their own ministerial responsibilities. When a consensus—or, occasionally, a majority vote—is obtained, the law is enacted. The process for amending the constitution is quite similar.

The Peruvian public sometimes first learns that a law is under consideration when the mass media inform them that it has been promulgated. In most cases, however, laws are drafted by civilian technicians in the relevant ministries; an informal but effective network of consultations gives at least some of the interested parties a chance to present their views to a staff advisory group (COAP) that reviews draft legislation and makes recommendations to the president and cabinet.

In Chile, Allende had to operate within a very different setting. The legislative power and courts were intact, and he had promised to respect pluralism and to work with these constitutional institutions. The legislative process was further extended by an important political step—Allende obtained a consensus of the heads of the political parties and movements making up the UP, before he submitted a bill to the congress.

Although opposition parties hold a majority of the seats in both houses, they began as a loyal opposition, rather than trying to block Allende at every turn. There are provisions for a plebiscite in certain cases of disagreement between the president and the congress, and the UP talked of using this route in 1971 but shunned an opportunity to use it in early 1973. The problem was to find an issue popular enough to be sure of winning, since a defeat could be disastrous to the UP's momentum and sense of "majority." Also, the UP seemed reluctant to set up a plebiscite mechanism, since even if it won the first test the opposition might then use the plebiscite route to block the UP on some other, less popular, aspect of its program.

President Allende was further restrained—unduly so, according to his more impatient supporters—by his pledge to maintain democracy, pluralism, freedom of the press, freedom to operate private schools and the like. Several of these pledges were made explicit in the constitution, as part of a pact between the UP and the Christian Democratic Party, ensuring Allende's nearly unanimous election by the congress after he won a relatively modest plurality from the voters in a three-man race.

Civilians and the armed forces

To some extent, the presence of ranking military officers at all major events and Allende's frequent meetings with them suggested an informal kind of consultation there, as well. This relationship was formalized when several officers were named as ministers in 1972, serving between a general strike of the Opposition and the regular 1973 parliamentary elections, and after a second strike later in 1973. In Peru, where the heads of the armed forces *are* the government, certain leading civilian spokesmen of the private sector take a regular part in the deliberations at the top staff level, the COAP. Although there are no civilian ministers, there does appear to be a trend toward moving civilians back into middle-level posts in the ministries and operating agencies, when officers at the level of majors and colonels are promoted or reassigned to military units. In both countries, the officers and the civilians are getting to know each other. The cardinals and bishops of the Catholic church, and sometimes Protestant leaders as well, also play a minor but visible role in the dialogue of both governments with their citizens.

The difference in the way laws are enacted obviously affects the style of both presidents. The speed and ease of legislation in Peru leads to many laws, some of which inevitably are enacted without sufficient study. In such cases, problems are resolved in the drafting of regulations, or by amendment through a further decree-law. The comparative slowness of the parliamentary process in Chile encouraged Allende to dust off old legislation already on the books whenever he could—which was quite often. It is important to remember that each of these methods constitutes due process of law in the country concerned, is fully constitutional and, through 1972, was respected as legitimate by most jurists and laymen alike. More recently, in Chile, the Opposition of some of the courts have attacked certain executive acts which were not consistent with existing jurisprudence, or on which there is some constitutional ambiguity. Either the pace of change or "due process" had to yield; the government could have gotten back into legalistic form by beginning a "consolidation" of the revolution, but neither its more ardent partisans nor the Opposition seemed willing to permit this. The attempted revolt by one armored unit in July 1973, inspired by the extreme Right, also made it easier for Allende's supporters to justify illegal measures in the name of "national security." And these in turn fueled the movement leading to the coup of September 11, 1973.

The Struggle for Autonomy and Redistribution of Wealth

Both President Allende and President Velasco were obviously determined to reduce their nations' vulnerability to economic decisions taken elsewhere. Past international economic arrangements have led to an outflow of interest, profit and depreciation remittances in recent years far greater than new investments and loans coming in. Technology and know-how have been acquired on terms that now appear unreasonably harsh, and the transnational corporation is better able to take advantage of regional integration than are locally owned enterprises somewhat in the negotiations for a common policy on third-country capital for the Andean Common Market. Among the biggest escape clauses is one enabling firms in member countries to continue more or less indefinitely with foreign ownership, so long as they do not export to other Andean Pact countries. On the other hand, since the industrial community law promises that, in time, the workers of every firm will come to own 50 percent of that firm, it seems likely that the Velasco Doctrine will apply to most foreign-owned manufacturing firms in Peru.

In Chile, many of the larger manufacturing firms were nationalized through negotiated purchase (under duress, of course). In the cases of certain high-technology firms, no action was taken, but there was talk of a mixed-society solution for cases such as the IBM subsidiary and the Philipps electronics factory. RCA Victor sold a majority interest in its electronics factory to the government, but continued to provide technology and imported components as a minority partner.

We turn now to specific examples of the tactics used to increase the role of the state and decrease foreign domination of manufacturing and mining, under Allende and Velasco. Here again, the differences are often as striking as the similarities.

Mining

Chile and Peru: Two different situations

The trend is unmistakable; large mines are no longer politically acceptable objects of direct foreign investment in Latin America, just as public utilities became unacceptable to intellectuals and populist politicians several decades ago. The process of nationalization, begun under Belaúnde and Frei, was accelerated by Velasco and Allende—but their strategies were quite different, because the objective situation of mining in Chile and in Peru is very different. In Chile, almost every large valuable mineral deposit was already in production or was opened in the process of Chileanization under Frei. In Peru, on the other hand, two large copper mines were producing, along with an iron ore field—but six other deposits with proved reserves and engineering studies nearly completed remained untouched. The Chileans thus face problems of maintaining the operation of going concerns, in taking over the mines, whereas the Peruvians face the much greater problem of overcoming both engineering and financing obstacles to bring new mines into production.

The Peruvian government is actively seeking foreign investment and know-how to open these other mines—and at least through 1972 took care to maintain good relations with the several companies then operating. Inevitably, however, the Peruvian search for foreign capital and know-how has been affected by events to the south: potential investors in Peru looked at neighboring Chile and feared that, as soon as their capital was invested and the mine in production, it would be taken over. Even though they have full confidence in the integrity of the present Peruvian government, investors know that it takes five years or so to open a mine and 10 to 20 years more to recover their capital and profits at a level similar to those they can earn elsewhere. By that time, they fear, there may be another government which will change the tax laws or other "rules of the game." Potential investors have therefore been investing heavily in mines in countries with Anglo-Saxon laws and traditions: Australia, Canada and the United States, but thus far they have ignored Peru. The one newly activated mine, Cuajones, is being opened largely through the reinvestment of depreciation and profits from the other Peruvian mines owned by the same U.S. corporations; European and Japanese capitalists considered, but eventually refused to make major commitments to, the estimated $385 million needed to bring Cuajones into production by 1975.

Foreign companies are quite willing, however, to bring in their technology to help solve the engineering problems involved—for a fee. If Peru doesn't have the capital to open the mines and build smelting facilities, it can borrow it from abroad—but only as a loan which is to be repaid at a definite time and with a specific rate of interest, rather than with the future profits which the investors know will be attacked by politicians almost as soon as they begin to flow. In fact, this is what Peru is now doing. Belgian and British interests competed aggressively for the job of financing the opening of the Cerro Verde mine and the building of a copper refinery at Ilo. The operation is being handled as a loan to the government, which will be the sole owner and operator of the mine and refinery.

Peru's "mine it or lose it" policy

To carry out this policy, the government must be able to dispose freely of Peru's mineral deposits without having to pay anyone for them. The Revolutionary Military Government can do so legally, thanks to a "mine it or lose it" law enacted under Belaúnde, but first enforced by the present government. Drawing on the traditional Spanish doctrine that the subsoil belongs to the state and is inalienable, this law declared that the function of a mining claim is to protect the investment of a company or person that is actively bringing it into production, but not to protect the investment of speculators who hold a claim in hopes of reselling it at a profit. This law, passed in 1965, ordered all holders of large mining claims to either get them into production by 1975 or else renounce them. The Revolutionary Military Government passed a complementary law in 1969, ordering such holders to submit detailed plans, engineering and geological information to the government by December 31, 1969, showing how they intended to get the mines into production by 1975, or else suffer immediate reversion. The following year, another deadline was set for the filing of proof of sufficient assured funding to carry out the investment; again, reversion without compensation could be decreed for deposits for which no funding was in sight. These laws have been enforced and various large and small ore bodies reverted, without compensation. Moreover, this step-by-step process meant that government files already contained considerable information about most potential mines and the cost and steps needed to bring them into production. This strategy is a particularly intelligent way of trying to get mines opened by private capital, while ensuring that, if this does not happen, the state will obtain the results of the exploration and planning work gratis, in exchange for the time during which the investors held, but did not use, an exclusive mining right.

The Allende Doctrine: A retroactive excess profits tax

In Chile, the objective was the comparatively simple task of taking over existing mines already in production. The Allende Doctrine required a constitutional amendment, which was enacted with overwhelming support from all political parties. This reform specified several means of reducing the compensation to be paid. The logic of some of these concepts is obvious, such as the deduction of the reserves for future pensions which will now have to be paid by the government. Engineers will determine the amount to deduct for equipment or installations that are in bad repair and not already depreciated on the books, just as might be done when one private company sells a mine to another. Allende obtained reports from Soviet and French mining consultants to back up the opinion of Chilean technicians regarding how much should be deducted on this score.

The new concept in compensation disputes, however, is a retroactive excess profits tax: Allende and the Chilean congress agreed that it was unacceptable that the foreign copper companies had earned higher profits in Chile than at their mines in other countries, even after the "Chileanization" measures established under Frei had taken effect. While Chile could have taxed them more heavily at the time, this was not done—in part because the record prices for copper were unexpected. Through constitutional amendment, the higher tax was in effect levied ex post facto. This is of course unfortunate for the stockholders who bought and held shares at prices reflecting the high dividends of recent years. The result was that the Anaconda and Kennecott operations wound up owing money to Chile, rather than vice versa. (Cerro, whose mine had just come into production in 1971, is supposed to recover its full investment, with interest but no profits.)

Legal scholars will undoubtedly argue the Allende Doctrine for years to come, but the traditional Anglo-Saxon rejection of ex post facto legislation might well be tempered with some consideration for the unequal bargaining power and negotiating skills of those who negotiated the past arrangements in Chile. In addition, I believe the constitutional ban on retroactive legislation in Chile and Anglo-Saxon countries sought to prevent human beings from being punished for acts that were not crimes when performed, rather than to protect wealth, no matter how it had been acquired. Corporations, after all, enjoyed perpetual life—which mortals do not yet enjoy on earth —so perhaps it is arguable that they could be subject to ex post facto taxation.

On the other hand, as noted above, the Chilean policy prevented Peru from obtaining new direct foreign mine investments in the traditional way—this was to Peru's benefit, I believe. And, although legally valid in Chile, the ex post facto action appears to be confiscation under the laws of many copper-importing countries. Spurred on by the threat of class-action lawsuits from its own indignant stockholders, the Kennecott Corporation has initiated lawsuits in various European countries, seeking to collect the value of shipments of copper from its former mines. In the 1973 seller's market for copper, this harassment did not prevent Chile from finding customers, but it has occupied government energy and resources in legal actions abroad, at some cost. Kennecott's suits also enabled Allende to accuse the company of "economic aggression," providing a rallying cry with which to unite the UP coalition, at times when unity was not its most notable characteristic.

Manufacturing: Creation of the "Social Area" in Chile

In Peru, the government has not sought to take over existing manufacturing firms. On the contrary, W.R. Grace has tried to *persuade* the government to buy its paper, chemical and other plants. (Grace is also asking for cash, now, in exchange for the long-term bonds it received for its sugar plantations taken during the land reform.) In Chile, the UP moved rapidly to acquire the principal business firms (numbering about 100) without having to ask the opposition-controlled Congress to vote expropriation. This was done through a variety of pressures and tactics. While many have been used before in isolated instances, in Chile and elsewhere, seldom have they been used so intensively or with such artistry, across such a wide spectrum of industries. And the opposition has responded, first in the courts and—when these proved slow and ineffectual—with increasing vehemence and a constitutional amendment intended to ban all forms of expropriation except through a specific law aimed at the company involved. Allende vetoed the amendment, but the government and Opposition differ as to whether or not the presidential veto could be overridden by a simple majority—this was important, since the Opposition did not have a ⅔ majority on its side. While such an impasse between the president and the Congress would presumably be resolved by the citizenry through a plebiscite, the UP was reluctant to establish that precedent. At any rate, before turning to new forms of worker participation in Peru, it may be useful to review the steps used to socialize most of the manufacturing sector in Chile.

The wage-price squeeze

As part of the general UP economic policy for 1971, Chilean business had to operate under a rigid price freeze, but it still had to pay legal increases in wages on the order from 35 to 40 percent. For firms with idle capacity and products bought by that part of the population receiving these wage boosts, greater sales offset the lower profit margins; for other firms, profits vanished. This process, plus the potential loss of bank credit now largely controlled by the state, weakened both the will and the ability of some firms to resist efforts to take them over for the state or "social area" of the economy. In Peru, by contrast, inflation has been moderate (under 10 percent a year), and a general price freeze was only decreed in 1973, when a reform of sales taxation created confusion and many firms raised prices out of apprehension about the new tax, or because their suppliers had done so.

Intervention

Existing laws in Chile allow the government to seize or "intervene" in a firm for a variety of reasons, all of which boil down to a failure to supply the market with essential products in sufficient quantity. Firms can be and have been seized for ignoring price controls and for shutting down production lines without official permission. A number of plants were seized even though their threat to supplies consisted solely of a shutdown caused by worker seizure of the plant—a seizure which took place in most cases just after the government had announced its interest in nationalizing that company; sometimes this seizure occurred on the initiative of the union itself, in an effort to push the government into acting sooner than it planned.

The first months: Improvisation

To make this process clearer, we will describe the principal cases in which manufacturing plants passed to the "social area" during the UP's first year. The UP program called for the nationalization of all "monopolies," a tentative list of which was released before the election. There was no definitive calendar to follow, but three firms in the light metalworking, poultry feed and textile lines closed down shortly after the election and thereby forced the government to act in order to preserve the jobs and output of those firms, which were needed as inputs by other firms. In the Nibco and Purina cases, the majority partner (a man from Indiana and a Chilean, respectively) was apparently unwilling to continue under the new political situation, and ordered activities slowed or halted right after Allende's election. Then the Bellavista Tome textile factory was driven into bankruptcy by labor problems, and probably mismanagement as well; its owner fled to Argentina. In all three cases, by invoking emergency legislation enacted during the 30-day government of a socialist regime in 1930 but never repealed, the UP was able to seize the plant, name an intervenor to run it (with full power to dispose of its assets, including the owner's checking account and any cash on hand). Theoretically, the owners could recover possession as soon as they had corrected the causes for intervention; in practice, Nibco and Purina reached amicable agreements with the Development Corporation to sell a majority interest, while the owner had no equity left in the bankrupt textile mill. During the same period, a few firms were also seized in order to halt flagrant violations of price or foreign exchange controls; this made price controls much more effective than they had been under previous governments.

Second stage: Purchase of shares

The next step in this process was the purchase of bank stocks directly from the public. Announcing that a law would soon be submitted to the congress providing for expropriation on much less attractive terms, President Allende asked bank shareholders to sell out voluntarily at prices based on the average market quotation for 1970—which was considerably above the stock market quotations following his election on September 4. Most of the shareholders did this and most of the banks are now state-owned or—as in the case of the Banco de Chile—operating with a strong state voice in management. It was unnecessary even to submit the draft law to the congress. Instead, the Development Corporation (CORFO) bought the shares invoking its general mandate to make investments that "promote development." Control of the banking system in turn facilitated further nationalization, because the banks could acquire shares of an enterprise with their investment funds, or lend to CORFO for the same purpose, without the need for a budget appropriation which the opposition majority in the congress might well defeat.

Control of the banks serves another purpose, as well: it reduces the ability of opposition groups and politicians to obtain loans with which to finance their campaigns—or their business operations, whose profits finance their campaigns. There is also much discussion in Chile about whether or not control of the banks ends the secretive nature of client-banker relations. The occasional publication in pro-government papers and magazines of the borrowings, net worth, protested checks, etc., of opposition politicians suggests that bank files have not been inviolable, although this probably reflects the zeal of individuals rather than official policy. The government's possession of the balance sheets and lists of assets and liabilities of the wealthy and the interlocking economic elite, also made it easy to pressure the weak to sell shares of those firms the state wants to acquire, or to cooperate in other ways to bring about the economic destruction of their class.

In Peru, as in Chile, the state has acquired most of the banks. The Banco Popular, largest in the country in terms of both deposits and branches, was on the verge of bankruptcy as a result of high costs and bad loans, many allegedly given to members of the bank's stockholders and their relatives for real estate speculation. The government took it over, contributing badly needed new working capital as its investment, and reducing the former ownership interest to a nominal 15 million soles. Several other banks were purchased outright, while a few important banks remain in the private sector. In Peru, the objective is clearly rationalizing the sector and channeling credit to productive uses rather than merely taking over all banks because they are a form of power.

Third stage: Intervention with assistance by unions

Once the bank purchase operation was well underway in Chile, the next target was the textile industry, traditionally a sector of high labor combativeness. The UP program called for its nationalization, but rather than submitting a bill in this regard to the congress, the government used existing legislation to accomplish its desires. For this, it was necessary to state that the textile industry was in a "state of crisis," as described in the appropriate 1930 laws. The Minister of Economy made an address announcing the nationalization of the textile plants, and called on the owners to cooperate. However, the morning after his speech most of the major plants were seized by the unions, which demanded the nationalization of the plants—then the government seized the factories, on the grounds that consumer supplies were endangered by the union strike and seizure. In due course, the Contraloria General rejected the decrees of intervention on the grounds that the threat to essential consumer supplies was not immediate, and in any case an illegal act by third parties (the seizure of the plants by their unions) could not be used as a pretext for taking the plants away from their owners. However, the government could hardly accept the loss of face (and momentum) of going back, so it overruled the Contraloria through a Decree of Insistence. (Such decrees must be signed by all members of the Cabinet, and serve mainly to give publicity to the fact that in the opinion of the Contraloria an illegal administrative act has taken place. Such conflicts and "insistences" are not new with the UP; Frei had also used such decrees at various times.)

The congress would no doubt have approved the taking over of the textile mills in 1971, but with lengthy debate over how many other sectors would also be taken, the future of suppliers and specialized finishing plants, and of course the question of compensation to the owners. Meanwhile, the owners would have been depleting inventories, destroying all evidence of illegal practices (tax evasion, false invoicing of imports, etc.) and generally letting the industries run down. If a large, complex operation is going to be seized against the wishes of its owner, the social and economic cost will normally be much lower if there is no time lag between the announcement and effective seizure. (Note the parallel between this analysis and the almost instantaneous seizure of the sugar plantations during Peru's agrarian reform.)

No compensation has yet been paid the owners of those textile firms, and it is not clear when—or if—they ever will be paid at all. Technically, they are being operated by the intervenors for the account of the owners, but all vestiges of the past management were being wiped out (e.g., the toppling of the statue of the founder on the grounds of one plant). The sudden seizure had another advantage, too: any claim for indemnization could be greatly reduced by assessments for back taxes and fines for irregularities discovered by the intervenors as they went over the books. All of these firms apparently underinvoiced and sold goods without invoices, in order to evade the sales and income taxes. It is also alleged that they arranged for false invoicing of imported raw materials, in order to cut taxable profits and send dollars abroad at the unrealistic official exchange rate.

With the textiles and banks in hand, the government next turned to the cement plants, the tire factories and the only privately owned paper company. The cement industry was taken over with the aid of a strike and government intervention, but the tire company shares were bought up by CORFO, along the model used with the banks. This difference in treatment may reflect the fact that the biggest cement company is a traditional "villain" in Chilean politics. The tire companies are smaller, and have foreign as well as Chilean shareholders. (The latter protested the "better treatment" of foreign shareholders, who were paid in dollars and marks, while the Chileans received *escudos*.) The government also began buying shares of the paper company, but failed to acquire control, though the battle was intense. The opposition naturally spoke of the issue as a threat to the freedom of the press, and the paper company union refused to assist a takeover by "intervention." After Allende's first year there were rising pressures for the government to announce at once which other firms would be taken over, so that the "exempt" could invest, as was clearly needed, to meet the expanding demand arising from a near-100 percent increase in the money supply during the UP's first year of power. The government submitted a bill in October 1971, to define the limits of the social, mixed and private sectors. In terms of this chapter, the key decision was that all firms with capital in excess of E° 14 million (about $500,000) as of December 31, 1969 would be taken eventually, and would constitute the "social area" of production. The government issued a list of the firms that qualified as "social," with a "clarification" that newspapers and radio stations would not be nationalized, even if they were above the E° 14 million in capital. *El Mercurio,* the largest newspaper enterprise in Chile, and on the whole the best-run one, had a capital of E° 106 million, according to the list. Its continued existence as a widely read opposition family of papers was naturally an annoyance to the UP and to extremist groups on the Left. (Its exposés are received about as graciously by President Allende, as were the Watergate stories by President Nixon. However, its editorials are much harsher than those of the *Washington Post,* and it saw itself, correctly, as being in a life-or-death struggle for survival.)

No Peruvian paper would dare to be as outspoken as are all of Chile's papers; and the timidity of the press in Lima explains the importance of rumors—*bolas*—there. In Santiago, both pro- and anti-UP rumors were immediately printed in whatever paper was politically most pleased with the impact such publication might have. As in New York, the wilder rumors appear in the tabloids, while the "serious" press—in this case: *El Mercurio, El Siglo, La Prensa* and *Ultima Hora*—made some effort to check out these stories.

Returning to the government's bill, it provided that firms with E° 14 million or more in capital could be acquired on the Chilean president's initiative. Indemnization would be paid owners according to the president's choice of one of these three formulas:

1. the average of market quotations for a company's stock during the year prior to nationalization;
2. the book value of the property as of the December 31 preceding takeover, less deductions for any revaluation of assets (to compensate for inflation) that may have been made after February 14, 1964; or
3. an average of the amounts calculated by the first two methods.

This bill would also exempt the government from responsibility for the debts of any company it takes over. This clause, of course, would make it virtually impossible for any privately owned Chilean firm to obtain credit abroad unless a government agency guarantees payment. The bill went to the congress, where it was amended to be consistent with a constitutional reform submitted by the Christian Democrats. The main difference was that the latter establishes a fourth sector, that of worker-management *(auto-gestion),* provides for more significant worker participation in the decision-making process of all firms, rules out any further use of intervention to take over firms, and requires congressional approval for each expropriation or purchase of shares. The reason the Christian Democrats submitted their bill as a constitutional amendment, however, is that this permitted work on it to continue during the Extraordinary Session (when congress can only act on legislation proposed by the executive, and on constitutional amendments). Since many of the changes were unacceptable to the UP, the matter was unresolved and stalemated at least through mid-1973.

In Chile, then, there have been three main methods of state acquisition of manufacturing enterprises: intervention when owners closed plants or violated price control and foreign exchange laws; intervention when plants were seized by workers; and purchase of shares. In Peru, on the other hand, the state has sought to stimulate new investment and has generally resisted even the offers made it to sell the existing plants at their book values.

Worker Participation in Enterprise Management

Many of the debates over the role of foreign capital, and of the state, are familiar from other countries and other times. The question of auto-gestion is newer, and more intellectually attractive to several of the principal academic economists and planners in Chile—and, especially, in Peru.

In Chile, many UP spokesmen regularly attacked auto-gestion as a fraud or a counterrevolutionary plot, even though it is openly advocated by the Christian Left, within the UP coalition. Fidel Castro criticized this concept in speeches made to miners while touring Chile. If understood as ownership and the right to all the products of the copper mines, few would disagree with him. However, economists advocating auto-gestion would solve that problem by taxing away the economic rents.[7] In Chile, in any case, the auto-gestion advocates generally refer to agriculture and to small and medium-sized industry, where the results depend partly on worker productivity and a surplus (profit) is by no means assured.

The UP opposition to worker management may derive from the fact that Yugoslavia, the most successful economy based on auto-gestion, and the only one with much of its production organized on that basis, is not really regarded as one of the "club" by other communists. Perhaps the UP also tended to oppose this concept simply because it was advocated by the Christian Democrats; this was the one point in Tomic's unsuccessful 1970 campaign on which he really differed from Allende. The UP did stress worker participation in various committees, both in the plant and in Santiago, but the state, in the name of all the people, was clearly the ultimate authority.

In additon to worker management, the related concept of decentralized planning under socialism has been getting attention for some time in Chilean university circles.[8] Under Frei, CORFO's Servicio de Cooperación Técnica gave assistance to several dozen small plants owned by their workers—often due to a desperate situation when the owner went bankrupt and gave the plant to them in lieu of back wages, severance pay, etc. Curiously, while the Christian Democrats have failed to create a large sector of auto-gestion by statute, many plants have approximated self-government with an assist from the Federation of Revolutionary Workers (FTR), an affiliate of the Movement of the Revolutionary Left (MIR), which is not part of the UP, but which has often helped to seize plants in order to bring about intervention and state ownership. If the FTR doesn't like the intervenor's performance, they expel him from the plant and demand a replacement—which is one version of worker self-government. This practice was particularly resented by the parties to which the expelled *interventores* belonged, but in practice there is little they could do about it. FTR pressure also perhaps made the Central Labor Federation (CUT), dominated by UP parties, remain attentive to worker concerns even when these run contrary to the wishes of UP planners.

In Peru, on the other hand, the concept of participation "came from nowhere" and suddenly appeared as a key part of the Industries Law of 1970. That law provided that 15 percent of each year's profits were to be set aside and reinvested in the firm (or in other "approved" investments). The corresponding newly issued shares were to be given to the "Industrial Community," made up of everyone from manager to janitor. The personnel was to elect one member to the Board of Directors immediately, and more as their shareholdings rose. Eventually, the Community would come to hold 50 percent of the shares; dividends on these shares were to be added income for the workers.

A host of details had to be worked out afterwards, and a few are still unclear. After an initial panic, the industrialists have accepted the fact that the law and regulations as they stand are neither an immediate threat to their control, nor a heavy financial burden. At the same time, neither do they bring overnight revolution in labor-management power relations, as some union spokesmen had expected. There is no doubt that this law was an innovation, however. The creation of the industrial community added a new concept to the Peruvian Revolution. Intended to be distinctively Peruvian, it quickly spread to other sectors of production as well, and has been used by the government to dramatize its desire to find a middle way between capitalism and communism.

There were a number of theories circulating through Lima about the origin of this law and the concept behind it, with paternity attributed to various people—and denied by some of them. One plausible theory, however, traces the idea to a sudden compromise between some industrialists and the most zealous planners—a spokesman for the former offering to accept some degree of worker participation in profits if the latter would scrap a draft law providing for state control of the minute details of factory operations and decision-making.

Once the word "participation" had been introduced, the ideologues of the Revolution quickly went beyond a share in profits, to include participation in ownership and a voice on the board of directors as well. Agreement in principle was reached among the advisors; the planning group at the Ministry of Industries and Trade drew up the legislation rather quickly; and it became law, although it required a great deal of subsequent study and clarification. As in the reorganization of the sugar plantations (see chapter 12 on Agrarian Reform), part of the government saw the "Community" as another step toward harmony in people's places of work, which would tend to make the unions and strikes unnecessary. One of the drafters of the legislation, Professor Virgilio Roel, was later dismissed from the ministry for stating, in an academic forum, that the "Community" would intensify, not end, the class struggle in the factories. The minister himself later resigned.

In 1970 President Velasco stressed that 50 percent ownership of industries by their workers was the government's goal, not 100 percent. The goal, he said, is co-gestion, not auto-gestion. At any rate, companies operating at a loss, or with low taxable profits, move slowly if at all toward that goal, and even highly profitable companies will not reach the level of 50 percent for many years.

The whole concept of auto-gestion has received intensive review in Peru, in the light of a year's experience under both the Industries and the Agrarian Reform Laws. The result has been a variation on the original model, for fisheries (both seamen and packing plant workers), miners and telecommunications workers. In particular, a large part of the Community's profits is shared with the Communities of other firms or mines. While this will obviously reduce the intended stimulus to harmony and productivity, statements made at the time clearly indicated that this measure was intended to produce greater equity between workers in fishing companies or mines that are profitable, and those in others that are not.

The percentage of pretax profits given the Community varied, too: instead of 15 percent as in manufacturing, it was 12 percent in fishing and 6 percent in mining. In addition, workers also receive directly, in cash, either 10 percent (manufacturing), 8 percent (fisheries) or 4 percent (mining), in lieu of all previous statutory profit-sharing arrangements.[9] This system corresponds roughly to that in force under previous laws, but is much simpler. Half of the funds are distributed equally among all workers, according to the number of days worked during the year, and half are distributed in proportion to wages or salaries received.

Although it is still too early for a thorough evaluation of this situation, the labor communities are no longer popular among Peruvian intellectuals, nor are industrialists so threatened by them as they were in 1970. In many cases, the communities are reported to be most cooperative with management—and just as adamantly opposed to the entry of any new worker into the firm. According to several cases described to me on a visit to Peru in May 1973, the obligatory reinvestment is apparently being channeled largely into labor-saving equipment to increase output without hiring more workers. It has now become obvious to Peruvian planners that the Communities are fine for those already employed, but counterproductive to the government's goal of 500,000 new jobs in the 1973–74 biennium.[10]

To deal with this problem, and to devise a new form of organization, less prone to turn workers into "sub-capitalists," Peru's planners in 1973 were trying to develop a different set of working rules for what will be called the "social area" of production in Peru. Details were being kept secret, although a few glimpses appeared in statements by cabinet members. For instance, these firms will definitely not be state-owned (unlike the "social area" in Chile), yet they are to be financed by the government. This new area is to be "predominant," although it has not yet been announced in what respect or time period. And it has been suggested that the area will consist mostly of new enterprises, though a few existing firms may be converted. If so, that brings the planners right back to the same problem that has hampered Peru's industrial growth for the last decade: a shortage of viable, new, profitable projects ready to be launched.

Economic Performance

It is difficult to obtain adequate data for an evaluation of the performance of these economies under their very different approaches to nonviolent "Revolution." For Chile, in particular, it appears that the first year (1971) was highly successful—if anything, it was *too* successful. GDP rose about 8 percent in real terms, and the share of labor in national income rose from 49 to 59 percent, approximately. In 1972, growth slowed and redistribution may have regressed somewhat; at the same time inflation reached a record rate of 180 percent. In 1973, strikes, shortages and general confusion, as well as continuing inflation, led to stagnation equal to or worse than that found by Allende when he took office. Nonetheless, right up to the coup of September 1973, employment was high and UP mass communications specialists successfully persuaded many workers that the shortages were largely the fault of the Opposition, which they certainly were. A truckowners' strike, for instance, was to blame for the scarcity of bread, because imported flour was piled on the docks but couldn't reach Santiago.

The Chilean foreign exchange situation was particularly critical in 1973, although the loss of considerable copper output from strikes and shortages of parts and technicians is offset somewhat by the record-high copper prices, reaching 97 cents a pound in July 1973. Although Chile remains a member of the Andean Common Market, her exchange rate structure and domestic situation seem to preclude much progress at the moment toward effective integration.

In Peru, growth has been steadier, although published current statistics are scarce. There is a conspicuous lack of new private investment in medium-sized manufacturing activities—those necessary to achieve the "linkages" economists seek in development, yet too small to warrant special contracts with the state, of the sort given to "basic" or "strategic" industries. There is significant reinvestment in existing firms, however, and new plant investment and employment could increase, once the government defines the rules for the new collectively owned, worker-managed firms. Pending that, as well as some further definition of the boundary between private enterprise and the activities reserved for the state or the new labor-managed firms, investors seem to prefer to wait.

There is no such reticence on the part of oil companies, however, given the high probability of finding oil and the simple, unambiguous contracts which Peru offers. Foreign commercial banks indicated their confidence in Peru in mid-1973, by extending $100 million in long-term credits.[11] A consortium led by the Wells-Fargo Bank provided the funds for 8 and one-half years, with four years' initial grace period. Peru is also seeking $390 million from Japan, to build the trans-Andean oil pipeline. Whereas in 1971 Peru sought a refinancing of old loans, now the banks seem to come to Peru. The rates, too, are better—instead of 2¼ percent over the London Interbank rate, as in 1971, the recent operations are at a premium of 2 percent or 1¾ percent. (This may, of course, reflect an excess supply of Euro-dollars, in addition to well-founded confidence in Peru's future balance of payments.)

Even the "official" international lenders seem to be coming around, despite Exxon's pressures. The Interamerican Development Bank approved a $6 million dollar loan to the *Banco Minero* in early 1973, for relending to 58 small and medium mines, to create 8,000 new jobs and raise output by $49 million per year. This was a drop in the bucket compared to Peru's $3 billion list of projects, presented in June 1973 to the World Bank's Consultative Group for Peru. Of that amount, $1.5 billion are the estimated foreign expenditures, and Peru hopes to borrow a total of $1.9 billion between 1973 and 1975. Of course, much of this will be supplier credit, as was the $114 million obtained through the same group after its meeting in February 1972. The World Bank itself made a $25 million agricultural loan in August 1973, and resumed active study and negotiation of other requests. This was the first loan to Peru by the World Bank in several years, except for an earthquake reconstruction loan, and it was correctly interpreted as proof that no veto was being exercised by anyone because of Peru's past or present policies. Cerra Corporation attempted to bring pressure in September

1973, over the price and other aspects of its proposed sale of the Cerro de Pasco mine to the Peruvian government, but there was no indication that Cerro's arrogant press releases influenced lenders.[12] The Bank is highly influential with other lenders, and it had already helped Peru by convening the "Consultative Group" and by providing a thorough, highly constructive economic report on Peru as a background to discussion among potential lenders in the group. Even before the new loans, however—and without significant fish meal exports for 1972 and 1973, since the fish simply disappeared—Peru was clearly in a better financial position in 1973 than it was when it sought the refinancing of its existing debt in 1971. Part of the credit for this improvement goes to Petroperu's oil finds, but a good deal also reflects an intelligent balance, by the military government, between social change and rational economic policies. In Chile, the priorities, policies and results were quite different, ending tragically in bloodshed, and in the closing of parliament, political parties, many university departments and most of the press.

Velasco and Allende shared a concern for autonomy and the redistribution of power in favor of those now governing. They have both shown imagination in approaching economic problems, and ingenuity in finding legal ways to cut the compensation to the people whose lands and industries were expropriated. Nonetheless, the two countries' historical and ideological differences are substantial, and by now it is clear that their priorities are as different as their political settings. Sister republics and neighbors, they are traveling different roads. However, both will be providing economists (and other social scientists) with invaluable research materials over the next several years. Like Cuba and Brazil during the last decade, they provide testing grounds for alternative engines of development, sovereignty and national dignity.

NOTES

1. For example, apart from the essays herein, see: José Iglesias, "Report from Peru: The Reformers in Brass Hats," *New York Times Magazine,* December 14, 1969; E.J.

Hobsbawn, "Chile: Year One," *New York Review of Books,* September 23, 1971; Carlos Delgado, *Problemas Sociales en el Peru Contemporáneo* (Peru: Instituto de Estudios Peruanos, 1971); Carlos Delgado, *El Proceso Revolucionario Peruano: Testimonio de lucha* (Mexico: Siglo 11, 1972); and James Petras, "The Transition to Socialism in Chile: Perspectives and Problems," *Monthly Review* (October 1971).

2. *Estadísticas 1969,* Republica de Chile, Servicio de Seguro Social.

3. Figures from the U.N. Statistical Yearbook, for calendar year 1968. Official figures given by government agencies are somewhat higher. For instance, ODEPLAN estimated Chile's 1969 GDP per capita at $550, while the United Nations put it at $520. Obviously, the choice of an exchange rate is critical and thus makes post-1970 income figures particularly hard to estimate in terms of dollars. (By 1973, there were more than five "official" exchange rates.)

4. CEPAL, "Informe acerca de Chile, 1970," according to *La Prensa* (Santiago), April 11, 1971.

5. On the long history of Belaúnde's efforts to persuade Standard Oil (now Exxon) to give up an oil field, its title to which was based on little but the Statute of Limitations, see Richard Goodwin, "Letter from Peru," *The New Yorker* (May 17, 1969), pp. 41–109. In Chile, otherwise competent negotiators seem to have failed to foresee the possibility that copper prices might rise far above the level prevailing at the time of negotiation for "Chileanization" of 51 percent of Kennecott's mine. They therefore neglected to stipulate that any such windfalls would accrue entirely to Chile. Likewise, the "nationalization by contract" of Anaconda's mines in 1969 contained contract terms that gave Anaconda strong incentives to "high-grade" the mine, and to spend as little as possible on removing the burden or making other expenditures that would be repaid in increased copper output only in 1972 or thereafter.

6. On the Chilean election of 1970 and subsequent events, including the assassination of the army's chief of the general staff and the "Pact of Guarantees" obtained by the Christian Democrats as the price of support for Allende in the congress, there are various sources. One of the most complete is Edmundo Labarca Goddard, *Chile al Rojo* (Santiago: Editorial Austral, 1971).

7. See Jaroslav Vanek, *The General Theory of Labor-Managed Economies* (Ithaca: Cornell, 1970), chapters 14 and 15. Professor Vanek visited Peru in 1972 at the invitation of the development finance agency, COFIDE.

8. A. Foxley, ed., *Chile: Busqueda de un Nuevo Socialismo* (Santiago: Universidad Catolica, CEPLAN, 1971).

9. The relevant legislation, with concordances, regulations and a manual of instructions, may be found in Miguel A. Suarez Sandoval, *La Comunidad Laboral Perana* (Lima: Impresiones Moreno, 1973.)

10. The goal of 500,000 new jobs was stated in the Budget Message for the 1973–74 Biennium. See the transcription of the press conference of December 29, 1972, given by the Minister of Economy and Finance, General Francisco Morales Bermúdez C., and the Chief of the National Planning Institute, General Guillermo Marco del Pont S. (Lima: Department of Public Relations, Ministry of Economy and Finance, 1973).

11. Figures in this section are taken from the *Peruvian Times* (June 8, 1973), and other recent issues.

12. Cerro's indignant accusations appeared as an advertisement in the *New York Times*, September 25, 1973, and Peru's reply appeared about two weeks later. I am in no position to evaluate the truth of Cerro's allegations, nor do I know whether the successful coup against Allende on September 11 prompted Cerro to take a harder line in Peru.

Shane Hunt

14.

Distribution, Growth and Government Economic Behavior in Peru

The original purpose of this study was to set forth the means by which policy instruments have been used by the Peruvian government to affect that nation's rate of economic growth. After their initiation, however, essays tend to lead lives of their own, and this one has chosen to broaden itself in one direction and narrow down in another.

It is broader because it could not deal with growth policy alone. Growth is of course a Good Thing, and any government would prefer to foster rather than retard it.* Nevertheless, the urgency of pursuing other policy goals, such as stabilization and distribution, frequently leaves a government with few effective instruments left for growth policy. This has generally been the case in Peru, and so the history of growth policy in that country is largely a history of the secondary effects on growth resulting from policies designed with other goals primarily in mind.

Secondary growth effects produced by the pursuit of other policy goals are not necessarily random; in the case of policies for improved distribution, they are generally unfavorable. Yet the conflict between growth and distribution is not inevitable. It can be avoided by redistributing claims on future income generated by present investment, instead of redistributing present income. It can also be avoided by the behavior of the rich; if they love luxury so much that their marginal

---

* Sometimes it is argued that what is important is not growth but development, the difference being that development involves both growth and additional changes that permit a more equitable income distribution. Growth without development, as a separate policy goal, would therefore seem best defined as growth with unchanging income distribution, and that is the sense in which I use it in this essay.

propensity to save is no higher than anybody else's, then the dilemma disappears.

But in fact, this dilemma of choosing between growth and distribution appears to be very real in Latin America. It seems no accident that the countries which have suffered the most unhappy growth performances in the last twenty years—Argentina, Chile and Uruguay—are precisely those in which the middle and lower classes have become most powerful politically, most disaffected with the existing social structure and income distribution and most forceful in demanding distributive change. This close, inverse connection between growth and distribution demands that if policy toward one is to be studied, then policies toward both must be studied. That is the case in this chapter.

This essay is narrowed down in that it deals only with budget policy—i.e., the use of taxation and expenditure to achieve combinations of the policy goals already mentioned. This leaves out tremendously important policy fields, such as those dealing with industrial development, public enterprise and exchange rates.

For two reasons, I do not wish to view policymaking as a technical problem of correctly turning the handles of instrument variables in order to achieve exogenously determined targets. First, this approach is better suited to policy planning than to the analysis of past policymaking, since for the latter one is likely to find the exercise of the instrument as the only evidence suggesting what the target was. Second, the process of choosing targets is very important and should not be left out of consideration. Just as consumer expenditure is determined by the behavior of individuals, as expressed by a consumption function, so is government expenditure and taxation determined by society's behavior, as expressed by the choice of policy targets. Society's preferences, thus filtered through the mechanism of government, are nothing more than a reasonably pacific resolution of the preferences of different competing groups. The policy targets chosen are a reflection of the power of these various groups in the political arena; they are also a major determinant of the net benefit these groups receive from the political process in general and the budgetary process in particular.

Before looking at the taxation and expenditure patterns that have been the result of political struggle over the Peruvian budget, first we will look at the political environment itself, as it has been analyzed by various noneconomists. We seek the political origin of the economic behavior embodied in the particular combinations of growth and distribution policies pursued over the years.

Political Origins of Budget Policy

Political systems in Latin America run to a pattern, the major features of which are known to every educated layman. It is generally recognized that a small upper class, fully Westernized, exercises a commanding position in the political process, that a slow-to-emerge middle class is still numerically small and fairly powerless, that an enormous gulf in living standards exists between rich and poor, and that rumblings of unrest within the political system are frequently heard but usually deflected or suppressed. The political system has been described, in a word, as oligarchic.

Oligarchies are relative things, however, since all nations have groups that exercise political power disproportionate to their numbers. With few exceptions, these same groups also maintain much higher living standards than do the less fortunate of the same society. Therefore we must say that the political and social features listed above are merely more characteristic of Latin American political systems than of systems elsewhere in the world.

Moreover, since Latin America has its own diversity, they apply better to some Latin countries than to others. It is generally thought, however, that they apply particularly well to Peru. Nowhere else does the gulf between rich and poor seem so great. There are few other areas in Latin America with poverty comparable to that endured by the peasants of Peru's southern sierra, but at the same time, in the same country, a century of development in the other half of a dualistic economy has produced great wealth. The gulf seems great in social mobility as well as in income; it is an "often made observation that Peruvian society is rigidly structured and barriers between social classes are unusually difficult to cross—even in comparison with other Latin American countries." [1]

It is this view of society that has led most Peruvian intellectuals to speak of domination, rather than some form of reciprocal accommodation, as the essence of political and economic relationships between classes as well as between nations. Domination, it is argued, is exercised by whites and mestizos over the Indian peasants,[2] and by foreign interests over a small open economy such as Peru's. It is also the essence of the relationship between oligarchy and masses. Thus a typical description of Peruvian class structure differentiates between *clase baja, clase media,* and *clase dominante.*[3] Not only is the latter's power emphasized, but its numerical smallness as well. Some make reference to 30 families, some to 40, others to 100;[4] nobody has attempted to say with any precision exactly which families are on the list,[5] but the impression of smallness, exclusiveness, and monopolization of power remains strong in both popular and academic minds.* A summary assessment of the society of domination is put most bitterly and succinctly by the revolutionary de la Puente: "I think there is not a country in America where infra- and superstructural conditions are so unjust, so rotten, so archaic as in ours."[6]

Of the various forms of domination, the one most extensively studied over the years concerns relations between the national, Spanish-speaking society, represented by white and mestizo, and the Indians. A number of studies document the mechanisms whereby the Indian is excluded from political participation, since he is illiterate and not eligible to vote; from legal redress, since the courts require the use of Spanish; and from economic opportunity.[7] It is quite appropriate that anthropologists and sociologists have focused particularly on this issue, because the assimilation of the Indian into national life remains the overridingly important social problem of the country.

A few years ago the other power relationships to which the term domination is applied had been much less well studied. In the case of relationships between oligarchy and masses, however, a spate of recent studies, begun by the work of Bourricaud and continued in a recent publication of the Instituto de Estudios Peruanos, has thrust this aspect of domination to the forefront of interest.[8]

---

* Evidently this is the popular view from within as well as without the oligarchy. Robert Triffin tells the story of attending a large bankers' luncheon in Lima in the 1940s, where he was told, "There are only 100 people in Peru who really matter, of whom 50 are in this room. If we stick together we will be all right."

The debate thus stirred up has centered on whether a Peruvian oligarchy really exists. This would be a difficult empirical problem under any circumstances, and it is made more difficult in the present context by the absence of any careful attempt at defining terms. Criteria for separating the confusing variety of social systems into the oligarchic and the nonoligarchic remain obscure.

Two principal lines of argument suggest that an oligarchy does not exist. One maintains that even within the closed elitist societies of Latin America there are many competing political groups, and that the traditional aristocracy takes its share of lumps in the domestic political arena.[9] Thus a study of legislative performance can show that the aristocracy loses as many battles as it wins, but the meaning of such a rigorous approach is undermined by the consideration that other groups may bring up only those issues on which they think they have a chance of winning.[10] On the other hand, it is a bit bewildering to assess the elite's strength, and thus whether or not it is an oligarchy, from its performance on unfought political battles. In a less quantitative way, Bourricaud and Favre also emphasize the weakness of the elite's power today by stressing the losses of its power suffered over the past 10 or 15 years. Thus Bourricaud speaks, somewhat obscurely, of a "shift from absolute to relative domination." [11] Without being overly specific, he suggests that the shift is a rather recent phenomenon, caused particularly by the changing role of the armed forces. Favre places the elite's decline at about the same time but associates it with the rise of inexorable pressure for agrarian reform, since he gives particular emphasis to landholding as the basis of oligarchic power.[12]

An entirely different argument against the existence of oligarchy comes from Bravo Bresani, who feels that the upper classes of Peru do not exercise power independently, but instead derive power exclusively from their being the intermediaries of foreign economic interests.[13] Thus landholding per se ceases to be the source of power, since land provides power only if it generates wealth, and this it has done in the past principally by producing crops for export. Bravo's line of reasoning is also followed by Piel, who arrives at a Hobsonian view of imperialism: that the real power lies not with the landowners but with the international financial system, which together with its Peruvian affiliates provides the finance required for export production.[14]

This argument is of enormous practical importance, for at issue is the idea that concentration of domestic power can be understood and combated only by understanding and combating a more fundamental power relationship—the domination of Peru by foreigners. No assessment of the argument seems possible at present, however, until further analysis is directed at evaluating the freedom of maneuver available to domestic elites having economic ties to foreign markets. The thrust of the Bravo-Piel view is that markets, especially world commodity markets, are essentially manipulative rather than impersonal, better formalized by the theory of games than by atomistic models. It is a startling argument to the ears of economists trained in the Anglo-Saxon tradition, but in Latin America it runs far stronger and deeper than does the Marshallian demand curve.[15]

For this study of public finances, however, the Bravo-Piel argument is not particularly important, except insofar as it suggests that the nation is not a meaningful unit of study. Nevertheless, a fiscal system is nation-specific, so we have no choice but to deal with that unit of analysis. For our purposes it is enough to know that a small group possesses a large share of domestic political power, without needing to know if the ultimate source of that power is domestic or foreign.

But how can one assert the existence of this concentration of power if a methodologically rigorous approach cannot establish its existence? I think one must remain satisfied, for the moment, with the unrigorous, essayist approach of Bourricaud and others. One may supplement this by considering the vast gulf between the commonly held understanding of the requisites for a just society and the legislative accomplishments of any popularly elected administration in recent Peruvian history. A reformist government such as that of Belaúnde will chip away where it can, but even its apparent victories such as agrarian reform were easily frustrated through ineffective implementation. This chronic gap between what is widely desired and what is politically feasible is the power of the elite. In Peru the gap has been wide, at least until the present military government came to power, and the elite that maintained the gap has been cohesive on vital issues. As the term is used, therefore, it has been an oligarchy.

Peru's traditional oligarchy is now quite evidently in retreat, however, and by now has perhaps retreated past any reasonably drawn line of demarcation between oligarchic and nonoligarchic systems. The time at which the decline began is not fixed with any certainty at all. While Bourricaud and Favre place the moment somewhere within the last 20 years, nevertheless, the heyday of Peruvian oligarchy was long before that, in the first decades of this century, when the República Aristocrática held sway through its political instrument, the Civilista party, and the oligarchy's rule was direct and effective.[16] Peru's political and social history in the past 75 years is therefore a story of very gradual erosion in oligarchic power, as other groups have developed the leverage to obtain a share of the political system's output.

At the beginning of the century these other groups were exclusively urban; the political system recognized the growing power of urban workers and the middle classes by enacting social legislation, encouraging collective bargaining, and setting the urban beginnings to a national system of public education.[17] Over the decades the process of social mobilization has continued, to the point that in recent years the political system has begun to grant some of its benefits to the Indian peasant—i.e., two agrarian reform laws, the earlier law of 1964 being a direct response to the peasants' newly acquired ability in political organizations.[18]

Many of the new, challenging groups have relied on mass action and threatened violence as their bargaining tools in the political process.[19] The oligarchy has receded, but slowly, since in the past it has known that excessive instability would bring the armed forces to the rescue. A few years ago, therefore, Peru was most appropriately described as a military guardianship, where the armed forces permitted the oligarchy to employ "a defensive and delaying tactic which realistically has estimated the possibilities of defeat of the traditional ways but wishes to soften its impact." [20]

This political description of Peru, only a few years old, is already obsolete. The present military government, which took power in October 1968, has assumed an entirely new role for itself. Far from being the traditional defender of oligarchic interests, it represents the triumph of a new, assertive middle class against a weakened oligarchy.

Since this political summary gives particular emphasis to the distribution of political power, it has direct implications for the distributive impact of governmental economic policy. In this case, the thrust of political argument is that power is distributed discontinuously among three groups—oligarchy, Indian peasants and a middle group which is merely the nonoligarchic, non-Indian residual. If political power is thus distributed as a three-step function, we should expect the same of economic benefit derived from the budgetary process.*

Specifically, taxation and expenditure should reflect oligarchic power by being relatively regressive in upper income ranges, and should reflect domination of the Indian by being relatively regressive in the income range that separates incomes of most Indians from incomes of most mestizos and whites. Moreover, the regression, or weak progression, of the system should be changing over time in the direction of greater progression, but the beginning of such change might be located anywhere between 1900 and 1955.

These expectations about incidence, as well as the earlier description of the distribution of power in the political system, are couched in relative terms, and therefore before examining the Peruvian fiscal system we must say something about patterns of expenditure and taxation in other countries, so that standards of comparison will be at hand.

Patterns of Taxation and Expenditure
In Developing Countries

Very little work has been done on estimating the incidence of taxation and expenditure in less developed countries. Within Latin America, the few studies to be found have, to my knowledge, all focused exclusively on tax incidence. Carefully done studies in El Salvador and Venezuela both conclude that these tax systems are mildly progressive.[21] A study of Colombia, which dealt only with quartile groups and was therefore quite undifferentiated by the upper end of the income distribution found tax proportionality but no progression.[22] On the other hand, a more ambitious but looser study by Musgrave showed quite different results: that in all South American countries except Venezuela, families ranking between the 25th and 50th percentiles in income suffered the highest average tax rate. These

---

* That is, if individuals were arrayed by amount of political power, and if political power could be satisfactorily quantified, a step function would result. If instead the vertical measure were *cumulated* total power, the result would be a political Lorenz curve consisting of three linear segments.

tax systems therefore seemed to be progressive only below the 25th percentile, and regressive over the wide range above it.[23] In the case of Argentina, the conclusion of tax regressiveness was confirmed independently by Herschel.[24]

The redistributive impact of taxation appears more certain in industrial countries, which generally place greater reliance on income taxation. Yet even in the United States, a country that gives particularly strong emphasis to income taxation, incidence studies have shown that progression of the total tax system is weak in both lower- and middle-income brackets; significant progression is to be found only in the upper brackets.[25]

One concludes that there are probably no tax systems in the Western Hemisphere which are strongly redistributive in either direction. For significant redistributive impact, one must look to the expenditure side of government fiscal activity, even though empirical studies are harder to find there. The exercise of assigning benefits from government expenditure to various income classes involves such arbitrariness that few have attempted it.[26] No studies come to mind for Latin America; for the United States, the estimates show strongly regressive expenditure favoring the lowest income groups, but also a milder yet still significant redistributive impact running through the full range of income classes.[27]

The evolution over time in patterns of redistribution can be approximated through studies of expenditure and revenue patterns among countries at different levels of per capita income.[28] These studies show that government expenditures, expressed as shares of GNP, typically rise from about 12 percent to about 20 percent of GNP as per capita income increases from $100 to $600. Among the elements of expenditure whose rapid increase causes this percentage share to rise, education and health seem to be the most important. Kuznets calculated from a small sample that education and health expenditures are 3.8 percent of GNP for poor countries and 5.5 percent for rich countries.[29]

On the side of revenue, the predominant characteristic of cross-country studies is the relative growth of direct taxes, especially personal and corporate income taxes, and the relative decline of indirect taxes. Hinrichs pointed out that the direct-indirect tax ratio actually follows a U-shaped curve, with the earliest stages of modernization having been characterized by the relative decline of traditional direct taxes, particularly land and head taxes, and the rise of indirect taxes on foreign trade.[30] In the world today, however, this earlier stage is largely a matter of economic history. All recent cross-section studies show a strong relation between the share of direct taxes in GNP and per capita income. Expressed again in GNP shares, direct taxes run 2 to 4 percent for a country with per capita income of $100, and 6 to 11 percent for a country with a $600 per capita income.[31] Most of this growth is attributable to personal income taxes. Corporate tax shares show some upward trend, but they also show great variability among countries.

Indirect tax shares are only slightly greater for $600 than for $100 countries, about 9.5 percent of GNP in the former and 8.5 percent in the latter. This represents a substantial decline in relative importance in the budget, from about two thirds of revenues to less than one half.[32]

It therefore appears that tax systems have been getting more progressive, or less regressive, over time, as individual and business income taxes become increasingly important.* The particularly rapid growth of expenditures on education, health and transfers suggests growing redistributive significance on the expenditure side as well.

The growing government share associated with rising per capita income therefore has clear and favorable distributional significance. Its significance for growth is by no means so clear. A growing share has generally been considered good for growth, since it is expected that government's marginal propensity to save will be higher than the private sector's propensity to save less because of marginal tax increases. As growth proceeds this becomes an increasingly questionable assumption, however, since the high elasticity of direct taxes means that marginal increases in tax collections bear increasingly on saving. Nevertheless, government's commitment to steer expenditure increases into development projects and education is frequently thought sufficiently strong to outweigh the negative growth effects of increasing tax progression.

This view cannot be accepted so sanguinely in Latin America. A glance at the expenditure patterns is sufficient to convince that the richer countries do indeed have a larger share of GNP devoted to

---

* This conclusion is not certain, since the relative expansion of direct taxes is partly at the expense of import taxes, which could themselves be quite progressive.

government expenditure, but that this expenditure runs particularly heavily to transfer payments instead of to investment. Since part of this redistribution is from rich savers to middle-class nonsavers, the impact on growth of an expanding government share is probably perverse.

The Incidence of Taxation and Expenditure in Peru

Unfortunately, nobody has done the careful statistical work that the question of tax incidence in Peru deserves. In fact, the only estimates I have seen are the exceedingly rough ones put together by Musgrave.[33] Rough estimates have their place, of course, and are generally better than nothing, but in this case the dangers of roughness are compounded by the fact that the estimating method used is particularly liable to large error in result caused by small errors in data. Accordingly the conclusion of this procedure, that the Peruvian tax system is regressive, is very much open to question. Some alternative calculations, based on a comparison of results for Colombia obtained by Musgrave and by the Joint Tax Program, produced the following estimates of burden by income quartile:

	I (Poorest)	II	III	IV (Richest)
Tax incidence (%)	19.5	17.4	20.6	16.9
Total incidence (%) (taxes minus expenditure)	16.3	15.3	7.6	13.6

We conclude that the Peruvian tax system has no noticeable redistributive impact one way or the other. The weakness of the evidence supporting this conclusion is such that the conclusion is best stated negatively: there is no clear evidence of either progression or regression.

If redistributive effect is to be found, therefore, it must be found on the expenditure side of the budget, despite the fact that most types of expenditure defy assignment of benefit to particular groups. Expenditures for general administration, defense, justice and police are of this nature and must be ignored here. That is, they must be assumed to have their benefits distributed proportional to income. From an a priori standpoint, only social and development expenditures (education, health, agriculture, transport, public works) can be assigned with some confidence, and even here data problems make it impossible to say anything about the grab bag that is public works.

Transport expenditure benefits probably accrue particularly to the poor, since over the years a large share has been devoted to expanding and improving the national highway network, thus making it possible for Indian peasants to migrate to the city and to escape the age-old domination exercised over them by mestizos and whites. Expenditure on agriculture could also be regressive, since incomes are lower in the agriculture sector than elsewhere, but in practice the experience of Latin American agricultural programs has been that the power of the few wealthy farmers has permitted them to appropriate most of the benefit.[34] Peru is no exception to this experience.

For a quantitative assessment of expenditure incidence, however, we must be restricted to a partial estimate involving only education and health, which together accounted for little more than a quarter of government expenditure in 1961. We may concentrate on this portion with some confidence that the other three quarters of expenditure has an incidence that, like the tax system, shows no obvious departure from proportionality. The benefits of education and health expenditures are treated as transfers received—i.e., negative taxes—in the estimate above of total budget incidence. This estimate shows the expenditure advantages gained by urban lower and middle classes, who comprise all of the third and part of the fourth and highest quartile. The public school system functions for them; in 1961 it had not yet been extended greatly to the rural poor, and it is not used by the upper class.* As for health expenditures, they are largely located in urban areas, where income levels are higher. The hospitals and clinics built and subsidized are more available to urban residents, while the water and sewage systems provide exclusively urban benefits.

We concluded earlier that the Peruvian tax system, with its absence of strong deviation from proportionality, is not greatly unlike the other systems of the Western Hemisphere. The incidence of expendi-

* In the 1961 census, only 52 percent of the 7–14 age group was enrolled in school.

ture, however, is wholly different from that of the United States, the only other country for which we possess similar estimates. Whereas social expenditures were seen to accrue particularly to the benefit of the poorest sectors in the United States, in Peru the lower half of the income distribution is effectively excluded from such benefits and thus experiences a high net tax incidence. This is the statistical reflection of the domination of the Indian peasant referred to previously. Virtually no government services are made available to him, but some taxation is levied upon him, particularly the turnover tax and the excises or monopoly prices charged to coca, alcohol and tobacco.

In making this comparison, the obvious should be emphasized: that in recent years the United States has been forced to recognize that the extent of redistribution it effects through government expenditure is no cause for smugness. However, in the present instance this condition makes U.S. expenditure incidence all the more interesting as a standard of comparison. It also makes the enormity of the challenge facing Peruvian reformers all the more evident.

While the poor have therefore gained little, neither has great redistributive advantage accrued to the oligarchy. It would be argued by some that common governmental functions such as defense and the police should be assigned to the benefit of the oligarchy, since they help preserve a political system possessed of obvious benefit for the oligarchy. This seems too tenuous an assignment in the technical framework that governs studies of incidence, however. Rather it should be considered the achievement of oligarchy that, in a world of tax progression, it has survived with a proportional levy. The price it has paid is assent to fiscal advantage obtained by the new groups diluting oligarchic power.

The Evolution of Peruvian Expenditure Incidence

Next to be considered is the trend over time in the redistributive impact of the Peruvian budget. Compared to the assessment of incidence in a given year, trend over time can be assessed more accurately and more easily, merely by examining the trend in size and composition of expenditures and revenues. It is here that the cross-country experience of the 1950s will aid in giving perspective to the evolution of Peruvian public finances.

By the standard of these cross-country estimates, we can see that in the 1950s Peru was a country with a small governmental sector. For example, Williamson's regression, dealing with the period 1951–56, predicted a government share of 14.6 percent for a per capita income corresponding to Peru's, but his figure for Peru was only 11 percent.[35] But how different things were in the 1960s. By the middle of the decade government expenditure had risen to just a shade below 20 percent of GNP, while per capita income was not even half way to $600.[36] A substantial allocative shift had taken place.

We can never be sure that cross-section studies are accurate predictors of change over time, however. It may be that government expenditure functions, where the observations are countries, exhibit the same upward drift commonly associated with the consumption function, where the observations are individuals. If upward drift is widespread, then many less developed countries must be given credit for improved fiscal capability in the 1960s, but regardless of behavior elsewhere the government of Peru must be given such credit. This capability is important for the redistributive and growth-inducing potential that it represents, but clearly the realization of the potential depends on the political forces determining government economic behavior.

A look at the evolving composition of Peruvian expenditure shows that government's expanding share has indeed been associated with increasing redistributive impact, through the growing importance of education and health expenditure. It will be recalled that the figures of Kuznets, derived largely from 1958, indicated a rise in the GNP share of education and health from 3.8 percent for poor countries to 5.5 percent for rich countries. Peru was one of the poor countries included in Kuznets's sample, and in 1958 its GNP share devoted to education and health was exactly 3.8 percent. This ratio had risen sharply from abysmal levels during the early 1940s, however, and during the 1960s the rise was even more rapid. By 1965 the ratio had risen fully to 6 percent, and for education alone it was 5.1 percent.

It should be noted that this educational expansion is not merely the reflection of an upward drift in expenditure common to all poor countries. Although educational expansion has taken place elsewhere, nevertheless the Peruvian expansion was extraordinary, so that by 1963 its share of GNP devoted to education was exceeded only by Cuba and

Puerto Rico among Latin American countries.[37] Moreover, this expansion did not proceed independently of the particular administration that was in power; the residuals tabulated in Table 1 show that the administration of Odría deemphasized education. The nature of the deemphasis is more clearly demonstrated by the figures showing education's share of government expenditure. With every other new presidency, education's share jumped significantly. Odría did not cut back, but he held the line, even though as a result he had to cut a year out of the primary school curriculum, thus forcing two cohort groups to compete for admission to secondary schools at the same time.

Table 1
COMPONENTS OF GOVERNMENT EXPENDITURE

	Real GNP per capita (1963 prices)	Government expenditure as percentage of current price GNP			Total minus education and defense
		Education	Education and health	Defense	
1942–45	$156	1.13	1.83	2.46	5.1
1945–50	164	1.67	2.44	2.61	4.9
1950–55	200	1.77	2.60	2.70	5.45
1955–60	223	2.52	3.57	3.17	5.2
1960–65	261	3.60	4.78	2.92	5.2

		Deviations from trend of regressions					
		Education/ GNP		Defense/ GNP		Total gov't. expenditure minus education and defense GNP		Education as percentage of total gov't. expenditure
Presidency	Period	Pos.	Neg.	Pos.	Neg.	Pos.	Neg.	
Prado	1942–45	1	3	2	2	2	2	13.0
Bustamante	1946–48	3	0	2	1	3	0	18.5
Odría	1949–56	1	7	2	6	4	4	18.4
Prado	1957–62	4	2	4	2	2	4	26.4
Belaúnde	1963–65	3	0	0	3	2	1	33.4

Sources: 1950–63: BCR, Cuentas nacionales del Perú, 1950–1965, Tables 1, 2, 3, 4, 12, 1964–67: Cuentas nacionales del Perú, 1950–1967, 1942–49: author's estimates, based on current price GNP in BCR, Renta nacional de Perú (issues of 1947–51) and government expenditure detail in Contraloría General de la República, Balance y cuenta general de la república (annual). Figures refer to resource-using (exhaustive) expenditure only. Transfer payments not included.

As the statistics on incidence showed, in education we see most clearly the pressures on the government budget for allocating a greater share of political and economic output to groups newly arrived in the political arena. Whether these groups are residents of provincial towns or new migrants to Lima, perhaps their first and strongest demand of government is education for their children.[38] Education is a derived demand, however; the primary demand is for occupational advancement. The expansion of educational expenditure under Belaúnde had as its purpose the expansion of employment and income for prospective teachers, as much as the expansion of educational opportunity for children.

Table 2 gives an indication of the different sources of pressure for increasing education expenditures. The growth of government spending on education, expressed in current prices, is divided into four components: increases in the number of public school teachers, in the cost of living, in the average real wage level in the economy, and in the real wage differential existing between teachers and the economy's average. The expansion of the stock of teachers follows a growth path suggested by the pattern of residuals in the previous table; a spurt during the administration of Bustamante (11 percent annually from 1946 to 1948), rather slower growth during Odría (4.4 percent annually from 1949 to 1956), a faster 8.0 percent rate during Prado's administration, and a remarkable 12 percent annual growth in the first years of Belaúnde. The growth rates vary by presidency, but within the period of a given presidency the rate does not show systematic variation.

It is quite different in the case of teachers' real wages. The characteristic pattern is for real wages to take a big jump with the coming to power of a new administration, either immediately before or immediately after the election; but between elections the teacher, and the civil servant in general, is lucky if his money wage merely keeps pace with the cost of living. After an increase of 31 percent in Bustamante's first year, real wages declined so much that two years later teachers were worse off than they had been before Bustamante came to power. We see other strong spurts in wages from 1949 to 1951, in 1956, and again in 1961 and 1962.

These election-oriented spurts are testament to the political importance of teachers in particular and civil servants in general. Expansion of the stock of teachers and classrooms involves lags and cannot be so

Table 2
INDEXES RELATING TO EDUCATION
(1960 = 100)

	Total number of public school teachers	Total expenditure on education (current prices)	Implicit education price index	Cost of living	Implicit real wage of teachers	Real GNP per capita	Teachers' real wage differential
	(1)	(2)	(3)	(4)	(5)	(6)	(7)
1942	27.3	1.88	6.9	13.21	52.2	66.6	78.4
1943	33.0	2.21	6.7	14.81	45.2	64.6	70.0
1944	34.0	3.44	10.1	16.92	59.7	65.9	90.6
1945	36.8	4.06	11.0	18.80	58.5	66.7	87.7
1946	45.1	7.08	15.7	20.54	76.4	71.3	107.2
1947	51.3	9.32	18.2	27.26	66.8	67.5	99.0
1948	55.7	9.59	17.2	35.2	48.9	63.9	76.5
1949	55.3	13.04	23.6	41.3	57.1	70.4	81.1
1950	56.9	17.44	30.7	47.0	65.3	76.2	85.7
1951	58.4	22.7	38.9	52.4	74.2	82.6	89.8
1952	62.4	25.2	40.4	57.2	70.6	83.5	84.6
1953	63.4	28.1	44.3	60.6	73.1	83.7	87.3
1954	67.9	31.6	46.5	62.2	74.8	90.0	83.1
1955	69.7	35.0	50.2	65.3	76.9	92.4	83.2
1956	74.5	52.3	70.2	68.7	102.2	94.3	108.4
1957	77.5	60.4	77.9	74.9	104.0	92.9	111.9
1958	84.7	75.7	89.4	81.7	109.4	93.5	117.0
1959	90.6	88.5	97.7	91.0	107.4	94.3	113.9
1960	100.0	100.0	100.0	100.0	100.0	100.0	100.0
1961	107.4	129.5	120.6	105.1	114.7	105.1	109.1
1962	114.0	158.8	139.3	108.3	128.6	111.5	115.3
1963	121.2	194.8	160.7	112.4	143.0	112.3	127.3
1964	136.9	241.8	176.6	122.7	143.9	116.8	123.2
1965	152.2	385.1	253.0	143.8	175.9	118.4	148.6

Sources: Column 1: Author's compilation, derived mainly from Ministerio de Educación Pública, *Estadística educativa* and *La educación en el Perú* (Lima, 1967); also *Anuario estadístico del Perú.* Column 4: Author's compilation from *Balance y cuenta general de la república.* Column 4: For 1950–65, BCR, *Cuentas nacionales del Perú, 1950–65* (Lima, 1966). Table 9. For 1942–49, *Anuario estadístico del Perú.* Column 6: Same as Table 11.2 (in the original version of this chapter in Ranis). Columns 3, 5, and 7: derivative from columns 1, 2, 4, and 6.

neatly timed for the politically sensitive year. Despite the irregularity of wage advances, it is noteworthy that from 1942 to 1956 the long-run trend in teachers' real wages was just the same as for real wages in the whole economy. Since that time, however, the teachers have opened up a lead which widened greatly during the 1960s.

In the 1960s we see their expanding political power quite clearly.

Between 1960 and 1965, an expansion of 285 percent in education expenditures is decomposed into a 52 percent increase in the number of teachers, a 44 percent increase in the cost of living, an 18 percent increase in real wages throughout the economy, and a 49 percent increase in the real wages differential between teachers and the general labor force.[39] The increases corresponding to the cost of living and the expansion of real wages elsewhere may be labeled unavoidable, in the medium run if not in the short run; strong pressures to expand expenditure by that amount could be expected under any conceivable circumstances. The remarkable overall expansion of this five-year period is shown in the other two components, an almost equal percentage growth in the number and relative real wage of teachers. The expansion in numbers may be attributed both to parents' demand for education of their children and to university students' demand for places as teachers. It permitted an equal expansion in the total number of students in the system.[40] The equal expansion in relative real wages is attributable exclusively to the political power of teachers, however, and so we must conclude that the expansion of educational expenditure was more a response to the demands of teachers than of the families of school children.

Much of this increase originated in the famous Law 15215, which decreed a 100 percent increase in all teachers' salaries, to be provided in four annual steps of 25 percent each, a great expansion of teacher-training facilities, and the guarantee of a job with the government for every graduating teacher. This extraordinary law provoked hardly any opposition when it was introduced in Congress in 1964, so eager were all political parties to look good before so large and influential a block of voters, despite the fact that the fiscal planning required for implementing the law was, to say the least, inadequate. Within two years this fiscal commitment, among others, provoked an economic crisis from which Peru has not yet fully recovered. The last two of the four 25 percent increments were canceled, as was the commitment to hire all graduates of teachers' colleges. In the meantime, however, the expansion of enrollment in the teachers' colleges had proceeded apace, from 4,008 in 1960 to 14,718 in 1965, an increase of 267 percent. By 1967 the government needed fewer than 2,000 new teachers, but the teachers' colleges were graduating 9,000.

We hardly need say that in previous decades, particularly before World War II, it was never necessary to make such fiscal commitments in order to secure the support of public-school teachers. Comparisons with GNP are not possible for these early years, because GNP estimates begin only in 1942, but it is possible to examine the importance of educational expenditure through the evolving composition of total government expenditure. This is done in Table 3, which gives a long-term perspective of Peruvian budgetary development. From this table we see that the functions of government at the beginning of this century were largely restricted to the maintenance of domestic tranquillity and national defense. The essential change over the course of the decades has been the slow but inexorable expansion of demands for governmental participation in economic and social development. We have already traced that development in the case of education for the period since 1942. We can now see from Table 3 that Peru was virtually without a system of national public education in 1900, but that the decade following was a highly important one for educational development, marking the beginning of a commitment to universal public education. At first it applied only to Lima and other accessible coastal areas, but later, in the 1940s, the geographical outward expansion of universal education began in earnest.

It is significant to note that the first important steps toward educational expansion, made between 1900 and 1910, were the handiwork of the quintessential oligarchic government in Peru's history. They came as the result, not of immediate pressure from below, but of enlighten-

Table 3
PERCENTAGE DISTRIBUTION OF GOVERNMENT EXPENDITURE

	General adminis- tration	Armed forces	Justice and police	Educa- tion	Health	Develop- ment	Transfers	Other
1900	28.5	25.1	22.2	2.9	0.7	2.0	9.6	9.0
1905	23.8	35.6	14.3	4.5	2.9	3.3	13.9	1.7
1910	12.5	52.9	11.3	8.1	1.2	2.1	9.4	2.4
1915	18.6	27.4	17.7	10.1	0.7	1.7	16.3	7.4
1920	21.5	23.4	14.6	10.6	5.9	11.0	11.3	1.7
1929	25.8	22.8	14.5	11.7	4.9	8.3	10.9	1.1
1942	19.4	24.7	15.5	10.5	6.4	11.8	11.0	0.6
1945	14.7	26.3	14.8	13.3	7.7	10.9	11.6	0.7
1950	13.3	24.6	15.2	16.0	5.2	14.5	10.6	0.5
1955	11.8	23.8	13.9	14.8	9.4	15.3	10.4	0.6
1960	11.4	21.6	12.1	20.6	8.3	12.1	13.3	0.7
1965	9.6	15.6	12.2	29.4	6.4	16.8	9.3	0.7

Source: Author's compilation, derived from *Balance y cuentas general de la república.*

ment from above. One may reasonably doubt that this enlightenment was motivated by pure charity, however, but rather by a recognition of the likely course of future events. Oligarchic power was built on economic advancement, particularly export development, and this in turn was producing urbanization and social mobilization of the masses. Oligarchic power thus possessed the elements of its own decay, but it is nevertheless to the credit of José Prado, president of Peru from 1904 to 1908, and other relatively liberal Civilistas like him, that they recognized this and began an early and graceful retreat.

Public health and development expenditures did not acquire a significant share of budgetary allocations until the 1920s, during the eleven-year presidency of Leguía (1919–30). This was a period of big construction activity, financed in part by big foreign loans and devoted largely to national integration and further development of an export economy. Water and sewer systems, hospitals, irrigation works, port works, and, most of all, roads were the newly emphasized responsibilities of government. As mentioned above, many of these types of expenditure probably had an incidence that was not particularly beneficial to the poor. All urban dwellers did benefit from public health investments, however, and perhaps the poorer urban dwellers benefited most. The purely economic investments generally represented a response to the demands of capitalists who required government infrastructure investment complementary to their own private investments. The upsurge in development expenditures during Leguía's period is therefore a statistical manifestation of the historian's view of his presidency: a period of capitalist expansion undertaken by a new group of entrepreneurs who were not well-established members of the old Civilista oligarchy.[41]

Principally through education, therefore, we can see that the expansion of governmental activity was associated with an increasing redistributive impact which may be traced back to the very beginning of this century. Although the first steps in this educational redistribution may be attributed to anticipated rather than actual power possessed by newly emerging beneficiary groups, real power was not far behind. The political power of the urban masses was manifest at least as early as 1912, with the election to the presidency of Guillermo Billinghurst, although it is more obvious in the last twenty years.

It was mentioned earlier that the educational cutback of the relatively conservative administration of Odría illustrates that this particular component of expenditure did not expand independently of presidential administration. In the case of total government expenditure, however, it is surprising how little the overall expansion was influenced by differences in the combinations of political forces that brought successive presidents to power. This is not immediately apparent, if we happen to look at the pattern of residuals which comes from a regression of the expenditure/GNP ratio on real per capita income. The administrations of Bustamante and Belaúnde were founded more substantially on the power of emerging middle and lower-middle classes, and, as Table 4 shows, they have a much higher proportion of positive residuals.

There is some deception in this result, however. A closer look

Table 4
DEVIATIONS FROM TREND

	Real growth in GNP from preceding years (percentage)	Position in cycle (boom +, recession −)	Sign of regression residual	Presidency	Total residuals for presidency	
					Pos.	Neg.
1942			−	Prado	2	2
1943	−1.2	−	+			
1944	3.7	−	+			
1945	3.1	−	−			
1946	8.7	+	+	Bustamante	3	0
1947	−3.7	−	+			
1948	−3.6	−	+			
1949	12.3	+	−	Odría	4	4
1950	10.1	+	−			
1951	10.5	+	−			
1952	2.9	−	+			
1953	2.2	−	+			
1954	9.6	+	−			
1955	4.9	+	+			
1956	4.6	+	+			
1957	1.0	−	+	Prado	3	3
1958	3.4	−	+			
1959	3.5	−	+			
1960	9.1	+	−			
1961	8.2	+	−			
1962	9.3	+	−			
1963	3.8	+	+	Belaúnde	3	0
1964	6.8	+	+			
1965	4.8	+	+			

Sources: Same as table 2. Residuals calculated from regression of the form *in* (G/GNP/P) = a_0 + a_1 *in (GNP/P)* where G is total government expenditures including transfers, both G and GNP are in current prices, P = population.

suggests a ratchet effect in government expenditures over the cycle; thus government expenditure is maintained when GNP declines in a recession, causing the ratio to rise, while government expenditure expands with a lag in a boom, causing the ratio to fall at first, then to rise in the boom's later stages as the government's expenditure share surges to a new higher level. This evidence is also summarized in Table 4, where the two columns of signs show a remarkable parallelism. The signs tend to be opposite except for the late stages of a boom, when government expenditure also is booming, as in 1955–56 and 1963–65. Thus we conclude that the overall growth in government expenditure has not proceeded independent of the business cycle, but it is independent of the political representation of various presidential administrations.

The expansion of government expenditure thus appears inexorable, a fact of political life against which neither an Odría government in Peru nor an Eisenhower government in the United States could do much. Although on the one hand Odría reduced the redistributive significance of expansion by cutting back on education, his alternative emphasis on labor-intensive public works expenditure was certainly not without redistributive impact. Indeed by this emphasis he probably favored still poorer groups; aspiring manual laborers instead of aspiring public-school teachers. No government in recent decades has been able to afford the luxury of throwing away the additional political advantage to be gained from additional expenditure programs.

The Evolution of Peruvian Tax Incidence

In similar fashion, we now examine the evolution of tax incidence over the years. As was the case with total expenditure, the ratio of total revenue to GNP shows a clear and steady growth over time. Also as before, however, we can make no inferences about redistributive impact merely by looking at the trend of the aggregate, but must instead look directly at the trends of component parts.

Indeed, the recent evolution of revenue structure in Peru is quite atypical. The first unusual feature we note is that the expansion of indirect taxes, not direct taxes, has enabled the revenue system as a whole to collect an increasing share of total income. All direct taxes,

Table 5
GROWTH OF GOVERNMENT REVENUE
(Revenues expressed as percentage of current price GNP)

	Total revenue	Indirect taxes	Taxes on imports	Excise taxes	Turn- over tax	Direct taxes	Major taxes on income from: Labor	Capital
1942-45	11.2	—a	—	0.83	0.17	—	—	—
1945-50	11.6	—	—	0.42	0.27	—	0.65	4.3
1950-55	12.7	6.3	2.8	0.30	0.23	5.8	0.67	3.9
1955-60	13.3	7.4	2.9	0.35	0.46	5.3	0.73	3.0
1960-65	16.0	9.2	3.4	0.29	2.49	6.1	0.72	3.2

a Dash indicates data not available.
Sources: same as Table 1.

taken as a group, have just kept up with GNP growth since 1950, their share of GNP being a more or less constant 5.5-6 percent. In fact, the major component, consisting of a group of the principal taxes on income from capital has grown less rapidly than GNP.* Although the growth of direct taxes is therefore surprisingly low, their recent level is not; rather by the cross-section standard the level was unusually high in 1950, given the low per capita income which existed, but this same level in 1965 was about average for countries of Peru's 1965 per capita income.

It is important to note, however, that this reasonably high level of direct taxes has not been produced by a widely cast tax-collecting net. While direct taxes have been levied against personal income ever since 1926, they have never attained great fiscal importance, and direct taxes have been, essentially, taxes on businesses, particularly large businesses in the modern sector.

At first sight, the sluggish growth of taxes on capital income seems paradoxical. Decline in the ratio of tax base to GNP seems unlikely, as the modern sector expands, but decline in the ratio of tax collections

*This group consists of the cedular taxes on business and interest income, the excess profits tax, the tax on retained earnings, the business license tax (patentes), the complementary fixed tax that is applied to dividend and interest payments, and all export taxes. Most export tax payments may be credited against liabilities for business income taxes, and so merely represent an advance payment of a profits tax. Those export taxes that cannot be so credited are nevertheless taxes on income, since world market prices are given for a small country and the tax therefore cannot be shifted forward in the short run.

to base is also refuted by prima facie evidence—i.e., the tax rates. The tax rate on commercial and industrial profits has been going up steadily. From a top rate of 10 percent established in 1941, it has risen to 15 percent in 1942, 20 percent in 1947, and 35 percent in 1959. Further change in 1968 did not raise the top rate but raised the lower rates substantially.[42]

There remains only one reason by which this strange sluggishness of profits tax expansion may be explained; it is the continuing erosion of the tax base through special exonerations of continuing taxes and abolition of minor taxes. Most exonerations have come through the Industrial Promotion Law, which has provided generous deductions for reinvested profits and further tax reductions for locating manufacturing establishments outside Lima. Important beneficiaries of this latter provision are mine smelters, none of which were located in Lima before passage of the law.[43] Beyond this, however, not only have mining companies secured the right to special tax provisions, through the Mining Code of 1950, but also the most significant new mining venture of the last two decades was undertaken through a special contract containing even more generous terms. Essentially, the Southern Peru Coppor Company was accorded the privilege of a special low tax rate until such time as it had recovered its enormous investment in the Toquepala mine. "Recovery" was defined to have taken place when accumulated profits equaled the original investment, where these profits were calculated *net of depreciation and depletion.**

The lack of emphasis on personal income taxation is another curiosity of the Peruvian tax system. It is well documented that personal income taxes in less developed countries generally have about the same exemption levels and structure of progressivity as do similar taxes in developed countries, but that income levels are so low as to convert an important mass tax in developed countries into something fiscally far less important, levied only on the well-to-do.[44] This situation is acutely and particularly true for Peru. A number of alternative calculations show that personal income tax exemptions, when expressed as a multiple of per capita income are higher in Peru than in any other South American country.[45]

---

* A public uproar over this contract occurred in 1967, some 14 years after it first went into effect, and brought about a change in terms.

Table 6
EXEMPTIONS IN PERSONAL INCOME TAX
(Impuesto Complementario de Tasa Progresiva)

	Annual exemptions Single male (in soles)	Family of 4 (in soles)	Personal income per capita (in soles)	Price index of consumer goods	Number of taxpayers	Taxpayers as percentage of white-collar workers
1950	S/.12,000	S/.22,800	S/.1586	41.8	5,308	2.0
1961	30,000	66,000	4827	93.5	8,740	2.2
1963	30,000	66,000	5787	100.0	—a	—
1964	48,000	114,000	6619	109.2	—	—
1968	98,000 b	164,000 b	—	—	—	—
1950	100	100	100	100	—	—
1961	250	289	304	224	—	—
1963	250	289	365	239	—	—
1964	400	500	417	261	—	—
1968	817 b	719 b	—	—	—	—

a Dash indicates data not available.

b Income from labor only.

Sources: Joint Tax Program, *Estudio fiscal del Perú,* Chapter 2; Ministerio de Hacienda, *La reform tributaria de 1968,* pp. 35–36; BCR, *Cuentas nacionales del Perú,* Tables 1, 6, 9 and 11.

The problem of excessively high exemption levels could have been solved by inaction, by allowing rising price levels to scale down the real value of exemptions. Unfortunately, pressures to raise these levels have been periodic and irresistible. As Table 6 shows, the number of taxpayers was minuscule during the 1950s and early 1960s, and this small number may be expected to decline further, as exemption levels have recently gone shooting up much more rapidly than has average money income. Meanwhile, the cedular tax on wages and salaries was abolished in 1964 and replaced by a stamp tax. This was indeed a curious change. Payments to labor for services rendered are now counted merely as another form of transaction, to be covered by the ubiquitous turnover tax.[46] In place of a 5 percent cedular tax levied with a 30,000 soles exemption (about $1,000), there was instituted a 1 percent tax with an exemption of only 2,400 soles annually (about $100). The middle classes, those with 1963 incomes above 30,000 soles annually, were clearly the winners in the important tax changes of the 1960s. If their income was above 66,000 soles, a family of four gained tax relief on two fronts, as Table 6 shows, for their liability was reduced for complementary as well as for cedular taxes.

But rich and poor alike paid substantially more in indirect taxes. As in the case of direct taxes, an unusual evolution over the past 15 years has produced a tax/GNP ratio much more in line with the experience of other countries. Both $100 and $600 countries, it will be recalled, tended to collect indirect taxes amounting to 8.5–9.5 percent of GNP, and by the 1960s Peru's indirect tax revenues had risen to just that range.

Excise taxes did nothing to contribute to the rapid expansion of indirect taxes. These most traditional of internal indirect taxes have never been levied on a wide variety of goods, and the few goods involved are among the least income-elastic. In fact, more than half of the pure excises represented by the appropriate column in Table 5 are received from taxes on alcohol alone. In addition to these pure excises, however, the net surpluses of the traditional government monopolies in tobacco, salt, and a few other basic commodities should be considered disguised excises. Most such products are both price and income-inelastic, so even if we include them in a broader definition of excise taxes, the resulting aggregate is still strongly inelastic. For example, excises and government monopoly surpluses together averaged some 1.55 percent of GNP in 1942–45 and had declined to 0.63 percent of GNP by 1962–65.

Import taxes were subject to the same process of erosion through exoneration which seems to have so undercut the potential elasticity of taxes on business income, so it is surprising to see that they expanded more rapidly than GNP during 1950–65. Moreover, this expansion occurred precisely during that period in the 1960s when exonerations from the Industrial Promotion Law were becoming particularly numerous. The cause lay in a series of major tariff increases which occurred at the same time.

These tariff increases were made mostly for revenue purposes, but protection was also an important motive. The 1960–67 period was one of export boom and domestic inflation associated with the luxury of exchange-rate stability. Therefore, domestic industry was progressively robbed of protection by diverging price movements; tariff increases helped offset this effect. Moreover, the tariff levels prevalent in the 1950s, while high by worldwide standards, were quite low by the standards of the amazing tariff rates generally prevalent elsewhere in Latin America.[47] A government hard pressed to find new revenue sources found room for maneuver in import taxation, since in Peru as in neighboring countries tariff increases were welcomed and supported by important segments of society as harbingers of prosperity through industrialization.

Over this postwar period, therefore, the dominant trend in incidence of the Peruvian tax system has been toward increased regression (or decreased progression). This is the result of an increased relative importance of indirect taxes and the continued erosion of direct taxes on both individuals and businesses, an evolution that represents a continuing expansion in the power of domestic entrepreneurs and the salaried middle class.

Looking at revenue structure in a longer perspective, our conclusions must be less certain, but it seems most likely that tendencies toward greater regression in the last 20 years represent a backsliding from a longer-term trend toward somewhat greater progression in the tax system. This trend may be traced back as far as 1854, when President Castilla abolished the head tax on Indians, a levy that was clearly the most regressive element in the tax system of colonial Peru. For several decades thereafter, the overwhelming important source of revenue was not taxation, but instead the income deriving from Peru's possession of a world guano monopoly. It was only with the collapse of guano revenues in the 1870s that the country was obliged to begin construction of a modern tax system.

The reconstructed tax system relied principally on customs duties supplemented by a few internal excises, and we can see from Table 7 that the job had been done by 1900. The system was effective, but regressive. The few direct taxes included in the revenue mix were of trivial importance.

The incidence of Peruvian revenue structure did not change greatly between 1900 and the advent of World War I, but thereafter the major changes in taxation were all in the direction of greater progression. First there were export taxes introduced during the war itself, then a regular system of business and personal income taxation, a process begun in 1926 and greatly advanced with the reform and consolidation of income tax laws in 1934. The share of major taxes paid by the richest quartile of the population was 51 percent in 1900 and rose to 65 percent

Table 7
PERCENTAGE DISTRIBUTION OF GOVERNMENT REVENUE

	Export taxes	Other profits taxes	Personal income taxes	Import taxes	Turnover taxes	Excise taxes and monopoly revenue	Other revenue
1900	0	2.9	0	59.5	1.6	27.7	8.3
1905	0	3.6	0	50.9	1.4	35.1	8.9
1910	0	4.2	0	49.9	1.2	29.0	15.7
1915	0	5.5	0	28.5	1.4	39.1	25.5
1920	32.6	3.4	0	26.1	0.9	17.7	19.3
1929	7.1	6.2	0.9	30.3	1.8	27.0	26.7
1942	16.0	15.0		11.1	1.5	15.9	40.6
1945	16.5	16.1	5.7	9.0	1.6	11.7	39.4
1950	27.5	13.9	5.4	8.5 (13.0)	2.4	7.0	30.7
1955	11.0	12.3	5.4	18.1 (21.7)	1.5	6.7	41.4
1960	8.9	15.6	5.5	8.5 (19.6)	8.3	5.8	36.2
1965	4.0	10.4	3.5	18.1 (23.9)	19.6	3.6	35.0

Source: Author's compilation, derived from *Balance y cuentas general de la república.* Figures in parentheses are total import taxes, including those collected under various special accounts, as reported by BCR, *Cuentas nacionales del Perú,* Table 13.

in 1920, 70 percent in 1945, and 76 percent in 1950. By 1961, however, this share was back to 62 percent.

The sources of possible error in such calculations are numerous, but perhaps the most obvious is the assumption that the burden of a given tax among quartile groups is constant over time. In the case of import taxes this seems particularly questionable; high transport costs and the low degree of urbanization in 1900 suggest that in fact import tax incidence might have fallen much more heavily on the rich than it does today. If this is the case, the redistributive backsliding of the recent decades may have been sufficient to return the incidence of the Peruvian tax system not just to what it was in 1920, but even to what it was in 1900.

These trends are dangerous for making inferences about the evolution of oligarchic power, however, since the richest 25 percent of the population consists largely of middle-class wage earners. The introduction of taxation on exports, business income, and personal income in the second and third decades of this century undoubtedly hurt the oligarchy, but in Peru as in other countries the problems of tax compliance and loophole plugging are so serious that an effective fiscal attack on the oligarchy is evidently a matter not of legislation but of tax administration, a far more difficult challenge. Moreover, legislative attacks on the rich hit even more effectively at the salaried middle classes, the group that now challenges the oligarchy's traditional power most seriously. For this reason, in Peru as in so many other countries, the use of taxation as an instrument for achieving distributive equity has ground to a halt. The theorist's heady talk about making efficiency and equity compatible through more or less competitive markets, lump-sum taxation, and redistribution seems applicable only in another world, perhaps somewhere above the clouds.

Meanwhile, back on the Andean earth, we find the long-run redistributive impact of the Peruvian budget lying almost entirely on the side of expenditure, with the expansion of education and public health programs. But an expanding revenue system with unchanging tax incidence does have redistributive significance if it makes possible the expansion of redistributive expenditure, and it is from this viewpoint that a favorable assessment may be given to the most important tax change since 1934. This is the recent development, in the early 1960s, of an effective and significant system of internal indirect taxation.

There remains a further significant tax development which has not yet occurred; this is the transformation of personal income taxes from minor levies on the elite to important levies collected on a mass basis. It took the belt-tightening esprit of total warfare to persuade the American public to permit the transition to this type of income tax. Naturally, it cannot be accomplished so quickly without so dramatic an external threat, but it is discouraging to see that in Peru progress seems to have been backwards on this issue. Personal income tax reform must remain the great challenge of Peruvian public finance in the coming decade.

Budget Policy and Growth

In an environment of continuing political conflict over distributive issues, what have Peruvian budget policies been able to contribute to accelerated growth? Part of an answer comes from the first column of Table 8, which shows that growth of government investment has kept up with GNP growth, but in a very erratic fashion. During periods of

Table 8
GOVERNMENT INVESTMENT

	Government fixed investment percentage GNP	Percentage of total government exhaustive expenditure	Private fixed investment as percentage of private consumption plus investment
1950	1.14	13.5	15.8
1951	1.10	11.9	19.8
1952	2.47	23.6	21.0
1953	2.14	19.7	23.3
1954	1.56	16.6	17.5
1955	3.30	29.9	17.3
1956	2.55	21.8	23.2
1957	2.08	19.1	24.5
1958	2.27	20.4	22.3
1959	1.49	14.1	18.4
1960	1.19	12.1	18.8
1961	1.97	17.1	20.5
1962	2.15	18.6	21.5
1963	1.26	11.4	19.8
1964	1.87	14.8	17.0
1965	2.70	19.5	16.4
1950–55	1.95	19.2	19.1
1955–60	2.15	19.6	20.8
1960–65	1.86	15.6	19.0

Source: BCR, *Cuentas nacionales del Perú,* Tables 1, 2, 5.

fiscal crisis, investment programs are among the expenditure components easiest to cut, so they show marked cyclical instability, with serious slumps in 1954, 1959–60, and 1963.

Table 8 also shows that the expenditure shares devoted to fixed investment are about the same in public and private sectors. It might seem surprising that the investment share is not larger in the public sector; certainly economists seem to assume a larger share when they view with evident favor the expansion of government's share of GNP in a developing economy.* In fact, in Peru the similarity of invest-

---

* The investment share of government is in fact substantially higher in the only other South American country for which data were readily available. This is Uruguay, certainly not a country noted for the overzealous investment programs of its government, but possessing a government investment rate of 20.5 percent for 1960–63, as compared to the private sector's rate of only 13.6 percent for the same period. Cf. United Nations Economic Commission for Latin America, *Boletín Estadístico de América Latina* 4, no. 1 (February 1967): 245.

ment shares is prima facie evidence that the substantial expansion of government's GNP share in the past 20 years has had no significance for the long-run growth rate.

This conclusion is subject to two important qualifications, however. First, it is based on terribly inadequate accounting conventions about what constitutes investment and what constitutes consumption. A far more analytically useful definition of investment would not include durable consumer goods, e.g., residential construction, but would include all productivity-increasing expenditure even if not embodied in material output—e.g., education. If we assume that only half of educational expenditure is properly treated as investment, government investment as a percent of total governmental exhaustive expenditures is changed from something less than 20 percent to something more than 30 percent.

The second qualification is that the comparison of Table 8 between public and private average rates, does not fully suit our purpose. Marginal investment rates are more suitable, since our analysis concerns the growth consequences of expanding the government sector, not of creating it. However, a comparison of marginal rather than average rates changes our conclusions very little. Government and private sector investment propensities remain the same over the 1950–65 period.[48]

Such comparisons assume implicitly that increases in government expenditure are financed by withdrawing resources proportionally from private investment and consumption, leaving the private investment rate unchanged. Our knowledge of the evolving pattern of government revenue conflicts with this assumption. Despite limited detailed knowledge of sources of saving in the Peruvian private sector, we may be quite certain that the general source is income from capital. Therefore, the surprising inelasticity of tax revenues on income from capital, so unfortunate from a distributive standpoint, is not at all unfortunate from the standpoint of growth. As taxation has become more regressive in recent years, it has shifted more and more away from saving and investment and on to consumption.

These various qualifications therefore give support to the earlier conclusion: *the expansion of the government sector, as it has taken place in Peru in the past 20 years, has been good for growth.*[49]

Two Final Issues

The various results of previous sections need not be restated in conclusion, but two issues touched on at different points in this chapter need to be drawn together and summarized. These are the extent to which this budgetary study complements the political studies mentioned earlier, and the extent of conflict between policies for growth and policies for distribution.

It will be remembered that the budgetary inferences drawn from the studies of domination were that the fiscal system would be regressive, probably in two discrete jumps at income levels corresponding to the transition from Indian to non-Indian and from masses to oligarchy, but that the degree of regressivity would have diminished over the years. Our statistical results give only partial confirmation to these expectations. We did find that the exclusion of the Indian from expenditure benefit was evident, even dramatic; here indeed was the fiscal manifestation of domination. The domination of masses by oligarchy was not to be seen in expenditure incidence, however, and neither aspect of domination was reflected in the present tax structure, whose wandering proportionality is not very unlike the structure of the United States or any other American country. We are left with a paradox: if an oligarchy has preponderant, dominating power, then why should it not derive greater benefit from the state mechanism which it controls?

There are four possible answers to this paradox. The first and most obvious is simply that an oligarchy does not exist. Unfortunately, this resolution may be little more than a word game; we may well say there is no oligarchy, but we are still left with the impression of nearly every social observer that all kinds of inequalities—income, influence, education—are substantially greater in Peru than in rich countries. It would be foolhardy to discard those impressions on the strength of the statistics in this essay. Nevertheless, these statistics emphasize the point that all non-Indian groups receive benefit from the budgetary process and therefore must have power. In this context the use of the loosely defined term domination can be deceptive, since some mechanism of accommodation must exist in a national political environment where all groups have some power, yet are not engaged in civil war.

The second possibility is that a more careful examination of incidence, particularly on the side of expenditure, would reveal favors to the rich that are hidden in the crudeness of present estimates. While this outcome cannot be denied, I must confess to a skeptical view of the possibility that more refined studies would change the conclusions radically.

Third, the oligarchy's benefit from governmental action may derive from economic policy measures operating outside the budget, such as those determining exchange rates, exchange freedom and tariff protection. Although these areas are not covered in this chapter, I will hazard an armchair conclusion that here, as in the field of taxation, the oligarchy's triumph is largely the negative one of keeping policies from being turned against it.

That leaves one final explanation, which seems to me the most plausible. It derives from the idea that the oligarchy's favored economic position is created and maintained by its control over natural resources, particularly land, and by its monopoly of contact with the world economy. The oligarchy is the primary beneficiary of capitalism's invasion into a traditional society, and for its purposes it has remained satisfied with a state that is merely permissive, rather than directly augmenting of oligarchic income. To the extent that the state's policies have given direct aid, this has probably occurred mostly in police and judicial administration rather than in economic and budgetary policy.

Viewed in this context, a proportional tax system in a country with income distribution as unequal as Peru's, seems a substantial triumph for the upper classes. Furthermore, the triumph is greater than the mere maintenance of proportionality; the tax system has in fact become more regressive in recent decades, at precisely the period when the oligarchy is most evidently in retreat. For reasons described earlier, the oligarchy seems in little danger of attack through increased tax progression. The dangers were increased substantially when the present radical-reformist military government came to power in 1968, but even now, as the antioligarchy attack develops a momentum never before seen in Peruvian history, it is curious to see how lightly regarded tax reform is as a weapon of attack.

To be sure, the secular diminution of oligarchic power may be seen on the expenditure side of the budget, where over the decades the share devoted to educational and social purposes has risen inexorably. This is only one facet of the state's changing role, by which it has slowly become less permissive and more controlling toward the oligarchy. Outside of the budget, this evolution can be traced from the modest beginnings of social legislation in the first decades of this century, through acquiescence to the rising trade union movement and the extension of unionization to coastal farm workers.

With all these various measures, the oligarchy has retained its property and simply has had to mend its ways in labor relations. The direct attack on ownership and uses of property, particularly land, is of a more recent vintage. Various measures attempted in the late 1940s were frustrated by ineffective implementation,* but today agrarian reform is on the march, and prospects for implementation are decidedly better. It remains to be seen, however, if land is sufficiently important in the oligarchic portfolio to make this the knockout blow Favre suggests it will be.[50]

We come next to the issue of conflict between the goals of growth and distribution. There are indeed several instances in which these goals have come into conflict, with quite opposite outcomes. On the side of taxation, the most obvious and difficult conflict has concerned the severity with which income from capital is to be taxed. In this case growth won over distribution, partly because the growth significance of unequal distribution was obvious and persuasive to policymakers and to public opinion. This is particularly the case with tax exonerations; the entrepreneur who wishes to introduce a new industry to his country, for the small consideration of not having to pay taxes, is a culture hero, and the size of his personal income after taxes does not come to issue.

On the expenditure side, growth and distribution came into conflict on the issue of teachers' salaries, and this time distribution won the day with ease, partly because the growth-promoting alternatives could not be specified. In both of these instances, the "conflict" was an intellectual dilemma which we may view in hindsight. In fact, neither of these issues provoked growth-versus-distribution political debates at the time, because the alternatives being decided upon were not clearly stated.

---

* For example, a 1947 law intended to improve the lot of sharecroppers resulted principally in their being expelled from the land and replaced by more centralized and capital-intensive production.

The mechanism by which distribution-motivated expenditure affects growth objectives can be particularly pernicious. In the case of the 1964 education program mentioned previously, it was not a question of reallocating tax revenues away from growth-oriented projects. Rather, there were no tax revenues; distribution expenditure was financed by fiscal deficits which, in their ultimate effect on the economy, did far more damage to growth than one might reasonably have expected from mere tax reallocation. Inflation, balance of payments deficits, exchange speculation, credit tightening on the private sector and a substantial cutback in private investment, caused partly by uncertainty, partly by unavailability of funds and partly by domestic recession—these have all been the unhappy growth consequences in the last few years of massive, distribution-oriented expenditure programs a few years earlier.

This particular outcome was, of course, not an efficient one among the feasible set of growth-distribution options. In fact, we have also mentioned several instances of more efficiently chosen programs in which there was essentially no conflict of goals. This was the case, for example, for that portion of expanded educational expenditure that represented the incorporation of new resources into the sector, rather than merely the higher remuneration of already active teachers, and was also within the capacity of the tax system. It was also the case in many other smaller government investment programs, such as those involving road building and settlement in high jungle regions, or systematic assistance to small farmers on the coast.

On the other hand, there are some policy outcomes which have not had favorable results, for either growth or distribution. In this class I would put the continued undermining of the personal income tax system. The unfavorable distributional consequences are evident, and it is most unlikely that the beneficiary middle-class groups have high marginal savings propensities.

The growth-distribution conflict exists; it crops up time and time again, in different places, under different guises. Its resolution is essentially a political rather than a technical problem, but it should be a cause for the comfort of technicians to see how random and inefficient some outcomes have been, and how much better served the nation would have been if technicians had done their job of spelling out options and making sure that superior opportunities were not overlooked at the moment of decision.

NOTES

1. Richard Patch, "La Parada, Lima's Market: A Study of Class and Assimilation," *West Coast South America Series,* American Universities Field Staff 14, no. 3 (February 1967): 13.
2. See Julio Cotler, Chapter 2 of this volume.
3. José Matos Mar, "Consideraciones sobre la situación social del Perú," *America Latina* 7, no. 1 (January/March 1964): 62. In recent years the most extensive analysis of the concept of domination comes from François Perroux, whose intellectual influence in Peru and elsewhere in Latin America is profound. See his *La economía del siglo XX* (Barcelona: Ariel, 1964). One of the few examples of his work that appears in English is "The Domination Effect and Modern Economic Theory," *Social Research* 17 (June 1950).
4. Luis Alberto Sánchez, *El Peru: retrato de un pais adolescente* (Lima: Universidad de San Marcos, 1963), p. 150; Matos Mar, "Consideraciones," p. 60; François Bourricaud, Chapter 1 of this volume.
5. A rather casual attempt has been made by Carlos Malpica, *Guerra a muerte al latifundismo* (Lima: Ediciones Voz Rebelde, n.d.), Part 4.
6. Luis F. de la Puente Uceda, "The Peruvian Revolution: Concepts and Perspectives," *Monthly Review* 17, no. 6 (November 1965): 21.
7. E.g. Cótler, Chapter 2 of this volume.
8. François Bourricaud, *Poder y sociedad en el Perú contemporáneo* (Buenos Aires, Editorial Sur, 1967); Bourricaud, et all., *La oligarqua en el Perú* (Lima: Moncloa-Campodónico for the Instituto de Estudios Peruanos, 1969).
9. James Payne, "The Oligarchy Muddle," *World Politics* 20, no. 3 (April 1968): 439-53.
10. Ibid., pp. 449-51.
11. François Bourricaud, "Structure and Function of the Peruvian Oligarchy," *Studies in Comparative International Development* 2, no. 2.
12. Henri Favre, "El desarrollo y las formas del poder oligárquico en el Perú," in Bourricaud, et al., *La oligarquía en el Perú.*
13. Jorge Bravo Bresani, "Mito y realidad de la oligarquía peruana," in Bourricaud, et al., *La oligarquía en el Perú.*
14. Jean Piel, "La oligarquía peruana y las estructuras del poder," in Bourricaud, et al., *La oligarqua en el Perú,* p. 188.
15. In a famous polemic of the 1920s, this is one point on which Marxist and Catholic traditionalists could agree. See José Carlos Mariátegui, *Siete ensayos de interpretación de la realidad peruana,* 13th ed. (Lima: Amauta, 1968), pp. 80-82, and Victor Andrés Belaúnde, *La realidad nacional,* 3rd ed. (Lima, 1963), p. 29.
16. Bourricaud, "Structure and Function," gives the impression that oligarchy *prefers* indirect rule, and that the Civilista period was an aberration. It seems to me, rather, that indirect rule has been the best that oligarchy could manage during other periods. See Fredrick Pike, *The Modern History of Peru* (New York: Praeger, 1967), pp. 192-200.
17. Jorge Basadre, *Historia de la república del Perú,* 6th ed. (Lima: Editorial Universitaria, 1969), vol. 15, pp. 7-53.
18. Hugo Neira, *Cuzco: tierra y muerte* (Lima, Problemas de Hoy, 1964).

19. James Payne, "Peru: The Politics of Structured Violence," *Journal of Politics* 27, no. 2 (May 1965).

20. Rosendo Gomez, "Peru: The Politics of Military Guardianship," in Martin Needler, ed., *Political Systems of Latin America* (Princeton: Van Nostrand, 1964), p. 300.

21. Henry Wallich and John Adler, *Public Finance in a Developing Country; El Salvador: A Case Study* (Cambridge: Harvard University Press, 1951), pp. 132–33; Commission to Study the Fiscal System of Venezuela, *The Fiscal System of Venezuela* (Baltimore: Johns Hopkins Press, 1959), p. 40.

22. Joint Tax Program (hereafter cited as JTP), *Fiscal Survey of Colombia* (Baltimore: Johns Hopkins Press, 1965).

23. Richard Musgrave, "Estimating the Distribution of the Tax Burden," in Conference on Tax Administration, *Problems of Tax Administration in Latin America*, for the Joint Tax Program (Baltimore, Johns Hopkins Press, 1965), p. 63. The apparent progression in Musgrave's Venezuelan estimate appears erroneous, however, as a result of including taxes on foreign companies in a distribution that pertains only to residents of the country.

24. Ibid, p. 86.

25. George Bishop, "The Tax Burden by Income Class, 1958," *National Tax Journal* 14, no. 1 (March 1961): 54.

26. For a brief bibliography, see W. Irwin Gillespie, "Effect of Public Expenditures on the Distribution of Income," in Richard Musgrave, ed., *Essays in Fiscal Federalism* (Washington: The Brookings Institution, 1965), pp. 122–23.

27. Gillespie, "Effect of Public Expenditures," p. 162. Also Eugene Schlesinger, Appendix to John Adler, "The Fiscal System, the Distribution of Income, and the Public Welfare," in *Fiscal Policies and the American Economy*, ed. Kenyon Poole (New York: Prentice-Hall, 1951), pp. 418–20.

28. Alison Martin and W. A. Lewis, "Patterns of Public Revenue and Expenditure," *Manchester School* 24, no. 3 (September 1956); Jeffrey Williamson, "Public Expenditure and Revenue: An International Comparison," *Manchester School* 29, no. 1 (January 1961); Harley Hinrichs, *A General Theory of Tax Structure Change during Economic Development* (Cambridge: Harvard Law School, 1966); Simon Kuznets, "Quantitative Aspects of Economic Growth of Nations: VII. The Share and Structure of Consumption," *Economic Development and Cultural Change* 10 (January 1962), part 2; Richard Thorn, "The Evolution of Public Finances during Economic Development," *Manchester School* 35, no. 1 (January 1967). For a more complete bibliography, see Thorn, "The Evolution."

29. Kuznets, "Quantitative Aspects of Economic Growth of Nations," p. 10. Relation of government expenditure shares to income per capita calculated from regression equations in Hinrichs, "A General Theory," p. 13; Thorn, "The Evolution," p. 40; and Williamson, "Public Expenditure," p. 50. The correspondence between the results from these three sources is only fair.

30. Hinrichs, "A General Theory," pp. 73.

31. Calculated from regressions in Thorn, "The Evolution," p. 48, and Williamson, "Public Expenditure," p. 52. Also Kuznets, "Quantitative Aspects," p. 8.

32. Kuznets, "Quantitative Aspects," p. 8; Williamson, "Public Expenditures," pp. 52, 54.

33. Musgrave, "Distribution of the Tax Burden."

34. Solon Barraclough, "Agricultural Policy and Land Reform," Conference on Key

Problems of Economic Policy in Latin America, University of Chicago, mimeo. (1966), pp. 11–29.

35. Williamson, "Public Expenditure," pp. 50, 56. Note that his figures pertain to the share of government current expenditure only.

36. In 1965, per capital income is estimated at 280 dollars of 1963 vintage, and the government expenditure share, including transfers, at 19.7 percent. In 1967, the last year for which data are available, the corresponding figures are $363 and 22.3 percent. BCR, *Cuentas nacionales del Perú 1950–1967* (Lima, 1968), Tables 1, 12.

37. UNESCO, *Statistical Yearbook, 1965,* Table 21.

38. William Mangin has pointed this out in the case of residents of Lima *barriadas.* Cf., "Urbanization Case History in Peru," *Architectural Design* 33, no. 8 (August 1963).

39. That is, (1.52) (1.44) (1.18) (1.49) = 3.85. Since the quantum index refers only to teachers, rather than to all educational personnel, this assumes that the growth of administrative personnel is proportional to the expansion in the number of teachers. If administrative growth has been more rapid, then the real wage differential growth rate is too high.

40. The number of students in both public and private schools grew by 50 percent during 1960–65. Ministerio de Educación Pública. *La educación en el Perú* (Lima, 1967), p. 51.

41. Jorge Basadre, *Perú; problema y posibilidad* (Lima: F. y E. Rosay, 1931), chapter 8; Pike, *Modern History of Peru,* chapter 8.

42. JTP, *Estudio fiscal de Perú,* chapter 2; Ministerio de Hacienda, *La reforma tributaria de 1968* (Lima, 1968), p. 38.

43. See the excellent study by Charles Farnsworth, "The Application and Impact of Tax Incentives for Industrial Promotion in Peru," mimeographed (BCR, 1967).

44. U Tun Wai, "Taxation Problems and Policies of Underdeveloped Countries," *IMF Staff Papers* 9, no. 3 (November 1962), pp. 432–33.

45. Musgrave, "Distribution of the Tax Burden," pp. 64–65. For example, in 1958 the income of a single person had to be 12 times the national average before he became liable to tax payments, and 14 times before his tax liability rose to 1 percent of his income. The corresponding multiples for a family of four were 26 and 32. The highest corresponding multiples to be found anywhere else in South America were 6, 25, 9 and 17, respectively.

46. Thus we have a part of income taxes masquerading as an indirect tax in our figures. This wage tax amounted to some 7 percent of total turnover taxes in 1967, and is so small a share that its transfer to direct taxes would not greatly affect any of the data or conclusions of this essay.

47. Santiago Macario calculates the average Peruvian tariff at 22 percent for 1959, as compared to 29 percent for Brazil, 32 percent for Colombia, 38 percent for Chile, and 53 percent for Argentina. See his "Protectionism and Industrialization in Latin America," *Economic Bulletin for Latin America* 9, no. 1 (March 1964), Table 2.

48. The elasticity of investment expenditure with respect to total expenditure, which equals the ratio of marginal to average investment rates, was 0.972 for government and 0.975 for the private sector. However, any one of a number of small definitional changes upsets this equality between marginal rates and shows a somewhat higher rate in the government sector. These changes include increasing the span of years to 1967, using constant price data, regressing first differences, or, most significant of all, redefining investment to include education.

49. Two other factors, not dealt with in this paper, are also important for assessing the desirability of an expanded government sector. The first is possible complementarity between private and public investment, but this represents only one aspect of the second, larger issue: the relative social profitability of public and private investment in Peru.

50. Favre, "El desarrollo y las formas del poder oligárquico."

The Military
and the Church

Luigi R. Einaudi

15.

Revolution from Within?
Military Rule in Peru
Since 1968

In 1871, Karl Marx wrote to Ernst Kugelmann that the fate of the Paris Commune demonstrated that henceforth popular revolutions could not succeed without first smashing the increasingly powerful repressive arm of the modern bureaucratic state: the armed forces.

In 1954, the dominant elements of the Guatemalan military, acting with the support of the United States, helped to overthrow the elected government of Colonel Jacobo Arbenz and reversed what was beginning to be an increasingly radical agrarian reform program.

In 1959, a triumphant Fidel Castro took what he considered the first key steps toward consolidating his power by declaring himself Commander-in-Chief of the Cuban armed forces and placing his brother and his most trusted guerrilla *comandantes* in charge of a program of restructuring the Cuban officer corps, thereby insuring himself against internal counterrevolution. Only then did he turn to the agrarian reform that was to prove the symbol of the Cuban revolution.

In 1968, in direct contrast to these previous events and to the generalizations commonly drawn from them, Peru's armed forces, acting (in exemplary bureaucratic fashion) under the command of the military chief of staff and the commanders of the three services, seized power from an elected but ineffectual liberal democratic regime, nationalized without compensation the local subsidiary of Standard Oil of New Jersey, and set in motion a revolutionary process that has included Latin America's most radical agrarian reform program since Cuba.

What makes these Peruvian events doubly puzzling is the fact that the revolution was led by many of the same officers who in 1965 had supervised the bloody destruction of the guerrillas of the Movement of the Revolutionary Left (MIR), led by Luis de la Puente. Could it really be, as Fidel Castro colorfully stated in August of 1970, with his characteristic sense for the jugular, that "the fire has broken out in the firehouse"?

This chapter seeks to answer Castro's question about Peru by looking first at the firehouse and then at the fire. First, it briefly considers the military forces of Peru and some sources of their political behavior, which has so strikingly contradicted the stereotypical view of the military as committed to preserving the status quo through repression. It then touches on the nature of the military government, and some of the innovations which it has attempted to bring to Peru since 1968, in order to conclude by suggesting some implications of these events for strategies of change in general.

The Military Sources of the 1968 Revolution in Peru

The evolution of the political style of the Peruvian military is complex and halting, as befits the behavior of an organized bureaucracy in a rapidly if unevenly developing society.[1] It could nonetheless be argued that events since October 3, 1968 mark a qualitative shift in military participation in politics, from a generally cautious political stance dedicated primarily to arbitrating between the policies and leaders advanced by civilian political groups, to an even more dominant role, placing military leaders directly in policymaking positions to the point of virtually excluding civilians. Military rule, previously conservative and caretaker in style, now claims to be revolutionary, and is introducing innovations in public policy that, when considered in the past, were regularly rejected.

The origins of this pronounced leftward shift in the style and substance of military political activity are rooted in a complicated combination of institutional military factors, the personal experiences of members of the military officer corps, particularly in the army, and the course of Peruvian society in recent decades. What happened may be summarized at one level by saying that military leaders began to perceive national security problems as extending beyond conventional military operations. They did so in large part because many of the existing social and economic structures seemed so inefficient or unjust as to create the conditions for, and give legitimacy to, revolutionary protest—and hence constitute a security threat. Even conservative officers came to feel that these conditions could ultimately become a threat to the military, as an institution.

In the late 1950s and early 1960s, Peruvian officers increasingly came to see their society as caught up in a fundamental, long-term crisis that threatened them both as military men and personally, as members of an often hard-pressed middle class. Land invasions, guerrilla movements and acts of political terrorism were seen as the top of an iceberg of inexorably mounting social pressures caused by exploding populations that would, in the long run, overwhelm traditional social structures. Military officers in the national war college, Centro de Altos Estudios Militares (CAEM), studied a wide range of social problems. These included questions of land reform, tax structure, foreign policy and insurgency, and involved the formulation of policies and reforms that the military felt necessary to ensure stability. The result was that military policy became much more closely linked to political policy than it had been in the past.

The guerrilla experience of 1965, while successfully controlled in military terms, underscored for the military the importance of social change. It also raised fundamental doubts about the capacity of civilian-directed efforts to achieve that change—despite the fact that the military junta of 1962–63 had helped install Fernando Belaúnde as president with the hope that he would prove to be a successful reformer. By 1966, military men were ready to admit Belaúnde was a failure, particularly since many of them envied the power and the activity of the civilian professionals around Belaúnde, many of whom were financially rewarded beyond the highest expectations of general officers, although they were often far less competent.

The impotence of the Belaúnde government, together with the continuing presence of the aging and by then largely complacent Apristas, heightened the military's anger. Their frustration was continuously fed by incidents of social rejection by the pretentious "whiter" social elites of the coastal cities, and by the antimilitary arrogance of the United States, whose efforts to promote the Alliance for Progress often appeared to many army officers as anti-Peruvian meddling, limited to the defense of U.S. economic interests.

These shifts are of sufficient interest to warrant a more detailed examination, in both theory and practice, from the viewpoint of the Peruvian military leadership, as traditional military resentment of civilians, plutocrats and foreigners increasingly became focused on organized political parties, which were in turn viewed as hopelessly committed to an unjust social, political and economic order. These views, together with the wider concerns over economic backwardness and social instability, gradually permeated the training and operations of two major institutions: the military schools and the military intelligence services.

Theoretical Perception of Threats: The Military School System and the CAEM

Ever since the founding of the Center for Military Instruction (CIMP) and the Center for Higher Military Studies (CAEM) in the first years after World War II, military education in Peru had improved and expanded to include socioeconomic concerns.[2] The CIMP opened in 1948; it pulled together military education under a single command, laying the basis for greatly expanded emphasis on continuing post-Academy training. The CAEM, which opened in 1950, offered a one-year course, largely devoted to social, economic and political problems, to select classes of colonels and generals. Moreover, officers were encouraged to follow specialized military or civilian courses both in Peru and abroad, usually at government expense. Members of the officer corps had studied military affairs in Europe and the United States since the turn of the century, often winning recognition as the best foreign students. In the 1950s and 1960s, Peruvian officers studied economics under United Nations auspices with the Economic Commission for Latin America (ECLA) in Chile, attempted unsuccessfully to import the Belgian Catholic sociologist Frère L. J. Lebret to teach, and made innovative policy suggestions to the conservative Prado government, some of whose members in turn became concerned at "Communist" infiltration of the CAEM.

As William F. Whyte has suggested, most Peruvians do not believe that success in life is based on merit.[3] In the military, however, the emphasis on professional training and education in the promotion process, particularly since World War II, has made its members among the most merit oriented within the state bureaucracy, if not the entire society. All navy and air force officers, and more than 90 percent of all army officers, are Academy graduates. The continuing value of education in the Peruvian military career may be inferred from the fact that, of the division generals on active duty between 1940 and 1965, no fewer than 80 percent had graduated in the top quarter of their class at the Military Academy. In addition, the expansion and improvement of advanced military training after 1945 introduced a new element of competition into the officer corps, and improved the life chances of officers previously stymied by the promotion system's dependence on class standing at the time of graduation from the Military Academy. The final Academy class standings, determined on the basis of combined academic and discipline performance, were often stifling to bright men who were deficient in discipline or conduct, but who, in the 1950s and 1960s, were given new chances to prove themselves in advanced education, much as the air force, during the 1920s and 30s, had provided an outlet for energetic and talented officers who had been "burned" in the regular army.

The CAEM is probably the most important center for the development of Peruvian national security strategy.* Many of the changed military perceptions have crystallized in CAEM studies and class exercises. Of the first 19 cabinet ministers after the 1968 revolution, 13 were CAEM graduates, including the Prime Minister and the Chief of the Council of Presidential Advisors (COAP). The director of the CAEM is a general appointed by the Joint Command (Comando Conjuto) of the Armed Forces. The Director has a small staff, three departments and three directorates under him. These departments include the *Deputy Director,* who is in charge of administration and through whom the three directorates report; the *Academic Council,* made up of the heads of the directorates and selected professors; and, finally, an optional body called the *Consultative Council,* which may be convened at the director's discretion to study special problems. Of the

---

* National planning, conceived of less as general theory and more as related to immediate government policies, is carried out elsewhere, of course, primarily at the National Planning Institute (INP), originally established with mixed civilian and military personnel by the 1962 military junta. Civilian institutions, including universities and the research-oriented Institute of Peruvian Studies (IEP), are important primarily through the impact achieved on CAEM doctrine by individual faculty members.

directorates, the *Academic Directorate* is responsible for plans, academic programs and the actual content of instruction. To it are assigned the students, mainly officers in the rank of full colonel, known as "participants." The *Directorate of National Strategy and Special Studies* deals with contemporary problems of national security, special problems and the strategies of foreign powers, including the United States. The third directorate, *Research and Development,* is concerned exclusively with the future.

CAEM courses in 1970 opened with an introductory study of methodology, sociology and similar general principles.[4] This was followed by the first major curriculum segment, the study of national reality, which in turn was followed by the analysis of national potential, defined as constantly moving and changing. The contrast between reality and potential establishes national objectives, which are to eliminate this differential between reality and potential. National problems are studied from economic, social, military and psychological viewpoints, each of which was represented in the second major part of the course, the study of national strategy. National strategy consists of the actual programs designed to attain national objectives. The final portion of the course is devoted to individual case studies. These studies, drawn up by the participants in the CAEM, benefit from the experiences of the military participants, and also those of the civilians. Although occasional civilian students attended CAEM classes as early as 1961, it was not until the mid and late sixties that their numbers became significant on a routine basis. In 1971, 16 students out of 43 were civilians.

Since its founding in 1950, the CAEM has consistently taught, in accordance with Article 213 of the Peruvian Constitution, that the military must defend national sovereignty. Specifically, this is defined as an obligation to increase Peru's capacity for maneuverability vis-à-vis the outside world, and particularly the United States. Recognition of the Soviet Union, coupled with some trade, is in harmony with this interpretation of the constitutional mandate. Similarly, the constitutional prescription for the maintenance of order is now interpreted at the CAEM as the need to ensure an order conducive to "national well-being," that is, the well-being of all Peruvians, not just the dominant social classes.

To argue in favor of economic development and social justice is not, however, to have a clear plan for how to bring them about. Military men have a strong tendency to view politics in a fundamentally apolitical light. This contradiction is exemplified in the opening paragraph of the action program adopted in 1944 by a secret military lodge, the Comando Revolucionario de Oficiales del Ejército (CROE):

> CROE has no political implications of any kind. It is a revolutionary organization of the officers of the Army who aspire to lead the country within a democratic and strictly constitutional order.[5]

The failure to realize that revolution involves politics, while an old problem, is still typical today, as is CROE's stress on the need for "morality" in public life. As recently as 1970, General Velasco was proclaiming that he was a "soldier and a revolutionary, not a politician." [6]

To say that the traditional military prescription for good government is morality, discipline and patriotism is to be reasonably close to the fundamental, old-line military attitudes. There has always been some tension, however, between these views of politics and the military's sense of inferiority in cultural and social matters. "When a general met an ambassador, he turned red in the face and trembled," said a former minister of war, one of Peru's leading military intellectuals.* Traditionally, the thought persisted that successful politics might require more than could be brought to it by the military.

Peruvian officers' attitudes toward civilians and toward politics have historically combined into a powerful dislike for civilian politicians. Their attitude toward politics, along with their self-image of discipline and efficiency, leads some officers to believe that they are the elect and must therefore lead the nation. Typically, however, these same attitudes also lead to another and somewhat contradictory sense of contempt for officers who "play politics" within the military, thus undermining discipline and efficiency. With these conflicting attitudes to overcome, even among their fellow officers, it is not surprising that

---

* General José del Carmen Marín, who made this particular comment to the author in 1964, was referring primarily to the 1930s. By the 1960s and 1970s, partly because of Marín's efforts as an educator and, more importantly, because of the strengthening of the military as an institution, these roles were frequently reversed.

the military leaders who ultimately do assume national leadership tend to be both tactically astute and politically tough.

The military's proposed solution to these conflicts, however, has generally been typically apolitical: officers should be better trained. The Center for Higher Military Studies—whose directors have proudly proclaimed it, not a "school for presidents," but a "school for statesmen"—has not only improved military training, but it has also retained the traditional military prescription for national health, adding only "technology." And the means by which it instills morality, discipline, patriotism and technology remains one of the traditional panaceas of the Peruvian military: education. As with other military attitudes, the origins of this emphasis on education lie in a mixture of institutional and social factors. The importance of education to the promotion process (a step that has revolutionized the military career since the 1930s) reflects, among other things, the concerns of men sensitized by the knowledge that low social standing and limited finances had, during their adolescence, precluded their attending civilian universities.

Even at the CAEM, however, politics in Peru, and especially good government, was still seen in the early 1960s as an imponderable, fraught with difficulties and beset by devils. Bolívar's statement that he had "ploughed the sea" in trying to govern, reflects a common military attitude. "So long as Peru does not have programmatic and well-organized political parties, *the country will continue to be ungovernable.*"[7] This ungovernability, however, was not attributed to the traditional and well-known civilian defects alone:

> The sad and desperate truth is that in Peru, the real powers are not the Executive, the Legislative, the Judicial or the Electoral, but the *latifundists,* the exporters, the bankers, and the American [U.S.] investors.[8]

And the oligarchic and foreign devils are joined by the APRA party —"a form of national cancer," according to the same military planners.

Despite their hostility toward politics and the tendency to oversimplify complicated issues for the sake of action, Peruvian military leaders have frequently demonstrated considerable flexibility and political skill. That some officers are capable of being *criollo* (clever

and sometimes unscrupulous realists) does not alter their suspicion that political compromise is fundamentally a betrayal of military values, but it may enable them to put some of their theories to a rather effective test.

Practical Threat Perception:
Guerrillas, Intelligence Organization and Petroleum

The military educational system, as we have seen, developed some interesting doctrines. Nonetheless, it took the guerrilla campaigns of 1965–66 to force social theory out of the schools and into the barracks, thereby making the political immobilism and economic decline of the late 1960s a matter of urgent military concern. In the summer of 1965, two separately organized guerrilla fronts began their activities in the central and southern Andes with ambushes of police units. Within a month, these outbreaks had led to the displacement of the relatively ineffective rural police by a joint military command and martial law in the affected forces. This, in turn, led to the discovery of other fronts still formed in other parts of the country. Within six months, despite forebodings in elite political circles about "revolution in the Andes," the military forces completely eliminated the guerrilla pockets and almost entirely wiped out the MIR leadership. And they did this without forcing a change in government, and without the prolonged suffering and mounting casualties characteristic of other cases of political violence (Guatemala and Colombia among them).[9]

Containment of the guerrilla threat also confirmed the military in their commitment to reform. The guerrillas had chosen for their headquarters a remote mountaintop called "Mesa Pelada" near the Convención Valley in the Province of Cuzco, where the famous Trotskyist labor organizer, Hugo Blanco, had successfully organized peasant unions in the early 1960s, before his capture in 1963. But the Convención Valley had also been the scene of construction of a penetration road from Colca to Amparaes by military engineer battalions, and had been the site of a pilot agrarian reform program by the military junta of 1962–63. The failure of the region's peasants to provide significant support to the insurgents appeared in military circles to confirm the wisdom of the earlier reform policies.

The sense of success was tempered, however, by fear of a reoccurrence of violence. If a handful of radicalized urban intellectuals could occupy thousands of troops for months, what would happen if popular forces and the peasantry were enlisted in future disorders? The Ministry of War's published account of the guerrilla campaign concluded that Peru had entered a period of "latent insurgency."

Nor was this a matter to be readily resolved with foreign assistance. Guerrilla war had proved the undoing of France, first in Indochina and then in Algeria. French military operations had been observed by Peruvian officers with French training and connections. Now Vietnam was proving the Achilles heel to the United States, demonstrating the difficulties that irregular warfare could create even for the world's foremost military power. The conclusion that the fate of these two historic military mentors seemed to suggest for Peru was that internal subversion would have to be controlled by Peruvians alone, if indeed it could be controlled at all.

The "latent insurgency" dilemma appeared to convince many officers that Peru needed agrarian reform combined with industrialization, or, in the more abstract language of the Ministry of War, a "General Policy of Economic and Social Development." [10] According to this view, similar to the McNamara-Rostow thesis that violence springs from economic backwardness, conditions of injustice in the countryside needed to be removed, so that the absentee landowner and his local henchmen no longer would exploit and oppress the rural peasant masses, whose marginal living conditions were making them potential recruits for future subversion and movements directed against military and governmental authorities.

Elimination of the latent state of subversion now became the primary objective of military action. In a formal intelligence analysis by General Mercado, the man who was to become Peru's foreign minister after the 1968 revolution, the "latent state of subversion" was defined as the presence of Communist activity exploiting national weaknesses.[11] This Communist activity, which took a variety of forms—military, political, economic and social—was containable for the present. But the existence of national weaknesses continually threatened to tip the balance against the forces of progress and order.

National weaks spots were defined, in General Mercado's remarkable statement of this theory, to cover a wide range of organizational, economic, technical and political elements. His list of national weaknesses included fiscal crises, scarcity of trained personnel, resistance to change by privileged groups, inadequate scientific and technical development, lack of unity and coordination of efforts, absence of effective international security cooperation, lack of governmental control and communication with the rural areas and, finally, lack of identification by the population with national political objectives. The reforms introduced by the revolutionary military government that took office less than a year after Mercado's article had appeared, were largely meant to offset these weaknesses.

But threat perceptions, fear and antisubversive warfare were not the only wellsprings of action. Genuine compassion for the conditions of the rural population was quite common among officers who had served in rural areas during the regular tours as well as during the guerrilla campaign, and who often found emotional and ideological support for such feelings in paternalist Catholic social doctrines, which stressed that every man had a right to an existence offering material and spiritual dignity. In fact, there can be little doubt that among the major intellectual and moral forces impelling the largely Catholic military to action, were the progressive priests and scholars who in the 1960s helped move the hierarchy of the Church in Peru to reorient its political participation in the direction of greater social justice for all Peruvians, including the poor.[12]

Communists, of whatever variety, were not the only enemies of order and security in Peru. Many officers, accustomed since the War of the Pacific in 1879 to seeing external enemies exploit internal weaknesses, had come to believe that the United States, in alliance with Peru's "oligarchy," favored Peru's continuing in a state of underdevelopment. This view associated the United States with Peru's vulnerability to subversion, as well as to more traditional external threats. The Belaúnde government had been strongly supported by most military men as a reformist movement dedicated to national progress. Its fumbling, which some attributed to American interests, only added to this theorizing, which to outsiders sometimes seems to verge on paranoia.

"Foreign interests, the oligarchy, and the decrepit politicians in their pay," was the way President Velasco later characterized this new subversive force, or *"anti-Patria."* [13] Although one result of studying political and social problems may be to realize their complexity, another may be to undermine the credibility of solutions advanced by political parties, thereby weakening the claim of civilian leadership to sole legitimacy. The legitimacy of civilian leadership was further eroded in Peru during the 1960s, by the information collected through the increased activity of military intelligence services. The military command developed evidence of the corruption and compromises that were the daily fare of Peruvian politics. Even normal political compromise finds little acceptance in the military's values, as we have already discussed. Peruvian politics have never been very clean, yet not every form of misconduct provokes indignation. A particularly messy smuggling scandal became known during the Belaúnde administration, in early 1968. But smuggling, to military people, was sufficiently common not to be in itself cause to unseat Belaúnde. However, in the context of the payment by private interests of "contributions" to political parties and leaders, of continuing inaction on basic reforms and of Congressional privilege, it was enough to lead increasing portions of the military, including nationalist elements in the intelligence services, to side with Catholic priests and others who denounced "corruption" in government.

All of these complicated matters were involved in the explosive petroleum issue that came to a head in the proposed Talara Agreement of 1968, providing the immediate impetus behind the overthrow of Belaúnde and the installation of the government that still rules Peru today, seven years later. This is not the place to review the petroleum affair,[14] except to point out that the debate over IPC became pivotal in helping to associate the United States government with the Peruvian and American private interests which military officers were already perceiving to be inimical to Peruvian security and development.*

---

* Perhaps even more than the fishing industry (in which Peru now competes with Japan for world primacy), petroleum fits the category of a basic national resource. Contrary to some suspicions in the United States at the time, that President Velasco had been irresponsible and unrepresentative, he almost certainly acted with broad military support in the IPC case. As early as February 5, 1960, the Joint Staff, over the signature of the Commanding General of the Army, publicly recorded its belief that the *La Brea y*

As General Arturo Cavero later explained to a group of visiting American military officers, threats to the internal security of Peru could originate in the plotting of groups committed to peaceful revolution, as well as in the efforts of groups seeking to impose revolution by violence.[16] General Cavero, then the director of CAEM, said this when Peruvian relations with the United States had improved from their low point in early 1969, when application of the Hickenlooper Amendment seemed imminent, threatening to cut U.S. economic assistance and sugar quotas in response to the IPC nationalization. But Cavero began his remarks to the U.S. officers by pointedly quoting General Mercado's speech before the United Nations in April of 1969:

> The threat has varied over time. At first it was narrowly military in nature. Then new and subtler psychological and ideological threats arose against the security of each country. Today we face a new threat: Economic aggression. Just as we fought against the violent aggression generated by guerrillas and by different forms of terrorism, so we are now fighting against economic aggression.

Cavero's U.S. military audience can have had no doubts about the direction of these remarks. Nor could they have doubted that the Peruvians meant what they said: in May 1969, less than a year before, Peru's military government had expelled the U.S. military missions from Peru.*

Parinas agreements were "harmful to national sovereignty." That it took nearly nine years to put belief into practice is a sign of institutional caution, rather than individual recklessness. An "inside dopester" account of the political history of the petroleum issue from the Peruvian perspective, of additional interest because shortly after writing it its author moved from the conservative newspaper *El Comercio* to the directorship of the Government Information Bureau run by the presidency, is Augusto Zimmerman Zavala, *La Historia Secreta del Petroleo.*[15]

* The immediate cause of this expulsion was an attempt to retaliate for prior U.S. suspension of military sales—imposed in accordance with the requirements of the Pelly Act, as a result of the perennial tuna disputes arising from Peru's insistence on a 200-mile-wide oceanic border, while the U.S. recognizes only a 12-mile limit. The departure of the missions was also, however, delayed proof of the deterioration in both political and military relations between the two countries during the mid and late 1960s.[17]

For a combination of reasons, then, many officers, particularly in the army, moved in the late 1960s toward an authoritarian preemption of what had traditionally been nationalist and left-wing positions, especially on the issues of petroleum and agrarian reform. But unlike the Left, most of whose leaders dreamed of guerrillas or elections, the military were to impose their views under the aegis of a nationalist military dictatorship pledged to the nonviolent restructuring of Peruvian society.

The Nature of the Regime

Peru has been governed since 1968 by a unique blend of personal leadership and institutional military commitment. The president, General Juan Velasco Alvarado, is tough, with an acute political sense, committed to his own power as a means of implementing the policies he supports. But all of Velasco's decrees must be countersigned by the commanding generals of the three armed services, who have assumed powers combining the executive and legislative functions. By statute, these commanders can be changed only in accord with the regulations in force on October 3, 1968, the date of the revolution. These regulations are largely based on seniority, and guarantee a continuing rotation among the generals holding a veto power over government policies. All ministers and the heads of all important public agencies are military officers. Government policies and access to the president are coordinated through an all-military Council of Presidential Advisors (COAP). The absence of significant politically organized civilian support or opposition further underscores the military nature of the regime.

This unusually militarized government has embarked on a thoroughgoing reform of Peruvian society. The government's basic hypothesis is that Peru's global security requires more balanced social and economic development, and that this can only be obtained at present through authoritarian and nationalist policies.[18] Although government programs are generally moderate in application, and most officers personally conservative, their "revolutionary" rhetoric, their lack of personal ties to economic interest groups and their sense of anger at Peru's traditional social and political leaders, give the regime a radical tone. Wide-ranging agrarian reform and social mobilization programs have combined with an expanding government role in the economy, particularly in banking and in basic industries such as mining and petroleum, to give Peruvian policies a strong statist flavor, despite the continued presence of a large private sector. Sensitivity to criticism has led at times to the intimidation of the private sector, and, more particularly, of the press.

Military pragmatism

The first year after the coup of October 3, 1968, may be characterized as a period in which Peru's military leaders consolidated their power and shed some of their illusions about the world around them. In particular, they began to realize that the United States was not likely to be as hostile as many had predicted, and that some of their internal enemies and allies were weaker than they had expected. These realizations came slowly and are still by no means complete, but they have led military leaders to discard some of the theoretical baggage with which they came to power. During the second year of the revolution, military leaders, freed from their fear of confrontations, gained self-knowledge and began to realize their own limits. Whereas previously they had felt that their technical competence and discipline would suffice to set the country right, they began to learn the limits of the possible, and to be aware of their need for civilian allies and technicians.

The greatest virtue of the Peruvian military is that they have capable leaders who are committed to action. Intelligence and the resolve to act have enabled military leaders to overcome much of their previous inexperience and many of their preconceptions, but without abandoning their original objectives. In the investment sphere, for example, General Fernandez Baca, the very able president of Petro Peru, the national oil company, quickly learned that the issue is not so much whether to accept foreign capital, but rather under what conditions to seek and control it. As a result of increased self-confidence, institutional changes and a system of limited-duration contracts and shared production, foreign petroleum companies have been converted in the space of three years from potential enemies of the state into instruments of Peruvian development. A similar evolution is beginning with regard to the "industrial communities," which seek to give workers a share of both profits and management: government leaders are willing to minimize the fears of entrepreneurs by modifying implementing regulations, but they are not prepared to surrender the essential principle of increased worker participation and responsibility.

Throughout, the military government has shown considerable flexibility and a capacity to learn from its mistakes. But mistakes there have been, and before turning to the present and potential future of the Peruvian "Revolution of the Armed Forces," it is necessary to consider the internal political processes of the military government.

Internal regime politics

The absence of a strong civilian political class and restrictions on freedom of the press have caused public criticism to be muted—except for occasional student-led outbursts. They have also channeled political debates largely within the military "family," where the major actors are the army officer corps, air force and navy commanders and secondarily, the military staffs, particularly the Joint Chiefs *(comando conjunto)* and the National War College (CAEM), which has the explicit mission of analyzing government policies as part of its elaboration of national security doctrine.

Sentiments expressed within the military act as a major constraint on the government, because the generals in power are responsible to the military institutions. This dependence of the government on the military institutions rests formally on the need for the endorsement of legislation by the commanding generals of the three services, and informally on the role of the officer corps as the primary source of governing personnel and political support. Under the leadership of General Graham Hurtado, the Council of Presidential Advisors (COAP) plays a key role in coordinating government policies and ensuring support for them.

There are several sources of potential discontent within the military. Personnel policies and pay differentials between officers in line assignments and officers in government jobs create a potential for unrest that is occasionally heightened by personal rivalries. Communications between officers in government posts and those remaining "in the barracks" are often sporadic or incomplete, and contribute to a tendency for "second-guessing" government policies by officers not responsible for their execution. Many officers have essentially middle-class life-styles and outlooks, if not social origins, and they tend to be suspicious of government policies criticized as "radical" in middle-class circles. Normal political differences within the military are played upon by civilian politicians and other social groups within Peru who see themselves threatened by government policies, or who seek special favors.

These vague tensions are frequently crystallized in the minds of military traditionalists by the fear that the total commitment of the military institutions to government since 1968 may damage the military institutions themselves, by provoking internal dissensions or by weakening the public standing of the military profession. The revolutionary statute sets harmony and national unity among Peruvians as a major government goal. Unrest, for whatever cause, is thus a sign of failure to accomplish a revolutionary goal, and thus it becomes a cause for pressure on the government.

The potential significance of these internal military tensions is difficult to gauge. The unexpected illness of President Velasco in February 1973 revealed some internal differences, but these were impressively overcome by an acceptance of internal debate and diversity. Given the lack of civilian political leaders capable of organizing an effective alternative government, neither the current rulers nor their internal military critics see much prospect for a return to civilian rule. For the foreseeable future, therefore, political instability or shifts in government policy are likely to result only from changes in the ruling military coalition. The question about political change in Peru, therefore, given the absence of a viable civilian alternative, is not whether the military will stay in power, but how well it performs, and what specific policies it adopts to implement its general goals of restructuring Peruvian society—which is the subject of the next section.

Peru After Five Years of Military Rule

Conflicts among government goals

The major policy goals of the Peruvian government may be summed up as: increased control over Peru's national destiny, structural change and income redistribution to foster social development, and economic growth. Programs have been adopted to further each of these goals. Characteristically, however, the goals and therefore the programs are sometimes in conflict.

The assertion of "national sovereignty" contributed greatly to the 1968–1969 seizure of the International Petroleum Company. The same objective is reflected in the search for new formulas for the import of foreign capital and technology in ways that are both less costly economically and less damaging to Peruvian concepts of sovereignty.

The goal of structural change and income redistribution led to agrarian reform and to the formation of worker-management "communities" that have been decreed into existence—often without a significant prior preparation—in most of the modern industrial sector. Similar profit-sharing arrangements in the coastal sugar cooperatives and in the fishing and mining industries combine with price controls to demonstrate the government's interest in giving the working classes a "stake in the system."

The outcome of these initiatives clearly depends heavily on the state of Peru's economy, which is generally good, but which includes some major uncertainties. Exports are more diversified than those of most Latin American countries, and prices have been good, offsetting a decline in fishmeal production due to an apparently cyclical disappearance of the anchovy. Prudent management, successful rescheduling of Peru's relatively moderate debt load and repatriation of capital have led to substantial foreign exchange reserves ($380 million in January 1973). Per capita GNP has grown at an annual rate of about 3 percent since 1970 (about double the rate for the last two years of the Belaúnde regime and the first year of the revolution). Gross National Product showed a real increase of 5.8 percent in 1972, and prospects are at least as good for 1973. Inflation has been kept within reasonable limits. Government fiscal and monetary policies have been conservative, and have received good marks from the IMF, IBRD and the CIAP, whose June 1972 report also criticized the slowness of multilateral financing of Peruvian projects.

Unfortunately for the regime, the emphasis on nationalism and social change have tended to slow down private investment activity. Initially, the government concentrated on reforms which did not require immediate capital outlays. Now, however, the short-term need is for a positive investment climate. The Finance Minister, General Morales Bermúdez, the Director of the National Planning Institute, General Marcó del Pont, and the Minister of Industries, Admiral Jiménez de Lucio, are all respected for their moderation and seriousness. Private investment rose some 8 percent in 1972, while government investment rose by nearly 25 percent. But Peru's ambitious national development plan also requires substantial foreign investments, both public and private, if it is to meet its economic growth goals.[19] Despite recent investment of almost $100 million by U.S. oil companies, an apparent Japanese commitment to finance a $330 million pipeline, and projected investments by European and Japanese sources of roughly another $300 million, chiefly in mining, and despite generally optimistic 1972 and 1973 meetings in Paris of the Consultative Group for Peru, much of the development plan remains unfinanced.

Uncertainties are not restricted to the foreign sector alone. The government's ambitious plans are placing a great strain on the Peruvian civil service. The public bureaucracy is already upset by administrative reforms and jurisdictional confusion; its limited technical competence is likely to weaken the implementation of the projected heavy expansion in public investment. In the private sector, although 1971 and 1972 saw increased domestic reinvestment, many Peruvian businessmen remain skeptical and ambiguous in their plans.

If the government fails to mobilize increased domestic and foreign private investment and obtain at least some external public financing, it will face major political and economic problems. Peru's middle and professional classes are strongly oriented toward the urban areas and can translate their high consumption requirements into strong political pressures. A level of financing below the ambitious amounts envisioned in the Development Plan could force upon the government an unpalatable choice between abandoning its distributive goals in an effort to improve the climate for investment, or attempting to further expand the public sector in an effort to make up shortages of private capital with public investment.

The conflict among advocates of growth and distribution is not likely to be resolved easily. Should economic conditions deteriorate, the regime's internal cohesion could be affected enough to limit its governing effectiveness. Because Japanese and European investors and many U.S. banks and oil companies seem to consider Peru creditworthy, and have continued or resumed investments, there can be little doubt that generalized unavailability of Export-Import Bank financing and multilateral credits will produce sharp criticism of U.S. policies and lead many to hold the United States at least partially responsible for the difficulties involved.

Government planners have told the author privately that they are prepared to accept a halving of their projected growth rates rather than risk the regime's first goal—national control, symbolized by the nearly unanimous domestic support for the 1968 seizure of the International Petroleum Company. Despite the pragmatism of military leaders on most other issues, settlement with IPC is ruled out by ineradicable anger at the colonial past: as the collapse of the secret multiparty negotiations in April 1972 and the exclusion of the IPC issue from the bilateral U.S.-Peruvian negotiations begun in August 1973 strongly imply, the Velasco government is as unlikely to be swayed by blandishments as by pressure. It is an ironic truth that Peru will be more likely to give good terms to private capital if Peru triumphs on the IPC question. As occurred in Mexico after the crises of the 1930s, the capacity to successfully confront a major international giant contributes to confidence that new contracts need not damage national sovereignty. The Peruvian government may need foreign investment for economic reasons, but not as much as it needs IPC for political and psychological reasons.

Future prospects

Since 1972 there have been periods of noticeable unrest within the population, which is beset by food shortages and uncertainty provoked by the government's many reforms and compounded by covert censorship of the media, which often hinders an accurate expression of views. The leading group, the military officer corps, and within it the government leaders, sometimes seems worried over the breadth of problems unleashed by its very activism, and uncertain as to whether it will find the creativity necessary to overcome them. Despite the government's deep commitment to nonviolence, the potential for repressing its critics—at least in the form of muzzling the press and intervening in universities—remains a source of concern.

Over the next two or three years, however, there seems little likelihood of an effective political alternative to the current government. In the longer run, alternatives will depend largely on whether government policies are successful or whether they lead to economic stagnation and general deterioration in the conditions of life. If the government is successful, military rule can be expected to last at least until the late seventies, giving way to some form of corporate political regime with electoral support. In the unlikely event that the situation were to deteriorate badly, opposition within the officer corps could conceivably lead to a precipitous military "withdrawal" through elections as occurred in Argentina in 1973.

The political consequences of any military retreat from power are as difficult to gauge as it is unlikely. The Aprista Party is not capable of providing more than verbal opposition, and the government's cooption of some of its previous leadership through government jobs and elections in the sugar cooperatives further limits its potential for opposition. Were elections to be held, one potential outcome would be a victory for the civilian radicals (including many ex-Apristas) currently organizing the "popular mobilization" system (SINAMOS), but presently counterbalanced within SINAMOS by military zone commanders. But Peru's political parties, including APRA, are probably too weak to carry out an effective campaign without extensive time, and even SINAMOS would be unable to become an official government party soon. If a prolonged crisis took place, therefore, an outcome more likely than elections would be a strong radicalization of internal policies under a dictatorship that would repress internal demand—precisely what the current government seeks to avoid.

Future oil and copper revenues may be the regime's ace in the hole. The rapid development of these reserves, by the late 1970s, could enable Peru to finance significant development activity without either foreign aid or forced internal savings. But their development would require in the short run either foreign exchange or a greater internal economic mobilization than anything yet attempted. As of mid-1973, it appeared that foreign private investors, aware that Peru's new "rules of the game" were stable, if not always palatable, were once again prepared to invest. But should new initiatives not coincide with Peruvian priorities, or if the financing does not materialize as expected the lure of future profits and the needs of development increase the likelihood that the Peruvian government itself will adopt stringent self-help measures limiting consumption and perhaps strengthening tendencies toward authoritarian economic statism.

Peru's leaders are thus increasingly aware that they have started a complicated process that will continue to generate new problems as it develops. Because the leadership is military, and hence both activist and pragmatic, there is little ritualized ideological thinking. Because Peru's "national revolution" is still recent, there is little uncertainty and general tiredness. Military support is a source of strength as well as a constraint, and the Peruvian government can still draw upon the support of the Catholic Church and most intellectuals, and it is not blocked by organized political parties or trade unions. Nor is political stability threatened by large unincorporated but demanding political masses. Most military leaders feel the relatively low level of popular consciousness is likely to provide the government more time than one might suspect to work out its problems. Indeed, SINAMOS, the "system for national support for popular mobilization," may help to buy time, whether by channeling support toward the government and ultimately providing a civilian apparatus that could help the military to withdraw from direct rule, or simply by acting as a lightning rod for criticism.

Peru "represents the ultimate social paradox: an authoritarian government which claims to be building a participatory social system." [20] But it is not likely to be the last such challenge to the views we have traditionally taken of Latin America. The current Latin American context is one of increasing economic and political experimentation by governments operating within a nationalist framework and seeking to redefine international as well as domestic relationships. Peru's military leaders are at the forefront of changing military perspectives that have already affected developments in Panama, Ecuador and Bolivia, and have considerable influence in Brazil, Argentina and Venezuela. The recent reorientation of church as well as military roles suggests that change in Latin America has profound roots, and is finding institutional expressions that guarantee permanence as well as continued conflict.[21] Peru is both unique and successful, but it is not alone.

Revolution in Latin America in Light of the Peruvian Experience

The military government that has ruled Peru since October 1968 has clearly unleashed a process that is reshaping Peruvian society. Whether this process is called a "revolution" or not is, of course, largely a matter of perspective. For some, no process that is essentially nonviolent, or that leaves many traditional institutions formally intact, or that is led by military forces, or that is not led by a Communist Party, can be called a revolution. And it is difficult to quarrel with such viewpoints, because the Peruvian government is led by the military, has avoided political repression, is willing to accept the Catholic Church and to defend private property, and has only the support, not the leadership, of the Communist Party.

But the real point is that, while revolution can be *defined* in many ways, it is important not to lose sight of the social and political reality with which words are meant to deal. And the process under way in Peru today is clearly unprecedented. Parliament may return; some future government may decide to pay Standard Oil an indemnity for the Talara Oil Fields formerly operated by the IPC and now administered by Petro Peru; some of the military ministers who have fought corruption may succumb to the temptations of power.

Yet should all this happen, Peru will still have changed in ways this writer considers decisive. The government has gone well beyond attempts that tinker with the status quo so as to "modernize" it or otherwise render it less objectionable. The agrarian reform begun in 1969 with the cooperativization of the productive coastal estates and the passage of the water rights law, and the subjection of new investment to the establishment of Worker's Communities *(comunidades laborales)* for profit-sharing under the terms of the new industrial, fishing and mining laws, are acts whose impact is more than legal.[22] They affect the fabric of Peruvian life in ways that cannot be reversed by changes in government or by new laws.

It is not yet entirely clear precisely what that impact will be. It is also difficult, therefore, to identify who will be favored most by the process underway. If the middle classes and the foreign investors can take heart in the thought that the government does not in principle oppose the idea of private profit or property, the lower classes can also take heart in the government's willingness to recognize violent seizures of public lands for the purposes of private home construction by the landless poor and in the government's attempt to limit profits and ensure their equitable distribution.

Let us suppose, however, that much will go wrong, and also that some social sectors will profit considerably more than others in the changes under way. Let us even suppose that the one third of Peru that is Indian in culture and life-styles profits least from what is now happening. Should we then argue that this is no revolution, or that this is just another military dictatorship to be opposed by all progressive and civilized people?

Three major points should be borne in mind while seeking the answer to this question:

1. What has already been done, under present historical circumstances, is a great deal for Peru. Peru has not only one third of its population unable to speak Spanish (and thus not easily mobilizable for national political—even revolutionary—purposes), but it also has twice the population spread over ten times the territory with one fifth the television sets per capita that Cuba has. Revolution in Peru, Cuban-style, would seem difficult even if a charismatic leader and an obligingly terrifying (and foolish) foreign enemy could be found.

2. The changes that have taken place in Peru have come from within the system, not from outside it. Since the Cuban revolution, and especially since the rise of guerrilla movements, much attention has been focused on "outside strategies" of change. Little hope was expressed for political leaders following "inside

strategies" of change—that is, utilizing traditional institutions, like the military or the church, for innovative political ends.

3. We should not, however, assume, because of the relative success of the Peruvian military and the relative failure of Ché Guevara, that inside strategies will automatically work where outside strategies have failed, or, alternatively, that the military have in the current decade become an inevitable force for progress. In the first place, the limits set by bureaucracy, internal divisions and resource scarcity may in the long run produce a conservative reaction within the military even in Peru, where the process of military reorientation toward structural change has gone very far.[23] And finally, as our Peruvian case study has also made clear, those military intellectuals who argued for the "inside strategy" and for revolution from within, gained their audience among their fellow officers and comrades at arms not just because they were working within an institution with a highly developed educational system, but also because young civilian students and intellectuals gave their lives in following an outside strategy, and with their sacrifice gave the "insiders" a chance to make their views felt.

NOTES

1. Military politics in Peru has been one of the author's primary intellectual concerns for some years, leading most recently to the Peruvian section of *Latin American Institutional Development: Changing Military Perspectives in Peru and Brazil* (R-586, The Rand Corporation, 1971), written with Alfred C. Stepan III. The discussion in this section is largely drawn from that document, particularly pp. 16–31.

2. A readily available (but sketchy) summary of the structure and function of military educational institutions, emphasizing the role of General José del Carmen Marín in the founding of CAEM, will be found in Luis Valdez Pallete, "Antecedentes de la nueva orientación de las Fuerzas Armadas en el Perú," *Aportes*, no. 19 (January 1971).

3. William F. Whyte and Graciela Flores, *Los Valores y el Crecimiento Económico en el Perú* (Lima: SENATI, 1963).

4. This paragraph, like the preceding one, is partially based on an interview with General Augusto Freyre García, Director of National Strategy and Special Studies at the CAEM.

5. Victor Villaneuva gives the complete text in the Appendix to the 1956 Peruvian edition of his classic *La Tragedia de un Pueblo y un Partido*.

6. As the president put it in a speech in Trujillo, October 11, 1969: "We are not politicians, professional or otherwise. We are soldiers and we are revolutionaries." (Version issued by the Oficina Nacional de Información, Lima, n.d., p. 36.)

7. CAEM, *El Estado y la Política General* (Chorrillos, 1963), p. 89. Emphasis added.

8. Ibid., p. 92.

9. The official account of the campaign is in *Las guerrillas en el Perú y su represión* (The Guerrillas in Peru and Their Repression), published by the Peruvian Ministry of War, Lima, 1966. See also Hector Béjar Riveria, *Perú 1965: Apuntes sobre una experiencia guerrillera* (Havana: Casa de las Americas, 1969), for an intelligent analysis by one of the few surviving leaders, who was captured and then freed by the junta, and appointed to a post in SINAMOS (see chapter 16 of this volume).

10. *Las guerillas en el Perú y su represión*, p. 80.

11. General de Brigada E. P. Edgardo Mercado Jarrín, "Política y Estrategia Militar en la Guerra Anti-Subversiva," *Revista Militar del Perú*, Chorrillos, (November-December 1967): 4–33. An English-language summary of this article, "Insurgency in Latin America—Its Impact on Political and Military Strategy," by General Edgardo Mercado Jarrín, Peruvian Army, appeared in the *Military Review* (March 1969): 10–20.

12. See the discussion in Luigi Einaudi, Richard Maullin, Alfred Stepan, and Michael Fleet, *Latin American Institutional Development: The Changing Catholic Church,* (The Rand Corporation, RM-6136-DOS, October 1969), especially pp. 51–55.

13. In a speech given at Talara, October 9, 1969, commemorating the takeover of the International Petroleum Company. *Mensaje a la nación dirigido por el Señor General de División Presidente de la República, desde Talara, en el primer aniversario del día de la dignidad nacional* (Lima: Oficina Nacional de Información, 1969), p. 7.

14. Richard Goodwin described the intricate historical and legal background of the *La Brea y Pariñas* deposits, and the incredible ineptitude that marked the company's

and Belaúnde's dealings with each other in his "Letter from Peru," *The New Yorker,* May 17, 1969.

15. Lima, August 29, 1968.

16. General Arturo Cavero Calixto, "Threats to the National Security of Peru and Their Implications for Hemispheric Security," a lecture delivered in Chorrillos at CAEM in April 1970.

17. See Luigi R. Einaudi, "Peruvian Military Relations with the United States," in *U.S. Foreign Policy and Peru,* ed. Daniel Sharp (Austin: University of Texas Press, 1972), pp. 15–56.

18. A very useful 14-page pamphlet on government objectives and programs was released in English by the CAEM in June 1972. Republica Peruana, Comando Conjunto de la Fuerza Armada, Centro de Altos Estudios Militares, *Today's Peru* (Chorrillos, 1972).

19. See Robert E. Klitgaard, "Observations on the Peruvian National Plan for Development, 1971–1975," *Inter-American Economic Affairs* 25, no. 3 (Winter 1971): 3–22.

20. William F. Whyte, personal communication, 1972.

21. See, in this context, Luigi R. Einaudi, *Beyond Cuba: Latin America Takes Charge of Its Future* (New York, Crane, Russak, 1973).

22. The purposes of these and other laws are detailed by the Chief of the Presidential Advisory Committee (COAP), General de Brigada E. P. José Graham Hurtado, in his *Filosofía de la Revolución Peruana* (Lima: Oficina Nacional de Información, 14 de Abril de 1971).

23. This is essentially the limiting argument I present in "The Military and Progress in the Third World," *Foreign Service Journal* (February 1971).

David Scott Palmer
and
Kevin Jay Middlebrook

16.   Corporatist Participation under Military Rule in Peru *

Since the October 3, 1968 coup d'état which overthrew President Fernando Belaúnde Terry's constitutional government, Peru's military regime has significantly altered the conventional image of the Latin American military, by pursuing a vigorous policy of socioeconomic reform.[1] What soon became apparent following the 1968 coup was the military's unwillingness to withdraw from active politics without achieving certain basic reforms. Rather than merely exercising a veto over political developments, the Peruvian armed forces now see themselves as the long-term initiators and managers of socioeconomic change. The self-titled Revolutionary Military Government, headed by General Juan Velasco Alvarado, has nationalized several foreign property holdings, revised the acceptable conditions for foreign investments, implemented an agrarian reform program at the expense of the landed elite, and stimulated an increase in the social property**sector of the economy through reforms in fishing, manufacturing and mining.

* The financial support of the Latin American Teaching Fellowship, Fletcher School of Law and Diplomacy, and the Latin American Studies Program, Cornell University made possible the field research in Peru on which this essay is based. The authors are grateful to Jorge Domínguez and Samuel Huntington of Harvard University and Christian P. Potholm of Bowdoin College for their careful reading of and comments on an earlier draft.

** The basic principle underlying the concept of social property in the fishing, manufacturing and mining sectors of Peru is the construction of institutions in which labor and capital are treated as imputs of equal weight in the enterprise.

The military reformers also see themselves as political organizers working toward the creation of what they call a "social democracy of full participation." [2] Most of the abundant literature on military governments emphasize the military's hesitancy with regard to political organization and assumes a fundamental incompatibility between political participation by the citizenry—understood as the presence of institutionalized opportunities to influence the decision-making process—and direct political control by the military.[3] Thus the novelty of the Peruvian case is twofold: not only is the Peruvian military government playing the role of political organizer, but it is also attempting to institutionalize citizen participation along lines compatible with its Hispanic tradition, rather than with Western democracy.*

This chapter focuses on initiatives regarding participation within the military's agrarian reform policy. Not only was the June 24, 1969 agrarian reform law the Revolutionary Military Government's first major step regarding participation, but it also represents, in theory at least, the one policy designed specifically to incorporate the population's most marginal sectors into the national system. After outlining the basic tenets of the present military government's ideology of participation, the major policy initiatives in this area to date, and the analytical model of participation which they appear to suggest, we shall turn to the presentation and evaluation of a number of case studies within the agricultural sector.

The Ideology of Participation

During the Velasco government's first year in power, the military establishment was concerned principally with constructing a working alliance among the various internal factions of the military and stimulating an affective bond between the military elite and the

---

* The term "Western democracy" refers here to the institutional framework of political parties and pressure groups as interest aggregation and interest articulation structures, respectively, along with a national legislature of popularly elected representatives from these parties. Organized opposition is legitimate, and alternation of different parties in power is routinized. The term "Hispanic tradition" refers to the structural and cultural inheritance of Spanish and Portuguese colonial rule.

general population. Julio Cotler has labeled this latter process "military populism";[4] that is, an attempt to break down old institutional loyalties to party and union and to stimulate loyalty to the military government, through a number of noninstitutional mechanisms. The extraordinary expropriation of the International Petroleum Company, a long-disputed and highly nationalistic issue, the barrage of speeches by the president and ministers in all parts of the country and the weekly food handouts in Greater Lima's squatter settlements, are examples of such mechanisms.

Only after a large number of more or less spontaneous organizational efforts from below (called "Committees for the Defense of the Revolution")[5] threatened to get beyond the military's direct control, did the Velasco government attempt to institutionalize from above the citizen's relationship to the national political system. Starting in April 1970,[6] ideological formulations concerning this relationship began to be articulated. Two major expressions of this ideology may be found in President Velasco's speech to the Ministerial Meeting of the Developing Nations, held in Lima in October 1971, and the National Development Plan published in July 1971.

> Our position is defined in terms of a revolutionary humanism.... This position picks up the best of the legacies of the Christian, libertarian, and socialist traditions ... [and] represents the confluence of the most illustrious streams of revolutionary thought of our own historic tradition. It constitutes the basis for a new socio-political conceptualization in Peru ... which has as its object the construction of a fully participatory social democracy ... a system based on a moral order of solidarity, not individualism.... [In such a system] the means of production are predominantly social property, under the direct control of those who generate the wealth from their work. [Within the] political order [of such a system] the power of decision ... is diffuse and rests essentially in social, economic, and political institutions which are conducted by the men and women who make them up, with a minimum of intermediaries, or with no intermediaries whatsoever....[7]

The National Development Plan spells out the way in which these objectives, as articulated by President Velasco, will be implemented. "Social Mobilization" is defined as "the process by which the emerging groups come to exercise a basic or structural participation by gaining access to the control of the society's key resources. [These key resources] are basically the ownership of the means of production and the making of the central decisions which affect the most important aspects of society as a whole." The Plan goes on to note the responsibility of the state to "stimulate, channel, and consolidate" the participation of the people, reasoning that "[our] people are relatively untrained and incapable of assuming fully and in the short run [their] responsibilities [under the present dynamic of change]." [8]

The Plan emphasizes that Social Mobilization, as an instrument of policy, prevents conservative elements from working to maintain their dominant position; furthermore, it excludes those elements which "would pretend to introduce ideologies foreign to the essence of the Peruvian Revolution." [9] The Plan goes on to argue that the failure to pursue this policy in the face of rapid changes in the population's aspiration levels, as well as demographic pressures, would bring about a social dynamic which would jeopardize the continued existence of the state.

According to the Plan, organization is the central objective of the Social Mobilization policy. Officials will work with such local units of participation as cooperatives, peasant communities and neighborhood organizations. The Plan argues, however, that it will not be sufficient to emphasize organization only at the local level.

> This organization ... must be shaped into horizontal and vertical nets of integration ... [in order to take] the decisive step for the construction of a society of solidarity. ... This organization provides the bases for effective participation ... and a rational structure of communication with the Government assists the process. ... But special mechanisms will be needed to promote the direct and effective participation of the population in the process of decision-making and the carrying out of programs and projects of development. These go along with the formal instruments to be established at the level of administrative regions and municipal organization. This refers specifically to the organization of the bases of a system of interaction, consultation, and joint programming among the development services and the organized population. [10]

This system is to be built from the base up to the regional level, at which point "it will be made compatible with the objectives and goals formulated at the national level." [11]

The ideology of Peru's Revolutionary Military Government recognizes the crucial definition of political participation: the need for the citizenry to control the making of key decisions which affect society as a whole. Furthermore, the ideology asserts that this participation is to be achieved within Peruvian Hispanic traditions. The central government's control of the entire process is stressed on the grounds of internal security, and justified as compatible with the historical tradition of the Spanish world. In terms of implementing this ideology, government agency rather than political party becomes the means of transmission for the expression and resolution of citizen concerns. All local units of participation—even those the government is not anxious to encourage, such as unions and the "Committees for the Defense of the Revolution"—are included, in order to insure control.

However, ultimate authority remains outside the control of these functionally organized units. They increasingly participate in the decision-implementing process at the local and regional levels, but always in concordance with government officials at that same level. Basic policies continue to be determined by the governing apparatus at the center, and all actions at the local or regional levels must be taken as a function of those decisions. This tension between the ideological commitment to full citizen participation and the felt need to control each aspect of participation from the center is the major paradox in the Revolutionary Military Government's ideology of political participation.

The Practice of Participation

During the first four years under Peru's Revolutionary Military Government, the ideology of participation and the emphasis on the accompanying "revolutionary mystique" have been complemented by a number of efforts to create or to stimulate participatory institutions.

The agrarian reform law of June 1969 * reaffirmed the Belaúnde

---

* Decree-Law #17716, June 24, 1969. Under the provisions of this law it is estimated that 24,822 farms encompassing 11,387,000 hectares (1 hectare = 2.5 acres) and benefiting 242,088 families. Ministerio de Agicultura, Oficina Sectorial de Planificación Agraria, *Resumen del Plan Agropecuario a Mediano Plazo, 1971-1975,* Tomo 1, October 1970, Lima, pp. 89-99. This report estimates that there are about 1.1 million farm families in Peru, and that about 700,000 families need additional land to move above a subsistence existence.

government's emphasis on cooperatives and strengthened it in a number of ways. Even though the Velasco government did not initially emphasize these collective forms of property ownership, the agrarian reform law names the cooperative as the preferred form of land ownership for reform beneficiaries. Land formerly worked for the owner is now to be worked cooperatively, and decisions regarding land use and the distribution of agricultural products are to be made by the cooperative's governing institutions. Under the Peasant Communities Statute of February 1970, the cooperative concept is extended to recognized peasant communities. All pasture land and much cultivated land are to be held cooperatively if they are not so owned already. The law itself gives a clear preference to cooperatives for the form of adjudication and for the allotment of farm credits.* Here, too, decisions regarding land use are to be made by the governing administrative council.

Between July and September 1970, the Industrial Community concept was implemented into law. Under the Community plan, an enterprise's workers share equal control with those who provide investment capital. Workers elect representatives to the Board of Directors (comprising up to 50 percent of the Board) in proportion to the ownership in the enterprise which the Industrial Community has purchased through its 15 percent share of annual profits.[12] Workers also receive individually an additional 10 percent of net profits.[13] This plan, initially applicable to enterprises employing six or more workers in the manufacturing sector, was later applied to the fishing and mining sectors as well.[14] However, the proportion of annual profits allocated toward the purchase of ownership for the Community was lower than in the manufacturing sector, 12 percent and 6 percent, respectively. Direct local control over decisions was diluted by the addition of a superordinate coordinating entity for the channeling of profits among the Communities in each functional sector.**

* Contrary to the popular belief that communal property predominates in Peru's estimated 5,600 peasant communities (of which 2,377 are recognized officially by the government), only about 600 of these communities considered that their lands were predominantly communal, according to the 1961 Census.

** In May, 1973 the government expropriated the fishmeal industry (Decree-Law # 20000, May 7, 1973), thereby nullifying the provisions of the Fishing Community Statute. The Community concept outlined above does not apply to state enterprises under the debatable argument that such companies are in the public domain.

In June 1971, the "National System of Support for Social Mobilization" (SINAMOS) was established by government decree. Implementing legislation was delayed until April 1972, largely because of strong differences among military factions over the role which this agency should play. SINAMOS's main purpose is to provide official coordination, stimulation and channeling for all initiatives relating to citizen participation. The organization includes a number of previously functioning government agencies whose responsibilities related to participation in one way or another: the "Young Towns" Development Office, the National Development Fund, the National Cooperative and National Community Development Offices, the Peasant Communities and Peasant Organizations Offices and the Community and Agrarian Reform Promotion Offices. Total personnel numbered approximately 4,500, and the 1971-1972 budget amounted to about $92,000,000. It functions, in theory at least, as an intragovernmental "transmission belt" institution for citizen concerns, bypassing the ministerial bureaucracies. The body also operates as a "participation promotion" entity.

SINAMOS is directly tied to the Council of Ministers at the national level—the Director sits on the Council but has no vote—and has zonal (department level) and regional (province level) units which enjoy some degree of autonomy within national guidelines to adapt policies regarding participation to local realities. Opportunities are provided at the regional level for the inclusion of local participation units' citizen representatives on a consultative basis. Resources for the stimulation of citizen participation under SINAMOS's aegis are to be dramatically increased in 1973-1974.* However, because an extra layer of bureaucracy was added without increasing budgets, the short-run impact through 1972 was actually to reduce funds available for infrastructure projects at the local level.

In May 1972, the National Agrarian Society (SNA), an old-line organization dominated by large farming interests, was abolished on the grounds that it did not fully represent agricultural interests. The National Agrarian Confederation (CNA) was established in its place,

* According to Iván Pardo F., Director of SINAMOS's Peasant Organizations group for the Lima-Ica Zone, the number of anthropologists with "contact point" field responsibilities is to increase from the 20 now employed in this office to over 200.

as the one legitimate organ of expression for farm interests.[15] Political activity is not permitted within the CNA, although existing agrarian unions may join. Membership is open to individual owners as well as to members of cooperatives and communities. The legislation contains provisions for regional and zonal subunits. Elected local delegates choose representatives for each higher organizational level.

These developments represent the Revolutionary Military Government's major efforts to date to provide a new institutional framework for citizen participation. They are characterized thus far by an emphasis on functionally organized, all-inclusive local organizations of participation. The mechanisms through which citizen concerns might influence decisions at the center have not been clearly defined. Emphasis has been on official sponsorship of all initiatives regarding participation on the grounds that anything else is "chaotic" and subject to "manipulation." [16] In terms of allocated resources and expressed concern, stress has been placed on the most mobilized areas. This is in part due to the need to react to periodic crises provoked by the most mobilized sectors in reaction to the insistence on central control, and the large number of restrictions implicit in such insistence.

A Corporatist Model of Political Participation

The formula for the citizen's relationship to the political system outlined in ideology and in practice by the Revolutionary Military Government may be conceptualized as a corporatist model of political participation.[17] Actions taken to date represent an attempt to construct the participatory mechanisms which will form the base of a larger corporatist model.

The model involves a highly centralized, hierarchical decision-making process, dominated by top-down government initiative, in which the ruling elite directs the political process through a chain of vertically aligned government agencies. In the model's ideal form, popular pressures are channeled through the ministries' local "contact points" to affect the governing elite indirectly. "Local participation units" organized by functional area serve as the mechanism by which local problems are resolved and demands on the governmental hierarchy are articulated. In short, the central government's control is both direct and pervasive; citizen influence is localized and indirect.

PALMER, MIDDLEBROOK

The theory of corporatist participation internalizes the entire political process in the governmental structure. The governing elite's ability to make rational decisions on the basis of sufficient information thus presumes near-perfect receptivity by the governmental "contact points" in touch with the participation units. Also assumed is the government's ability to provide sufficient demand satisfaction so as to eliminate the need for demand articulation through mechanisms external to the operation of the model itself. These "escape mechanisms," such as land invasions, strikes, marches, violence and the like, allow popular pressures to bypass the administrative hierarchy and to affect the governing elite directly.

The corporatist model of political participation is rooted in the Iberic-Latin culture's concept of the organic state, which has been described as "a hierarchically and vertically-segmented structure of class and caste stratifications, social rank orders, functional corporations, estates, juridical groupings and *intereses*, all fairly well-defined in law and in terms of their respective stations in life, a rigid yet infinitely adaptable scheme whose component parts are tied to and derive legitimacy from the authority of the central state or its leader." [18] This system of licensed, structured participation effects limited change through the incorporation of emerging social and political forces into the local participation unit structure. The corporatist framework thus serves the interests of the ruling elite by subordinating rising social forces to the authority of the elite-dominated state apparatus.

This model follows closely the developmental model of the Hispanic tradition.*

Beginning in the mid-to-late 19th century there began to be articulated in the Iberic-Latin nations a developmental ideology of their own, uniquely attuned to their own tradition, which was positive and progressive and which serves as the Iberic-Latin counterpart to the modernizing ideologies evolved elsewhere. . . . The Iberic-Latin writers built upon the newer and

---

* This developmentalist ideology has been implemented in whole or in part in Italy from 1922 until World War II, in Spain since 1938, in Argentina under Juan Perón, and in Brazil under Getulio Vargas. While "Hispanic corporatism" shares obvious structural parallels with "corporatist fascism," the Hispanic model does not include fascism's more virulent ideological components, such as ethnic superiority, a territorial imperative, and a continually utilized, massive repressive apparatus. The repressive capability of an authoritarian government is, of course, much greater than under a nonauthoritarian alternative. The specific case of Peru, under a military government, is no exception.

reformist currents emanating from the Church and also drew upon their own considerable historical tradition. Still within the corporate-organic mold, they sought to fashion a framework for thought and action which blended the traditional regard for order and hierarchy with the newer imperative of change and modernization. They attempted, for instance, to deal with the new phenomenon of mass man through the erection of corporate structures that would provide for class harmony rather than conflict, togetherness and structured participation rather than rootlessness and alienation. Representation was generally to be determined by functions (labor, business, agriculture, religion, etc.) rather than through divisive interest groups and political parties. The state was to regulate, oversee, and harmonize the entire process. In this way the articulators of the new Iberic-Latin development ethic sought to face up to the realities of the modern era without sacrificing the organic corporate structures of the past.[19]

The corporatist model indicates the lines along which the Peruvian military seeks to organize popular political participation. In practice, however, the corporatist model is still largely an objective rather than an accomplished reality. "Escape mechanisms" persist at the present time, reflecting the continued existence of political parties, pressure groups and social forces mobilized prior to the assumption of political power by the present military government. Their presence, like the government's use of repressive tactics or its "populist" solicitation of support through noninstitutionalized mechanisms, indicates how incompletely developed the corporatist model is, at the present time.

The popular base presently remains largely undifferentiated as the local participation units begin to appear.[20] Intersectoral political organizations such as unions persist. Unsatisfied demands cause popular sectors to express their interests through mechanisms external to the corporatist system, resulting in sporadic bottom-up initiative and an intermittent upward information flow. The imperfect receptivity of the governmental "contact points" further limits the central government's ability to consider local problems accurately. The governmental elite is, therefore, less likely to make rational policy decisions which accord with external reality. Decision-making often occurs through gross reorientation as feedback comes largely from dysfunctional outbursts, at times the result of government repression. Legislation thus often takes on a "tentative" quality, subject to adjustment in accordance with its implementation in concrete reality.

The Case Studies

Five case studies taken from the Velasco government's agrarian reform program present the corporatist model in the context of socioeconomic changes actually undertaken by the regime in the agricultural sector. The cases range from highly mobilized, politicized coastal sugar cane haciendas to peasant communities in the Peruvian sierra which evidence a generally low level of social and political mobilization. Presented in the order of decreasing levels of social and political mobilization, the cases reflect the dynamics of the developing local participation units and their relationship to the national system.

On the coastal sugar cane plantations, the military's attempts to create worker cooperatives—the corporatist model's local participation units—have been motivated by a determination to maintain strict government control over the productive resources deemed crucial for national development. The military's reform initiative on the northern coast was also designed to undermine APRA,* Peru's most institutionalized mass-based political party. The well-organized labor unions on 10 of the 11 coastal sugar plantations had long constituted a key source of APRA strength. Local forces, including the APRA unions, have strenuously resisted this effort to restrict all political activity to the closely regulated interaction between these newly established participatory structures and corresponding governmental agency "contact points."

Because the regime's political and economic priorities have required the agrarian reform program to focus primarily on the most mobilized areas, most of the sierra, with lower levels of political mobilization and economic importance, has generally been neglected

---

* The Alianza Popular Revolucionaria Americana (APRA) founded in Peru in 1930 by Victor Raúl Haya de la Torre. The deep-seated animosity between APRA and the military stems from an abortive barracks revolt led by APRA forces in Trujillo in 1932, in which hundreds perished on either side. Between 1932 and 1948 there were at least six other major attempts by APRA to subvert elements of the armed forces in attempted coups. This suggests that military hostility toward APRA is based less on ideological grounds than on the real threat which the party represented to the institutional unity of the military establishment.

by the reform process. Established channels of political activity have been proscribed, but new participatory mechanisms have not replaced them effectively. These marginal sectors remain unincorporated into the national political system.

Tumán

Tumán is located near Chiclayo on Peru's northern coast. Its 5,500 hectares of sugar cane support 2,400 workers and a total of 12,500 inhabitants.[21] Tumán has long ranked as Peru's most productive sugar cane hacienda, and under the Pardo family its workers received more basic social services than were available on any of the other sugar estates. At the time of the agrarian reform Tumán was the only hacienda which lacked a labor union.

Tumán was among the first of the coastal "agro-industrial complexes" expropriated in the wake of the military's June 1969 agrarian reform. For the next 11 months the estate received high priority in the government's attempt to prepare the population for the formation of a worker cooperative. The National Office of Cooperative Development (ONDECOOP) took the lead in these efforts at worker socialization, emphasizing cooperative ownership and effective local control under the reform's "Land for the Tiller" theme. A military priest toured Tumán, stirring up the workers with radical rhetoric and urging the formation of a "Committee for the Defense of the Revolution." Twelve ONDECOOP officials and some 30 students conducted a broad series of classes explaining the agrarian reform and the theory of cooperative ownership.[22]

When technicians protested the proposed worker control and threatened to paralyze production by resigning en masse, the government was forced to impose restrictions on the coastal sugar cane haciendas. As a result, immediately before the scheduled formation of worker cooperatives in June 1970, measures were introduced which severely limited popular participation within the cooperative structure.[23] First, a specially constructed Agrarian Reform Control System (SAF) guaranteed military control by placing an officer from the Army Intelligence Service on each complex. Second, labor leaders were barred from elected office within the cooperative for a period equal to the total time they had held union office. Third, rather than choosing the cooperative's 120-seat general assembly in open elections, four worker groups were established corresponding to field, factory, office and technical workers; and thirty delegates were chosen from each group. Control of the cooperative's administration and vigilance councils (whose members were elected from the general assembly) was thus given to the technicians and administrators, groups which constituted only 15 percent of the worker population. Finally, the government reserved the right to select delegates in proportion to the amount of funds "loaned" to the cooperative for expropriation purposes. The government named 98 delegates outright at Tumán and enjoyed majority control on all of the highly capitalized *complejos* except Cayaltí.

ONDECOOP's role as a government "contact point" was virtually eliminated. In part this was the result of a power struggle among government bureaucracies, but it was also due to the actions of several disillusioned ONDECOOP officials at Tumán who supported the workers' disruptive tactics to show their opposition to the new restrictions. Only one ONDECOOP agent presently remains at Tumán, and his function is severely circumscribed as a technical counsel whose only role is to advise the cooperative's formal operation. Not only does ONDECOOP avoid handling workers' grievances, but since June 1970, there has also been no effort to stimulate popular participation through widespread training courses.

The Center of Agrarian Production Sugar Cooperatives (CE-COAAP) constitutes an additional restriction on the cooperative's autonomy. CECOAAP was organized to provide national coordination for the sugar cooperatives, lending economies of scale to resource acquisitions and marketing procedures. The body supposedly provides only technical advice to the cooperatives, but in practical terms CECOAAP's ability to make credit and resources available gives it effective control over decisions reached at the local level.

Under the theory of corporatist participation, effective local influence is to be exercised through local participation units and responsive government "contact points." At Tumán, however, the cooperative structure was dominated by the same technocratic interests which had held power under the former owners. Governmental "contact points" such as ONDECOOP, CECOAAP and the resident military coordinator also proved ineffective in transmitting participant demands and encouraging popular participation. Finding the intended participatory structures closed to popular demands, either because they were blocked by established power interests or subject to direct government control, Tumán's workers have been able to show their discontent and exert real influence only through "escape mechanisms" which fall outside the boundaries of the corporatist model.

In the absence of a labor union capable of organizing demands collectively, the workers' disillusionment with the restrictions imposed by the central government was manifested in spontaneous violent outbursts. A bitter dispute over the distribution of the cooperative's profits, in which the workers demanded cash payments while the government argued that all profits should be reinvested, resulted in the Minister of Agriculture's resignation after he was held captive at a general assembly meeting.[24] The incidence and severity of such outbreaks increased throughout 1970 and 1971, and a small local group called the "Tupamaros" *(Vanguardia Revolucionaria)* gradually emerged to exert pressure on the cooperative's governing bodies. In response to this climate of discord, in January 1972, the government used army troops to intervene forcibly on what had once been considered a model complex. Twenty-three worker leaders were arrested and the cooperative was placed under direct state administration.[25]

In the face of similar disturbances on several of the northern sugar cane cooperatives, the Velasco government hurried SINAMOS into operation in March and April 1972, and transferred responsibility for the complejos to that agency. SINAMOS's appearance was used as an opportunity to remove virtually all the restrictions on delegate selection. In mid-April open elections were held on each of the cooperatives, and antigovernment worker leaders won control of the general assembly and governing councils in each case. At Tumán, the Tupamaros' winning electoral list contained no technicians.[26]

The elimination of restrictions within the cooperative has not broadened the scope of local influence. Tumán's military coordinator, now responsible to SINAMOS rather than to the Army Intelligence Service, and CECOAAP still retain the effective decision-making power. Furthermore, the persistence of volatile social tensions between technicians and manual laborers challenges the corporatist model's underlying assumption that different hierarchical levels in a single functional area can cooperate through a solidarity of interests.

Cayaltí

Cayaltí is another agroindustrial complex located in the department of Lambayeque near Chiclayo. Prior to the agrarian reform, some 2,300 workers were employed there in the cultivation of 4,500 hectares of sugar cane and approximately 4,900 hectares of rice and other foodstuffs.[27] Suffering from poor management and low capital reinvestment, Cayaltí was in many ways Tumán's opposite. Its living standards and productivity were the lowest of all the sugar haciendas. Adverse working conditions and a history of brutal repression under the Aspíllaga family accounted for the existence of a vigorous, respected labor union.

As at Tumán, Cayaltí's workers initially greeted the agrarian reform with enthusiastic support. ONDECOOP pursued a program similar to that implemented at Tumán, and the labor union offered its own assistance in preparing the population for the organization of a worker cooperative. Yet, when the government's restrictions on popular participation were announced, Cayaltí's labor force also expressed its extreme disillusionment. Because Cayaltí was in bankruptcy at the time of the agrarian reform, the government was entitled to select only 22 of the general assembly's delegates. But the formation of the four worker categories permitted the technicians and administrators to exercise disproportionate influence and give them control of the governing councils. For example, in clear violation of the reform statutes, the administration council contained no delegate representing the field workers.[28]

Popular resistance to government control at Cayaltí was channeled through the existing union. The labor union initiated a series of work stoppages between June 1970 and July 1971. Its strength was revealed when a massive 72-hour work halt in July 1971 forced the government to return top union leaders to the cooperative's payroll in apparent violation of existing legislation.[29] Government restrictions served to maintain the union's vitality, and the strike reaffirmed the organization's functional importance as the workers' means of expressing material and political demands.

The government's perception of the basic incompatibility between the labor union and the cooperative structure was evidenced in ONDECOOP's effort to undermine the union organization through the creation of "study circles." [30] In the early months of 1971, ONDECOOP attempted to establish new communications channels between the popular base and the unresponsive cooperative administration, in the form of small discussion groups (with 10 to 15 members each) meeting in weekly two-hour sessions. The study circles' success depended upon general assembly delegates serving as group moderators, thus placing cooperative officials in direct contact with small, organized worker groups. ONDECOOP's initial efforts, however, encountered both widespread apathy—as delegates failed to attend a preliminary training course—and outright hostility, as the technician-dominated governing councils attempted to censor the group's discussion topics. As a result, ONDECOOP watered down its study circle plan to include volunteers, rather than elected delegates, as group leaders. This modification, while satisfactory to the governing councils, rendered the study circles meaningless as communications mechanisms between workers and officials.

Another strike broke out at Cayaltí when a key union leader was arrested in January 1972, on charges of "sabotaging the agrarian reform." [31] Part of Tumán's work force organized a sympathy strike, precipitating the crisis on the northern coast which led to the repeal of the government's onerous restrictions. At Cayaltí the union's Aprista leadership won the ensuing elections.[32] As at Tumán, power within the cooperative was monopolized by precisely those elements which had dominated the decision-making process under the former landowners, and strict government control rendered the governmental "contact points" meaningless. Significantly, effective popular influence was exercised through an organization external to the cooperative mechanism.

Pucará

Pucará is an officially recognized peasant community of approximately 1,600 inhabitants located in the central sierra's fertile Mantaro Valley. Three quarters of the families living there are engaged in agriculture (wheat, oats, potatoes, onions) and livestock raising.[33] Perhaps reflecting its relatively high level of modernization by sierra standards, Pucará suffers from problems of communal land fragmentation and internal domination by an entrenched local elite.

The Peasant Communities Statute, decreed in February 1970, established a community governmental structure based on the cooperative framework. Cooperative membership was originally limited to those who were both permanent community residents and full-time agricultural workers. The Statute also sought to consolidate communal lands, thus reducing the local elite's power resources. By forbidding a member to receive his major source of income from outside the community, the legislation challenged the community's most influential figures, whose wealth did not justify their participation in the community's already inadequate resources.

Pucará formally accepted the cooperative administrative structure when elections were held to choose administration and vigilance councils in November 1970. Contrary to official expectations, however, the winning electoral list was comprised of the same political and economic elite which had previously dominated community affairs. Indeed, due to the local Office of Peasant Community's extreme resource shortage and its subsequent inability to enforce a satisfactory qualification of community members, the administration council contained three individuals who should have been legally excluded from cooperative membership.[34]

Even though Pucará is a modernized community in the sierra's most progressive area, it has had only minimal contact with government reform agencies. Infrequent contact with these local "contact points" prolonged a dispute over a communal livestock farm, heightening internal tensions and undermining the success of community development projects.

In effect, the individual peasant cooperative represents an atomized local participation unit which restricts participation to the local level. The only external linkages are through intermittent contact with relevant government reform agencies and the embryonic state-controlled cooperative federations, sectoral organizations which seek to replace traditional participatory patterns at the national level. These channels have not replaced those previously maintained by APRA and Acción Popular peasant unions, now effectively proscribed. The new cooperative structure thus reflects no qualitative improvement to date in the community members' relationship to the national political system.

Chuschi [35]

Chuschi is a relatively large and prosperous officially recognized peasant community of 1,100 inhabitants in the isolated department of Ayacucho. Located at the end of a torturous one-lane dirt road, the community serves as the market center for the surrounding area. Agriculture is the principal occupation, as it is in all peasant communities in Ayacucho, but there are also several stores, a small hotel, the government's agricultural extension office and the residence of the parish priest.

Implementation of the Peasant Communities Statute in Chuschi set the stage for a massive power struggle within the community. The community's modernization, stimulated by the arrival of the road in 1961, permitted privileged groups within the community—such as the merchants and the priest—to increase their wealth at the expense of the majority. After his arrival in Chuschi in 1962, the priest worked to increase the size of the church's lands and flocks. These resources ostensibly provided the church's income in the parish, but they in fact benefited the priest himself. He sided increasingly with the community's more prosperous elements and tenaciously opposed all change which would benefit the less privileged majority.

An extremely active community association (containing some 250 members) of Chuschi natives who had migrated to Lima viewed the implementation of the new community statutes as an opportunity to change the internal balance of power, and a number of the group's leaders returned to Chuschi to see what could be done. Two of their number were elected to the presidencies of both the community's governing councils, even though they would not have qualified for community membership if the Statute's membership requirements had been strictly followed. The two elected leaders, who had worked in Lima factories for several years, had strong union ties and considerable political experience.

The attempt by ONDECOOP representatives to establish a cooperative in Chuschi gave these leaders their chance to carry out their plans. They immediately established close relationships with the government officials and loudly espoused the cause of cooperativism within the community. Their goal was to use the cooperative as the mechanism to take over the church lands and flocks—about 40 hectares of the community's best irrigated land and some 800 head of cattle—and to use the good offices of the ONDECOOP officials to remove the priest from the community.

The priest, however, had his own power resources. He succeeded in getting the national police to jail the community authorities on at least three occasions. ONDECOOP officials, seeing their infant cooperative threatened by the removal of its two most ardent spokesmen, worked just as hard to get the leaders out of jail. The first time, they hired Ayacucho's leading lawyer; on the second occasion they intervened directly with the department prefect. With the third jailing, ONDECOOP enlisted the support of the Public Defender, the Agrarian Reform Office and the office of Peasant Communities. Each time they were successful. In February 1972, Ayacucho's bishop made a "routine" transfer of the priest out of Chuschi. As of May 1972, the cooperative had yet to become a viable entity in Chuschi.

Slack control by government officials from the Office of Peasant Communities in the application of the Peasant Communities Statute provided an opportunity for experienced elements identified with the community's general welfare to take positions of authority. These leaders then utilized the clientelistic ties which they had established with ONDECOOP officials to accomplish a goal with important implications for local power relationships, but with little connection to the government officials' original objectives. While local power holders could depend upon individually formed clientelistic ties, the unconstituted cooperative structure left the community as a whole without an institutionalized means of expressing its interests in the national corporatist framework.

Chupis and El Porvenir [36]

Chupis and El Porvenir are two small adjacent haciendas situated in Ayacucho near the provincial capital of Huanta. The properties total about 250 hectares and contain 83 families as beneficiaries of the agrarian reform. While Chupis averages only one hectare of cultivated land per peasant family, El Porvenir boasts four times this amount.

Chupis, formerly owned by Ayacucho's departmental welfare organization, was invaded in 1963 by a large number of landless peasants with the encouragement of several of the property's subrenters. However, the subrenters kept the more valuable irrigated land for themselves and left the invaders with the dry lands. The invaders' rights were legitimized in 1968 under the Belaúnde agrarian reform law, but the property was adjudicated in 1970 without resolving the fundamental dispute over the maldistribution of resources.

In spite of the majority's strenuous efforts to resolve the conflict by organizing themselves and carrying their case to the subzonal, zonal and national levels, they had not succeeded as of December 1971, due to the privileged few's successful exploitation of close ties with subzonal agrarian reform officials. These clientelistic relationships were originally established through this minority's formation of a "Committee for the Defense of the Revolution" and their ardent and vocal support of the present government. In turn, the agrarian reform officials named members of this privileged minority to the directorship of Chupis's precooperative Farmers' Council. Government officials frequently call upon these directors to serve as the peasants' spokesmen at official gatherings and celebrations.

In clear violation of reform statutes, two of the leaders of the Farmers' Council in Chupis are also considered beneficiaries in El Porvenir. They serve as directors of the Farmers' Council there as well, where some peasants have accused them of using common property for their private benefit. The obvious solution to Chupis's difficulties, relocating those beneficiaries with claims on both properties in El Porvenir where more land is available, has not been implemented because of the entrenched elite's close relationship with agrarian reform officials.

In both Chupis and El Porvenir, the agrarian reform has increased internal tensions due to the privileged few's ability to maintain their exploitive position. An effective reform presence would require governmental agency "contact points" responsive to the majority's interests and local participatory structures capable of expressing popular demands. These crucial linkages to the national corporatist system are absent, leaving the local population without an institutionalized means of political participation.

Conclusions: The Participation–Control Paradox

From the viewpoint of the Peruvian military government, it is apparent that the goal of "social democracy of full participation" can be achieved only by continued careful control from above. The corporatist model of participation suggests that the only institutionalized form of citizen participation which is compatible with it is local, rather than national, in nature. Furthermore, the fact that it is a military institution which holds political power at the present time suggests that the regime's general reform orientation and its particular concern with the institutionalization of local participation stem from an underlying concern for internal security.[37] The military perceives an inherent conflict between the goals of internal security and full participation, and the Revolutionary Military Government's tendency to date is to emphasize control, rather than freedom.

The corporatist model is in principle admirably suited to these purposes. It follows from the Hispanic and Catholic traditions and is, therefore, congruent with the Peruvian past.* This heritage justifies a strong element of central direction and rationalizes placing ultimate responsibility for the reform process with the military government. There is also a strong element of tutelary guidance: the populace is to learn while doing and to walk before it runs.

As the case studies indicate, a number of problems have arisen in the construction of participatory mechanisms which constitute the basis for a national corporatist system. First, the successful implementation of the proposed participatory model assumes a malleable and receptive population. The more mobilized the

---

* This is not entirely correct. About half of Peru's population is probably closer to Peru's Indian heritage (47 percent of the population, according to the 1961 Census, speaks an Indian language as its mother tongue). The Incaic tradition which dominated Peru at the time of the conquest included a highly centralized theocracy, better organized than, but in many ways parallel to the Hispanic institutions which formally took over after 1532. However, this Incaic heritage was widely influenced by the three centuries of colonial rule which followed.

populace, the less receptive it is to the imposition of new structural arrangements from above and the more able it is to neutralize such efforts or to impose its own conditions. As for Peru, considerable variety exists within the country's overall level of relatively low social mobilization. The areas of highest mobilization are precisely those areas deemed crucial by the military government for "production for development" goals. Local forces resist strict government control and successfully realize their demands by taking action outside the corporatist framework's formal boundaries. In Peru's areas of lower social mobilization, where ties between government "contact points" and the central government are often lax, there is a greater tendency to maximize advantages *within* the system through clientelistic devices. At this level, those with greater local power resources usually win.

Second, the successful implementation of the corporatist model requires nearly perfect control from the center at all levels. In practice, however, the government has insufficient resources and personnel to orchestrate the development of corporatist participation as it would like. Although this provides a margin of flexibility at the local level which keeps tensions lower, it also introduces "tentativeness" to legislation and perpetuates levels of relative incompetence at the government's local "contact points." The quality of these local contacts is crucial to the successful implementation of the corporatist model, but in practice both power and priorities have been concentrated in the center and in certain key, highly mobilized regions. The center perceives these local "contact points" as the last outposts of government, rather than as the citizen's first contact with the government. Local agencies, especially in marginal areas, tend to receive low pay and low support.

Although local participation units in the form of agricultural cooperatives, neighborhood committees and industrial communities now exist in several sectors, local political influence remains sporadic and inadequate. The Peruvian military appears generally hesitant to acknowledge the importance of bottom-up initiative. Some form of hierarchically organized functional representation institutions, such as the embryonic National Agrarian Confederation, may gradually assume policy-making responsibilities.[38] However, political participation in practice under the corporatist framework as it has been articulated thus far by the military government, does not encompass popular control or influence over the national decision-making process. Rather, the Velasco government seeks to guarantee the citizenry's loyalty through a skillfully employed "revolutionary mystique," and attempts to involve popular sectors in socioeconomic changes undertaken by the government through local organizational reforms, such as cooperatives. Such popular acceptance and nominal participation are necessary to maintain political stability and internal security without resorting to political repression.

The Revolutionary Military Government's design for corporatist participation holds important implications for the Peruvian political system. The corporatist model simultaneously attempts to reorient existing political forces and to establish an institutional framework capable of incorporating new social actors mobilized as a result of socioeconomic reforms. Spontaneous, self-initiated popular participation is incompatible with the government's effort to restrict all political action to the regulated, localized interaction between established government "contact points" and the local participation units.

In the short run, the gap in citizen expectations resulting from a "revolutionary ideology" which endorses a form of popular political participation the military is not yet able to accept, may lead to an increase in political conflict. The corporatist model suggests—and the case studies confirm—that where ties between government "contact points" and local participation units are strictly regulated and local influence is denied, local forces often express their demands through escape mechanisms which forcibly bypass the corporatist framework.

In the long run, the crucial question is the extent to which political influence and decision-making responsibilities are devolved to the local level under the corporatist model. The extreme regulatory power over emerging social forces which the corporatist framework grants to the ruling elite, plus the Velasco government's inclination to limit popular participation to a nominal involvement in socioeconomic changes through organizational reforms, constitute fundamental obstacles to popular political participation. Such an alteration of surface structures through "revolution from above" is insufficient to change Peru's underlying social reality. While perhaps offering political challenges and potential disruption, effective popular participation is precisely the dynamic force necessary to change permanently the face of the social order.

NOTES

1. Literature on the conservative role of the Latin American military abounds. Recent examples include Eric Nordlinger, "Soldiers in Mufti: The Impact of Military Rule upon Economic and Social Change in the Non-Western States," *American Political Science Review* 64 (December 1970) 4: 1131–1148. Also Amos Perlmutter, "The Praetorian State and the Praetorian Army: Toward a Taxonomy of Civil-Military Relations in Developing Politics," *Comparative Politics* 1 (April 1969) 3: 382–404.

2. This has been one of the Peruvian military government's persistent themes since its original formulation in President Velasco's speech for the Sesquicentennial of Peruvian Independence, July 28, 1971.

3. See, for example, Samuel Huntington, *Political Order in Changing Societies* (New Haven: Yale University Press, 1968), p. 243; Henry Bienen, ed., *The Military Intervenes; Case Studies in Political Development* (New York: Russell Sage Foundation, 1968), p. xix; and Martin Needler, *Political Development in Latin America: Instability, Violence, and Evolutionary Change* (New York: Random House, 1968), pp. 59–76.

4. "El Populismo Militar como Modelo de Desarrollo Nacional: El Caso Peruvano," Instituto de Estudios Peruanos, Lima, October 1969.

5. Nicole Bosquet, "The Committees for the Defense of the Revolution in Peru," Department of Sociology, McGill University, Montreal, Canada, unpublished manuscript.

6. In a speech by President Velasco to the National Veterans Association, April 19, 1970.

7. Reprinted in *Expreso*, October 29, 1971. This is a succinct summary of the ideology's initial formulation in the president's speech marking the sesquicentennial of Peruvian independence, July 28, 1971.

8. República Peruana, Presidencia de la República, Instituto Nacional de Planificación, *Plan Nacional de Desarrollo para 1971–1975, Plan Global*, vol. 1 (July 1971), pp. 31, 32.

9. Ibid., p. 32.

10. Ibid., p. 34.

11. Ibid.

12. Decree-Law No. 18384 (The Industrial Community Law), September 1, 1970. The Industrial Community concept was first established in Decree-Law No. 18350 (The General Law of Industries), July 27, 1970. It is estimated that approximately 200,000 workers are included, or about 5 percent of the economically active population as of 1971.

13. Legislation enacted in 1946–1947 originally provided for profit-sharing, but it was never implemented.

14. Decree-Law No. 18810 (The General Fishing Law), June 9, 1971 (implementing law, July 1, 1971); and Decree-Law No. 18880 (The General Mining Law), June 9, 1971 (implementing law, April 21, 1972). It is estimated that approximately 70,000 workers are included under the provisions of both laws, or a little under 2 percent of the 1971 estimated economically active population.

15. Decree-Law No. 19400, May 9, 1972.

16. These terms were used by President Velasco to characterize the Committees for the Defense of the Revolution in an interview recorded in the Argentine weekly, *Panorama* (July 6, 1971), p. 57.

17. For recent work in this area see Howard Wiarda, "Toward a Framework for the Study of Political Change in the Iberic-Latin Tradition: The Corporative Model," *World Politics* 25 (January 1973) 1. Also see Melvin Burke and James M. Malloy, "Del populismo nacional al corporativismo nacional: El caso de Bolivia, 1952-70," *Aportes,* no. 26 (October 1972): 66-96; Julio Cotler, "Bases del corporativismo en el Peru, *Sociedad y Politica,* no. 2 (October 1972): 3-12; D.S. Palmer, "Revolution from Above: Military Government and Popular Participation In Peru, 1968-1972," Ph. D. diss. in political science, Cornell University, January 1973.

18. Wiarda, "Toward a Framework," p. 3.

19. Ibid., p. 6.

20. About 550 cooperatives of all types were established during the first 39 months of the present government (October 1968-December 1971). This compares with about 700 established during the five years of the Belaúnde government (July 1963-October 1968)—ONDECOOP, *Anuario estadistico, 1971* (Lima: May, 1972). As of June, 1971, 2,834 Industrial Communities had been officially recognized out of approximately 4,000 companies eligible—*Siete Dias* (May 28, 1971) and *El Comercio* (January 13, 1972).

21. Information Bulletin, Agrarian Reform Office, Zone II, Lambayeque, Peru.

22. Information about the training programs at Tumán is from interviews with ONDECOOP's resident advisor at Tumán (August 3, 1971) and ONDECOOP's regional director in Chiclayo (August 7, 1971). See Kevin Middlebrook, "Land for the Tiller: Political Participation and the Peruvian Military's Agrarian Reform," B.A. thesis, Harvard College, March 1972.

23. Delegate election restrictions were decreed May 29, 1970, in Supreme Decree 019-70-PM and Decree-Law 18299. The Agrarian Reform Control System was created by Supreme Decree 51-70-AG, March 10, 1970.

24. This episode was first related to both authors by a student at Pomalca (a nearby *complejo*), and later verified by personnel in the Agrarian Reform Office in Lima.

25. ONDECOOP Resolution 040-72; *El Comercio* (February 3, 1972), p. 4; and *Caretas,* no. 452 (February 22-March 9, 1972): 18.

26. *Caretas,* no. 455 (April 17-27, 1972): 6.

27. Information Bulletin, Agrarian Reform Office, Zone II, Lambayeque, Peru.

28. Field notes taken at Cayaltí by Kevin Middlebrook, August 8, 1971.

29. *El Comercio,* July 26, 1971.

30. ONDECOOP, "Projecto para los círculos de estudios," January, 1971; and interview with Cayaltí's resident ONDECOOP representative by Kevin Middlebrook, August 4, 1971.

31. *El Comercio,* February 8 and 12, 1972.

32. *Caretas,* no. 455, April 17-27, 1972, p. 6.

33. *Atlas Comunal,* June 1964, vol. 2 (Ministry of Labor, Lima).

34. Field notes taken by Kevin Middlebrook at Pucará, September 1972, courtesy of Dr. Norman Long, University of Manchester.

35. D. S. Palmer's field notes taken in September and November 1971, at Chuschi, assisted by F. Angelino and H. Rojas. Additional background information courtesy of Billy-Jean Isbell, Department of Anthropology, State University of New York, Binghamton.

36. D.S. Palmer's field notes taken in November 1971, at Chupis and El Porvenir, assisted by G. Mítrovič and R. García.

37. The "internal security" motive for reform by military governments is explored in Victor Villanueva, *El CAEM y la revolucion de la fuerza armada* (Lima: Instituto de Estudios Peruanos, Campodonico, 1972).

38. As expressed by a number of SINAMOS officials in interviews with D. S. Palmer in Lima in April and May 1972.

Carlos Alberto Astiz

17.   The Catholic Church in the Peruvian Political System

Historically, the Catholic Church has publicly admonished the faithful: "Render unto Caesar that which is Caesar's and unto God that which is God's." This advice is very wise, provided that Caesar and God agree about who is to get what and so long as the contributors, in turn, accept the agreement. History shows that the representatives of the temporal and spiritual realms have had many disagreements regarding such distribution, and that the faithful were often dissatisfied, even when the other two parties did agree. In the 1970s, the Catholic Church and the Latin American Caesars seem to be going through a period of particularly acrimonious disagreements; what is worse (or better, as the case may be) is that the faithful demand a voice in the settlement of these disputes and threaten to withdraw their support if this demand is not honored. This threat is more effective against the church, which lacks the means to coerce support, than against the state, which under certain conditions can enforce its policies regardless of the will of the majority.

Such conflict has occurred more in certain Latin American countries than in others. During the year 1971, no less than 52 Catholic priests were arrested in Argentina for political reasons; demonstrations led by clergymen were repressed and some of their leaders manhandled by the police and military authorities.[1] The jailing and torture of religious personnel by the Brazilian political police and the armed forces has been widely covered in the press; the political disagreements that brought about such actions still exist. Similar accounts have been made public in reference to Colombia and Paraguay, among other countries.[2] The growth in the literature dealing with this topic provides quantitative confirmation of the widespread recognition that the Catholic Church is involved in that which is

Caesar's and that, in turn, Caesar is involved in that which is the church's.

Within the available space, then, this chapter will explore some of the avenues and mechanisms employed by the Peruvian Catholic Church to participate in politics, the course and extent of its power, the processes employed to articulate its interests and the possibility of altering its political role. This analysis deals with one country only; thus its findings may not be transferable beyond Peru's national boundaries. Much more data needs to be uncovered before broader comparisons can be made.

It is not necessary to discuss here the historical factors which gave Catholicism a religious monopoly in the nation-states of Latin America, converting the Catholic Church into an essential element of the national struggles for political power. It should be pointed out, however, that the intimate relationship between church and state transferred to this region by the Spanish political system at the time of discovery and conquest was adjusted, but not essentially altered, by the processes of independence.[3] The political elites of the republics that finally emerged chose to retain the close relationship inherited from the colonial powers, and the Catholic Church found the maintenance of this status quo equally attractive.

Some writers have maintained that the Catholic Church is simply another of the pressure groups operating within the traditional political systems of countries such as Peru. While this view is occasionally warranted, it fails to explain the essential role played by the church in the domestic politics of Latin American political systems; the political power of the Catholic Church is derived from its role, through a series historical circumstances, as the provider of the ideology of the status quo. Consequently, as the author has maintained elsewhere, the traditional upper class and other elements which make up Peru's status quo defenders have not needed to develop an ideological foundation which would intellectually justify and support their privileged share of societal rewards.[4] Strangely enough, in a country where the overwhelming majority of the population are Indian or mestizo, Peru's ruling elites have not even attempted—except for some *Hispanista* pronouncements—to provide a coherent explanation of their role and status: as some members of the clergy indicated, they were there by the will of God. The irreverent but precise description of the relationship between the power-holders and the church, provided by one character in a celebrated Spanish novel, can be transferred to Peru: "I go to Mass to serve as an example; I give alms to the priests; I protect an orphanage. Religion is useful. We help priests to live, and they defend us from the poor with the threat of hell." [5] A Philippine landowner, who was having difficulties with his plantation workers, provided a more pragmatic outlook on the use of religion to protect the status quo; he was quoted as saying: "My biggest problem right now is the fact that there is only one Mass a year held for the workers of my plantation; I am trying to see that they can have Mass once a week." [6] A keen observer of the Peruvian political scene demonstrates that Peruvian landowners had developed a similar approach to religion. He writes that, in the Peruvian sierra:

> the chapel is the required complement of the landlord's residence; Mass is celebrated there when there is a priest available, and always on the birthday of the Patron Saint who protects the fields, harvests and cattle, prevents droughts, and offers heaven in exchange for obedience and resignation in this world; these are the Christian virtues which the priest emphasizes in his sermons. [7]

In a fictional series of vignettes describing Peruvian society, a Peruvian writer presents a description of the typical sierra priest, his contempt for the people under his spiritual guidance, and the reactions of a peasant youngster who has his first contact with the church. The writer points out that, while he is transmitting the "word of God" to the faithful, the priest takes the opportunity

> to refer to the struggle among the political parties. He vehemently attacks left-wing ideas, and advises resignation and peace before the power of the strong, who, in a certain way, "are the representatives of the Supreme Judge of Heaven and Earth. He, then, is the only one entitled to judge them, not men." Solna [the peasant youngster], who has listened carefully, is confused. His teacher's book advised effort, action and pride before the strong. [Yet] the Priest recommends resignation, humbleness, meekness, submission before abuse and exploitation. [8]

Returning from fiction to reality, in the late 1930s the archbishop of Peru, Pedro Pascual Farfán, clearly indicated the ideological role to be played by the Catholic Church in regard to Peru's political structure: he announced that poverty was the road to eternal happiness and that the solution of socioeconomic problems was based on the ability of the state (with the support and assistance of the church) to make the poor recognize the virtue of their plight.[9] The similarities between the fictional and nonfictional descriptions quoted above need not be emphasized. Nevertheless, it would be both unfair and erroneous to say that Catholicism's main objective, as a world religion, is either the maintenance or the alteration of the political, social and economic status quo. Like most religions, Catholicism is made up of a collection of texts, often obscure and contradictory, which lend themselves to varying interpretations.

In discussing the political role of the Catholic Church in the context already outlined, we must identify the various levels from which pronouncements with an ideological content might originate: (1) the supranational level, made up of the Holy See and international meetings, such as Vatican II and, within the region, the Latin American Episcopal Council, better known as CELAM; (2) the national level—the archbishop, the bishops acting collectively (usually through national episcopal conferences), the Papal Nuncio, and the hierarchy located mostly in the capital city; and (3) the local level, essentially represented by the parish priest and all other religious personnel working directly with the rank-and-file faithful, as well as their immediate supervisors. It must be remembered, however, that access to church pronouncements made at the supranational and, occasionally, even at the national levels, requires a high degree of education and the availability of sophisticated sources which provide texts, background information and commentaries. These sources are available only to a small minority of Latin Americans, those with enough training, time and means to keep up with reinterpretations of the Catholic dogma. Most believers, members of the urban and rural lower class, and of the lower middle class, do not belong in this category. Particularly in the case of illiterates, but also in the case of the majority of those who have received elementary schooling, Catholic dogma tends to mean what the local priest says it means; in other words, the local level is in a position to effectively amend or remake the political ideology to which all good Catholics are expected to subscribe. Obviously, the national level can act as an ideological filter in regard to supranational pronouncements; it also has the power to police the interpretations transmitted by the local level to the people.

Available evidence indicates that, at least throughout this century, the members of the local level of the Catholic Church in Latin America have in fact employed their powers to give specific political meaning to general supranational and national pronouncements, as well as to downplay those which would interfere with their own political role. In the case of Peru, local priests have tended to support the status quo and challenge those who favor effective reform. In the 1920s and 1930s, when APRA developed as a reformist party, with a political ideology which at the time ran counter to that of the Catholic Church, many sermons became forums for the denunciation of APRA, whose leaders and followers were accused of planning to murder priests and laymen, burn churches and rape nuns. As election time approached, the clergy, often speaking from the pulpit, threatened damnation to those who acted against their political directives, choosing to support APRA. One witness reports,

> I heard a priest's sermon in one of the churches of Huancayo in 1932; he was addressing the faithful on political subjects. He showed that APRA was the work of the devil, and that it should be feared and hated since its own leader, because of the profile of his nose, looked exactly like Satan.[10]

Well-timed pastoral letters reminded Peruvians of the errors contained in APRA's ideology and platform, as well as of the consequences, both in this world and the next, of going along with those errors. Since the end of the Second World War, and as APRA shifted its stand to become a defender of the status quo, the Catholic church of Peru directed its attention to more immediate ideological threats; political organizations such as APRA Rebelde, MIR, FIR and some peasant groups became its new rivals. Reports maintain that, in the early 1960s,

> the Catholic Church, at least at the parish level . . . joined in this campaign against the peasant movement. The priests of the region refused to baptize the sons of those peasants who belonged to the unions directed by Hugo Blanco. . . . If the cultural level of the Cuzco peasantry is taken into account

and if the religious beliefs of the Peruvian people in general are remembered, the fear by these peasants because of the priests' refusal to baptize their children will be easily understood.[11]

Pressures for Change in Peru

The traditional position of the Catholic Church of Peru as the ideological mainstay of the traditional upper class has been subject to increasing pressures since the late 1950s. Domestically, the "revolution of rising expectations" attracted Peruvians at the lower levels of society. This new set of ideas contradicted that interpretation of the dogma which counseled patience and resignation, on the grounds that little could be done to upgrade the status of those who were not getting what they thought was their share of socioeconomic rewards. When the peasantry was told by educated outsiders that they, the peasants, were in fact entitled to own the land they were working and to receive a larger share of the profits for their work, they found nothing wrong with the idea. When the ideological struggle developed between these "outside agitators" and the local clergy, the peasants were forced to choose between what they thought was just, fair, and in their own interest, and the mandate of the Catholic Church. It is not surprising that a significant number chose that ideology which offered them, at least on paper, an immediate solution to their economic plight, even if it was at the expense of achieving salvation after death.

With respect to the decline in religious participation, a conservative member of the Peruvian clergy wrote:

It cannot be denied that the percentage of adults who attended mass weekly is low, and the percentage of those who follow the precepts of yearly confession and communion is even lower. . . .

The Protestant propaganda, particularly that of the Adventists, Baptists, Jehovah's Witnesses, Mormons, *but above all Marxist and atheist propaganda, have grown greatly.* This propaganda has had contributing parties, unbelieving intellectuals, and press organs. It increased . . . after the triumph of Castroism in Cuba. . . . Although in the 1940 census those who stated that they did not have any religion were very few. I fear that their number has grown a great deal in the last twenty-two years.[12]

More importantly, a study conducted by social scientists of the Catholic University of Peru in the department of Puno found that only 27 percent of a representative sample were aware of the religious organizations available in their communities, 8 percent showed appreciation of them, and only 6 percent actually belonged to at least one religious organization—furthermore, one third of those who belonged indicated that they were somehow coerced into membership. According to the data from a survey of the town of Sicuani,[13] 8.3 percent of the sample surveyed belonged to Catholic organizations. However, when the universe is taken into account, that figure appears as less than 3 percent of the actual population—again, a low level of participation in a locality that offers very little else to do. The group of researchers that conducted the survey of Puno stated that:

> The religious organizations seem to have significantly less importance than we thought before beginning to conduct this research. Only one-third of the sample is aware of their existence, and less than one-third of these appreciate and belong to them.[14]

Since the political efforts of the Catholic Church were directed during the late 1950s and most of the 1960s against its ideological competitors, the parties of the left, it should be noted that the above testimony and data are confirmed by the electoral returns in some of the latest elections that were held before the military takeover of October 1968. While the left-wing parties, because of their own political incompetence and considerable police hostility, had not been able to show any electoral strength until the mid-1960s, in the 1966 municipal elections their candidates obtained 20.7 percent of the vote in Arequipa, 12.8 percent of the vote in Cuzco, and an impressive 33.9 percent in Puno, where religious organizations were found to be extremely weak, as indicated above. These electoral returns acquire even more significance when we remember that illiterates are not allowed to vote, and that more than 80 percent of the population of Puno was classified as illiterate. Only 7.8 percent of the total population, and 15.2 percent of the voting-age population, exercised the franchise in Puno; since 15.8 percent of the voting-age population was legally permitted to register, the percentage of those entitled to vote who failed to do so was minimal.[15] Those deprived of the franchise belong to the lower layers of society, which is where the ideological conflict between Catholic dogma, as interpreted by the local level, and anti-status quo political philosophies collide; therefore, it is fair to assume that, in the last few years, left-wing candidates would have done better if more people had been enfranchised and other elections held.

Ideological Changes Within the Peruvian Catholic Church

The deterioration of the position of the church, particularly among the lower and lower-middle classes of Peru, did not go unnoticed by the clergy. As elsewhere, the parish priests and other religious personnel—such as nuns working in free schools and hospitals—were the first to perceive that Catholicism was losing out to the anti-status quo ideologies. Relatively little was done about this within the church until the late 1960s, although reference should be made here to two clergymen who were pioneers in this area. Salomón Bolo Hidalgo, a well-known figure in Peruvian politics, the organizer and leading member of the country's National Liberation Front, began opposing the church's traditional role in politics in the 1950s. Although Bolo Hidalgo has been largely ignored by his fellow countrymen, he developed the line of reasoning which, during the last two years, has been adopted by the reformist group within the Peruvian clergy. In a proclamation issued in 1961, Bolo Hidalgo stated:

> Everyone who speaks the truth is called communist in today's Peru. I have waited ... but even the Archbishop of Lima and the Papal Nuncio follow the "fashion" of attacking communism, indirectly favoring the selfish interests of the oligarchs, the landowners, and the political bosses. That is why I speak up, *as a Peruvian citizen and as a Minister of Christ,* so that it cannot be said that the Catholic priests forget our mission and become servants of the exploiters.[16]

Predictably, Bolo Hidalgo's pronouncements and his involvement with the National Liberation Front brought about his immediate suspension as a priest. In explaining this measure, his bishop wrote that Bolo Hidalgo had "lent his name and his assistance to movements which threaten the integrity and the security of the Catholic Church

462   CARLOS ALBERTO ASTIZ

and of the Peruvian people." [17] It should be emphasized that this early
reformer has repeatedly disclaimed being a communist, an accusation
hurled at him by some conservative Peruvian newspapers. In so doing,
he uses an argument which constitutes one of the potentially most
powerful weapons of the Catholic Left: that they cannot possibly have
anything to do with Communism because they are devout Catholics.[18]
He has consistently emphasized, and still emphasizes, that Communism has nothing to do with the political insecurity which exists in
Peru; he blames it on the extremely uneven distribution of wealth and
other socioeconomic rewards; and he has not hesitated to attack the
cardinal, the nuncio and the clergy as a whole for their position on these
matters.

> Those bishops who issue pastoral letters to take votes away but do not issue
> them to require the wealthy to give something to the poor, to pay just
> salaries, to stop the exploitation of miners, peasants and workers; those
> bishops who photograph themselves with the "jet set" but who forget the
> undernourished children and do not issue pastoral letters against those
> responsible for the massive illiteracy and tuberculosis; those bishops who
> gain plenty of weight but only remember in their pastoral letters to favor
> the powerful of this country; those bishops, I repeat, are only merchants of
> religion.[19]

The other priest who should be mentioned here is the Jesuit Romeo
Luna Victoria; he is more of an intellectual reformer and less of a
"doer" than Bolo Hidalgo. At one time Luna Victoria taught political
science at a normal school; he has published an interesting manual
dealing with the theory and practice of revolution, addressed to political leaders. Although he does not single out any one country, outlining only a series of generalized conditions for violent revolution, his
other writings make it clear that Peru was foremost in his mind.[20]
Luna Victoria rejects the idea that Catholic doctrine forbids participation in strikes or in a bloody revolution; he feels that the contrary is
true, and that the scriptural advice to "turn the other cheek" does not
apply to sociopolitical matters. He concluded that the situation may
arise in which, to

> carry out that which is experimentally correct, unquestionably just, and
> extremely urgent, which we are sponsoring throughout this study, there
> may not be, in some areas of the world, any other alternative but to resort
> to armed revolution.[21]

Luna Victoria has recommended the redistribution of certain types of property: those items given by nature and not produced by an individual's work (which he calls "elastic property") are subject to confiscation, or at least the rent they produce is so subject.[22] Finally, he has shown the same frustration expressed by Bolo Hidalgo toward the Peruvian Catholic Church; pointing out that, when this institution receives money or other economic advantages from the state, the result often is "a 'satisfied' and 'silent' Church."

> I do not wish to cite contemporary names because I prefer to avoid damaging discords and arguments. The spectacle of a religious hierarchy that does not speak up when it should, that remains silent when it must denounce the obvious violation of sacred human rights, is extremely depressing.[23]

The political position of these two men, and their disagreement with the Peruvian Catholic Church, was further emphasized in 1965, when guerrilla groups began to operate in the Peruvian Andes. Both Bolo Hidalgo and Luna Victoria supported, or at least defended, the guerrillas, a position which contradicted that of the hierarchy; an organization led by Luna Victoria even rejected the government's branding of guerrillas and Communist supporters as traitors.[24]

During the last decade, many of the laymen and clergymen favoring drastic reforms in Peru attempted to channel their political activities through the Christian Democratic Party, an alternative that became attractive in Peru after the election of Christian Democrat Frei to the presidency of Chile. Ivan Vallier provides the following explanation:

> Is the rise of a reform-type Catholic party a condition for the long-term development of the new Church in Latin America? I suggest that it is, otherwise the latent political impulses that the theologies of the progressive Church stimulate become fused with Church-sponsored movements and organizations. If this happens, the Church re-enters politics via a two-stage sequence. First, the enthusiastic, progressive, and politically oriented lay movements begin to take sides in the central arenas of the total political system. By these actions, the Church becomes directly implicated in a political position on the left. Since this inevitably creates intense conflict and anxiety within the Church, the hierarchy is certain to reject the politicized groups or silence them. When this happens the Church swings back to a "neutral position" (or noninvolvement) which is equivalent to the legitimation of the status quo.[25]

Whatever the logic of this political strategy, it did not work out in Peru. It soon became apparent that the Christian Democratic party was failing to develop either the popular following or the political influence that Catholic reformers had been hoping for; because of its limited strength, the party made an agreement with Belaúnde Terry and supported his administration, thus sharing in the blame for his failures. Internal splits further diminished the party's role and, since the military regime took over in October 1968, the role of party politics in Peru has become marginal and its future cloudy.

Meanwhile, the ranks of the Catholic reformers within the clergy seem to have grown substantially during the late 1960s; they have organized themselves and entered their country's political arena as a group. Their activities have been particularly noticeable since the current military regime showed that it was prepared to carry out certain reforms. In a sense, the influence of Bolo Hidalgo and Luna Victoria has been reduced, or rather superseded, by a more highly organized group which, although still a minority of the clergy, no longer relies on a few individuals. The organization that seems to have evolved as the spokesman for these reformers' views on what the political ideology of the Peruvian Catholic Church ought to be, is the National Office of Social Information, or ONIS. While the author has been unable to obtain a complete list of its members, they apparently are less than one hundred, all clergymen. Their statement on agrarian reform, issued on June 20, 1969, shortly before the Peruvian military regime announced its Agrarian Reform Act, has 82 signatures. It was possible to obtain some information on 72 members of ONIS, which is summarized in Table 1.

Certain characteristics of this group are readily apparent: its members are young priests, mainly from the Lima metropolitan area; the proportion of those with advanced training in the social sciences and the humanities is high, and may be even higher than shown in the available data. Of those not located in Lima, the overwhelming majority were either in the dioceses of Arequipa or Trujillo. In fact, some of the signers participated in an incident which took place in the city of Trujillo during March and April of 1969; on that occasion they supported blue-collar workers on strike, and came into conflict with an upper-class club. The priests involved were attacked by the Papal Nuncio, who denounced them to the hierarchy and to the military

Table 1
COMPARISON OF ONIS MEMBERSHIP AND GENERAL PERUVIAN
CLERGY

	ONIS Members	All Priests
Percentage native Peruvian	57.5	38.0
Percentage located in Lima	62.5	32.5
Age breakdown—percentage distribution		
to 40 years of age	56.9	43.7
41–50	33.3	22.7
51–60	6.9	17.1
61 on	2.8	16.5
Average age	40.3 years	45.9 years

Source: Prepared by the author from data made available by the Peruvian Catholic Church.

government. This episode ended when both the government and the hierarchy refused to intervene, thus forcing the Vatican representative to resign his post.[26]

Finally, the proportion of Peruvians in ONIS is much higher than that of all priests working in Peru. While the matter of nationality does not seem particularly important for the organization, it was mentioned repeatedly by the reformist pioneers, mainly Bolo Hidalgo.[27] It is difficult at this time to determine to what extent the national origin of clergymen influences their ideological choices; there are indications, however, that the Holy See preferred to appoint non-Peruvians to high positions. Thus, to the extent that the appointment of Peruvian-born bishops is influenced by the government, the status quo forces Peruvian priests who are interested in being promoted to develop good relationships with the political authorities since, at least statistically, their chances outside this category are minimal.

At the level of speculation, it is possible that the reformers, particularly those who joined ONIS, have been motivated by indications that the movement away from the Catholic Church is being reflected in the relationship between the priest and the faithful, along the lines suggested by the data presented in Table 2.

After all, it should be obvious to everyone concerned that the foreign religious personnel can ask to be transferred from Peru, if they so desire, while those who are native Peruvians may not have such an easy way out, or else they may prefer to remain in their country of origin.

Table 2
OPINION OF PRIESTS HELD BY LAYMEN IN LIMA AND SICUANI

Activity	Percent Positive		Percent Approving Son as Priest	
	Lima	Sicuani	Lima	Sicuani
Blue-collar				
Peasant	29.0	—	39.0	27.6
White-Collar	54.0	—	61.0	41.9
Professional	33.0	—	50.0	41.1
Overall	36.0	41.1	49.0	—

Source: Prepared by the author from data made available by the Peruvian Catholic Church and from Pedro Negre Rigol and Franklin Bustillos Gálvez, *Sicuani, 1968: Estudio Socio Religioso* (Cuernavaca, Mexico: CIDOC, 1970).

Thus, the prestige enjoyed by the church and by the clergy may be more important to them than to the foreign missionaries.

These reformist elements have widely publicized their perception of what the church's position was and should have been. One of the leading spokesmen for this group has outlined the traditional role of the Peruvian church in no uncertain terms:

> The Church has been an easy, and often complacent, prey of those who in the name of a "western or Christian" world have used it to protect their interests and to defend an order created for their own benefit.
> It could be admitted, at the most, that the Church presents certain ethical requirements in the building of the eternal city; and this only when these requirements do not openly contradict the interests of those who have the reins of the economic and political domination of the people.

On the other hand, he sees the new role of the Peruvian Catholic Church as that of providing "a theology of man's liberation":

> For those who are trying to conform their lives to the evangelical requirements, it becomes constantly more difficult to accept vague and theoretical calls to fraternity and union of all Christians, without taking into account the deep causes of the present state of things and the concrete conditions of the building of a just society. It forgets that the universality of the Church is not something definitely acquired and which continues to exist at any price, but something that needs to be bravely, sacrificially, and willingly conquered. These invocations seem to be intended, consciously or not, to smooth real and necessary tensions and, in the last resort, to maintain the status quo. . . . The most dynamic sectors of the People of God in Latin America . . . are seeking two things: A theological base which encompasses all their actions in a continent in the process of liberation;

and new ecclesiastic structures which allow a life of total Faith, in accordance with the perception the Latin American man has of his own historic future.

To preach the evangelical message is not to preach an evasion of this world. On the contrary, the Word of the Lord tends to make deeper, to radicalize, our commitment in history. And this, concretely, means for us to solidarize with the oppressed of this continent, to participate in their efforts to become free, with the understanding that the history of salvation is a liberation in process.[28]

The Catholic Church and Peruvian Politics:
A Possible Course of Action

A careful exploration of events within the Catholic clergy of Peru shows that these views are held by the vanguard of the reformist group. It must also be remembered, however, that the Peruvian reformists and their more conservative colleagues are currently faced with a very special situation. It is not particularly difficult for the Catholic Church to place itself to the left of those controlling the government in countries such as Brazil and Paraguay; the church can do so without radically shifting its political ideology and without necessarily alienating the bulk of its upper and upper middle-class supporters. The abuses of power committed by those in control provide attractive short-term issues, without forcing the church to consider the more crucial redistribution of socioeconomic rewards.[29] But in Peru, since October 1968, the Catholic reformers—and the rest of the clergy—have been operating under an authoritarian military regime which has presented itself as the country's developmental elite. Furthermore, the Peruvian military officers now in control of the government have taken action in certain fields, such as agrarian reform, tighter control of economic penetrators, and greater supervision of foreign exchange operations, which lend some credence to their avowed intentions.[30]

The only situation which could be related to the one the Peruvian Catholic Church now faces is the Castro takeover in Cuba, and his later embrace, at least orally, of Communism. And even this situation is not really comparable. Both the supranational authorities of the Catholic Church and their national counterparts have clearly indicated their opposition to Communism, although the church has tried to continue its activities in countries controlled by people who subscribe to the competing ideology. The Peruvian military leaders, however, have clearly indicated that, while they are not particularly responsive to the wishes of one superpower, they have not moved very much closer to the other; and we must remember that some of the officers now occupying responsible positions were active in the elimination of the left-wing guerrilla bands in 1965. Therefore, the Catholic Church of Peru, and particularly its reformist wing, are faced with a regime that is taking the limelight away from them. The alternative of siding with the traditional upper class is no alternative at all, particularly for the reformist wing. If the church failed in its ideological competition with the left-wing ideologies when it could count on the resources of the state for help, and when it could accuse its ideological rivals of being Communists (that is, evil), how could the church expect to succeed against a military government which was able to convey a reformist image? By opposing reform, the church would alienate an even greater percentage of the lower and lower-middle class, as well as the few technocrats who still subscribe to the Catholic faith.

The choice was not too difficult for the reformist wing. Since its members noticed that there were policy cleavages within the armed forces, which could not all be solved by sudden retirements or diplomatic sinecures, and that these cleavages were reflected in extremely cautious and sometimes contradictory actions, the reformists placed themselves firmly to the left of the military regime. They supported those measures that seemed sufficiently reformist, and criticized those which did not go far enough. They also took the military regime to task when no action was forthcoming on items that, in the Catholic reformists' opinion, were in need of change. Consequently, although ONIS's declaration on agrarian reform appeared a few days before the military government issued its Agrarian Reform Act, it was already popular knowledge in Lima and the rest of the country that a decision on this matter was forthcoming. The ONIS declaration states: "It is our duty, as servants of the Lord's Word, to announce to all those who in one way or another return dignity, bread and justice to the peasant, that in doing so they are doing it to Christ himself." [31] The implication that ONIS is more reformist than the military is emphasized by Gutiérrez, who indicated in October 1969 that the steps taken so far by the government were "interesting, important, but insufficient. An authentic transformation suggests, for instance, greater popular participation; such a transformation cannot be made only from the top down." Another member of the organization stated that, "since before this revolution, we have been trying to develop a revolutionary consciousness." [32] A public declaration by ONIS, dated October 4, 1969, continued along the same lines:

> Social transformation is not merely a revolution for the people; the people themselves—particularly the peasants and the blue-collar sectors, exploited and unjustly marginalized—should be agents of their own liberation. . . . The steps recently taken in Peru [IPC's nationalization and agrarian reform] suffer obstacles and limitations in their application, owing to the pressures and the involvement of those sectors affected [by these measures] and to the negligence of some public officials. . . . We call the public's attention to the distrust and even the repression shown against just demands of unionized labor. . . .[33]

More recently, as the government became involved in negotiations with American corporations regarding the extraction of copper from the Cuajone area, ONIS warned the military that further concessions should not be granted. Members of ONIS have assisted workers who were striking for higher salaries or who had been laid off, while the organization questioned the military government's policy of ignoring the high unemployment rate and maintaining the freeze originally decreed on wages.[34] The workers have responded positively to this support and, when in conflict with the military government, have occupied churches, usually when the priest in charge subscribed to the reformist point of view. ONIS, in turn, has responded with statements of support for the workers and for their turning to sympathetic parishes for help. Since the conflicts were with the military government, the reformist wing challenged it to carry out real reforms.[35] Thus, in 1970, ONIS appeared to have succeeded in keeping the initiative in the area of structural change and in disassociating itself from the military regime.

The pioneers of the concept of political change within the church have pursued the same course. Bolo Hidalgo writes:

> Let us not delude ourselves: there is even talk now of a military caste. There are huge deficiencies. If we don't criticize them immediately we may end up in a terrifying civil war. . . . The revolution reaches neither the people, nor the churches, not even the police itself yet.[36]

A similar position has been adopted by Luna Victoria, recently living in London but writing often in the magazine *Oiga*. This political position has had its consequences; Father Harold Griffiths Escardó, sympathetic to the reformists, indicated that the powerful economic groups, for instance, have rejected this

> new attitude [of the Church] and have refused, in retaliation, their economic assistance to the works of the Church. This attitude, however, has only served to assess the depth of the belief of many of those Christians and to painfully ascertain the limitations of the serious training provided in Catholic schools and pulpits.... Unfortunately, the January calls of Medellín and of the national hierarchy have not been sufficiently heard or sufficiently implemented.[37]

What may have been more surprising for both interested and neutral observers is that the bulk of the Peruvian Catholic Church, as represented by the hierarchy, has maneuvered itself into a position that parallels that of its reformist wing, but a few degrees to the Right. This equivocal attitude of the Peruvian hierarchy has existed since the 1960s, and was reflected in the public positions taken in the Second Vatican Council, as indicated in Table 3. Thus, while the hierarchy did not punish the early reformist priests, such as Luna Victoria, and did not support the Papal Nuncio's attack in the Trujillo episode, it also did nothing to prevent the use of the faith in combating left-wing organizations, particularly in the sierra region.

Table 3
PUBLIC POSITIONS OF PERUVIAN REPRESENTATIVES IN VATICAN
COUNCIL II

| | Conservative | | Liberal | |
	Absolute	Percentage	Absolute	Percentage
Cardinals	4	66.6	2	33.3
Bishops	3	50.0	3	50.0
All	7	58.3	5	41.7

Source: Prepared by the author from information published in Xavier Rynne, *Letters from Vatican City* (New York: Farrar, Straus, Giroux, 1963–66), four volumes.

The relationship of the hierarchy and the military government has been, at best, an uneasy one. Cardinal Juan Landázuri Ricketts, the head of the Peruvian Catholic Church, supported those measures which had obvious popular appeal, such as the takeover of the International Petroleum Company assets and the conflict with the United States over the purchase of military equipment. His support of government actions on the IPC question, however, was coupled with a call for prompt elections and a return to civilian government.[38] The bishops of Chimbote and Cajamarca took the side of workers and peasants and severely criticized the authorities; the bishops also stated that the Agrarian Reform Law passed by the military regime had serious deficiencies, and called for its improvement. The position of the bishop of Chimbote in favor of blue-collar workers was so forceful that he was reported to have been detained by Peru's secret police.[39] Bishop Bambaren, who was appointed bishop of the shanty towns not too long ago, heads an organization which advises shanty town dwellers on possible improvements. When General Artola, then Minister of the Interior (and thus in charge of internal security), tried to develop popular support by distributing presents among these people, he was rebuffed by Bambaren, who pointed out that, "instead of calming the poor with cake and used clothing, it is necessary to reform society." [40] After this, General Artola ceased in his token attempts.

The conflict between Auxiliary Bishop Bambaren and Interior Minister Artola came into the open once more in May of 1971. Shanty town dwellers invaded urban land in a newly developed area of Lima. While Bambaren does not seem to have encouraged the move, he went to the area being occupied, made some apparently inflammatory remarks, and celebrated mass. Artola took an ambivalent attitude toward the episode, but finally decided to authorize the use of force to expel the invaders. When the confrontation took place, Artola accused Bambaren of being an agitator and ordered him jailed. Although President Velasco freed the auxiliary bishop of Lima the same evening, the event caused the urgent return of Cardinal Landázuri Ricketts from abroad, urgent meetings between the principals, apologies and, after a few days, Artola's resignation. In the process the participants made certain remarks which indicated that the settlement had been, at best, a tactical one. President Velasco reiterated that the land invasions had been the work of agitators, planned by enemies of the government; however, Bambaren was not involved and everything relating to his involvement had been a misunderstanding. In fact, according to the president, the clergy was supporting the administration and there was no conflict between the two. Bambaren issued a press release in which he distinguished carefully between the government and the minister of the interior; the auxiliary bishop was apparently willing to absolve the former, but not the latter, and reminded the public that he had not been treated in accordance with his position. Cardinal Landázuri Ricketts, after meeting with President Velasco, tried to play down the episode (he had complained bitterly and publicly at the airport, upon his hurried return to the country). In general terms, he agreed with the president and indicated that there was no struggle taking place between church and state. He then stated that:

> What we should make very clear is that to solve [the problem posed by the land invasions] lack of respect for private property cannot possibly be admitted; if private property is not respected, then the juridical order, the legal procedures established in our nation, are attacked. If there is no respect for private property, guaranteed by the Constitution, by our laws, then, naturally, there will be chaos, lawlessness.[41]

While the Archbishop was reiterating his support of private property, however, a gathering of Catholic organizations assembled by ONIS, with representatives from blue-collar and white-collar groups in various parts of the country, concluded that the church should aim at establishing "a classless society, with collective ownership of the means of production." They also pointed out that, "it will be necessary to change the privileged status of the church, expressed in its property, in its union with the state, in congregations that manage schools for the wealthy and in certain pastoral activities which are repressive, since they prevent the concretion of a committed Faith." Finally, they recommended that the organizations attending the gathering become pressure groups within and without the church.[42]

Apparently these groups were relatively effective. A few months later, the Episcopal Assembly issued a statement entitled "Justice in the World," in which it rejected capitalism, both economically and ideologically, and called for "the social ownership of the means of production." The specific meaning, however, is not quite clear, since the statement also rejected "certain historical socialisms." The bishops called on the Peruvian military government to make the necessary adjustments in the agrarian reform program so as "to avoid inequalities between the new owners and the exclusion of large groups of peasants." Finally, they called for "a qualitatively different society . . . in which democracy would become real through the effective participation of the members of such society." [43] Whatever the specific meaning of this pronouncement, through it the Catholic Church appears to have increased its political standing among the population.[44]

Perhaps the most serious conflict between the hierarchy and the military regime came about as a consequence of university reforms enacted by the government. Students of the Catholic University demonstrated in opposition to the new university reform law, and the police entered the buildings and beat up faculty, students and even the university president. Cardinal Landázuri Ricketts chastised the government for this action, even after official apologies had been made. The conservative newspaper *La Prensa,* which articulates the views of the coastal sector of the traditional upper class, praised the Cardinal's position:

> These exhortations should be taken very much into account, because they show the preoccupation of the primate of the Peruvian Church for the commission of acts which injure the rights that constitute the spiritual and human patrimony of Peru's Catholics, as citizens.

But the newspaper felt that it should distinguish between the Cardinal and the reformist wing. In a different article, printed on the same editorial page, *La Prensa* attacked change in the church by saying:

> In wanting to renew the Church in order to bring it up to date, those who wish an "incarnation" of the Church as close to the present world as possible, as modern as possible, should remember what happened in the Middle Ages: a tie between the Christians and what then was "the present" world. And it cannot escape our attention that, in those procedures, there was a large share of legitimate drowning of the Christian in the profane; and this is what is dangerous in a too definitive "incarnation," of too steep a renewal toward that which is temporal.[45]

When it came to deeds that affected their immediate interest, the hierarchy was extremely cautious, and the reformist wing lost its precision and sense of urgency. ONIS agreed in October 1969, "to make a very real effort to eliminate in our communities the system of payments for the administration of sacraments." [46] A meeting of Peruvian bishops, held in July 1969, agreed to review the church's relations with the state and indicated that a committee was studying the matter of church property in relation to urban reform; at the same time, the bishops demanded social security and other social benefits for the clergy. Cardinal Landázuri Ricketts decided to move from his official residence into a less pretentious house; he also donated suburban land near Lima to build 600 houses for people of limited means, although it was not made clear to whom the donation had been made or who was going to build the houses.[47] More recently ONIS has continued in this general fashion by criticizing as insufficient the reformist measures taken by the military regime and by calling for effective popular participation in national politics and collective ownership of the means of production.[48] However, there was still no indication of the measures that ONIS was prepared to take toward solving concrete problems, such as the above mentioned system of payment for the adminstration of the sacraments. While ONIS and, more recently, the bulk of the Peruvian Catholic Church and its hierarchy, have grown highly critical of the capitalist system—both as it existed and as it currently exists in the country—they have shown far greater prudence in offering specific alternatives, as well as in taking concrete measures to disassociate themselves from those aspects that bind the church to the capitalist society which they unequivocally reject. Perhaps it is this policy of caution that has made it possible for the Peruvian Catholic Church to avoid the open cleavages, expulsions and persecutions which have occurred in other Latin American countries. On the other hand, when certain priests or bishops have attempted to move decisively to implement the church's pronouncements in this area, either the national hierarchy or the supranational church authorities have moved decisively to maintain the status quo. Such appears to be the case of Monsignor Julio González Ruiz, bishop of Puno, who was removed by decision of the Holy See in May 1972, when he was proceeding to divide and distribute church property.[49] Episodes of this nature, when compared with the abundance of aggressive rhetoric and the shortage of specific actions, have prompted charges of deception by anti-Catholic writers:

> The Church pretends, through spectacular postures such as the already-mentioned encyclical [Populorum Progressio], to place itself in a more or less "advanced" strategic position. In such a way, it plans to imitate what happens in road bicycle races, when a team captain sends one of his assistants to lead the group, in order to slow it down with the appearance of giving it more impetus.[50]

This line of thinking, however, appears to be erroneous. If—as this chapter maintains—the core of the Catholic Church's political power in countries such as Peru has come from its being the supplier of a political ideology ratified by the word of God, which justified the status quo; and if the "revolution of rising expectations" has reduced the effectiveness of that ideology and turned people away from the Catholic faith, it would seem that the only realistic alternative, if those souls are to be regained, is to shift the ideological content of Catholicism and turn it into a political ideology of change. This shift in content can be achieved at the national and local levels, through the reinterpretation of existing supranational documents, such as *Rerum Novarum*, *Quadragesimo Anno* and *Populorum Progressio*. This interpretation is generally the responsibility of the parish priests and of all other religious personnel working directly with the poor. It is they who have to be convinced of the necessity to change their focus, before the Catholic Church, as an institution, can provide ideological support to social and political reform in Peru.

The general tone of this chapter may give the impression that the only problem of survival faced by the Catholic Church as a political institution, both in Peru and in the rest of Latin America, is the type of ideological guidance it provides to the faithful. However, at least a brief reference should be made here to the problem of personnel recruitment, which also threatens the existence of the church as an institution and which, therefore, is an important factor in Latin American politics. In Peru, the number of priests has grown during the 1960s at the average rate of slightly over 3.5 percent per year, thus keeping up with the growth of the general population. The situation with nuns is different, however; their average yearly increase of less than 0.5 percent reflects an increasing gap with population growth. These figures also include the foreign-born religious personnel, whose continued inflow in the future is far from assured. The concentration of clergymen in the large cities and in the more highly developed areas, documented by Table 4, further complicates the situation. Without sufficient religious personnel who are readily available to all the people, the Catholic Church will find it impossible to supply *any* political ideology, thus severely compromising its political influence by default.

While there are many reasons that account for the inability of the Catholic Church to attract personnel, its traditional political philosophy undoubtedly plays a significant role in this area. Since

religious personnel tend to be recruited from among the strongest
believers, the more cleavages the political role of the church produces
among Catholics, the smaller the pool from which to recruit, the greater
the doubts about the validity and relevance of the institution, the
fewer the number of those who would be willing to become its active
representatives.

Table 4
VACANT PARISHES IN SELECTED AREAS OF PERU AND IN THE
ENTIRE COUNTRY
1969

Location	Parishes		
	Total Number	Total Vacant	Percentage Vacant
Lima*	114	0	0.0
Arequipa*	41	9	22.0
Trujillo*	35	4	11.4
Callao*	9	0	0.0
Piura*	34	2	5.9
Abancay †	37	23	62.2
Puno †	37	21	56.8
Ayaviri †	29	15	51.7
Sicuani†	22	12	54.5
Chuquibamba †	20	10	50.0
Entire Country	991	234	23.6

(*) Urban and/or relatively developed areas; (†) rural and relatively backward areas.

Source: Prepared by the author from data made available by the Peruvian Catholic
Church.

The data currently available tend to indicate that the majority of the
clergy in Peru do not yet favor the ideological change proposed by its
reformist elements. In terms of Peru, it is realistic to think that the
presence in power of a group of military officers prepared to carry out
some reforms, and the benevolent neutrality of the hierarchy, together
with pressures which develop at the supranational level, will give ONIS
and similar groups the opportunity to develop the widespread support
among their colleagues required to effect the desired ideological shift.
Such a shift, however, will have to transcend the declaratory stage and
be reflected in specific performances, if it is to reverse the move of
Peruvian laymen away from Catholic guidance and practice.

NOTES

1. For a brief description of the most important cases, see *La Opinión* (Buenos Aires), Dec. 28, 1971, p. 12.

2. For information on Brazil, see *El Universal* (Mexico), Dec. 13, 1969, section 1, p. 4, and the *New York Times*, Jan. 9, 1972, p. 14; on Colombia, see *Excelsior* (Mexico), Jan. 12, 1970, sports section, p. 7; on Paraguay, see *Excelsior*, Jan. 13, 1970, p. 2-A.

3. According to a Peruvian clergyman, the postindependence period, with the possible exception of the first 40 years, was better for the Catholic Church in Peru than the years prior to independence. See Luis Lituma P., "La Iglesia Peruana en el Siglo XX," in *Visión del Perú en el Siglo XX*, vol. 2, ed. Jose Pareja Paz-Soldán (Lima: Ediciones Librería Studium, 1963), p. 478.

4. These topics have been discussed in Carlos A. Astiz, *Pressure Groups and Power Elites in Peruvian Politics* (Ithaca: Cornell University Press, 1969), particularly chapter 8, and in "La Iglesia Católica como Factor de Poder Político: El Caso Peruano," *Revista Mexicana de Ciencia Política* 15 (October-December 1969): 453-78.

5. Gonzalo Torrente Ballester, *Off-Side* (Barcelona: Ediciones Destino, 1969), p. 180.

6. *New York Times*, March 8, 1970, p. 14.

7. Víctor Villanueva, *Hugo Blanco y la Rebelión Campesina* (Lima: Librería-Editorial Juan Mejía Baca, 1967), p. 29.

8. Salomón Vilchez Murga, *Fusiles y Machetes* (Lima: 1960), pp. 50-51.

9. *Carta pastoral de Pedro Pascual Farfán con Motivo de la Próxima Festividad de Santa Rosa de Lima* (Lima: 1937).

10. F. M. Arriola Grande, *Discurso a la Nación Peruana* (Buenos Aires: Editorial Pueblo Continente, 1959), p. 237. Similar events are narrated by Luis Alberto Sánchez, *Aprismo y Religión* (Lima: Editorial Cooperativa Aprista Atahualpa, 1933), passim, and Harry Kantor, *El Movimiento Aprista Peruano* (Buenos Aires: Ediciones Pleamar, 1964), pp. 168-73.

11. Villanueva, *Hugo Blanco*, p. 149; a similar report is made by Hugo Neira, in *Cuzco: Tierra y Muerte* (Lima: Problemas de Hoy, 1964), p. 89.

12. Lituma, "La Iglesia Peruana," pp. 476 and 485-86 (emphasis added). This view is shared by reformist priests, in Peru and other countries. Segundo Galilea, a Chilean clergyman, warns that political ideologies often replace religion in Latin America—see *Oiga* (Lima), September 12, 1969, p. 33; and Jorge Alvarez Calderón, a Peruvian member of ONIS, has wondered whether the percentage of believers was actually decreasing in his country, *Caretas* (Lima), October 15-24, 1969, p. 20.

13. Pedro Negre Rigol and Franklin Bustillos Gálvez, *Sicuani, 1968: Estudio Socio Religioso* (Cuernavaca, Mexico: CIDOC, 1970), p. 336.

14. Christian J. L. Bertholet, et al., *Puno Rural* (Lima: CISEPA, 1969), p. 129.

15. The following year the extreme Left received 15 percent of the vote in the Lima municipal elections. The electoral data can be found in Astiz, *Pressure Groups*, chapters 4 and 6.

16. Reproduced in Salomón Bolo Hidalgo, *Cristianismo y Liberación Nacional* (Lima: Ediciones Liberación, 1962), p. 17.

17. Ibid., p. 43.

18. Although Bolo Hidalgo has employed this argument for a long time—see his *Cartas de mi Refugio* (Lima: Imprenta Gráfica T. Scheuch, 1963), pp. 136-37—since the 1968 military takeover he seems to be emphasizing the point that, although a radical reformist, he is as far away from Communism as he is from the traditional upper class. See some of his numerous letters to the editor, published in *Oiga*, August 15, 1969, p. 3; June 27, 1969, p. 3; September 3, 1969, p. 4; April 17, 1970, pp. 3 and 42; July 2, 1971, p. 4; and July 23, 1971, pp. 45 and 50. It would seem that, by so doing and by supporting specific measures of the military government, he is making himself and the National Liberation Front tolerable to the armed forces; occasionally, however, he has criticized specific measures of the present administration.

19. Bolo Hidalgo, *Cartas*, pp. 139-40.

20. The book being discussed here is Romeo Luna Victoria, *Ciencia y Práctica de la Revolución* (Lima: Editorial Studium, 1966). The author's views cannot be completely understood without reading his previous work, *El Problema Indígena y la Tenencia de Tierras en el Perú* (Trujillo, Peru: Cosmos, 1964), and his numerous articles in the nationalist reformist magazine *Oiga.*

21. Luna Victoria, *Ciencia y Práctica*, p. 280.

22. Ibid., pp. 190-203. The definition of "elastic property" is not quite clear, but Luna Victoria accepts confiscation of certain types of property.

23. Ibid., p. 26.

24. These statements are reprinted in Rogger Mercado, *Las Guerrillas del Perú—El MIR: De la Prédica Ideológica a la Acción Armada* (Lima: Fondo de Cultura Popular, 1967), pp. 140-45 and 183, respectively.

25. Ivan Vallier, *Catholicism, Social Control and Modernization in Latin America* (Englewood Cliffs, N.J.: Prentice-Hall, 1970), p. 93.

26. Apparently some of the same priests had also signed a letter to the Pope in November 1968, in which they opposed the Encyclical Letter *Humanae Vitae.* Some details about this incident were published in *Caretas,* May 8-22, 1969, p. 16.

27. Bolo Hidalgo, *Cristianismo*, pp. 16, 58, and 60.

28. Gustavo Guitérrez, in his introduction to *Signos de Renovación* (Lima: Comisión Episcopal de Acción Social, 1969), pp. 7 and 11-13. Father Gutiérrez, a member of the Faculty of the Catholic University of Peru, was involved in the exchange with the Papal Nuncio and is a member of ONIS. For a more recent statement of his views, see Gutiérrez, "Liberation and Development," *Cross Currents* 21 (Summer 1971): 243-56.

29. This is not to say that some reformist priests, in countries such as Brazil, have not addressed themselves to the more essential political issues of their country: in fact, they have done so. The numerous statements by Helder Camara and Valdir Calheiros, to mention just two bishops, prove this. But it should be emphasized that, to oppose the government, *they did not have to involve themselves in the larger socioeconomic question.*

30. For the author's view of some characteristics of the present Peruvian military regime, see Carlos A. Astiz and José Z. García, "The Peruvian Military: Achievement Orientation, Training, and Political Tendencies," *Western Political Quarterly* 25 (December 1972): 667-685. For somewhat different points of view, consult Luigi R. Einaudi and Alfred C. Stepan, *Latin American Institutional Development: Changing Military Perspectives in Peru and Brazil* (Santa Monica, Calif.: The Rand Corporation, 1971), pp. 9-70; Julio Cotler, "Crisis Política y Populismo Militar," in José Matos Mar, et al., *Perú: Hoy* (Mexico: Siglo Veintiuno Editores, 1971), pp. 87-174; and Victor Villanueva, *Nueva Mentalidad Militar en el Perú?* (Lima: Editorial Juan Mejía Baca, 1969).

31. The declaration was reproduced in *Oiga*, June 27, 1969, pp. 20–24; the quote is from p. 22.

32. *Caretas*, October 15–24, 1969, pp. 19–20.

33. *Oiga*, October 10, 1969, pp. 22–23.

34. *Oiga*, November 21, 1969, p. 11; January 9, 1970, pp. 42–43; and January 30, 1970, pp. 35–36. The military had no compunction about granting themselves a 30 percent pay raise; see *Caretas*, May 23–June 12, 1969, p. 13. The magazine was immediately closed down.

35. For specific cases of churches invaded by workers, see *Excelsior*, Jan. 5, 1970, p. 2-A, and Jan. 13, 1970, p. 3-A. For ONIS's reaction, see "Declaración ante los Problemas Laborales," in Movimiento Sacerdotal Onis, "Declaraciones" (Lima: June, 1970, mimeo.), pp. 35–37.

36. In a letter to the editor of *Oiga*, June 11, 1971, p. 5.

37. *Oiga*, July 11, 1969, p. 34.

38. *La Prensa* (Lima), October 11, 1968, p. 2, and *Caretas*, May 23–June 12, 1969, p. 15.

39. *Oiga*, March 7, 1969, p. 10; and November 14, 1969, pp. 12 and 33.

40. *Caretas*, May 23–June 12, 1969, p. 15; and July 10–23, 1969, p. 32.

41. News and commentaries of this episode were on the front pages of all Peruvian newspapers. The account is based on the information published in *Oiga*, May 14, 1971, pp. 10–12, 15–16, and 38; and *La Tribuna* (the official newspaper of the Peruvian government), May 13, 1971, pp. 1 and 3, and May 14, 1971, pp. 1 and 3. The quote is from this last issue of *El Peruano*, p. 3.

42. All the quotes are from *CIC Noticias*, May 10, 1971.

43. The main points of "La Justicia en el Mundo" appeared in *Oiga*, August 20, 1971, p. 14; and *Caretas*, September 6–16, 1971, p. 12.

44. See, for instance, the random survey conducted by *Oiga*, September 3, 1971, pp. 5–6.

45. Both articles in *La Prensa*, June 17, 1969, p. 8.

46. *Oiga*, October 10, 1969, p. 23.

47. *Oiga*, July 18, 1969, p. 41; and *La Prensa*, June 11, 1969, p. 7. In a follow-up note it was indicated that some of the holdings of the church, apparently including the property involved here, were a losing proposition and that the houses to be built were going to be rented with options to buy. Cardinal Landázuri Ricketts also appointed an advisory committee to gather facts and propose solutions and promised the future creation of a Permanent Bureau of Technical Advice, for further consultation. See *Siete Días de Perú y del Mundo* (supplement of *La Prensa*), June 15, 1969, p. 7.

48. See Centro de Estudios y Publicaciones, "Movimiento Sacerdotal ONIS: Declaraciones," mimeo. (Lima: June 1970), pp. 38–44; and the three-page release, "Propiedad Privada y Nueva Sociedad," mimeo. (Lima: August 15, 1970).

49. For a report of the episode, see *Jornal do Brasil* (Río de Janeiro), May 13, 1972, section 1, p. 9.

50. Elías Condal, "El Vaticano y el Tercer Mundo," in Bernardo Castro Villagrana, et al., *La Iglesia, el Subdesarrollo y la Revolución* (Mexico: Editorial Nuestro Tiempo, 1968), p. 196.

A Selected
Bibliography

BOOKS

Adams, Richard N. *A Community in the Andes: Problems and Progress in Muquiyauyo.* Seattle: University of Washington Press, 1959.

Alberti, Giorgio. "Inter-Village Systems and Deveopment: A Study of Social Change in Highland Peru." Dissertation Series No. 18, Latin American Studies Program, Cornell University, June 1970.

Alisky, Marvin. *Peruvian Political Perspective.* Tempe, Arizona: Center for Latin American Studies, Arizona State University, 1975.

Astiz, Carlos A. *Pressure Groups and Power Elites in Peruvian Politics.* Ithaca, New York: Cornell University Press, 1969.

Austin, Allan G., and Lewis, Sherman, *Urban Government for Metropolitan Lima.* New York: Praegar, 1970.

Beljar, Hector. *Peru 1965: Notes on a Guerrilla Experience.* New York: Monthly Review Press, 1969.

Blanco, Hugo. *Land or Death, The Peasant Struggle in Peru.* New York: Pathfinder Press, 1972.

Bourque, Susan Carolyn. "Cholification and the Campesino: A Study of Three Peruvian Peasant Organizations in the Process of Societal Change." Dissertation Series No. 21, Latin American Studies Program, Cornell University, January 1971.

Bourricaud, François. *Power and Society in Contemporary Peru.* New York: Praeger, 1970.

Carey, J. C. *Peru and the U.S. 1900–1962.* Notre Dame, Indiana: University of Notre Dame Press, 1964.

Chaplin David. *The Peruvian Industrial Labor force.* Princeton, New Jersey: Princeton University Press, 1967.

Cotler, Julio. "Traditional Haciendas and Communities in a Context of Political Mobilization in Peru." *Agrarian Problems and Peasant Movements in Latin America.* Edited by Rodolfo Stavenhagen. New York: Anchor Books, 1970.

Cotler, Julio, and Portocarreo, Felipe. "Peru: Peasant Organizations." *Latin American Peasant Movements.* Edited by Henry Landsberger. Ithaca, New York: Cornell University Press, 1969.

CIDA (Comité Interamericano de Desarrollo Agrícola). *Tenencia de la tierra y desarrollo socio-economico del sector agricola: Perú.* Washington, D.C.: Pan American Union, 1966.

Craig, Wesley W., Jr. "Peru: The Peasant Movement in La Convención." *Latin American Peasant Movements.* Edited by Henry Landsberger. Ithaca, New York: Cornell University Press, 1969.

480

Delgado, Carlos, *Problemas Sociales en el Perú Contemporaneo.* Lima: Campodon-ico-Instituto de Estudios Peruanos, 1971.
Dew, Edward, *Politics in the Altiplano.* Austin: University of Texas Press, 1969.
Gomez, Rudolph. *The Peruvian Administration.* Boulder, Colorado: University of Colorado, 1969.
Herbold, Carl, Jr., and Stein, Steve. *Guia bibliografcia para la historia social y politica del Peru en el siglo XX.* Lima: Ed Campodonico, 1971.
Hopkins, Jack W. *The Government Executive of Modern Peru.* Gainesville, Florida: Center for Latin American Studies, University of Florida, 1967.
Kantor, Harry. *The Ideology and Program of the Peruvian Aprista Movement.* Washington, D.C.: Savile Books, 1966.
Kilty, Dan R.*Planning for Development in Peru.* New York: Praegar, 1967.
Hilliker, Grant. *The Politics of Reform in Peru.* Baltimore: Johns Hopkins, 1971.
Himes, James R. "Peru." *Toward Strategies of Public Administration Development in Latin America.* Edited by John C. Honey. Syracuse: Syracuse University Press. 1968.
Jaquette, Jane S. *The Politics of Development in Peru.* Latin American Studies Program Dissertation Series, Cornell University, 1973.
Lewis, Robert Alden. *Employment, Income and the Growth of the Barriada in Lima, Peru.* Latin American Studies Program Dissertation Series, Cornell University, 1973.
Marett, Robert. *Peru.* New York: Praegar, 1969.
Matos Mar, Jose, et al. *El Peru Actual: Sociedad y Politica.* Mexico City, Mexico: Instituto de Investigaciones Sociales, Universidad Nacional Autonoma de Mexico, 1970.
Maynard, Eileen A. "Patterns of Community Service Development in Selected Communities of the Mantaro Valley, Peru." *Socio-Economic Development of Andean Communities, Report No. 3.* Itahaca, New York: Cornell University, Department of Anthropology, 1964.
McCoy, Terry L. "Congress, the President and Political Instability in Peru." *Latin American Legislatures.* Edited by Weston Agor. New York: Praeger, 1971.
Neira, Hugo. *Cuzco: Tierra y Muerte, Reportaje al Sur.* Lima: Problemas de Hoy, 1964.
——. *El golpe de Estado: Perú 1968.* Madrid: Editorial ZYX, 1969.
Paulston, Rolland G. *Society, Schools and Progress in Peru.* Oxford, England: Pergamon Press, 1971.
Payne, James. *Labor and Politics in Peru.* New Haven: Yale University Press, 1965.
Peru, Land and People: A Bibliography. Research and Training Series No. 15, Land Tenure Center. Madison, Wisconsin: University of Wisconsin, June, 1971.
Petras, J., and LaPorte, R. *Peru: ¿Transformación revolucionaria o modernización?.* Buenos Aires: Amorrortu Editores, 1971.
Pike, Frederick. *The Modern History of Peru.* New York: Praeger, 1967.
Quijano, Anibal. *Nationalism and Capitalism in Peru: A Study in Neo-Imperialsim.* New York: Monthly Review Press, 1971.
Robin, John P., and Terzo, Frederick C. *Urbanization in Peru.* New York: The Ford Foundation, n.d.
Roemer, Michael. *Fishing for Growth: Export-led Development in Peru, 1950–67.* Cambridge: Harvard University Press, 1970.
Sharp, Daniel. *U. S. Foreign Policy and Peru.* Austin: University of Texas Press, 1972.
Stephens, Richard H. *Wealth and Power in Peru.* Metuchen, N.J.: Scarecrow Press, 1971.
Tullis, F. LaMond. *Lord and Peasant in Peru.* Cambridge: Harvard University Press, 1970.

Villanueva, Victor. *¿Nueva mentalidad militar en el Peru?* Lima: Editorial Juan Mejía Baca, 1969.
————. *El Militarismo en el Peru.* Lima: Empresa Grafica T. Scheuch, 1962.
————. *La Tragedia de un Pueblo y un partido.* Lima: 1956.
————*Manual del Conspirador.* Lima: Empresa Grafica T. Scheuch, 1963.
————. *Un Año Bajo el sable.* Lima: Empresa Grafica T. Sheuch, 1963.
————. *Hugo Blanco y la Rebelión Campesina.* Lima: Librería Editorial Juan Mejía Baca, 1967.

PERIODICALS

Bourricaud, François. "Los Militares; ¿Porqué y Para qué?" *Aportes* (Paris) no. 16 (April 1970).
————. "Structure and Function of the Peruvian Oligarchy." *Studies in Comparative International Development* 2 (1966).
————. "Syndicalisme et politique, la cas Péruvien." *Sociologie du travail* 4 (Oct.-Dec. 1961).
————. "Remarques sur l'oligarchie péruvienne." *Revue Francaise de Science Politiaue* 14, no. 4 (Aug. 1964).
Bravo Bresani, Jorge. "Naturaleza del poder Peruano." *Aportes, no. 16 (April 1970).*
Campbell, Leon G. *"The Historiography of the Peruvian Guerrilla Movement 1960-1965."* Latin American Research Review 8, no. 1 (Spring 1973).
Chaplin, David. "Peruvian Social Mobility: Revolutionary and Developmental Potential." *Journal of Inter-American Studies* 10, no. 4 (1968).
Clinton, Richard. "The Modernizing Military: The Case of Peru." *Inter-american Economic Affairs* 24, no. 4 (Spring 1971).
Cohen, Alvin. "The Technology/Elite Approach to the Development Process: Peruvian Case Study." *Economic Development and Cultural Change* 14, no. 3 (April 1966).
Cotler, Julio. "Political Crisis and Military Populism in Peru." *Studies in Comparative International Development* 6, no. 5.
Gall, Norman. "The Master is Dead." *Dissent* (June 1971).
Goodsell, Charles T. "That Confounding Revolution in Peru." *Current History* (January 1975), pp. 20–23.
Goodwin, Richard N. "Letter from Peru." *New Yorker* (May 17, 1969).
Grayson, George W. "Peru's Revolutionary Government." *Current History* (February 1973), pp. 61–63, 87.
Hobsbawm, E. J. "Peru: The Peculiar Revolution." *New York Review of Books* (December 16, 1971).
Locker, Mike. "Perspective on the Peruvian Military—Parts I and II." *NACLA Newsletter* 3, no. 5 (September 1969).
Loeb, J. I. "Irony in Peru: Expropriation of the Cerro Corporation." *New Republic* (9 February 1974), pp. 8–9.
Lowenthal, A. F. "Peru's Ambitious Revolution." *Foreign Affairs* (July 1974), pp. 799–817.
Malloy, James M. "Authoritarianism, Corporatism, and Mobilization in Peru." *Review of Politics* (January 1974), pp. 52–84.
————, "Dissecting the Peruvian Military: Review Essay," *Journal of Interamerican Studies and World Affairs* (August 1973), pp. 375–382
Manaster, Kenneth A. "The Problem of Urban Squatters in Developing Countries: Peru." *Wisconsin Law Review* (Summer 1967).

Needler, Martin. "U. S. Recognition Policy and the Peruvian Case." *Interamerican Economic Affairs* (Spring 1963).

Niedergang, Marcel. "Revolutionary Nationalism in Peru." *Foreign Affairs* 49, no. 3 (April 1971): 454–463.

Patch, Richard. *American Universities Field Staff Newsletters:* "Peru Looks Toward the Elections of 1962" 8, no. 5 (May 1961). "Politics and the University" (May 1958). "The Indian Emergence in Cuzco" (August 1958). "La Parada, Lima's Market" 14, nos. 1, 2 and 3 (Jan., Feb., March 1967). "The Peruvian Agrarian Reform Bill" 11, no.3 (Feb.1964). "The Peruvian Elections of 1962 and Their Annulment" 9, no. 6 (June 1962). "The Peruvian Elections of 1963" 10, no. 1 (July 1963). "The Peruvian Earthquake of 1970," Parts 1–4, vol. 18 (March to July 1971), no. 6–9.

Payne, Arnold. "Peru: Latin America's Silent Revolution." *Interamerican Economic Affairs* 20, no. 3 (Winter 1966).

Payne, James. "Peru: The Politics of Structured Violence." *Journal of Politics* 27, no. 2 (May 1968).

Petras, James, and Rimensnyder, Nelson. "What is Happening in Peru?" *Monthly Review* 21 (Feb. 1970).

Pike, Frederick B. "The Old and the New APRA in Peru: Myth and Reality." *Interamerican Economic Affairs* 18, no. 2 (Autumn 1964).

———. "Peru and the Quest for Reform by Compromise." *Interamerican Economic Affairs* (Spring 1967).

Rozman, Stephen L. "The Evolution of the Political Role of the Peruvian Military." *Journal of Interamerican Studies and World Affairs* 12, no. 4 (October 1970).

Sanders, T. G. "Family Planning in Peru." *American Universities Field Staff Newsletter* 17, no. 6 (1970).

Taylor, Milton C. "Taxation and Economic Development: A Case Study of Peru." *Interamerican Economic Affairs* (Winter 1967).

———. "Problems of Development in Peru." *Journal of Inter-American Studies* 9, no. 1 (January 1967).

GOVERNMENTAL AND ORGANIZATIONAL PUBLICATIONS

Alisky, Marvin. *Peruvian Political Perspective.* Tempe: Center for Latin American Studies, Arizona State University (1975).

———. "Peru's SINAMOS Governmental Agency for Coordinating Reforms." Tempe: Institute of Public Administration, Arizona State University, vol. 11, no. 1 (1972).

Alliance for Progress, Panel of Nine. *Evaluation of the 1964-1965 Public Investment Program of Peru.* A Report to the Government of Peru (October 1964).

Brady, Eugene A. "The Distribution of Total Personal Income in Peru." *International Studies in Economics,* Department of Economics, Iowa State University (January 1968).

Carroll, Thomas F. *Land Reform in Peru.* AID Spring Review Country Paper, Department of State, Washington, D. C. (June 1970).

Einaudi, Luigi R. *The Peruvian Military: A Summary Political Analysis.* Memo RM-6048-RC, The Rand Corporation, Santa Monica, California (May 1969).

Estep, Raymond. *The Role of the Military in Peruvian Politics.* Documentary Research Study, Air University, Maxwell Air Force Base, Alabama (1970).

Larson, Magali S., and Bergman, Arlene E. *Social Stratification in Peru.* Politics of Modernization Series, no. 5. University of California, Berkeley (1969).

Little, Arthur D., Inc. *A Program for the Industrial and Regional Development of Peru.* A Report to the Government of Peru (1960).

Ministerio de Guerra. *Las Guerrillas en el Peru y su Represion.* (Lima: 1966).
North, Liisa. *Civil-Military Relations in Argentina, Chile, and Peru.* Politics of Modernization Series, no. 2, University of California, Berkeley (1966).
Payne, Arnold. *The Peruvian Coup D'Etat of 1962: The Overthrow of Manuel Prado.* Institute for the Comparative Study of Political Systems, Washington, D. C. (1968).
Thorp, Rosemary. "Inflation and Orthodox Economic Policy in Peru." *Bulletin of Oxford University Institute of Economics and Statistics* 29, no. 3 (August 1967): 185–210.
UN-ECLA, *The Industrial Development of Peru.* Mexico DF (1959).
U. S. Relations with Peru. Hearings before the Subcommittee on Western Hemisphere Affairs of the Committee on Foreign Relations, U. S. Senate, 91st Congress, First Session, April 14, 16 and 17, 1969. (Washington, D.C.: U.S.G.P.O., 1969).
Wils, Frits C. M. *Industry and Industrialists in the Metropolitan Area of Lima-Callao, Peru.* Institute of Social Studies, The Hague and C.I.S.E.P.A. Lima: Catholic University of Peru, 1970.

UNPUBLISHED MATERIALS

Deprospo, Ernest R., Jr. "The Administration of the Peruvian Land Reform Program." Ph.D. diss. Penn State University, September 1967.
Doughty, Paul L. "Community Response to Natural Disaster in the Peruvian Andes." Paper read at the 70th annual meeting of the American Anthropological Association, New York City, November 1971.
Dragisic, John. "Peruvian Stabilization Policies 1939–1968." Ph.D. diss. University of Wisconsin, 1971.
Handleman, Howard. "Struggle in the Andes: Peasant Political Mobilization in Peru." Ph.D. diss. University of Wisconsin, 1971.
Hawkins, Richard H., Jr. "The Washington-Lima Crisis of 1962: A Historical Perspective." Washington, D. C.: Foreign Service Institute, Department of State, May 1963.
Palmer, David Scott. "Revolution From Above: Military Government and Popular Participation in Peru, 1968–1972." Ph.D. diss., Cornell University, 1973.
Peeler, John A. "The Politics of the Alliance for Progress in Peru." Ph.D. diss., University of North Carolina, 1967.
Vandendries, Rene. "Foreign Trade and the Economic Development of Peru." Ph.D. diss., Iowa State University, 1967.
Webb, Richard. "Government Policy and the Distribution of Income in Peru 1963–73. Discussion Paper No. 39, Research Program in Economic Development, Woodrow Wilson School, Princeton University, 1973.

The Contributors

GIORGIO ALBERTI received a doctorate in Political Science from the University of Florence (Italy) in 1963 and Cornell University (Organizational Behavior) in 1970. He is currently a Principal Investigator with the Instituto de Estudios Peruanos (Lima) with which he has published numerous papers on peasant life and a book *Transformación Regional, Urbanización Rural, y Movimientos Campesinos en la Sierra Central* (Regional Transformation, Rural Urbanization and Peasant Movements in the Central Sierra).

CARLOS A. ASTIZ studied at the Law School of the University of Buenos Aires and at The Pennsylvania State University, where he received his Ph.D. in Political Science. He is now Associate Professor of Political Science at the Graduate School of Public Affairs and Associate of the Center for Inter-American Studies, both of the State University of New York at Albany. His publications include *Pressure Groups and Power Elites in Peruvian Politics, Latin American International Politics,* and the introduction and English version of *Los Que Mandan.* He has also written several papers on the military and on the Catholic Church in Latin America.

DAVID BAYER (M.S., Sociology, Cornell, 1971) was a Peace Corps volunteer in a barriada in Ica, Peru, from 1964 to 1966 under a community development program. He assisted in the direction of three barriada surveys, and worked with the Corporation for the Development and Reconstruction of Ica and with the Barriada Committee of Alfonso Ugarte to set up a housing cooperative. He returned to Peru in December 1971 and worked with peasants in the Ica Valley. (He is currently teaching at the Agrarian University [La Molina] in Peru.)

DAVID CHAPLIN, editor, is Professor of Sociology and Chairman at Western Michigan University. He received his doctorate from Princeton University in 1963 and is author of the *Peruvian Industrial Labor Force,* and editor of and contributor to *Population Policies and Growth in Latin America* as well as numerous articles on Peruvian society and politics.

DAVID COLLIER is Assistant Professor of Political Science at Indiana University. He received his Ph.D. from the University of Chicago. In addition to his work on Lima squatter settlements, he is engaged in comparative research on the timing and sequence of different aspects of development, in Latin America and more generally. This research focuses particularly on the analysis of regime characteristics and the timing of the introduction of policy innovations.

JULIO COTLER is a Professor of Sociology at the University of San Marcos and senior researcher at the Instituto de Estudios Peruanos. He received his doctorate in Sociology from the University of Bordeaux and has published numerous articles on Peruvian society and politics.

PAUL DOUGHTY is Chairman of the Anthropology Department at the University of Florida and President (1973–74) of the Latin American Studies Association. He received his doctorate in Anthropology from Cornell University in 1963 and has published a book, *Huaylas, An Andean District in Search of Progress,* and articles on Peruvian cultural and social change.

LUIGI R. EINAUDI has B.A. and Ph.D. degrees in Political Science from Harvard University, and has worked on Latin American problems since 1955. This article draws on a long-term research project on the Peruvian military. Dr. Einaudi was at the Rand Corporation from 1962 to 1973. He is currently a member of the Policy Planning Staff at the Department of State. He is the editor and principal author of *Beyond Cuba: Latin America Takes Charge of its Future* (New York: Crane, Russack & Company, 1974), and numerous research reports published by the Rand Corporation.

DANIEL GOLDRICH (Ph.D., Political Science, North Carolina, 1959), Professor and Chairman of Political Science Department, University of Oregon, is co-author of *The Rulers and the Ruled,* and author of *Sons of the Establishment.* He has published articles on the politics of Latin American students and of squatter settlers in Peru and Chile. Currently he is engaged in research with sociologists on the effect of the economic growth-steady state economy issue on perceptions of the corporate state and subsequent action to transform it.

SHANE HUNT is Professor of Economics at Boston University. He received his doctorate in Economics from Yale University in 1963. He lived in Peru during 1963–64 and 1969, working for Yale's Economic Growth Center and for the Ford Foundation. Aside from the contribution to this volume, his articles on Peru have dealt with economic statistics, economic history, and foreign investment.

KEVIN JAY MIDDLEBROOK is a 1972 graduate of Harvard College. His senior honors thesis, entitled "Land for the Tiller: Political Participation in the Peruvian Military's Agrarian Reform," analyzed the Peruvian military's policies regarding popular political participation as implemented in the 1969 agrarian reform. During 1972–73 he traveled in Europe and Africa on a Henry Russell Shaw Traveling Fellowship.

DAVID SCOTT PALMER is an Assistant Professor of Government at Bowdoin College. He received his Ph.D. from Cornell University in January 1973. He was a Visiting Professor at the Catholic University of Peru in Lima in 1971. Previously he had taught at the University of Huamanga, in Ayachucho, Peru (1962, 1963), while a Peace Corps Volunteer Leader. He has contributed articles to various journals and readers on Latin American politics.

SANDRA POWELL is an Associate Professor of Political Science at California State University, San Francisco. Her research interests include electoral behavior in Chile, political nonparticipation among the urban poor, and cross-national studies of violence.

RAYMOND B. PRATT is an Assistant Professor of Government at Montana State University. He is the author of several articles on urban politics in Latin America and is interested in national political strategies for overcoming economic dependence and achieving rapid economic growth in Latin America.

C. RICHARD SCHULLER is an Assistant Professor of Political Science at the University of Tennessee on leave to the Oak Ridge National Laboratory as a Research Associate in Environmental Studies. His current research and publications deal with U.S. Environmental Policy.

JOHN STRASMA is Professor of Economics and Agricultural Economics, University of Wisconsin (Madison), and has been Visiting Professor of Economics, University of Chile, first in 1959–64, then in 1966–68 and 1971–72. The author has also served as an advisor to the Peruvian Office of Tax Research and Development in 1970. He has also served in technical assistance missions in the F.A.O. and other U.N. agencies in Latin America and West Africa.

WILLIAM FOOTE WHYTE is Professor of Organization Behavior at the School of Industrial and Labor Relations, Cornell University. He is the author of numerous monographs and texts on industrial relations in the United States and was recently the Chairman of the Subcommittee on Research, National Manpower Advisory Committee, U.S. Department of Labor. Since 1961 he has been conducting research on human problems of development in Peru.

INDEX

PERUVIAN NATIONALISM
A Corporatist Revolution

Peru is the most interesting model of justice and development in Latin America today. To analyze the sociopolitical progress of this nation, David Chaplin has gathered together and edited this interdisciplinary collection of essays.

Peru's development is unique for several reasons. First, it has shown that a military force that was trained largely by the United States can employ its professional expertise not to remain a well-behaved ally but to pull off a genuinely radical nationalist revolution even at the expense of various interests of its "benefactor." Second, Peru has proven that successful economic development need be neither capitalist nor Socialist.

Peruvian Nationalism contains major papers by leading Peruvianists on the 1960s and on the current revolutionary military regime. The temporal focus is on the current (post-1968) revolutionary military government, with background material covering the early 1960s. Contributors are all social scientists — including American, Italian and Peruvian writers — who have carried out field research in Peru.